Integrating General and
Special Education

Integrating General and Special Education

Edited by

JOHN I. GOODLAD

Center for Educational Renewal
University of Washington

and

THOMAS C. LOVITT

Experimental Education Unit, College of Education
University of Washington

Merrill, an imprint of
Macmillan Publishing Company
New York

Maxwell Macmillan Canada
Toronto

Maxwell Macmillan International
New York   Oxford   Singapore   Sydney

Editors: Linda James Scharp and Ann Castel
Production Editor: Linda Hillis Bayma
Art Coordinator: Lorraine Woost
Text Designer: Susan Frankenberry
Cover Designer: Cathleen Norz
Production Buyer: Pamela D. Bennett
Electronic Text Management: Ben Ko, Marilyn Wilson Phelps
Illustrations: Jane Lopez

This book was set in New Baskerville by Macmillan Publishing Company and was printed and bound by Arcata Graphics/Martinsburg. The cover was printed by Phoenix Color Corp.

Macmillan Publishing Company
866 Third Avenue
New York, NY 10022

Macmillan Publishing Company is part of the
Maxwell Communication Group of Companies.

Maxwell Macmillan Canada, Inc.
1200 Eglinton Avenue East, Suite 200
Don Mills, Ontario M3C 3N1

Library of Congress Cataloging-in-Publication Data
Goodlad, John I.
    Integrating general and special education / John I. Goodlad and
  Thomas C. Lovitt.
      p. cm.
    Includes index.
    ISBN 0-02-344771-0
    1. Educational equalization—United States. 2. Special education—
  United States. 3. Educational planning—United States.
  I. Lovitt, Thomas C. II. Title.
  LC213.2.G66 1993
  371.9'046—dc20   92-25293
                                                          CIP

Printing: 1 2 3 4 5 6 7 8 9   Year: 3 4 5 6 7

Preface

This book addresses the daunting challenges of educating all children and youths equitably in the schools of our social and political democracy. Although the mission of enculturating all is at the core a moral one, it is now defined in part by legal terms. There are no legitimate arguments for denying access to knowledge. The educational environments provided in schools are to be minimally restrictive and maximally educative.

Clearly, our schools fall short of this ideal. Their tasks have been increasingly compounded by varying degrees of moral and legal commitment to this universal mission in the surrounding society. The student population to be educated has steadily increased in diversity while other segments of the educative infrastructure, especially families and religious institutions, have steadily declined in their effectiveness. Television contributes significantly—and unwittingly—to shaping manners and morals in the name of entertainment. For today's schools simply to cope and be regarded simultaneously as highly as yesterday's is a dual undertaking of major proportions.

These changes and their consequences surface in virtually every chapter of the book. The theme running through is that of more effectively integrating the general education of those students who most closely fit the norms of schooling and the special education of those who fit less well so that more of the education of both is common. Several of the authors argue that the need to provide for some what is not adequately provided for all within these norms has led to a second system of schooling. They provide data to both document and criticize this separation.

However, none argues for a fusion that would flatten out or reduce those provisions that extend well beyond the norms of schooling in order to provide educationally for children and youths with very special needs. Most argue instead for extending the range of normal schooling to encompass much of what is now labeled "special." But some sound a note of caution.

The road to public recognition and special funding of the unusual needs of disabled and learning impaired students, for example, has been bumpy. Although the concept of good education being adapted to the special needs of all makes sense, such rhetoric often obscures the difficulties of attaining this ideal. Hard-fought gains are easily lost and progress not yet made is thwarted in any system of schooling touted as encompassing all that fails to reach all. Sustained advocacy for the special educational needs of some, including legal provisions, appears to be a critically essential part of the moral imperative referred to earlier.

The title of this book might well include a question mark at its end. The issues addressed are not those of whether to integrate general and special education but of how and how much. All authors argue for bringing the two more closely together, but there is a considerable range of views regarding how close. For several authors, the merger implied or recommended brings the two almost but not quite together in common programs in common settings. Others stop much short of this. The more severe the disability or handicap, the closer the agreement on the need for educational provisions going beyond these commonalities. None eschews the necessity of at least part-time removal of some children from the regular classroom in order to ensure for them the special educational provisions that their circumstances require.

We have chosen not to summarize here the substance of each chapter. Much of this is done in chapter 3, which introduces the major issues and the chapters that address them. Then, the concluding chapter 11 provides a substantial summing up of all the chapters preceding it. We think it would be useful to the reader for us to present here what appear to be several major agreements or near agreements as well as disagreements among the several authors, each writing independently of the others. It is important to note that, although there are technical differences between *disability* and *handicap*, even most special educators commonly use the two words synonymously.

First and most obvious, they agree that there is undue and generally dysfunctional separation of what is offered as regular schooling for most children and youths and special for some. Perceptions of what is wrong range from there being two systems to there being one with a number of poorly articulated supplements and tack-ons. There is agreement on what is needed: close coordination and synchronization of the regular and special components of the K–12 system. Several authors include in the whole the preparation programs for those who teach in the schools. And some add to schools elements of the larger educational ecology.

There is agreement, too, that neither regular nor special schooling is sufficiently healthy. Consequently, integration combines ingredients falling short of educational excellence. For example, mainstreaming frequently brings students with special needs into classroom norms lacking the elasticity required to accommodate them. The goal of mainstreaming many students now segregated in various special programs and classrooms almost always requires for its adequate fulfillment substantial changes in the conduct of "regular" classrooms.

Indeed, succeeding chapters, each of which addresses various aspects of the integration theme, bring to the surface a problem of even greater magnitude: the necessity for and the difficulties of sustaining schools that continue, over time, to be responsive to their constituencies and diligently attentive to the needs of all students. There are some schools that have in place the necessary facilities, programs, and personnel. Their stewards are chronically dissatisfied with the status quo; they seek to sustain renewing schools.

Each of the chapters contributes to the design and conduct of such schools. Some describe alternative systems of evaluation or curricula or human connections. Some come close to describing whole schools and their accompanying support systems. There is considerable agreement on the importance of focusing on the individual site and directing support to it. But there is considerable disagreement among several of the authors regarding the role of "outside" intervention and particularly the impact of such on the desired "inside" processes of renewal.

One author views large-scale federal initiatives such as America 2000, ardently promulgated by President Bush and Lamar Alexander, secretary of education, as providing both the necessary goals and the leverage for widespread educational improvement. Several others view such as dysfunctional, as inhibiting rather than facilitating school renewal. Yet, they do not negate the need for federal and state policymakers to take strong action from time to time, especially to correct injustices and inequities. The balance between empowering those at the school level, on the one hand, and overregulating them, on the other, is a delicate one.

Although this book is one of advocacy with respect to the moral mission of educating all children and youths well, it stops short—by commission, not omission—of advocating a single, fixed route to fulfilling this mission. Indeed, the several authors were chosen for their area of expertise in relation to the rationale for the book and brief chapter outlines initially developed by the two editors. In their invitations to participate, the editors probed authors' interest in and enthusiasm for the theme but not their ideologies with respect to developing it.

The agreement at the outset, then, as stated earlier, was on the need for closely integrating general and special schooling so as to provide more common, high-quality, general education for all. Other agreements, some of them noted previously, emerged in the writing. The dissonance of disagreements may take away from coherence in the whole. But these disagreements make a positive contribution. They remind us that pursuit of the good in education rarely represents a single set of values. Instead, there are competing "goods," each deserving of close attention and careful analysis.

ACKNOWLEDGMENTS

Chapter 10 summarizes some of the findings of a comprehensive study of the education of educators carried out under the auspices of the Center for Educational Renewal, College of Education, University of Washington. Most of this work, conducted over a five-year period (1985–1990), is reported in several volumes published in 1990 and in a series of technical reports. Although the major focus was on the preservice preparation of "general" teachers, a considerable amount of data regarding programs for future "special" teachers was gathered, collated, and analyzed. There was not, however, a sufficient corpus of material to warrant a separate book.

When we, the editors of this book, drew up the preliminary outline, teacher education for both general and special teachers emerged as a significant topic. Sharon Field, coauthor of chapter 10, had contributed to the development of questions to be asked of future teachers of special education in the aforementioned study. Further, she had collated the several different kinds of data collected and had written the only document reporting this part of the research, the center's technical report 10. The current volume, *Integrating General and Special Education*, provided a unique opportunity to juxtapose different sets of data in order to make some comparisons of teacher preparation for general teachers, on the one hand, and special teachers, on the other, and to identify needed changes in both. Special thanks go to Dr. Field for both providing relevant background material and then sharing it with a wider audience through her contribution to chapter 10.

Currently, the Center for Educational Renewal is supported by grants from the Exxon Education, Mertz-Gilmore, and Southwestern Bell foundations and the Pew Charitable Trusts. Funds carried over from an earlier grant from the Exxon Education Foundation made it possible for the Center to complete its unfinished business regarding the component of its work addressed to special education, particularly through recruitment of the several authors. We are grateful to the foundation and to those who so enthusiastically accepted our invitation and produced the chapters.

It is not possible to list here all those individuals who contributed in various ways—from suggesting likely authors to reading parts or all of chapter drafts. Those who helped are aware of having done so; we thank them all.

From beginning to end, Joan Waiss of the Center staff maintained communication with the authors, reminding them of deadlines, matters of manuscript style, and demands of final editing, all the while providing central coordination for the two editors. We extend to her our appreciation.

John I. Goodlad
Thomas C. Lovitt

Contributors

CHARLES D. BERNSTEIN is the creator of the HeadsUp! approach to early learning and president of Early Learning Institute in California. He earned a Ph.D. from Stanford University and graduated magna cum laude from Princeton University. A governor's appointee for seven years to the California State Special Education Commission, he served as its chairman in 1984. Dr. Bernstein's research underlies the parent and early childhood education programs of the Early Learning Institute.

SHARON FIELD is associate professor (research) and program director for transition and employment at the Developmental Disabilities Institute, Wayne State University. Dr. Field directs several training, research, and demonstration projects related to education and employment for people with disabilities. She is a past president of the Division on Career Development of the Council for Exceptional Children. Her master's degree in special education and doctorate in educational policy, governance, and administration are from the University of Washington.

JOHN I. GOODLAD has held professorships at Agnes Scott College, Emory University, and the Universities of Chicago, California–Los Angeles, and Washington, where he now serves as director of the Center for Educational Renewal. He holds a Ph.D. from the University of Chicago and honorary doctorates from thirteen universities in Canada and the United States. Currently, he is involved in a comprehensive program of research and development directed to the simultaneous renewal of schooling and teacher education.

DANIEL P. HALLAHAN received his Ph.D. in education and psychology from the University of Michigan. He is currently professor of education at the University of Virginia, where he has been a faculty member since 1971. His primary areas of interest in special education are learning disabilities and attention deficit disorders. He is the coauthor, with James M. Kauffman, of *Exceptional Children: Introduction to Special Education*, one of the most widely used texts in special education.

IRVING G. HENDRICK earned his doctorate in the history of education from the University of California–Los Angeles. Currently, he is professor and dean of the School of Education, University of California–Riverside. Since 1983, his research has focused on the extension of the public school's mission in the United States to include responsibility for the education of "backward," "learning disabled," and "mentally retarded" children. This inquiry has encompassed historical examination of problems and issues in special education and to consideration of appropriate educational programs for the populations studied.

JAMES M. KAUFFMAN received his Ed.D. in special education from the University of Kansas. A former classroom teacher in both general and special education, he is now professor of education in the Department of Curriculum, Instruction, and Special Education at the University of Virginia, where he has been a faculty member since 1970. Dr. Kauffman served for eight years as senior editor of *Remedial and Special Education*. His primary interest in special education is children with emotional or behavioral disorders; he is a past president of the Council for Children with Behavioral Disorders. He is the coauthor, with Daniel P. Hallahan, of *Exceptional Children: Introduction to Special Education*.

THOMAS C. LOVITT is a professor of special education at the University of Washington where he is affiliated with the Experimental Education Unit, a division of the Child Development and Mental Retardation Center. Since 1982, Dr. Lovitt has been the principal investigator of five federally funded projects involving adolescents with mild disabilities who were mainstreamed into general education classes. He has written extensively in the general area of the mildly handicapped. His doctorate is from the University of Kansas.

DONALD L. MACMILLAN earned his Ed.D. from the University of California–Los Angeles, with a major in exceptional children and minors in educational psychology and clinical psychology. Currently, he is professor of education, University of California–Riverside and research educationist with the Pacific Neuropsychiatric Program of the Department of Psychiatry, University of California, Los Angeles. His research and writing have focused particularly on mental deficiencies. Dr. MacMillan's editorial appointments range across several of the most significant journals in his field.

LYNN BAKER MURRAY has overseen teacher preparation programs in elementary, secondary, special education, and early childhood education as chair of the education department at Trinity College in Vermont. She has provided staff development and evaluation training and consultation for school teams throughout the Northeast under the auspices of the Regional Laboratory for School Improvement for the Northeast and Islands. She has directed a regional office for the Regional Laboratory and codirected the Northeast Regional Resource Center, both at Trinity College. She is principal of Fairfield Center School in Fairfield, Vermont. Her Ed.D. in school administration, evaluation, and research is from Indiana University.

AUDREY J. NOBLE currently is engaged in graduate studies in educational policy studies at Arizona State University where she is employed in the Office of University Evaluation. She previously earned degrees at Pennsylvania State University in counseling psychology. She has spent thirteen years in public education as teacher, counselor, administrator, and director of student services.

MARLEEN C. PUGACH is associate professor of teacher education in the Department of Curriculum and Instruction at the University of Wisconsin–Milwaukee. Her research interests include the role of collaborative partnerships in restructuring urban schools to enhance the success of all students, including those with disabilities. She has written widely on special education in the context of the general education community, specifically with reference to the implications of the relationship between the two for the preparation of all teachers. Her doctorate is from the University of Illinois.

JUDY A. SCHRAG is currently the director of the Office of Special Education Programs, U.S. Department of Education. Prior to assuming this role in 1989, she was the assistant superintendent of public instruction in charge of special education and other special programs in the state of Washington. Dr. Schrag is a former local director of special education and a special and general education teacher. She earned her doctorate at the University of Idaho.

MARY LEE SMITH is professor in the Division of Educational Policy Studies, College of Education, Arizona State University. She earned a Ph.D. at the University of Colorado, Boulder, in research and evaluation methodology and counseling psychology. She has published widely in policy and evaluation methodology, qualitative research, and school policies relating to deviations in the pupil career.

CYNTHIA L. WARGER received her Ph.D. at the University of Michigan. She has been both a general education and special education teacher. While at the University of Toledo, she directed the teacher preparation programs in behavioral disorders, developed a graduate-level program in autism, and served as project director for a federally funded project on special education teacher consultation. Currently, she heads an educational consulting firm based in the Washington, D.C. area that specializes in providing services to educational associations, school districts, and educational agencies.

Brief Contents

Contents

1

Access to Knowledge

John I. Goodlad

Kelly qualified for almost all the special education programs in the Carver Elementary School. "In one day he was asked to respond to six different adults in six different classrooms with six different sets of classroom behavioral standards."[1] He tried to make friends wherever he went but was most of the time a social isolate. "Kelly had become, in a sense, a world traveler of special programs."[2] Such is the principal's description of good intentions run amok.

The principal and teachers of Montlake School transformed their small school, chopped into smaller pieces by specially funded programs, into a coherent entity through creatively integrating general and special education. Regular and special education teachers worked together in the same classrooms much of the time, which reduced the student-teacher ratio to one to sixteen, something that teachers in public schools usually are able only to dream about. But they also brought down upon them the wrath of regulatory agencies unable to identify the precise use of special funds, some obtained through the entrepreneurial skills of the principal and her associates.

The 1990s ushered in for many states and communities severe financial problems and accompanying cuts in allocations to public education. Local authorities pared school budgets, cutting especially deeply into "special" programs of all kinds. Many of these had been created during the 1980s in response to *A Nation at Risk*[3] and hundreds of commission reports on the urgent need to reconstruct our schools.

Increasingly realizing that top-down policies and mandates were having little impact on schools, many policymakers joined some grassroots reformers in proposing greater decentralization of district authority to individual sites. The school as the center of change and the empowerment of

1

principals and teachers to effect improvement were central to the rhetoric of reconstruction by the beginning of the 1990s.

The preceding anecdotes and brief descriptions pose for educators some daunting problems and dilemmas. The frustrations of the principal and teachers at the Carver and Montlake schools emanated from good intentions regarding children with special needs. We have come a long way in recognizing and providing for human variability since the early days of the century when H. H. Goddard used the Binet test in reaching the conclusion that huge numbers of foreign-speaking immigrants were feeble-minded.[4] Segregation was a popular solution, and we built mental institutions at a rapid pace. Segregation and isolation extended to many kinds of "deviation," color being one of the most obvious. I went through elementary school without encountering a cerebral-palsied classmate, although every day I walked past the home of one who should have been attending with me.

It is sobering to note, however, the extent to which government has had to intervene in the cause of justice. *Brown v. Board of Education* and PL 94-142, directed primarily to the inalienable rights of minorities and the handicapped, respectively, are highly visible examples. Public and professional enlightenment was insufficient antidote to widespread bigotry and ignorance. Government and the courts had to intervene.

Unfortunately, government intervention, such as in these two examples, seeks to translate a uniform egalitarian understanding of social justice into laws intended to prevail from sea to shining sea.[5] Well intentioned, they nonetheless present the stewards of schools such as Carver and Montlake with frustrating obstacles to dealing effectively with local circumstances and the multilayered complexity of student variability. Nonetheless, such interventions are likely to continue, in spite of the rhetoric of empowering teachers and principals to make decisions based on their professional know-how and special knowledge of the territory. What all educators must recognize and commit to as part of their professional creed is that their awareness of what is good, right, and beautiful is part of the defense against bureaucratic regulations. They must play a role in the nation's civility that goes far beyond classroom management. They must join with one another and with parents and their communities in creating humane, effective, just schools (see chap. 11).

The inequitable handling of budget exigencies illustrates that we have not yet built into the civility of our culture educational beliefs, policies, and practices fully reflective of a rhetorical commitment to education for all. We have not as a nation matured to widespread understanding of the role of education in gaining full participation in the human conversation, not merely a job.[6] When the curriculum is narrowed to include only subjects considered to have most economic utility and when budget cuts eliminate hard-fought gains for the handicapped and disadvantaged, the public (including educators spared the budget knife) is disappointingly mute.

Were the daily behaviors of our citizens closely allied with our democratic ideals, there would be very little need for government intervention, especially of the judicial branch. There would be very little need for schools, either. Educating would occur through paideia. If there were schools, they would be moral cultures.

But the schools into which today's teachers are socialized reflected from the outset the warts and blemishes of their larger context. School structures, curricula, and instructional practices solidified around a narrow conception of present and future clients, innocent of any research and inquiry regarding all of these. These commonplaces of schooling have been severely strained over the years, but they have been only stretched and modestly modified, not fundamentally changed. The necessary reinvention of schools has not occurred. Adaptation has been accompanied by serious omission and both constructive and ill-conceived commission, much of it thrust on schools from the outside.

As stated in the preface, this book addresses part of the necessary reconstruction—much greater fusion of general and special education. There is a delicate balance to be sustained. Many of the good things that have happened on the road to humane, effective schooling are the result of focusing on a special need and protecting resources earmarked for it. The admonition that all good education is special for the student has philosophical appeal but tends to blunt the edge of overdue intervention for the handicapped and disadvantaged. On the other hand, special education cannot afford the isolation and segregation that often attaches to "special" and the lack of the broad support that offers protection against the budget knife. Ensuring the special attention that children with disabilities need and simultaneously keeping them and their programs connected to a larger educational context present daunting challenges.

The greater integration of special and general education is an educational development long overdue. Effecting it stirs and rearranges an extraordinary political, economic, and educational network of agencies, institutions, and individuals, as succeeding chapters illustrate. Significant change affects entire ecosystems, arousing passions, changing human behaviors, and exposing reefs not marked on any charts.

Because significant change is tortuous and wearing for those involved and affected, major actors frequently become both tired and myopic and ultimately settle for something falling far short of what is necessary. This has been to a considerable degree the case in desegregating schools and mainstreaming. Gaining access often has been hardly worth it. Paraphrasing Oscar Wilde (*Lady Windemere's Fan*), there are two tragedies in life: one is not getting what one wants; the other is getting it—this is the greater tragedy.

A central argument of this and following chapters is that today's schools are blemished. Many of the things they do routinely are not well suited to their clients' needs; some are downright damaging and put children and youths at risk. I shall not list here the litany embracing home-school relationships, provisions for student mobility, conflicting expectations, reactions to race and poverty, sex discrimination, testing, the nature and organization of the curricula, methods of teaching, grouping and tracking, and more. Documentation and analyses are available elsewhere.[7] More serious is the alarming absence of reflection on these and other imperfections in "regular" school environments.[8]

And so I regard the need to more closely integrate general and special education—much of the present separation being itself a blemish—as a given. The common practice of many special education teachers being mere recipients of students sent to them rather than partners with other teachers in redesigning the school in order to rid it of conditions conducive of problems is dysfunctional. But we must be aware of the folly inherent in assuming that the implied process of renewal is generally characteristic of schools. It is not.[9] Few schools engage in critical self-appraisal and renewal.

Nor dare we assume that cadres of inquiring new teachers are coming into our schools prepared and eager to join into or initiate the site-based reconstruction or renewal for which they are to be empowered. Research into the education of educators described in chapter 10 reveals their preparation to be strangely separated from the moral, social, and political nature of the American democracy, almost devoid of attention to the school as an entity and the need for its reform, and engulfed by the demands and mechanisms of the classroom to the near exclusion of inquiry into major issues of excellence and equity embedded in the schooling enterprise.[10] Further, beginning teachers come into the schools as strangers, sharing very little in regard to mission, values, a base of professional knowledge, and the inclination and know-how essential to concerted group action.[11]

I leave further discussion of this dismaying conclusion and possible remedies to chapter 10. This chapter seeks to define the mission of schools committed to excellence and equity in the American democracy, describe some of their present shortcomings, and suggest the processes in which all connected with schools might engage in seeking to close this gap and create more nearly moral cultures.

TOWARD A MISSION OF SCHOOLING AND TEACHING

Early on in our comprehensive inquiry into the education of educators, my colleagues and I were surprised to discover that a seemingly natural connection—that of schools and the preparation of those who work in them—has entered only recently into proposals for the reform of schooling.[12] It came as no surprise, then, to find later in our work that the stated purposes of teacher education programs in colleges and universities turn in upon themselves in specifying knowledge and skills for future teachers devoid of any connection to the mission of schools and both practical and ideal delineations of the role of teachers. What we surmised from all of this—teacher education conducted as a largely dispassionate academic enterprise detached from moral imperatives—was confirmed in the data regarding extant conditions.[13] In effect, the preparation of teachers is without economic, social, political, or professional mission. Consequently, the programmatic incoherence identified by Howey and Zimpher in six case studies is to be expected.[14]

We set out in search of a credible mission, an exploration we had not initially thought to be necessary. Guided by a sense of minimal essentials, we postulated four legs to the professional stool of teaching and the teaching profession based on assumptions regarding the role of education and schooling in our society and the demands these place on schoolteachers.

The first of these is the critical enculturation of the young into a social and political democracy. The second is inculcation (in the best educational sense of disciplined encounters) in the knowledge, belief, and knowing systems of the human conversation. The third is thorough understanding of and expertise in the art and science of teaching (pedagogy) sufficient to encompass a wide range in students' styles and ways of knowing and to diagnose and remedy many of the conditions that impede learning. And the fourth pertains to stewardship—the ability to recognize deficiencies in the commonplaces of schooling and to pose viable alternatives, the commitment and the know-how to replace the ineffective with the more effective.

This short list appeared necessary but insufficient. All decisions in education are inherently value-laden. Schooling and education are moral endeavors.

We were about to distort the symmetry of our professional stool with a fifth leg when we realized that everything we wanted to say about the moral component is a dimension of one or more of the four. It is impossible to think or talk for long about enculturation, what knowledge is of most worth, teaching, or the proper stewardship of schools without encountering moral dilemmas and turning to moral argument.

To broaden and clarify our perspective on the significance of these moral dimensions (since they have played such a small part in recent discourse regarding educational reform), we commissioned a clutch of papers on teacher professionalism, moral considerations in teaching, the moral responsibilities of public schools and teachers, the school as a moral community, and more.[15] We then included exploration of this domain in the planned observation of teacher preparation settings and in the questionnaires for and interviews with administrators, professors, and students. We examined programs for the preparation of special teachers and first-level administrators (e.g., principals) as well as teachers for regular classrooms.

The results confirmed initial assumptions and hypotheses. Preparation programs devoid of mission could hardly be expected to have moral themes. Programs devoid of a moral mission could hardly be expected to be infused with the discussion of moral principles and the exploration of moral dilemmas rising out of our conduct of schooling. Yet, once we engaged them, professors and students entered freely and often enthusiastically into moral discourse, while readily admitting its general absence in programs. Students being inducted into the regularities of schooling had not often considered the need and possibilities for reform but sometimes were aware, for example, of inequities begging for attention. Students in special education preparatory programs, more than those preparing generally for elementary or secondary school teaching, readily spoke to the neglect of the handicapped and of the need for and enactment of regulatory legislation. Commonly, however, students sought to advance their positions through empirical or legal rather than normative argument. For example, they referred much more frequently to legislation governing educational requirements for the disabled than to moral imperatives regarding the education of all.

We should not be surprised that teachers-to-be, nearing entry into teaching careers, are preoccupied with their growing awareness of classroom demands and with fitting in. We cannot and should not expect them to be reformers at the outset. The cause for alarm, however, is that the settings into which they go also are caught up in these preoccupations, with little or no ongoing reflection on what they now do or inquiry into other possibilities. This alarm would quickly abate if we could have confidence in the claim that teachers "make decisions professionally and ethically, unaware of the complexity of what we do."[16] Unfortunately, ignorance and moral sensitivity are unlikely handmaidens.

This quote, from a teacher, serves to highlight the problem. Most teachers believe that they make decisions professionally and ethically and seek to avoid doing otherwise. Unfortunately, unawareness of complexity contributes to the preservation of immoral school practices to which they simply are not attuned.

TOWARD JUST SCHOOLS

The multilayered complexity of schools is such that all the elements of mission and stewardship interweave. Perhaps teachers are intuitively aware of this and so deliberately confine their span of attention to the already demanding complexities of the classroom simply to survive and manage each day. In so doing, however, they must come to understand the degree to which this is a kind of retreat, the result being that various agencies on the outside move into the vacuum and determine the school context in which teachers and students go about their work. Teachers often complain about the resulting expectations and frustrations, but, in a very real sense, their too narrow definition of role disenfranchises them in domains where major decisions that impact on them are made by others. McNeil effectively describes the dysfunctionalities in the classroom that result from bureaucratic policies bumping up against what teachers believe to be best but feel constrained not to do.[17] (See chap. 11 for further discussion.)

Toward a Moral Context

Unless they assume responsibility beyond the classroom, teachers become mere functionaries in a context determined for them. Ultimately, the context so intrudes that they find themselves in a legislated classroom.[18] The tragedy is that misguided requirements are rarely countered by the evidence teachers can provide regarding impact on their work and on students. A good and just system of education, good and just schools, and good and just classrooms depend on the active participation of both parents and teachers who must not by default give up the responsibilities and liberties intended by the framers of the Constitution.

As Nisbet points out, the framers hated the imperial powers of the Great Britain they had left and wrote the Constitution to ensure "a miscellany of cultures held together, but not otherwise much influenced by the federal government in Washington."[19] The underlying ideas were truths presumed to be self-evident: equality, inalienable rights, the pursuit of happiness, civil rights, the consent of the governed, the dissent of the governed.[20] These were assumed to be what people had come for, valued, and would seek to sustain. They provided a moral context for government, home, school, and the individual. Abiding by these truths would be the best defense against unwanted government intervention.

We managed for many years as a nation with extraordinary weak links between Americans and their national government. By 1913, we had added the federal income tax to the prevailing linkage of the postal system. But were the framers to look in on us today, they would be astonished and probably outraged by "the Leviathan-like presence of the national government in the affairs of states, towns, and cities, and in the lives, cradle to grave, of individuals."[21] We have not done too well in keeping government off our backs, in spite of the repeated promises of elected officials to do so.

Although the federal government has provided much of the rhetoric regarding the importance of education to the nation and the individual, most regulation and intervention have come from state governments—undoubtedly much more than the framers intended. But, in a diverse economy based heavily on an abundance of resources, there were many roads to opportunity—unless one were Black or Native American or Latino. Until recently, the common school occupied only a short span of years and months, serving more as a rite of passage than an obstacle, and shut the door to minorities. National and individual well-being depended much more on natural resources and expanding frontiers than on a highly developed, finely tuned school system, rhetoric extolling its excellence and benefits notwithstanding.

As Clark observes, "If individuals cannot get anywhere without some book learning, then the occupations richest in intellectual content move to the center of the stage."[22] And competition for these occupations and the most advantageous educational routes to them increases dramatically. The interesting side effect is that unfair and inappropriate inequities in regard to gaining access to these routes become more sharply apparent, if one is attuned to them. The shabby side of our democratic society is that the federal government has had to intervene because citizens have been insufficiently attuned. Oh, yes, the exercise of justice often was driven by agitation, but largely by those most disadvantaged, not by those whose present advantages might have sensitized them to their responsibility to the common weal. Not citizens educated through paideia in a moral culture characterized by moral schools led to sharp acceleration in access to schools and the best knowledge. The up side to *Brown v. Board of Education* and PL 94-142 is that they happened. The down side is that the government had to step in to enforce justice. The darkest side of the down side is the degree to which moral omission and commission in our polity made a shambles of the hoped-for equity. Government may be the last resort of scoundrels, but it is also, too often, the last resort for justice.

Until relatively recent times, there were very few culture-shaking federal interventions into the conduct of education. *Brown v. Board of Education* and PL 94-142 are virtually classic cases of seeking to incorporate into law a uniform, egalitarian understanding of social justice.[23] The need to mainstream visible segments of our population into schools and classrooms was overdue and increasingly obvious. The stakes of educational deprivation for minorities and the disabled were escalating at a rapid rate.

But so long as education and schooling are seen largely as individual opportunity, only loosely linked with social stratification (far less significant than color, e.g.) and only rhetorically associated with the wealth of the nation, all sorts of inequities, injustices, and malpractices in school can go relatively unnoticed. Charges of inequity are easily ignored, especially by the advantaged. Lack of success in the system can be accounted for on the basis of immutable inherited individual differences, lack of effort, family negligence, or whatever. The report cards I brought home from school featured a two-part summing up: a grade for overall achievement and another for "deportment." A low mark for deportment and a B in achievement (a rather unlikely combination) suggested to my parents that a little more attention by Johnny to his D in deportment might result in an A for achievement. In other words, the pony was on my back: I alone was responsible for success or failure. Only once in my growing up did my parents intervene to raise questions about what they considered a seriously out-of-line school decision. The school was right; the poorly performing student was wrong.

There is no way of raising the stakes in regard to the importance of schooling, however, without intensifying public and family scrutiny of school policies and practices. Interest in moral dimensions such as equity and justice also increases in intensity. Perhaps this is why there is today so little moral discourse surrounding current federal intervention in our schools. There may be government awareness that so many moral sand traps lie along the federal educational course projected for the year 2000 that the less said about them the better. On the other hand, if there is government unawareness, then land mines lie just under the sand.

To repeat, the context of schooling for more than the first half of this century has been morally inattentive. The most glaring inequities have brought forward government intervention in the cause of justice. But dozens of others are tolerated as a natural part of school culture or simply overlooked. Recent federal initiatives have raised the education stakes from the level of individual choice and opportunity to individual and national necessity. Either we must take account very soon of the moral implications so that schools become more just places, or we will have a major educational disaster. As schools become not just a rite of passage but a vital link to personal and national well-being, the conditions they provide for all children are subjected to increasingly close public scrutiny.

A Scenario for the Year 2000

In 1991 and 1992, the most visible educational initiative on the scene embraced two components: national goals and national systems of tests. The official federal strategy, America 2000, took its name from the target year 2000 for all children coming to school ready to learn; an increase in the high school graduation rate to at least 90 percent; all students demonstrating competency in challenging subject matter on leaving grades four, eight, and twelve; top standing in the world by students of the United States in science and mathematics; nationwide adult literacy; and drug- and violence-free schools offering a disciplined environment for learning. Corporate America was invited by President George Bush and Secretary of Education Lamar Alexander to contribute $200 million to a research and development effort behind the New Generation of American Schools—one in each congressional district.

A parallel initiative, also geared to the national goals, was taking shape. Advanced by the National Center on Education and the Economy, it already was influencing legislation in several states. Oregon, for example, had passed a reform plan based on a series of examinations that would culminate in a "Certificate of Initial Mastery" for tenth-grade students. Certificate in hand, a sixteen-year-old will qualify to choose a college preparatory or job training curriculum for his or her concluding years of high school. Some of the language of support for the plan endorses possession of the certificate as a prerequisite for entry into the work force.

Although the language of endorsement surrounding these goals-plus-tests proposals for educational excellence claims remarkably widespread support,[24] thoughtful rejoinders range from deep caution to alarm.[25] Some lauded intentions but doubted that the necessary financial commitments would be made. Some saw great danger in the widespread assumption that schools are at the heart of our economic decline and that good schools will turn the country around: "we are guilty of failing to examine the real root causes. . . . When Great Britain's economy hit the skids, no one blamed the schools."[26] Numerous critics viewed the national reform initiative as having disastrous implications for the handicapped and disadvantaged.

Let us put aside, however, the research-based economic issue of the shaky relationship between our productivity and schools. Let us put aside also the many questions one might raise about test-driven approaches to student motivation and educational excellence, even when the consequences of failure are dire. And let us put aside even the most obvious issue of the modest degree to which success in school predicts much in the way of human behavior beyond further success in school. Let us, instead, accept America 2000 (and related initiatives) as a serious, well-intentioned effort to produce the first-rate schools large numbers of us believe we do not but must have. Let us accept for the sake of discussion even the proposition that this strategy will stay on course to its ultimate culmination in the proposed tests and the building of national goals and national tests into the continuing fabric of schooling. For purposes of joining the argument that follows, assume that persons in and close to schools take the position that they have a responsibility to help strengthen this fabric within the conditions imposed by its larger context.

I have argued in preceding pages that the federal government, an increasingly significant part of this larger context, has had to intervene in matters of schooling for purposes of ensuring justice. The most visible issue has been access—first to schools and then to knowledge, with the latter access being by far the more obscure and subtle. Many of the subtleties have either been ignored in local practice or glossed over. "We've always done it this way" has proved to be an extraordinarily powerful justification for the status quo, serving to retain common practices in the face of both research and moral argument against their retention. Often, the changes called for were to benefit only a minority (frequently a relatively powerless minority), and so they were not powerfully motivating for the public as a whole. Frequently, too, many of those experiencing inequities and perceiving them as personal injustices did not connect them to major negative consequences to follow in the future. Success in school is not and has not been equally motivating for all.

In the scenario for the year 2000 sketched earlier, however, the game changes dramatically. The federal government has intervened both rhetorically and with a plan of action to raise enormously the stakes involved in gaining access not just to schools but to knowledge. Both individual and national well-being are at stake.

Instead of a federal policy largely of omission with respect to education and schooling, we suddenly have commission. Instead of commission spurred by a need to correct injustice, we have a commitment that puts education almost at the level of defense in federal policy. Suddenly, instead of the federal government becoming the last resort for individual justice in matters of education and schooling, it must become its own watchdog in regard to equity and other moral matters surrounding its own initiative.

The language of America 2000 addresses the involvement of "states and communities all over the country."[27] In the words "a nine-year crusade,"[28] it invokes a mission. There cannot be a mission without moral imperatives. With the stakes of this crusade so high, the federal government cannot settle for the role of cheerleader. Having set the goals and announced such a critical role for tests, it is morally and strategically obliged to ensure what inescapably goes between—the conditions necessary to accessing the requisite knowledge. Nor can the judiciary branch of government eschew its role of ensuring equity through equal access for all. Ultimately, for sure, it will be called on to pass judgment on the adequacy and even-handedness of its sister branches.

One wonders how much those calling for the crusade and for the local and state commitments it entails have thought about their responsibility to the crusaders. One wonders, too, how much they have thought about their ultimate accountability, especially if the crusade flounders. Perhaps someone already is greasing the hinges to the escape doors.

Clearly, two sets of conditions between the goals and the tests must be in place. First, there are those of the infrastructure surrounding schools—conditions of support funded collaboratively by local, state, and federal authorities. These must assure equal access to the requisite knowledge, whatever the school attended. Second, there are those thousands of schools that must be maximally educative, moral cultures. They must become inventively renewing.

THE EDUCATIONAL ECOSYSTEM

In an arresting paper, Welsh describes some of the parenting he and his colleagues take on every day in a school honored with one of the Reagan administration's first Excellence in Education awards.[29] Why, he asks, did Conant's vision[30] of a comprehensive high school meeting the educational needs of all youth in the community fail to become a reality? He answers, "It was swept away by demographic, cultural, economic, and technological changes that Conant did not foresee, and that American high schools and families are only beginning to recognize."[31]

Some critics, far removed from Welsh's daily encounters, give the back of their hand to these realities, maintaining them to be merely self-serving excuses of educators. Such assaults and educators' defenses get us nowhere. The fact is that recent, cataclysmic shifts in the moral fiber and supportive infrastructure surrounding schools have not only vastly complicated the school's tasks but also have disadvantaged, almost hopelessly, millions of young people in the education race elevated to high significance by America 2000. Without addressing the following points, at a minimum, the crusade is doomed to failure.

The first goal is for all children to start school ready to learn. How ready for what? Commonly, this question is answered by another: Is the child ready for school? Conventionally, this is determined by readiness tests—a measure now being proposed once again in relation to this goal.

Since tests in kindergarten or admission to the first grade measure predominantly what the child has learned prior to coming to school, states cannot stand idly by in the face of the diverse array of handicaps and disadvantages that children bring to classrooms. It becomes morally reprehensible, then, for a state using tests to determine later eligibility for higher education and jobs not to address itself to inequities early on. Consequently, a condition necessary to this nation's pursuit of its crusade is a comprehensive, nationwide family support system: early education in parenting, prenatal counseling, adequate nutrition for mother and child, a social and medical support system, and preschool educational programs such as Head Start.

The second goal is to increase high school graduation from the present figure of approximately 75 percent to 90 percent or more. The diploma is to "mean something," not merely seat time but satisfactory completion of a world-class curriculum as judged by performances on world-class tests. The crusade becomes accountable for whatever measures are needed to remove all barriers to access, whether the result of geography or individual handicap. For example, a technologically driven system may be the only feasible way to bring the basic curriculum measured by the tests to those students in very small high schools now getting only a whiff of a foreign language, mathematics, science, and perhaps other subjects. There must be in place a fifty-state educational delivery system, accompanied by a federal financial support commitment calibrated to each state's ability to pay that assures every child equal access to the necessary teachers, curriculum, and pedagogy. Our concept of "special" is vastly expanded until it blends with a norm of access encompassing all our children and youths.

The third goal takes us beyond English, history, mathematics, science, and geography to school responsibility for inculcating responsible citizenship, motivation for further learning, and whatever translates into productive employment. Enculturation has been established for some time as the overarching goal of schooling in the American democracy.[32] But the credentials requisite to advancing this goal never have been up front for teachers or teacher education programs. Ironically, the leaders of America 2000 and their advisers advocate alternative certification for teachers that would make no formal checks (such as examinations) on this requisite among candidates and would depend heavily on mentors who largely lack it. Must we write off, then, a condition critical to success of the crusade, namely, professional preparation for teachers? There is little dispute over what is required for the medical practitioner: "The combination of a vigorous assessment, an extended course of professional study, and a well-supervised practicum provides the strongest warrant of competence. Such a requirement answers not only that certain studies have been completed, but that certificate holders have been socialized in college and university settings where there is extended time for interaction and reflection with peers and faculty on matters of professional practice, ethics, and tradition."[33] Why not the same for the teachers who are to enculturate the young into the traits required to keep our nation strong and economically competitive?

The fourth goal will have us first in the world in science and mathematics achievement. Obviously, the educational delivery system required for achievement of the second goal pertains equally here. In addition, however, a massive overhaul of existing curricula is essential. For example, our underachieving mathematics curriculum is estimated to be at least a full year behind that of countries such as Japan.[34] Its redesign and that of other school subjects is one of the necessary conditions to be attended to both within and beyond schools.

The fifth goal calls for comprehensive literacy among adults—broad participation in the human conversation, if you will. Since the target date is the year 2000, we are talking about adults now beyond the K–12 system as well as future adults now well along in it. Both need extensive, accessible, continuing education, especially if the schooling they have had is anywhere near as bad as critics maintain. Today's and tomorrow's adults come into settings impatient with problems requiring complex, intellectual, and technical solutions, into a culture where a kind of educating through the media is pitched close to estimates of the lowest common denominator. Something more intellectually challenging is needed.

The time is come—long past come—for us to recognize and develop educational ecosystems for all ages in which schools play only a part, probably a much smaller part than is recognized in the strident calls for reform. Cremin put the argument well:

> My argument has been that profound . . . changes in the education proffered by families, day care centers, peer groups, television broadcasters, and work places have drastically altered the overall education being offered to the American people. The result has been a cacophony of teaching, the effects of which have been at best difficult to determine and even more difficult to assess. . . . I argue further that the phenomenon by its very nature calls for a much more extensive body of tested knowledge about the institutions and processes of education than is now available to those charged with the development of educational policy and the conduct of educational practice. In the absence of such knowledge, it is folly to talk about excellence in American education.[35]

There is plenty of talk about such excellence, all focused on schools. Not America 2000 or any of the other major goals-and-tests proposals talk about the total educative infrastructure Cremin discussed. If the schools count for only a small part of what is wrong in the United States, as Kerr contends,[36] then those pushing these initiatives have a moral responsibility at a minimum to invoke the rest of the educational ecosystem. Otherwise, the crusade will most certainly fail, and all those drawn in and the nation as a whole will fail to find the promised grail. And we will have sent our schools once more into the wilderness.

The sixth goal—school environments conducive to learning, free of drugs and violence—depends in large measure on all the others. We can afford no longer to shrug off, with a curl of the lip and the word *cop-out*, the problems young people bring into classrooms and the demands these place on teachers. For those who continue to do so, I recommend the sentence of a week or two of responsibility for six or seven classes a day in an inner-city high school. The school crusade will not reach its destination by the year 2000 in any case. But unless we mount a much larger crusade on our whole array of economic and social problems, even the *vision* of attaining the six education goals will fade and die.

Educators and the nation have much to gain and nothing to lose by continuing to strive toward school environments conducive to learning, whatever the current reform rhetoric. There are many such environments now. Furthermore, there is much agreement among those in renewing schools about the models they have in mind and some solid understandings of how to get them. Many critics and policymakers fail to take the time required to learn that such schools almost invariably have underpinnings in common and function according to many of the same principles. They write off such schools as unique and nonreplicable, looking endlessly for an elixir to bottle—education's Coca-Cola.

RENEWING SCHOOLS

The substance of preceding pages may be summarized as follows. A federally driven educational initiative, America 2000, promises to usher in a future when the personal and national stakes connected with gaining access to certain kinds of academic knowledge and skills will be very high. This initiative inescapably brings to the forefront exceedingly sensitive issues regarding the moral responsibility of the nation to assure not simply access but equitable access to the necessary learning. The monetary costs and the need for expertise are enormous. Failure on the part of the federal government to fulfill its responsibility to its own initiative while still pursuing it inevitably will result in suits carried all the way to its own judicial branch. There is precedent for federal intervention in educational matters in the cause of justice.

Not surprisingly, the rhetoric surrounding America 2000 speaks much to the involvement of states and local communities. Its success depends on fine-tuning local schools—something very difficult to do. But direct intervention in this fine-tuning must be in the name of justice and equity, or the federal government exceeds its constitutional rights in the educational domain. The legal issues raided by America 2000 have been in part side-stepped through creation of the New American Schools Development Corporation (NASDC) funded by contributions from the private sector. Grants from the NASDC to bidders are designed to stimulate the development and implementation of New American Schools.

Presumably, this part of America 2000 will be a resource for those hundreds of thousands of educators in thousands of schools who increasingly will be empowered (and held accountable) for fine-tuning their schools. In other words, much ado about schooling in high places ultimately comes down to school principals, teachers, students, and parents in local settings. It will be some years before the grants from NASDC bear fruit, some of which will be sour. In the meantime, toward what prior experience and ideas might local groups turn?

A scattered body of information provides two rather different sets of directions for responsible parties seeking to have good schools. The first has to do with a number of conditions characterizing those schools that have relatively high levels of parent, teacher, and student satisfaction. These are schools seeking to do better, to renew. The second body of information is mostly in the form of case studies or reports that provide individual examples of routes worth replicating. The general characteristics appear to be pervasive correlates of good schools that differ in their specific implementations. The message to those in individual school sites seeking to renew is both simple and frustrating: Do not look for general principles and generalizations to be accompanied simultaneously by "how to do it" manuals; if the principle appears to make sense, look to any success stories you can find and seek to adapt them to your own unique context.

Good schools are renewing schools. They remain quite stable while effecting systemic change. Their normal condition is one of continuously shedding old configurations while taking on new ones. Each new configuration is anticipated to serve as well or better than present ones in future circumstances that are perceived to differ from present ones. A school pronounced good cannot remain both unchanged and good over time.

Taking Care of School Business

Persons associated with renewing schools not only take care of school business but also perceive themselves as stewards of the whole.[37] Principals, teachers, parents, and students are organized over the long term into groups that worry about clusters of concerns: attending school regularly and on time and not dropping out, assuring a comprehensive curriculum for each student, creating and maintaining a school climate that emphasizes learning and embraces attention to the needs of all students, keeping good teaching high in the school's value system and assuring opportunities for teachers to renew, maintaining open channels of community-home-school communication, and more. Each group is chaired by a chief worrier. Short-term, unanticipated matters are addressed quickly by administrators who, in the toughest problem areas, are advised by working parties who are thanked and dismissed after completing their tasks. The agendas of faculty meetings and parent-student-teacher meetings address the reports of groups at work. These reports are subjected to a continuous cycle of dialogue, decisions, actions, and evaluation (DDAE).[38] All such meetings are preceded by distribution of reports to be considered and followed by reports of decisions made.

This scenario is a far cry from the way most schools address their affairs. Instead of making most decisions personally, principals must see that decisions are made and implemented. Instead of seeking control over only a single classroom, teachers must learn to be part of a span of control that encompasses an entire school. Instead of being told about only the progress of their children in school, parents must participate in determining what their school is for. Instead of merely fitting into decisions already made regarding organizational arrangements for children with special needs already in place, special education teachers must join with their general education colleagues in determining how best to take care of the needs of all children.

Things neglected deteriorate. A school is in many ways like a garden. In gardens unattended, weeds soon compete with vegetables for nutrients and sunlight. If schools are not carefully attended to by those in and close to them—parents, teachers, and students—nobody else will. Crusades will pass by, leaving only continuing decay.

The Human Connection

The human connections in healthy schools are markedly different from those in unhealthy schools. Principals set a tone that values good teaching but consider teachers as competent professionals who can be trusted to do their best in the classroom. Teachers regard one another in very much the same way. Further, they respect all students, eschewing sarcasm and favoritism. They are very sensitive with respect to the subtle ways racism is expressed, both overtly and covertly, by themselves and others alike, and work diligently to exclude it from the entire climate of school and classrooms.[39] Parents know their children's teachers, talk with them periodically during the school year, and perceive themselves as both having essential information about school programs and policies and being adequately involved in school affairs.[40]

All of these traits are quite different in most schools at the other end of the quality scale. In unhealthy schools, principals commonly perceive teachers to be part of the problem. They believe teachers to be far more involved in making schoolwide decisions than teachers perceive themselves to be. Teachers are more likely to view colleagues less generously, as less professional, than is the case in markedly healthier schools. Students are more likely to perceive their classrooms as marked by teachers' favoritism and sarcasm. Parents more frequently report having little information about school affairs, not knowing their children's teachers, and not being much involved.

It is significant to note that in schools where these human connections are in disarray, student preoccupation with things other than academic work is more likely to surface and, indeed, to characterize school climate. Being athletic or "good looking" dominates in the popularity of junior and senior high school students; being a gang member outweighs being a good student in the worst schools. An academic climate is hard to sustain in today's schools. But it can become a realistic expectation when the principal, parents, teachers, and students work together at attaining such.

School Size

Clearly, it is easier for all involved to work together toward shared values in the more intimate settings that small schools provide over large ones. In comparing the most healthy with the least healthy schools in our research sample, my colleagues and I noted that our smallest schools were consistently among the former and our largest among the latter. This does not mean that large schools are necessarily bad; it simply is harder to make and keep them good.

Small schools, it appears, necessarily depend on a large proportion of parents, teachers, and students to take care of ongoing business. A larger percentage of students participate in such so-called extracurricular activities as the student council, the yearbook, performances for parents and the community, athletics, and so on, whereas a much smaller percentage can and often does cover the whole in larger schools.[41] We need more definitive studies of the degree to which students who deviate from established norms are cut off more in large schools than in small schools from extracurricular activities often associated with the mainstream.

Budgetary and curricular advantages often associated with increasing school size appear not to be sustained as schools grow larger and larger.[42] And increases appear also to increase student anonymity and impersonality in the teacher-student relationship. The few studies that have been done suggest that assumed benefits no longer increase, but problems associated with size do increase when elementary, middle, and senior high schools grow beyond 400, 600, and 800 students, respectively. Of course, if one does not value the nature of the human connections in schools, their size probably will be of little interest.

Individualized Attention

When parents, teachers, and students are in close agreement that their school is of high quality, they all perceive students to be the locus of much individualized attention. Satisfied parents perceive their children to be known, safe, and attended to in school. This kind of security appears to be of more parental significance than the nature of the curriculum and teaching.[43] Perhaps they assume that the former is a correlate of the latter two.

In the most satisfying schools of the sample my colleagues and I studied, this perception of individualized attention extended beyond the gifted and disabled to include "normal" children. This is a rather significant finding within the theme of this book. It suggests that beyond whatever selfishness parents may display in regard to what they expect of their school for their own children, there is some parental recognition of the necessity to serve the needs of all children. Some of the excessive demands parents make might tend to fade with growing awareness that their school is serving all of its student population well and fairly.

Curriculum and Instruction

One of our most dismaying findings raises intriguing questions about how to get good schools as well as speculation running counter to some conventional wisdom regarding reform. The aforementioned generalizations regarding healthy and unhealthy schools were sharpened for us when we compared the most satisfying schools in our sample (the top quartile) with the least satisfying (the bottom quartile), leaving out the middle half. There was great variability in all of the areas that are very much at the discretion of school-based responsible parties: class climate, school climate, principal-teacher relations, teacher-teacher relations, teacher-student relations, parent-teacher relations, school-community relations, and so forth. It should be noted, also, that our smallest schools were in the top quartile and our largest in the bottom. Presumably, as stated earlier, it simply is easier to effect the human connections implied when a school is small.

One is inclined to conclude from this discussion that a good school is a good school in all of its characteristics, just as a bad one is bad. And to conclude that a good school tends to be small just as a bad school tends to be large. But I have said nothing as yet about the very heart of schooling—the curriculum and instruction. Our data, coming from various sources, including detailed descriptions of ongoing activity in 1,016 classrooms, revealed very little variability in regard to either. Indeed, both clustered narrowly around a mean that we considered unsatisfactory: a dominantly lecturing mode of instruction except at the primary level, becoming almost exclusive of all other methods in the senior high schools; a curriculum geared closely to courses of studies and textbooks and rarely balanced with respect to education in all the major domains of knowledge and knowing.

Reflecting on this finding brings into focus the degree to which the curriculum and instruction of schooling are determined outside of the dynamics of individual schools by tradition, state and district curriculum guides, and publishers of textbooks. The best examples of renewal among the schools of our sample fine-tuned the process in areas never legislated or prescribed. But even these schools tampered little with the renewal of instructional methods since these are largely handed down like heirlooms from teachers to teachers who were once their students. Principals and teachers in even the very best schools in our sample engaged hardly at all in fundamentally redesigning the curriculum. Clearly, self-renewal in schools is a far-off ideal.

THE MORAL IMPERATIVE

The incomplete list of characteristics of good schools suggests the malleability of major elements of school culture taken under control by those most intimately involved—principal, teachers, parents, students. Working collaboratively, they are able to construct settings of such nature that several correlates involving human connections add up to create good schools—safe, caring, learning environments. The absence of these characteristics reveals the decay that prevails when these connections are not made.

We shall see in chapter 10 that principals and teachers are not being prepared in present preparation programs, whether "regular" or "alternative," to effect this renewing process. Consequently, when it occurs, it is more by serendipity than by architectural intent and ability deliberately cultivated in the crucibles of preparation programs for administrators and both regular and special teachers. The apparent power of the renewing process is such, however, that it must not be left to chance. Preparing for it must be as much a part of teacher education as must be general and pedagogical education.

Indeed, the cultivation of the major human connections in schools and their mobilization for purposes of renewal appear to be so powerful as to be seductive in regard to matters of curriculum and instruction. Parental satisfaction with a child's daily enjoyment of a humane, caring school can come to be enough, and it is much to be thankful for. But it is not enough.

Whether or not the America 2000 crusade achieves or fails to achieve its goals, all our children—poor, handicapped, dwelling in remote places— must have access to the knowledge most likely to ensure their effectiveness as parents, workers, citizens, and individuals. Teachers prepared to be able stewards of schools that are good and just can carry us a long way toward the schools we need. But they are unlikely to have either the time or the resources necessary to the development, from top to bottom, of coherent, comprehensive curricula.

This nation must now add to its preoccupation with goals and tests delineation of the domains of knowledge and knowing to be encountered over time by all children and youths. Instead of pouring money into test construction, we would be better served by developing in each state a broad curricular framework from which teachers might creatively adapt—not a grade-by-grade specification but the fundamental concepts characterizing the world's knowledge systems. Currently, some of the California curriculum guides provide good examples of what is needed. Along with these, there should be recommendations regarding approximate percentages of time to be devoted over several years of schooling to language and literature, mathematics and science, the social studies, health and physical education, and the arts.

Finally, we appear incapable of getting beyond individuals as the units of assessment, with accompanying allocation of responsibility for success and failure. We must adopt as standard practice the kind of contextual appraisal that tells us whether schools have in place the curriculum, materials, pedagogy, and other conditions necessary to the good education of individuals. The absence of these exposes glaring inequities that are the moral responsibility of a caring people in a just society to correct. The higher we raise the educational stakes for individuals, the greater the responsibility of federal, state, and local agencies to provide the necessary conditions for learning and to ensure equal access for all. A system of compulsory schooling, whether or not its schools are ones of choice, geared closely to the economic well-being and general health of a democratic society carries with it sobering moral imperatives.[44]

NOTES

1. Suzanne Soo Hoo, "School Renewal: Taking Responsibility for Providing an Education of Value" in *Access to Knowledge: An Agenda for Our Nation's Schools,* ed. John I. Goodlad and Pamela Keating (New York: College Entrance Examination Board, 1990), 208.
2. Ibid., 209.
3. National Commission on Excellence in Education, *A Nation at Risk* (Washington, D.C.: Government Printing Office, 1983).
4. Thomas K. Gilhool, "From the Education of All Handicapped Children to the Effective Education of Every Child" (unpublished manuscript, 1984).
5. David L. Kirp, *Just Schools* (Berkeley: University of California Press, 1984), 5.
6. Michael Oakeshott, *Rationalism in Politics and Other Essays* (London: Methuen, 1962).
7. See, for example, *Access to Knowledge,* ed. Goodlad and Keating.
8. Dan C. Lortie, *Schoolteacher* (Chicago: University of Chicago Press, 1975).
9. John I. Goodlad, *A Place Called School* (New York: McGraw-Hill, 1984).
10. Regarding the moral, social, and political, see Kenneth A. Sirotnik, "Society, Schooling, Teaching, and Preparing to Teach" in *The Moral Dimensions of Teaching,* ed. John I. Goodlad, Roger Soder, and Kenneth A. Sirotnik (San Francisco: Jossey-Bass, 1990), 296–327; and Roger Soder and Kenneth A. Sirotnik, "Beyond Reinventing the Past: The Politics of Teacher Education" in *Places Where Teachers Are Taught,* ed. John I. Goodlad, Roger Soder, and Kenneth A. Sirotnik (San Francisco: Jossey-Bass, 1990), 385–411. For this mechanistic socialization into teaching, see Zhixin Su, "Exploring the Moral Socialization of Teacher Candidates," *Oxford Review of Education* 16, no. 3 (1990): 367–91.
11. John I. Goodlad, *Teachers for Our Nation's Schools* (San Francisco: Jossey-Bass, 1990).

12. Zhixin Su, *Teacher Education Reform in the United States (1890–1986)*. Occasional Paper 3 (Seattle: Center for Educational Renewal, College of Education, University of Washington, 1986).

13. See Kenneth A. Sirotnik, "On the Eroding Foundations of Teacher Education," *Phi Delta Kappan* 71 (May 1990): 710–16.

14. Kenneth R. Howey and Nancy L. Zimpher, *Profiles of Preservice Teacher Education* (Albany: State University of New York Press, 1989).

15. *The Moral Dimensions of Teaching*, ed. Goodlad et al.

16. Jo Ann Hines, "Exhaustive Inquiries into Teaching's Moral Nature, but Purely an Academic Restatement of the Obvious," *ATE* Newsletter 24, no. 5 (May–June 1991): 6.

17. Linda M. McNeil, *Contradictions of Control: School Structure and School Knowledge* (New York: Routledge, Chapman, & Hall, 1986).

18. Arthur E. Wise, *Legislated Learning: The Bureaucratization of the American Classroom* (Berkeley: University of California, 1979).

19. Robert Nisbet, *The Present Age* (New York: Harper, 1988), 2.

20. Mortimer J. Adler, *We Hold These Truths* (New York: Macmillan, 1987), 29.

21. Nisbet, *The Present Age*, xi.

22. Burton R. Clark, *The Academic Life* (Princeton, NJ: Carnegie Foundation for the Advancement of Teaching, 1987), xxi.

23. David L. Kirp, *Just Schools*, 5.

24. Lamar Alexander, "Dear Friends" (Washington: U.S. Department of Education, 2 Aug. 1991).

25. See, for example, *School Board News* 11, no.14 (23 July 1991); and articles in *Voices from the Field: 30 Expert Opinions on "America 2000"* (Washington, D.C.: William T. Grant Foundation Commission on Work, Family, and Citizenship and Institute for Education Leadership, 1991).

26. George Kaplan, "Scapegoating the Schools" in *Voices from the Field*, 11.

27. Alexander, "Dear Friends."

28. Bruno V. Manno, "From the Acting Assistant Secretary," *OERI Bulletin* (Summer 1991), 2.

29. Patrick Welsh, "A Teacher's View," *The Wilson Quarterly* 15, no. 4 (Autumn 1991): 77–87.

30. James B. Conant, *The American High School Today* (New York: McGraw-Hill, 1959).

31. Welsh, "A Teacher's View," 77.

32. Ernest L. Boyer, *High School* (New York: Harper & Row, 1983). See chap. 3.

33. National Board for Professional Teaching Standards, *Toward High and Rigorous Standards for the Teaching Profession* (Detroit: National Board, 1989), 49.

34. Curtis C. McKnight et al., *The Under-Achieving Curriculum: Assessing United States School Mathematics from an International Perspective* (Champaign, IL: Stipes, 1987).

35. Lawrence A. Cremin, *Popular Education and Its Discontents* (New York: Harper & Row, 1990), viii, 59.

36. Clark Kerr, "Is Education Really All That Guilty?" *Education Week*, 27 Feb. 1991, p. 30.

37. Paul E. Heckman, *Exploring the Concept of School Renewal: Cultural Differences and Similarities between More and Less Renewing Schools*. Technical Report 33 (Los Angeles: A Study of Schooling, Graduate School of Education, University of California, 1982).

38. Mary M. Bentzen, *Changing Schools: The Magic Feather Principle* (New York: McGraw-Hall, 1974).

39. See John Eggleston, David Dunn, and Madher Anjoli, *Education for Some* (Stoke-on-Trent: Trentham Books, 1986).

40. Many of the generalizations in this section are drawn from the several books and nearly three dozen technical reports presenting the data and findings from "A Study of Schooling in the United States." See particularly chap. 8 in Goodlad, *A Place Called School*.

41. R. G. Barker and P. V. Gump, *Big School, Small School* (Stanford: Stanford University Press, 1964).

42. John Ainley et al., *Resource Allocation in the Government Schools of Australia and New Zealand* (Melbourne: Australian Education Council, 1982).

43. Goodlad, *A Place Called School*. See particularly chaps. 3 and 8.

44. John I. Goodlad, "Beyond Half an Education," *Education Week*, 19 Feb. 1992, pp. 44, 34.

2

Evolution and Legacies

Donald L. MacMillan and Irving G. Hendrick

A serious late nineteenth-century commitment, especially in cities, to extend public education to nearly *all* children—children from working-class backgrounds, children from immigrant families, and children whose capabilities were in doubt—produced for public school officials more challenges than they likely had bargained for. A newly organized age-graded model of schooling appeared to be working quite well for *most* children. Experience with the system developed in teachers an expectation concerning what a child of a given age and grade should be able to learn and do. It was expected, of course, that some children would be able to learn faster and easier than others; such was the reality of life.

The major unanticipated urban reality was that *some* children did not seem to learn, or behave, even minimally up to normal expectations. Many of these children, especially those with no obvious physical disability, were already clients of the public schools and could not easily be dismissed. Their needs and the needs of the teachers who demanded that they be removed from regular classes cried out for special solutions, for example, ability groups and special classes.[1]

For children with more apparent disabilities, the evolution of services followed a more difficult and deliberate course. Efforts by public schools to adapt in order to meet the needs of disabled children began in earnest after the turn of the century. Services available prior to that time were privately, or at least locally, developed and usually included educational services as only a part of the treatment program. The focus in this chapter is on public

Authors' note: Preparation of this manuscript was supported in part by grant H023C80072 from the U.S. Department of Education. The opinions expressed are solely those of the authors and should not be interpreted to have agency endorsement.

school efforts since 1900 to serve children with various disabilities. Those collective efforts evolved into what is almost universally referred to in the United States as "special education." Throughout the chapter we examine the interface between special and general education as well as that between education and other professions and disciplines.

Children with sensory and physical disabilities (e.g., blind, deaf, orthopedically handicapped) have been recognized since well before 1900, as have children with severe mental disabilities. Other categories of children, particularly those with mild disabilities that exist primarily in the context of schools (e.g., mildly mentally retarded and learning disabled) emerged as potentially in need of special education considerably later. The latter group presented no physical symptomology; rather, these children constituted the lower portion of a normal distribution of individual differences. Interestingly, however, they came to be judged as sufficiently different to warrant special services by the educational community. Not surprisingly, this "mildly handicapped" group also became the subject of considerable controversy, debate, and even litigation.

Formal education for handicapped children has been shaped over a lengthy period, if one considers pioneering efforts of individuals and isolated treatment programs. The interested reader should consult one of several scholarly treatments concerning the history of treating individuals with handicaps.[2] Initial programs serving certain types of exceptional children in the United States are shown in Table 1.

Although deviance has been recognized throughout recorded history, categorization of exceptional children is a rather recent development.[3] Hewett and Forness comment that the only categories that counted in this

Table 1
Years in Which Special Classes for Various Types of Exceptional Children Were Instituted

Year	Type of Exceptionality	City
1869	Deaf	Boston
1874	Unruly or truant boys	New York City
1896 (or 1899)	Blind	Chicago
1899 (or 1900)	Orthopedically handicapped	Chicago
1908	Speech defective	New York City
1908	Pretuberculosis or malnourished	Providence
1909	Epileptics	Baltimore
1913	Partially sighted	Roxbury, MA
1920	Hard of hearing	Lynn, MA

Source: J. E. Wallin, *Education of Mentally Handicapped Children* (New York: Harper & Row, 1955), 18.

early period were the *weak*, the *odd*, and the *poor*.[4] Farber recalls that the mentally retarded, the blind, the lame, the mentally ill, and other handicapped persons were once lumped together in a category referred to as *misfits*.[5] The constant struggle for children and youth with physical impairments was for modifications of publicly funded facilities, special equipment, special instructional services, and special transportation. It can be arguably maintained that of all the groups with exceptional needs, children with physical handicaps have witnessed the greatest progress over the past century toward inclusion in the mainstream. This appears especially true since 1975.

Programs for children with sensory impairments were the earliest programs developed, which Pritchard has explained as resulting from greater sympathy aroused by blindness and deafness.[6] Major early efforts to educate deaf children included the work of Pedro Ponce de León on oral communication; a system of instruction based on finger spelling developed by Juan Donet; and the opening of the first public school for the deaf, the National Institute for Deaf-Mutes in Paris, in 1760 by Abbé Charles de L'Epée. During the past 100 years most educators have attempted, through the use of hearing aids for students with even slight physical capacity for hearing, to teach through the medium of voice transmission (i.e., through hearing and lip reading). The approach has not been without controversy.

In the area of blindness, Georg Philipp Harsdörfer in Germany introduced the use of wax tablets on which the blind could write, which was followed by Bernouilli's invention of a device that guided a pencil on paper. Later, Valentin Huay employed embossed print for use in reading by the blind. By the end of the eighteenth century, programs for children with sensory problems existed on a limited scale. Later, advances by Louis Braille, Samuel Howe, Thomas Hopkins Gallaudet, and others would further advance the education of blind and deaf children, but the initial efforts by these pioneers had been pivotal.

The writings and philosophies of many associated with the French Revolution were instrumental in advancing a sense of social responsibility for all individuals. Pioneering work by Jean Marc Gespard Itard and Édouard Seguin with mentally retarded persons and by Philippe Pinel with the mentally ill marked the beginning of humane and habilitative work with them. Samuel Howe, known primarily for his work with blind persons, was a major force in initiating programs for mentally retarded children. The initial direction that treatment took in the United States was with residential institutions, but the long-term impact would include expanding the mission of public schools.

MILDLY MENTALLY RETARDED: THE CONTROVERSIAL CATEGORY

No single category of exceptional children has been as politicized or has elicited as much controversy over definition as that now known as mildly mentally retarded (MMR). Children with sensory and physical impairments were evident to the teachers, the general public, and physicians alike. Their needs for "special" educational provisions appeared obvious to all. Thus, the education of blind and deaf children carried "face validity." Criteria for defining and identifying those children (e.g., determining the degree of visual or hearing impairment) could be measured objectively and with little controversy. Similarly, children with orthopedic problems and other physical impairments were obvious to the casual observer, and physicians identified the nature of their problems and the degree of their impairments.

In the case of children with severe mental retardation, problems of diagnosis were few. Failure of the child to meet developmental milestones was obvious, and the child's inability to succeed in public education was evident to virtually everyone. There was, to be certain, controversy over whether public schools had any responsibility for children with severe mental disabilities, and the topic was debated periodically. Yet, beyond argument was *whether* the children were mentally retarded.

The situation was quite different with MMR students, since this segment of the school population exhibited no readily apparent physical symptoms. It was thought that they *might* succeed in regular classes. Consequently, debate raged over whether they differed in "degree" but not in "kind" from "normal" children in regular classes.

MMR students, then, constituted a group around which controversy emerged from the turn of the century to the present time. Significant disagreement centered on the etiology of their condition (genetic vs. environmental), behavioral correlates of their condition (e.g., criminality, immorality), distribution among different ethnic or racial groups (e.g., overrepresentation of recent immigrant groups and blacks), and the relative benefits of various educational placements or curricula (e.g., special vs. regular class; EMR [educably mentally retarded] curriculum vs. standard curriculum). Furthermore, these children were traditionally identified only after beginning their formal education, and then by school personnel with only limited assistance from the medical profession.

By the 1960s another group, learning disabled (LD), emerged as a category of exceptional children who also, in the majority of cases, lacked biological etiology and were defined in terms of behavioral characteristics. Although definitional arguments have certainly been waged over LD children, this group has not been the subject of nearly as much debate as have MMR children.

INFLUENCE OF MEDICINE

The pioneers of special education were primarily physicians, and the impact of medicine on special education is apparent to this day. Approaches to the treatment of children with disabilities, both physical and mental, continue to recognize (1) definitions of disabilities that stress the sensory or biological system that is impaired or diseased and (2) the role of differential diagnosis if an effective treatment is to be devised. One might challenge the value of this legacy as classification systems used in special education are only tangentially related to educational functioning of children.[7] That is, children bearing the same categorical label based on their similarity on one or two dimensions (e.g., degree of hearing loss, ambulation, IQ, or achievement) invariably differ markedly on other dimensions not included in the definitional parameters for a particular category. Hence, children with approximately the same degree of visual impairment may differ significantly with respect to IQs or reading achievement. As a result of medicine's influence on classification, some have noted that while all tubercular children may be treated essentially the same, children classified as learning disabled or deaf cannot be.

INSTITUTIONS

In the early 1900s, children identified as mentally retarded were those with severe forms of mental retardation and those with physical stigmata. Professional opinion during this time held that the most appropriate agencies for serving mentally retarded children were residential institutions.[8] Original construction of residential institutions in the United States occurred in the late 1800s. These facilities were conceived of as schools where individuals with mental retardation would be brought, treated, and returned to society as productive members following their successful habilitation. Kanner characterized this early phase of the institutional movement as one in which the goal was habilitation, while Baumeister described the dominant model as the "educational model."[9] This initial optimism proved unfounded as few residents were able to return to the community, which thereby resulted in the eventual crowding of such facilities and a shift in their mission to custodial institutions. In Baumeister's terms, the "educational model" was replaced by a "pity model."[10]

One consequence of the failure of institutions to cure mental retardation was that the milder cases soon were found outside institutions where they became perceived as a social problem with which society must somehow deal.[11] By the late 1800s, special classes occasionally were being conducted outside of residential institutions.[12] According to Doll, by 1890 there was general acceptance of state responsibility for the care of mentally retarded children.[13] This did not imply, however, general state reimbursement for special education to local school districts until well into the twentieth century. And, although some special classes had been attempted earlier, the most common date cited for the establishment of special classes for retarded children is usually 1896.[14] The need for public schools to somehow cope with a segment of the population that was not so debilitated as to warrant placement in residential institutions but that clearly was not making adequate progress in the public schools was increasingly apparent. The means of coping would be shaped by several factors: public attitudes, compulsory attendance laws, challenges to public education in terms of its efficiency, and the structure of public education itself.

RECOGNITION OF THE MILDLY RETARDED

Early in the century, school officials recognized students whose advancement through the grades was slower than expected—that is, "retarded," to use the term of Ayres, writing as secretary for the Russell Sage Foundation's Backward Children Investigation. In his book *Laggards in Our Schools,* Ayres placed responsibility for the failure of students on city school officials, blaming them for a curriculum that matched the capabilities of only the brightest students.[15] Less adept students were forced to repeat grades or drop out. This provided further ammunition for critics of public education who saw the public schools as very inefficient.[16] Ayers documented the added costs of schooling resulting from grade repetition. Students who repeated grades and dropped out were not obviously mentally retarded but were able-bodied children who became "problems" only when asked to master the curriculum of the public schools.

As early as 1899 in New York City and 1902 in Los Angeles, efforts were made to establish special classes for "misfits"—students who appeared normal but who could not succeed in the graded school system. These classes, known as "ungraded" classes in large city school systems early in the 1900s, were developed in response to this very practical problem. In 1913, Goddard's report on the extent of retardation in New York schools acknowledged that the diagnosis and placement of children in ungraded classes was hardly an exact science. Many "feebleminded" children were remaining unserved while others in the ungraded classes were of normal intelligence.[17]

FORCES THAT SHAPED SPECIAL CLASSES

A reasonable question to ask is, Why was the mission of public schooling expanded to include responsibility for children with mental retardation? We have argued elsewhere that several theories probably explain various aspects of this development.[18] First, a "surplus population" theory best explains why the more severely mentally retarded children were ignored by the schools, whereas a "child saving" theory explains why the more mildly handicapped were not ignored altogether. Yet another theory, the "social control" argument, is advanced to explain such educational opportunities that were afforded to poor and ethnic minority children. All three theories hold some validity because multiple sets of facts, motives, and historical forces were simultaneously at work.

Lazerson describes how special education was shaped at the turn of the century by a public school system confronted with massive numbers of children to be educated at a limited cost, which led to concerns over efficiency.[19] As noted earlier, the schools were faulted for being inefficient, and the response was to alter the nature of special education. Several developments affected the future.

First, the public schools were the primary social institution in which social problems were to be considered. Cremin described this situation as one where, by 1920, any social problem was treated by making it an educational problem.[20] Thus, social problems like handicapping conditions or problems presented by children coming from culturally different backgrounds were viewed as problems that could be treated by the schools.

Second, public education adopted a corporate-industrial model of organization including centralization, specialization of function, administrative hierarchy, and cost accounting. This approach was used in an effort to become more efficient; however, it also brought with it a new definition of equality of educational opportunity. This definition rejected the notion that all children should be exposed to the same curriculum; instead, it emphasized relevance for those deemed unable to master the highly verbal traditional curriculum. This new definition gave rise to vocationalism, the third development listed by Lazerson.

Finally, Lazerson views the development of intelligence and achievement testing as providing the "scientific" basis for decisions concerning the specific curricular course appropriate for individual students.[21] While not denying the key emphasis that was eventually placed on scientific intelligence and achievement testing, our own reading of history has led us to downplay the extent and manner in which mental testing shaped special education programs.[22]

EUGENICS SCARE

The social attitudes dominant in the early 1900s played an important role in shaping special education. Most prominent of these attitudes in the minds of educated Americans were the orthodox and reform varieties of social Darwinism. The orthodox form led its adherents to view new immigrants as hopelessly defective and to recommend various forms of segregation. When applied to persons with mental retardation, the treatments that followed were even more severe. The "eugenics scare" was fueled by publication of several investigations, especially those by Dugale in 1877 and Goddard in 1912, that purported to show that mild mental retardation ran in families of particular racial, national, and ethnic backgrounds and was inevitably manifested in criminality, immoral behavior, and the need for public assistance.[23] Strong position papers of the era advocated treatment policies and placements that would protect society from this menace.[24] Among the policies enacted widely to control the threat of mental retardation were segregation and sterilization.[25]

Subsequent developments in the field would blunt the impact of the eugenics scare, and the evidence on which it was based would be roundly criticized.[26] Nevertheless, some of the early incentives for establishing special classes were to make teaching more palatable for regular class teachers and enhance the progress of nonhandicapped students. Furthermore, many highly regarded scholars of the day were aligned with the eugenics position and expressed concern over the menace of the mildly retarded and the need to control them. Consider the following commentary by Terman:

> Feebleminded school children are present everywhere. They linger in the third, fourth, fifth, and sixth grades until well into adolescent years. They consume a disproportionate amount of the teacher's time, they drag down the standards of achievement for normal children, they tend to become incorrigible and to feed the never ending stream of juvenile court cases. . . . Not until the borderline cases have been placed in special classes, can the work of the school with normal children proceed as it ought. Feebleminded children in the regular classes not only interfere with instruction, they are also likely to be a source of moral contagion.[27]

Although the eugenics movement began prior to intelligence test developments, the later widespread use of the Binet scales confirmed for some the threat that Goddard and others had described.[28]

SELECTION OF CHILDREN FOR SPECIAL CLASSES

Special or ungraded classes were established in America's large cities more than a decade prior to using intelligence tests in the United States. These classes reflected the trend toward efforts of schools to adjust the curriculum to reflect increasing student diversity, especially the growing numbers of foreign-speaking children. Ability classifications and adaptive curricula were logical recognition of individual differences in aptitude. In New York City, for example, selection of children for ungraded classes began with referrals from regular class teachers. Determining eligibility was more difficult with children from families that had recently immigrated, and school personnel were aware of the need to distinguish low aptitude from cultural differences. Principals were required to complete forms on children, and the item on nationality was considered extremely important. As described in one document,

> For one not familiar with national characteristics it is an easy thing to take the heavy sluggish response of the Slavic child as indicative of real mental ability, while the children of Latin Europe, with their lively shifting and seemingly inconsistent attention to school duties seem to the teacher to be unfitted for regular grade work.[29]

Initially, in New York, teacher and reformer Elizabeth Farrell sought to serve those children who were not succeeding in regular classes. Efforts to select which children were to be served did not reflect a fully developed policy. Rather, views and policies were shaped by social ideology, practical circumstances, and data collected on the program. The selection process required examination by physicians, review by school principals, and input from classroom teachers. Although time-consuming and labor intensive, this selection process was reported by Superintendent of New York City William Henry Maxwell as having "resulted most satisfactorily in preventing normal children who were only dull from being assigned to these classes."[30]

Under Farrell's guidance, ungraded classes concentrated on MMR children, which was a narrower focus than that envisioned by Maxwell. The superintendent instituted other special classes for children functioning in the normal range who suffered from anemia, tuberculosis, bad adenoids, and so forth, as well as those who were suffering from various physical handicaps. Special classes to serve children with varying special needs emerged during this early period with "C" classes serving non-English-speaking children, "D" classes for children about to reach fourteen years of age but remaining in lower grades who sought work certificates, and "E" classes for those who entered school late and "truants" and "incorrigibles." However, it was the "mentally defective" children who were the focus of Farrell's attention and effort.

Terman's publication of *The Measurement of Intelligence* (1916) and *The Intelligence of School Children* (1919) resulted in increased reliance on the use of mental tests, a new "scientific basis" for grouping, and appears to have stimulated increased use of ability grouping in the public schools.[31] Terman's views on the role of mental testing meshed with the problems confronting public school educators vis-à-vis educational retardation. As a former high school principal and normal school instructor, Terman was outspoken in his belief that "feebleminded" children did not belong in the public schools. Although he acknowledged that "special classes in great numbers will always be needed in the public schools," he believed that such classes should be reserved for "doubtful and borderline cases"—that is, higher-functioning children.[32]

Across the nation in Los Angeles, Arthur Sutherland, director of that school system's Division of Psychology and Research, began classifying some 2,000 students already enrolled in special classes by means of mental tests.[33] In New York, Farrell initially expressed reservations about mental testing. She recognized that the Binet-Simon scales measured variations of intelligence in different social classes. Further, she noted that (1) "scholastic and other attainments and not native ability are tested by the Binet-Simon tests," (2) a child could be at the mental age of six years in one capacity and twelve years in another, (3) mental testing is only one phase of mental diagnosis, (4) the Binet-Simon tests did not properly classify children for definite treatment or for detailed care, and (5) the Binet-Simon tests were "not infallible in determining the mental grade of a child."[34]

Gradually, however, Farrell came to recognize the savings in staff time resulting from the use of mental tests for identifying those to be served, and they provided a less capricious means for diagnosing children than the methods previously used. Between October 1916 and March 1917, Farrell tested children from the ungraded classes in the Bronx to establish the prevalence of "feeblemindedness." Her survey established the prevalence at approximately 2 percent, a figure reported previously by Goddard and earlier criticized by Farrell.[35] The survey also alerted Farrell to the far greater proportion of schoolchildren needing ungraded classes, which would have required the organization of sixty additional ungraded classes for the Bronx alone.[36] By 1920, intelligence testing greatly influenced the selection of children for ungraded classes.

Even during the early years of ungraded classes, there is evidence that city school officials were sensitive to assigning a disproportionate number of ethnic minority children to ungraded classes. There were no incentives for doing so, however, as these early programs were supported by city funds, with no special state incentives or reimbursements being available. When we analyzed the historical data from the Los Angeles schools, it was apparent that school personnel were sensitive to the issue of minority "overrepresentation," as it would come to be called. The Los Angeles schools reported from a survey in 1928 of 2,115 "subnormal" children enrolled in programs that a "large percentage" of the students were described as "foreign," presumably Mexican, based on photographs. Among the instruments used was the Stanford Revision of the Binet-Simon scale; however, in the case of some foreign students alternative scales (e.g., Pintner-Patterson, Kohs Block Design) were employed.[37] It seems fair to conclude that from the time intelligence tests were introduced into the selection process, "IQ data" were progressively weighted more and more heavily in establishing the eligibility of children for special classes. Yet, a child with a low IQ almost invariably could avoid a special class assignment with solid academic performance in his or her regular classroom.[38] As Scheerenberger has suggested, the total IQ became decisive as early as 1915 in precluding moderately and severely retarded children from attending schools; however, the role of IQ in determining who attended regular and special classes was considerably less.[39]

CURRICULUM FOR MMR STUDENTS

Now that a segment of students who were not succeeding had been recognized and means for identifying them established, the next issue concerned *what* and *how* they should be taught in the ungraded or special classes. It is noteworthy that for all categories of exceptional children other than mentally retarded, the essence of the special accommodations concerns *how* children are to be taught. With children with visual and auditory problems, for example, the instructional adaptation pertains to bypassing the impaired sensory system in order to teach the standard curriculum. A similar orientation applies for children with physical disabilities; that is, prosthetic devices may be employed and certain activities requiring physical skills may be adapted to accommodate the physical impairment.

For mentally retarded children, the nature of the adaptations involved both *what* and *how* they should be taught, although this was not necessarily the initial view. New York's Elizabeth Farrell, for one, believed that the curriculum for "mentally defective" children should emphasize more motor activity and be directed to the child's physical side. Furthermore, she denied that new or exclusive methods of instruction should be used with these children, since she held that "mentally defective" children differed from normally achieving children only in degree, not in kind.[40]

Interestingly, vocational or occupational training was not included in Farrell's plan. Not until the early 1940s did Richard Hungerford, perhaps her most notable successor in New York, move the curriculum decisively in that direction.[41] Farrell did recognize the need to reverse the failure set developed in mentally retarded children after repeated failures in regular classes. Instead of books, copy books, and written questions to answer, which she called "reminders of past failures," even in the earliest years of the century the ungraded curriculum emphasized "constructive, acquisitive and initiative instincts" in the child.[42]

Over the ensuing decades, considerable interest and discussion centered around how and what to teach. *The White House Conference Report* of 1930 included an extended discussion of curriculum that affirmed what was in place in the nation's schools. It recommended heavy emphasis on practical applications:

> Pre-vocational and vocational training, including homemaking, housekeeping, and serving for girls, along with woodworking and other shop skills for boys, were proposed in order to help the child develop as much social and economic independence as possible. Academic work was also advised, with an emphasis placed on arithmetic, reading and social science. Instruction focused on the very skills needed for economic and personal independence (e.g., reading want ads, making change, and local geography). While "academic" in nature, the direct instruction of practical applications reflected the prevalent belief that generalization and transfer skills were weak in mentally retarded children, and unless the applications were directly taught the children would not be able to make the needed transfer from academic instruction to practical demands.[43]

CONCERNS OVER SETTING: A LASTING LEGACY

In a thorough, thoughtful review, Polloway traces the persistent concern over the relative benefits accrued to MMR children as a function of their educational placement.[44] The specific placement alternatives changed over time (e.g., special school vs. regular school enrollment, special class vs. regular class, special class vs. resource or consultation model, etc.). The issue of setting assumes that *where* the child is taught is more important than what is done with the child once he or she is placed. Further, it assumes homogeneity of treatments within settings (i.e., the same thing goes on in all special classes) and ignores variation among MMR children, suggesting that all MMR children respond similarly to the same treatment. As Zigler and his associates explain, "we have conceptualized institutions, group homes, special education, and mainstreamed classes only as places, not as places *within which interactions occur.*"[45] It is a fallacy to assume that one setting is invariably preferable for all EMR children or that one setting is invariably bad for all EMR children.[46] Such positions ignore variation among EMR children.

The concern with setting variables has preoccupied many in the field and may be linked to the assessment by scholars, journalists, jurists, and some members of the general public concerning educators' motives in establishing special classes. That is, when children are placed in a self-contained special class for EMR children, it is possible to interpret the action as one motivated to best serve the child's interests through special instruction as well as protect the child from undue failure and ridicule. Alternatively, the action may be represented as malevolent segregation leading to negative stigma and lives of despair. The early period of special education contains written statements by leaders in the field that readily lend themselves selectively to validating either motivation. For those who assume that the central motive was to segregate EMR children in order to protect "normal" children, or worse, to harm those selected for separate instruction, special classes and everything associated with them are considered wrong.

PERIOD OF GROWTH AND DECLINE OF SPECIAL CLASSES

Society gradually assumed responsibility for children with handicaps, or at least with most handicaps. While the early programs were financed entirely by city school systems, states increasingly took responsibility for special education after World War I. The momentum picked up again in the 1930s when there was rapid growth in services for mentally retarded and other handicapped children.[47] The educational model of special classes as the way to educate children with special needs was rooted in the German system, and it provided a mechanism for reimbursement from state governments. By the late 1950s, most states were providing program support in the form of excess cost reimbursements for special classes for handicapped learners.

It is not coincidental that from the early 1930s to the late 1950s enrollments in special education increased dramatically. Importantly, the bulk of advocacy on behalf of children with mental retardation centered on providing special classes for them. In 1914, enrollments in classes for mentally subnormal children in the United States totaled 10,890; by 1922, this number had increased to 23,252; and by 1932, the figure had risen to 75,099.[48] Furthermore, by 1957, forty-six states supported special classes for mildly retarded students.[49] Between 1948 and 1966, there was a 400 percent increase in the number of mentally retarded children served by the public schools.[50] By 1966, 89.5 percent of all school districts provided programs, with the vast majority opting for self-contained classes.[51]

California, for example, made it mandatory in 1947 for public school counties and districts to serve EMR children. Children with other handicapping conditions were similarly provided for. Accordingly, the state offered school districts limited reimbursement for expenses associated with "excess" costs for physically handicapped minors, mentally retarded and severely mentally retarded minors, and special school transportation required for severely mentally retarded and certain groups of physically handicapped minors. The amount provided by states frequently was seen as inadequate when measured against what was required for effective services. On the other hand, the amount was more than the basic state allowance for normal children, which thereby tempted some county and district school officials to categorize more children than might be warranted as prospects for special classes for mentally retarded learners.

Although the proposition remains an arguable one, a reasonable historical inference is that it was a mix of racial prejudice and economic incentive, aided and abetted by the misuse of group intelligence testing, that produced the alleged overrepresentation of minority children in special classes. Thus, it became increasingly clear that intelligence testing could be used and misused as a two-edged sword. It could be used as Farrell did in New York as a means for *reducing* the number of pupils eligible for special classes from a much larger pool of candidates that had been referred by regular class teachers. Or, depending on where the cutoff score was drawn and how much attention was paid to a student's class performance, intelligence test results could be used to increase the pool of students eligible for special classes.

A possible economic motive for special class assignments can be found from state cost reimbursement data. In California during 1963–64, for example, that state allowed $356.62 for the excess of educating each minor with mental retardation and $637.16 for training each minor with severe mental retardation above and beyond the regular state apportionment.[52] That year the basic allocation from the state school fund was set at not less than $180 per unit of average daily attendance. At the time, California schools, like those in other states, received most of their basic support from local property taxes. Poorer districts received some additional state funding beyond the basic amount from what then and now is known as "state equalization aid." Still, after midcentury, urban school systems with large numbers of children categorized as mentally retarded stood to receive significantly more funding from their states than they otherwise would have received if fewer students had been classified as mentally retarded. Whether they profited, broke even, or lost money in the arrangement was a test of how conscientious they were in developing special programs at significantly higher cost.

By 1963, California also approved a general category of disability known as "educationally handicapped," which allowed as eligible up to 2 percent of the state's public school population. This category carried with it less "excess cost" reimbursement from the state than was allowed for other special programs. Notwithstanding that participation in the program was optional, by 1965–66, 77 percent of California schoolchildren attended school in districts that maintained such programs.[53]

During the years that shaped special education following the emergence of special classes, several developments in public education have been noted. First, school officials came to rely more heavily on intelligence tests for identifying children as MMR. Related to this was the fact that intelligence tests came to be viewed by many as the reason for placing disproportionate numbers of ethnic minority children into classes for the mildly retarded. A second issue that received increased attention was the extent to which children served in special education were isolated from or integrated with students without disabilities as a consequence of particular settings (e.g., special schools, special classes) in which services were delivered. These interrelated questions would ultimately be combined, and the overarching challenge to special education for mildly handicapped children would be cast in terms of the "efficacy" of these programs.[54]

ROLE OF IQ AND OVERREPRESENTATION

Although children were not placed in ungraded or special classes on the basis of low mental test scores alone, school officials over time became increasingly confident of the predictive value of intelligence tests. Even Farrell, who initially had been critical of tests, came to appreciate their value as a diagnostic tool for grouping children so that "unfair demands would not be made upon them."[55] Despite her reservations about the scales, she appreciated their efficiency in providing a less capricious basis for diagnosis than teacher referral alone was capable of producing. Farrell had become disenchanted with the tendency on the part of teachers and principals to refer all manner of troublesome students to special classes, whether or not they were mentally retarded.

As reimbursement programs emerged whereby states compensated districts on the basis of special education enrollments, the concern over reimbursement took another turn. Districts could not be given a "blank check" to capriciously identify inordinate numbers of children as "mentally retarded" in order to gain large sums of state money. Therefore, education codes increasingly specified criteria for eligibility in disability categories (e.g., degree of visual or hearing loss, IQ cutoff points, etc.) in order to restrict the number of children who could be identified and limit the amount of money that states would spend on special education. In the case of eligibility for categorization as mentally retarded, an IQ of 70 became the common upper limit for defining mental retardation.

As described previously, the initial efforts to establish ungraded classes were accompanied by concerns over possible misidentification of immigrant children. In the Eastern cities, southern European and Slavic children were considered to exhibit behaviors that might be misinterpreted as evidence of mental slowness. Experiences in Los Angeles prior to 1930 suggested that Black children were not being identified in disproportionate numbers for ungraded classes, but Hispanic children were presenting a unique problem to school officials.[56] School officials were sensitive to the possibility that language problems could erroneously be taken as evidence of feeblemindedness.[57] These early concerns over misidentification would later become the focus of heated debate and litigation. With the expansion of programs for mildly retarded children came recognition of and concern about overrepresentation of Black and Hispanic students in these programs.

As noted earlier, compulsory attendance laws and the failure of institutions to cure mental retardation swelled the ranks of children to be served by the public schools. Instead of serving only children from middle- and upper-income families, the public schools increased the range of individual differences by serving the entire socioeconomic range. Both immigration and scientific and social advances increased the special education clientele in public schools. After World War II, medical advances enabled children with severe health problems to survive. Such children often needed special educational services to accommodate their physical and mental problems.

Most importantly, by the late 1950s previously segregated white school districts began to enroll large numbers of minority children and allegedly implemented grouping practices designed to exclude Blacks and other minorities from classes attended by whites. One device to screen out minority students, which relied heavily on intelligence tests, may have been special education, especially classes for MMR students.[58] Mercer and Richardson describe how the repeal of a California law excluding Mexican-Americans from white schools coincided with legislation that created special programs for EMR students.[59]

Although public school officials noticed the overrepresentation of minority children in the EMR programs of the 1950s, the extent to which they used special education to exclude Black and Hispanic students from regular programs remains unclear. Our examination of data from Los Angeles city schools revealed no evidence suggesting that the use of mental tests and the establishment of special classes were undertaken to achieve racial and ethnic segregation of students. There is, to be sure, considerable evidence that Los Angeles school officials pursued a policy of racial segregation, but they did not require anything as subtle as intelligence testing or special education to achieve that objective. Prior to World War II, there were cheaper and more direct ways to segregate children, primarily through adjusting school attendance boundaries and establishing special language classes. In 1925 it cost nearly three times as much to operate the city's "development school" for MMR children than it cost to operate a regular elementary school in the same neighborhood.[60]

An influx of Black students into previously white school attendance areas and the immigration of large numbers of Hispanic students after

World War II eventually led to the overrepresentation of nonwhite students in special classes. It was also during this era that differential funding for special education became common and substantial. New child-based formulas, in which districts were provided standard average daily attendance (ADA) reimbursement, plus additional funds for children served in special education, provided strong incentives for identifying large numbers of children previously unserved.[61]

A combination of reimbursement monies from the state and a sociopolitical climate that required a "scientific basis" for cases of overrepresentation resulted in the use of mental tests as an instrument for securing maximum differential funding for school districts. After large special education enrollments became profitable, the magnitude of the overrepresentation reached its zenith and became the focus of special education critics. Resolution of the problem finally took place in the courts.

By the late 1960s, it was noticed that a large proportion of minority students were being enrolled in classes for EMR children. In California, that number grew to a peak of 57,146 in 1968–69, before declining again. By 1972–73, in spite of dramatic population growth in the state, the EMR population of 33,091 was lower than it had been any time since 1958–59.[62] Interestingly, standardized testing rather than administrative policy became the main target of many critics who had correctly observed the large number of Spanish-surnamed and Black children in special classes. One small irony in this is that it was the California Association of School Psychologists and Psychometrists that in 1959 had urged the State Board of Education to correct the structure of special education categories and end the alleged disproportionate number of minority children in classes for EMR children.[63] The major product of the reform effort became the California Master Plan for Special Education, approved in 1974.

Under the Master Plan, funding for special education was determined through a complex statutory formula that, among other things, limited special education funding to a maximum of 10 percent of K–12 enrollment in a particular jurisdiction, including a maximum of 2.8 percent of that jurisdiction's students in special day classes. A combination of administrative changes, state budget problems, and repeated attacks on special classes by the courts and elements of the public served to reduce substantially the alleged problem of using EMR classes as an excuse for segregating minority children.[64]

INTEGRATION OF SPECIAL EDUCATION STUDENTS

The impact of preplacement on the educational careers of children identified as mildly handicapped can best be described as abounding in school failure and social isolation. The regular class teacher initially referring the child for evaluation compares the target child to his or her classmates and judges the child to be substantially behind in academics or behavior. It cannot be stressed too strongly that since the inception of special classes, teacher judgment has always preceded assessment, regardless of whether that assessment included mental tests. Academic difficulty or behavioral problems invariably enter into the teacher's decision to refer the child for evaluation. We raise this point to provide a perspective against which to evaluate questions regarding "efficacy" of special education programming. Judgments concerning how a group of children served in special education is doing cannot be based on comparisons with nonhandicapped students whose progress in regular programs is at or above the norm.

Unfortunately, as pointed out by Polloway, the shifting nature of questions regarding the efficacy of special education for students with mental retardation make it impossible to research the questions, much less answer them.[65] Polloway does, however, identify five historical stages in which the issue of the most efficacious placement for mildly retarded children was examined over the past half century. During the 1930s and into the early 1940s, the major question concerned the relative benefits of special schools versus regular school enrollment of mentally retarded students. The placement in special schools versus regular schools was balanced against the need for exposure of persons with disabilities to more normal interactions. Polloway describes the general sentiments of the period as favoring regular school placement on the basis that it was more democratic and academic. Social benefits seemed to accrue to the special students from association with nonhandicapped children, and the appreciation gained by nonhandicapped children, and nonhandicapped children seemed to gain an appreciation of handicapped children. Proponents of special schools continued to cite greater efficiency, higher-quality services, availability of auxiliary services, and avoidance of an unhealthy competitive environment as reasons for continuing the separation of children with disabilities.

During the 1950s and early 1960s, the question of efficacy shifted to the extent to which student needs were best met in special class programs or by remaining in the regular class with no ancillary services.[66] The findings are about evenly split on this issue; nearly half of the studies present evidence showing that low-IQ children achieved higher in the regular classes, while the other half reports no differences in measured achievement. Special classes, on the other hand, appeared to yield more favorable social outcomes. Only one study, so far as we are able to determine (that of Goldstein, Moss, and Jordan in 1965), employed random assignment of subjects, and this investigation placed children at age six rather than the more common placement at about age eight after regular class failure had been experienced.[67]

Some ambiguity in these studies notwithstanding, special classes failed to demonstrate substantive advantages over regular classes, despite smaller class sizes, specially trained teachers, and a special curriculum. One problem inherent in this research is the use of achievement tests to assess academic status as students in regular classes were taught reading and mathematics, whereas the curriculum in the special classes stressed readiness and social skills. The curricular validity of standardized achievement tests was questionable in terms of reflecting the quality of instruction and learning that occurred in special EMR programs. Nevertheless, the failure to demonstrate advantages of special classes raised doubts and prompted criticism, leading to what Polloway calls "The Abolitionist Movement" of the late 1960s and early 1970s.[68]

Throughout the period from the inception of special classes until the 1970s, children with mental retardation were integrated with nonhandicapped children during their schooling to varying extents. Such integration usually occurred in those portions of the school day considered nonacademic—physical education, art, music, school assemblies, and lunch period. Contrary to the impression one might receive from critics of special classes, students with disabilities frequently had contact with nonhandicapped students. However, the amount and nature of the interaction and the educational settings in which it occurred varied from school to school.

Throughout the entire history of special education there has been a dilemma. That dilemma arose over the extent to which children with generalized learning problems could be integrated with nonhandicapped children and, at the same time, protect learners with disabilities from undue failure, frustration, and social rejection. This delicate balance between protection and opportunities for interaction with nonhandicapped children is a legacy that persists today.

As noted, the efficacy issue has been cast in terms of special school versus special class and special class versus regular class. The independent variable of importance when the question is posed in this fashion is *where* a child with disabilities is taught. At the same time, issues of what processes occur within a given setting are given lower priority and have seldom been captured in the research that has been conducted in special education. Even in recent years much of the literature concerning special education practices has emphasized resource room, consulting teacher models, and the like without detailed description of what actually goes on within these models. Preoccupation with setting variables has persisted over the years and, in our opinion, has proven to be a legacy limiting use of the knowledge base in seeking to improve special educational practices.

LEGAL CHALLENGES TO SPECIAL CLASSES

During the 1960s, several forces coalesced to result in challenges to the identification procedures for EMR children and the efficacy of special classes. The overrepresentation of certain minority groups in EMR programs became a major focus of civil rights concerns on the basis that EMR special classes constituted de facto segregation.[69] The means by which children were identified were also challenged, with the intelligence test being the major target of critics.[70] Even highly respected special educators questioned the efficacy of special classes.[71] To understand the foundation of this criticism, one must see the challenges to special classes as only part of the overall condemnation heaped on "institutions" serving handicapped individuals. That is, vocal advocates questioned the utility of large institutions serving mentally retarded clients, the effectiveness of mental hospitals for the mentally ill, residential schools for serving any disabled population of students, orphanages, and special classes. The critics' general message was that institutions are abusive to children. Another characteristic of the period was that "data were out" and "stories were in" as research evidence was discounted while anecdotes, often relaying atypical experiences, were persuasive.

A detailed examination of the research literature that pertained to many of the issues raised by critics is available elsewhere.[72] Suffice it to say that the evidence usually pointed to the complexities of the issues, yet the solutions offered were often simply cast—for example, close institutions, abolish special classes, stop labeling, and stop using tests of intelligence. It is reminiscent of a quote attributed to H. L. Mencken: "For every complex issue there is a simple answer, and it is wrong."[73]

The lasting legacy to special education from this period is that the nation's courts became the major sites for policymaking regarding special education. Instead of waiting for change to occur from within the educational system, dissatisfied parents and advocates sought redress through the judicial system. Lessons learned from civil rights cases during the decade earlier were used to challenge the denial of services or services perceived to be inappropriate. Several major "types" of litigation were initiated in order to remedy the perceived problems encountered by individuals with disabilities in receiving appropriate services: those concerned with "right to treatment" in residential facilities (e.g., *Wyatt v. Stickney*, 1971); "right to education" cases concerning public education's responsibility to severely retarded individuals (e.g., *Pennsylvania Association for Retarded Children [PARC] v. Commonwealth of Pennsylvania*, 1972); and cases pertaining to placement procedures alleged to be inappropriate to minority group children (e.g., *Diana v. State Board of Education*, 1970; *Larry P. v. Riles*, 1971, 1979, 1984; *Marshall et al. v. Georgia*, 1984; *PASE [Parents in Action on Special Education] v. Joseph P. Hannon*, 1980; and *S-1 v. Turlington*, 1986).

Cases pertaining to alleged bias in the placement of minority children into EMR programs are the ones most germane here. These cases turned on the issue of bias inherent in the use of tests of intelligence to identify children as eligible for EMR placement, particularly how the assessment process contributed to or was responsible for the overrepresentation of minority children in EMR programs.[74]

As Reschly has observed, these cases reflect a number of underlying issues and assumptions, including nature-nurture, meaning of IQ, role of intelligence tests in placement decisions, labeling effects, six-hour retardation, efficacy of special EMR classes, and concepts of test bias.[75] *Larry P.*, the most well known of the cases, was decided in favor of the plaintiffs and changed fundamentally the identification of EMR children in California. Furthermore, "Judge Peckham excoriated the efficacy of special classes no less than 27 times in his opinion through comments such as 'deadend,' 'inferior,' 'stigmatizing,' and so on."[76] The role of empirical data in deciding the case along with Judge Peckham's competence to evaluate these social science data raise some perplexing questions; nevertheless, educational practices in California were profoundly impacted by this litigation.

The direct impact of *Larry P.* has been restricted, since the decision is not binding outside of California. Three other cases (*Marshall*, 1984; *PASE*, 1980; *S-1*, 1986) were concerned with the same issues surrounding overrepresentation of Black students in EMR classes and the alleged bias of intelligence tests in the identification process. These three, however, were decided in favor of the defendants, as the courts were not persuaded of the undue reliance on IQ in the identification process. Moreover, in *Marshall* and *S-1*, the defendants persuaded the court that MMR did occur more often with lower socioeconomic status conditions and that the conditions of poverty in which disproportionate numbers of Blacks live provided a reasonable explanation for their overrepresentation in EMR programs.

The legacy of litigation as a major avenue for altering educational practice has been felt by special educators. Whether this role will be expanded remains to be seen, but its influence in the last two decades has been considerable.

THE ROLE OF RESEARCH IN A TIME
OF SLOGANS AND ADVOCACY

Special education practices, as noted earlier, have been modified as a result of litigation that in turn has frequently been influential in the drafting of legislation (e.g., PL 94-142). The past two decades have also seen an increase in the polarization of professionals on any number of issues: labeling, intelligence testing, special classes, and the use of aversives, to mention but a few.

During the 1970s when one would inquire as to the empirical evidence supporting a proposed "educational solution," it was not uncommon to be answered, "Lincoln did not require research to know that slavery was wrong." Since research activity during the past decade has increased in both quantity and quality, the tendency to discount its importance in the quest for appropriate and good education for handicapped students seems ill advised. Over a decade ago, Gottlieb noted that an "appropriate education for mentally retarded children has not yet been developed."[77]

Concepts (that required research to make them constructs) have been advanced, have attracted supporters (normalization, mainstreaming, deinstitutionalization), and have influenced practice. Too often, advocacy has emerged in support of these concepts when it is unknown whether programs and treatments considered consistent with the concept are beneficial, are of no consequence, or are detrimental to the very children who they are intended to help. Vocal advocates are advancing the Regular Education Initiative as though we know that it works.[78] The empirical evidence to date is lacking on many special education issues, and the need for research is paramount. Our concern is that when advocates convey the impression to legislators and other policymakers that we know what works, there is little incentive for legislators to support appropriations for research. A recent paper by Zigler et al. captures the complexities of several issues in the care and education of mentally retarded individuals and exposes the gaps in our understanding.[79] Research designed to capture these complexities, along with the complexities of individuals classified as mentally retarded, is sorely needed if progress is to be made toward appropriate and effective treatment.

A LEGACY AS FUTURE POLICY

Sadly, the controversy over the efficacy of special classes and other special services for MMR learners appears far from settled. Public Law 94-142 did much nationally to solidify and extend the rights of handicapped children to special services, even as it attempted to assure that this would be done in a "least restrictive environment." Interestingly, nearly a century of controversy concerning the wisdom of special education for MMR children has returned the debate back almost to where it began. Even as Elizabeth Farrell was laboring nearly ninety years ago to serve children with clearly apparent learning problems without the benefit (or curse) of intelligence testing, so today's educators have been moving, sometimes involuntarily through court decrees, to diagnose learning problems without the benefit of intelligence testing. Interestingly, the tests, more even than the special classes themselves, became the lightning rod in the debate over alleged stigma and other negative aspects of segregated learning environments.

Seventy years ago, standardized intelligence testing was viewed as a more objective way than personal observation for assessing the nature and extent of learning deficiencies. Today, as the special education legacy continues to unfold, the skeptics appear to outnumber the believers on that point. Political ideology and child advocacy have weighed in on both sides of the testing and special class controversy. The clear loser has been the claim of science, particularly in the realm of standardized intelligence testing. Far from clear at this writing is how much children with mental retardation have gained from a return to earlier forms of diagnosis. Moreover, many could be returned to the scene of their initial academic difficulty, the regular class, in the name of progress. Contrary to the beliefs of impassioned critics of testing, special education for MMR children did not owe its historical existence to standardized intelligence testing. Elimination of testing likely will not eliminate the need for special class services to children properly identified as being in need of those services. Old issues reemerge and live on, as becomes abundantly clear in succeeding chapters.

NOTES

1. Irving G. Hendrick and Donald L. MacMillan, "Selecting Children for Special Education in New York City: William Maxwell, Elizabeth Farrell, and the Development of Ungraded Classes, 1900-1920," *The Journal of Special Education* 22, no. 4 (Winter 1989): 395–417.
2. Stanley P. Davies and Katherine G. Ecob, *The Mentally Retarded in Society* (New York: Columbia University Press, 1959); Leo Kanner, *A History of the Care and Study of the Mentally Retarded* (Springfield, IL: Charles C. Thomas, 1964); Martin Lazerson, "Educational Institutions and Mental Subnormality: Notes on Writing a History" in *The Mentally Retarded and Society: A Social Science Perspective*, ed. Michael J. Begab and Stephen A. Richardson (Baltimore: University Park Press, 1975), 33–52; Martin Lazerson, "The Origins of Special Education" in *Special Education Policies: Their History, Implementation, and Finance*, ed. Jay G. Chambers and William T. Hartman (Philadelphia: Temple University Press, 1983), 15–47; David G. Pritchard, *Education of the Handicapped* (London: Routledge & Kegan Paul, 1963); Seymour B. Sarason and John Doris, *Psychological Problems in Mental Deficiency*, 4th ed. (New York: Harper & Row, 1969); Richard C. Scheerenberger, *A History of Mental Retardation* (Baltimore: Paul H. Brookes, 1983); J. Lee Wiederholt, "Historical Perspective on the Education of the Learning Disabled" in *The Second Review of Special Education*, ed. Lester Mann and David A. Sabatino (Philadelphia: JSE, 1974): 103-52; Gregory Zilboorg and George W. Henry, *A History of Medical Psychology* (New York: Norton, 1941).
3. Zilboorg and Henry, *A History of Medical Psychology.*
4. Frank M. Hewett and Steven R. Forness, *Education of Exceptional Children*, 2d ed. (Boston: Allyn & Bacon, 1977).
5. Bernard Farber, "Sociology" in *Mental Retardation and Developmental Disabilities, Vol. 6*, ed. Joseph Worfis (New York: Brunner-Mazel, 1974), 147–61.
6. Pritchard, *Education of the Handicapped.*
7. Herbert Goldstein, Claudia Arkell, Samuel C. Ashcroft, Oliver Hurley, and M. Steven Lilly, "Schools" in *Issues in the Classification of Children, Vol. 2*, ed. Nicholas Hobbs (San Francisco: Jossey-Bass, 1975), 4–61.
8. Irving G. Hendrick and Donald L. MacMillan, "Coping with Diversity in City School Systems: The Role of Mental Testing in Shaping Special Classes for Mentally Retarded Children in Los Angeles, 1900–1930," *Education and Training in Mental Retardation* 22, no. 1 (March 1987): 10–17.
9. Kanner, *A History of the Care and Study;* Alfred A. Baumeister, "The American Residential Institution: Its History and Character" in *Residential Facilities for the Mentally Retarded*, ed. Alfred A. Baumeister and Earl Butterfield (Chicago: Aldine, 1970), 1–28.
10. Baumeister, "The American Residential Institution."
11. Lazerson, "Educational Institutions."
12. Donald L. MacMillan and C. Edward Meyers, "Educational Labeling of Handicapped Learners" in *Review of Research in Education, Vol. 7*, ed. David C. Berliner (Washington, D.C.: American Educational Research Association, 1979), 151–94.
13. Eugene E. Doll, "Historical Review of Mental Retardation, 1800–1965: A Symposium," *American Journal of Mental Deficiency* 72, no. 2 (Sept. 1967): 165–89.
14. Edward Hoffman, *The Treatment of Deviance by the Education System* (Ann Arbor, MI: Institute for the Study of Mental Retardation and Related Disabilities, 1972).

15. Leonard Ayres, *Laggards in the Schools* (New York: Russell Sage Foundation, 1909).
16. Lazerson, "Educational Institutions."
17. Henry H. Goddard, *School Training of Defective Children* (New York: Word, 1914). Usage of the term *ungraded* in the early history of American special education should not be confused with usage of the same term during the late 1930s to describe a new form of school organization for normal children.
18. Hendrick and MacMillan, "Coping with Diversity."
19. Lazerson, "Educational Institutions."
20. Lawrence A. Cremin, *The Transformation of the School* (New York: Knopf, 1962).
21. Lazerson, "Educational Institutions."
22. Hendrick and MacMillan, "Coping with Diversity"; Hendrick and MacMillan, "Selecting Children for Special Education."
23. Richard L. Dugdale, *The Jukes* (New York: Putnam, 1877); Henry H. Goddard, *The Kallikak Family: A Study in the Heredity of Feeblemindedness* (New York: Macmillan, 1912).
24. For example, see Walter B. Pitkin, *Twilight of the American Mind* (New York: Simon & Schuster, 1928).
25. Kanner, "A History of the Care and Study."
26. Sarason and Doris, *Psychological Problems;* J. David Smith, *Minds Made Feeble: The Myth and Legacy of Kallikaks* (Rockville, MD: Aspen Systems, 1985).
27. Lewis M. Terman, "Feeble-minded Children in the Public Schools of California," *School and Society* 5 (1917): 164.
28. See Daniel J. Reschly, "Mental Retardation: Conceptual Foundations, Definitional Criteria, and Diagnostic Operations" in *Assessment and Diagnosis of Child and Adolescent Psychiatric Disorders,* ed. Stephen R. Hooper, George W. Hynd, and R. E. Mattison, *Developmental Disorders, Vol. 2* (Hillsdale, NJ: Erlbaum, in press).
29. New York City, Department of Education, *Ninth Annual Report of the City Superintendent of Schools to the Board of Education for the Year Ending July 31, 1907* (New York: Author, 1907), 169.
30. Ibid., 114.
31. Hendrick and MacMillan, "Coping with Diversity."
32. Terman, "Feeble-minded Children," 164.
33. Division of Psychology and Educational Research, "History and Present Status of the Division" in *Fourth Yearbook of the Division of Psychology and Educational Research* (Los Angeles: Los Angeles City School District, 1931), 7–10.
34. New York City, Department of Education, *Fifteenth Annual Report of the City Superintendent of Schools to the Board of Education for the Year Ending July 31, 1913* (New York: Author, 1913), 68.
35. Ibid., 68.
36. New York City, Department of Education, *Twentieth Annual Report of the City Superintendent of Schools to the Board of Education for the Year Ending July 31, 1920* (New York: Author, 1918-1920).
37. Hendrick and MacMillan, "Coping with Diversity."
38. Ibid.
39. Scheerenberger, *A History of Mental Retardation.*
40. Elizabeth E. Farrell, "The Problems of the Special Class," *Journal of Proceedings and Addresses of the 46th Annual Meeting of the National Education Association* (1908): 1131–36.

41. Richard H. Hungerford, Chris J. De Prospo, and Louis E. Rosenzweig, *The Non-Academic Pupil* (New York: Bureau for Children with Retarded Mental Development, Board of Education, 1947).

42. New York City, *Ninth Annual Report*, 616.

43. Irving G. Hendrick and Donald L. MacMillan, "Modifying the Public School Curriculum to Accommodate Mentally Retarded Students: Los Angeles in the 1920s," *Southern California Quarterly* 70, no. 4 (Winter 1988): 409.

44. Edward A. Polloway, "The Integration of Mildly Retarded Students in the Schools: A Historical Review," *Remedial and Special Education* 5, no. 4 (July/Aug. 1984): 18–28.

45. Edward Zigler, Robert M. Hodapp, and Mark R. Edison, "From Theory to Practice in the Care and Education of Mentally Retarded Individuals," *American Journal of Mental Retardation* 95, no. 1 (July 1990): 7.

46. Donald L. MacMillan, *Mental Retardation in School and Society*, 2d ed. (Boston: Little, Brown, 1982).

47. William I. Gardner and Herschel W. Nisonger, *A Manual on Program Development in Mental Retardation* (Washington, D.C.: American Association on Mental Deficiency, 1962); Polloway, "The Integration of Mildly Retarded Students."

48. Kirby A. Heller, Wayne H. Holtzman, and Samuel Messick, eds., *Placing Children in Special Education: A Strategy for Equity* (Washington, D.C.: National Academy Press, 1982), 30.

49. Francis A. Mullen and William Itkin, "The Value of Special Classes for the Mentally Handicapped: Regular Classes Can Serve Some Classified as EMH," *Chicago Schools Journal* 42 (1961): 353–63.

50. Romaine Mackie, *Special Education in the United States: Statistics 1948–1966* (New York: Teachers College Press, 1969).

51. Polloway, "The Integration of Mildly Retarded Students."

52. California, *The State School Fund and Educational Statistics for the Fiscal Year Ending June 30, 1964, Book One* (Sacramento: Department of Education, 1965).

53. California, *Report on Operation and Results of Special Educational Programs for Educationally Handicapped Minors* (Sacramento: Department of Education, 1967).

54. Lloyd M. Dunn, "Special Education for the Mildly Retarded: Is Much of It Justifiable?" *Exceptional Children* 35, no. 1 (Sept. 1968): 5–22.

55. New York City, *Twentieth Annual Report*, 7.

56. Hendrick and MacMillan, "Coping with Diversity."

57. Maud Whitlock, "Retarded Pupils in Primary Grades," *Educational Research Bulletin, Los Angeles City School District* 3, no. 7 (18 Feb. 1924): 3.

58. Heller et al., *Placing Children in Special Education*, 33.

59. Jane R. Mercer and John G. Richardson, "Mental Retardation as a Social Problem" in *Issues in the Classification of Children, Vol. 2*, ed. Nicholas Hobbs (San Francisco: Jossey-Bass, 1975): 463–96.

60. C. Amelia Winford, "A Follow-up Study of Subnormal Pupils," *Educational Research Bulletin, Los Angeles City School District* 6, no. 2 (Nov. 1926): 2–8.

61. Heller et al., *Placing Children in Special Education*.

62. California, *Programs for the Educable Mentally Retarded in California Public Schools* (Sacramento: Department of Education, 1974), 2.

63. California, *California Master Plan for Special Education* (Sacramento: Department of Education, 1974), 1.

64. California, *Special Education Fiscal Task Force Report* (Sacramento: Department of Education, 1988).
65. Polloway, "The Integration of Mildly Retarded Students."
66. Melvyn I. Semmel, Jay Gottlieb, and Nancy M. Robinson, "Mainstreaming: Perspectives on Educating Handicapped Children in the Public Schools" in *Review of Research in Education, Vol. 7,* ed. David Berliner (Washington, D.C.: American Educational Research Association, 1979): 223–79.
67. Herbert Goldstein, James W. Moss, and Laura J. Jordan, *The Efficacy of Special Class Training on the Development of Mentally Retarded Children,* U.S. Office of Education Cooperative Research Project 619 (ERIC Document Reproduction Service ED 002 907) (Urbana: University of Illinois, 1965).
68. Polloway, "The Integration of Mildly Retarded Students."
69. Daniel J. Reschly, "Minority Mild Mental Retardation Overrepresentation: Legal Issues, Research Findings, and Reform Trends" in *Handbook of Special Education: Research and Practice, Vol. 2,* ed. Margaret C. Wang, Maynard C. Reynolds, and Herbert J. Walberg (Oxford: Pergamon, 1988), 23–41.
70. Rogers Elliott, *Litigating Intelligence: IQ Tests, Special Education, and Social Science in the Courtroom* (Dover, MA: Auburn House, 1985).
71. One of the best-known senior spokespersons for the field articulated such a position in Dunn, "Special Education for the Mildly Retarded Students."
72. For reviews on the efficacy of special classes, see Walter M. Cegelka and James L. Tyler, "The Efficacy of Special Class Placement for the Mentally Retarded in Proper Perspective," *Training School Bulletin* 67, no. 1 (May 1970): 33–67; Samuel L. Guskin and Howard H. Spicker, "Educational Research in Mental Retardation" in *International Review of Research in Mental Retardation, Vol. 3,* ed. Norman R. Ellis (New York: Academic Press, 1968): 217–78; Donald L. MacMillan, "Special Education for the Mildly Retarded: Servant or Savant," *Focus on Exceptional Children* 2, no. 9 (Feb. 1971): 1–11; Semmel et al., "Mainstreaming: Perspectives." On bias in intelligence testing, see Lee J. Cronbach, "Five Decades of Public Controversy over Mental Testing," *American Psychologist* 30, no. 1 (Jan. 1975): 1–14; Arthur R. Jensen, *Bias in Mental Testing* (New York: Free Press, 1980); and Jane R. Mercer, *Labelling the Mentally Retarded* (Berkeley: University of California Press, 1973). On effects of labeling, see Donald L. MacMillan, Reginald L. Jones, and Gregory F. Aloia, "The Mentally Retarded Label: A Theoretical Analysis and Review of Research," *American Journal of Mental Deficiency* 79, no. 3 (Nov. 1974): 241–61; and Mercer, *Labelling the Mentally Retarded.* On "Self-fulfilling Prophecies," see Janet D. Elashoff and Richard E Snow, *Pygmalion Reconsidered* (Worthington, OH: C. A. Jones, 1971); Robert Rosenthal and Lenore Jacobson, *Pygmalion in the Classroom* (New York: Holt, Rinehart, & Winston, 1968); and Richard L. Snow, "Unfinished Pygmalion," *Contemporary Psychology* 14, no. 4 (April 1969): 197–99.
73. Edward Zigler and Robert M. Hodapp, *Understanding Mental Retardation* (New York: Cambridge University Press, 1986), 223.
74. Excellent analyses of these court cases can be found in several sources. Rogers Elliott, *Litigating Intelligence* (Dover, MA: Auburn House, 1987); Reschly, "Minority Mild Mental Retardation"; Daniel J. Reschly, Richard H. Kicklighter, and Patrick McKee, "Recent Placement Litigation. Part I: Regular Education Grouping; Comparison of *Marshall* (1984, 1985) and *Hobson* (1967, 1969)," *School Psy-*

chology Review 17 (Jan.–March 1988): 7–19; Daniel J. Reschly, Richard H. Kicklighter, and Patrick McKee, "Recent Placement Litigation. Part II: Minority EMR Overrepresentation; Comparison of *Larry P.* (1979, 1984, 1986) with *Marshall* (1984, 1985) and *S-1* (1986)," *School Psychology Review* 17 (Jan.–March 1988): 20–36; Daniel J. Reschly, Richard H. Kicklighter, and Patrick McKee, "Recent Placement Litigation. Part III: Analysis of Differences in *Larry P., Marshall,* and *S-1* and Implications for Future Practices," *School Psychology Review* 17 (Jan.–March 1988): 37–48.

75. Reschly, "Minority Mild Mental Retardation."
76. Ibid., 28.
77. Jay Gottlieb, "Mainstreaming: Fulfilling the Promise?" *American Journal of Mental Deficiency* 86, no. 2 (Sept. 1981): 115–26.
78. An informative discussion of this issue by James M. Kauffman and Daniel P. Hallahan is found in chap. 4 of this book.
79. Zigler et al., "From Theory to Practice."

3

Recurring Issues in
Special and General Education

Thomas C. Lovitt

In the public schools there have been two educational systems for some time: general and special. Back in the nineteenth century, when the public schools got off and running, there was only one system. In those days, children simply came to school and were educated together. At that time, little attention was given to different ages or abilities. That approach worked rather well for a number of years because not many children came to school, and those who did were much alike in their backgrounds. Later, when hundreds of immigrants entered the public schools and enrollments increased, youngsters were grouped by age and grade level, much as they are today. Since there was an increasing amount of intellectual, motivational, and experiential variability in these classes, most schools, particularly at the high school level, organized tracks of one form or another in efforts to deal with the heterogeneity.

Individuals with disabilities were generally not served at all in schools prior to about 1920. In the thirties and forties, some orthopedically handicapped, visually and hearing-impaired, and mentally retarded youngsters were accommodated in special schools and institutions. Shortly after World War II, children of those types were served in public schools in special classes. In the sixties and seventies, some situations were arranged in public schools for youngsters referred to as learning disabled, emotionally disturbed, neurologically impaired, and other such types.

When services were set up for individuals with disabilities in public schools, they were in "self-contained" classrooms—that is, classes made up of only children of a designated type. Ordinarily, children in those situations were managed by individuals presumably trained in the designated disability. The primary reason for separating special children from those who were not special was guided by the notion of homogeneity that had

49

prompted educators, several years earlier, to group children by age. I will comment a great deal more on that issue later in the chapter.

Actually, there appear to be four reasons (all of questionable validity) for separating special children and youth from those without handicaps. One, they generally function at lower levels than others, those said to be typical. Two, they acquire information and develop skills at different rates. Three, different techniques, procedures, and methods must be arranged to instruct them. Four, many of them should be taught different skills and behaviors than those offered their nonhandicapped peers. Throughout this chapter I reflect on these assumptions.

Following World War II, there was a wave of advocacy for mainstreaming that called for the integration of children with handicaps into regular classes. Several reasons were advanced for sending children with handicaps of various types back into regular classes. The primary justification for mainstreaming was based on data from studies that compared the benefits of placing children with handicaps (particularly the educably mentally retarded) in either special or regular classes (see chap. 2). Summary data from that research suggested that, generally, children with handicaps were better off academically in regular classes but gained more socially in special situations. Mainstreaming proponents at that time apparently believed that to be a good trade-off.

In the 1960s, educators and others who championed mainstreaming based their arguments for the merger of regular and special children on the spirit of civil rights. They maintained that numbers of special youngsters were not receiving the same benefits as others if they were being educated in self-contained special classes. According to them, separate was not always equal.

There was another burst of interest in mainstreaming in the seventies, this one stimulated by the enactment of the Education of the Handicapped Act (1975), with one of its major provisions being the education of children with handicaps in the least restrictive environment (LRE). The LRE provision required that all youngsters with disabilities be educated to the extent possible with and alongside their nonhandicapped peers. Although there was no mention of mainstreaming as such in the act, the LRE was largely interpreted as involving children with disabilities of all types in regular situations as much as possible.

In the 1980s, there was yet another boost to the mainstreaming movement, this time from the Regular Education Initiative.[1] This initiative, developed and promoted by special educators, not only called for the education of special students in regular classes but suggested that regular and special education teachers share the responsibility for the education of handicapped children.

There has always been resistance to this integration of special and regular students from some educators of both types. As for general educators, there has never been an outpouring of support from them to bring back the disabled. Many of them went through quite a process to have individuals with handicaps removed from their classes. Moreover, they were told by special educators that these special youngsters required unique services that only they could offer. Most general teachers also have not been adequately informed about those special techniques, whatever they might be. Meanwhile, numbers of special educators believe that many of their charges should not be transferred to general classrooms. Significant numbers of those specialists maintain that individuals with handicaps are served quite well in special situations.

PREVAILING ISSUES

As these opinions and positions for educating individuals with handicaps have been discussed by general and special educators, seven related and overlapping issues have been the primary topics:

- identification,
- delivery systems,
- curriculum,
- evaluation,
- funding,
- relationships and responsibilities, and
- homogeneity and heterogeneity.

In this chapter, as each issue is discussed, I will integrate comments or data from relevant research and provide personal comments.

Identification

When special education classes were first arranged, they were, as mentioned earlier, designed for individuals who were noticeably handicapped: blind, deaf, or physically disabled. The identification of individuals with those types of disabilities was not a problem. Later, as separate classes and different forms of instruction were provided for individuals with mental retardation, learning disabilities, and behavioral disorders, the matter of assessment became more complex; for now, the differences between them and others were based on cognitive, social, and emotional attributes that are not as obvious as the physical characteristics that distinguished sensory and physically impaired youth from others.

The apparent logic for identifying who is special and who is not has to do with homogeneity, placement, and instruction. The idea is relatively simple in its conception, if markedly flawed in its operation. It goes like this: Individuals of a certain type are identified, by administering a test or survey, by carrying out an interview or observation, then taken away from those who are not like them and placed with others who are. The rationale continues by suggesting that since those similarly identified youngsters are homogeneous with respect to the process that discriminated them from others, the same type of instruction can be provided all of them. Furthermore, the reasoning implies that the youngsters who were placed with others of their ilk will be better off for having had this different type of instruction, a form that was presumably designed just for them. Inherent consequences of all this might be that those individuals who were specifically identified and accordingly grouped stay in school longer, get more out of school while they are in it, and live more productive lives when they leave it than they would have had they not been specially dealt with.

This practice of identifying then separating individuals from the "mainstream" has not been the exclusive process of special education. Youngsters of other types have been identified, pulled out, placed together, and taught as groups: Chapter I, English as a second language (ESL), and gifted, to name three. In addition, several school districts have identified other types of youngsters as at risk or in need of remediation and have placed them in separate instructional situations.

Apropos of these expanding categories and services, Sapon-Shevin notes, "As the number of children served in various remedial, entitlement, and enrichment programs continues to grow, these programs often serve a majority of a school population."[2] According to an article in the *New York Times,*[3] one in every eight children in New York City's public schools is now classified as handicapped. In that city, about 33,000 children are tested and interviewed each year for special education at a cost of about $3,000 a child.

There is no indication that there will be fewer categories and special types of youngsters in the future. According to the most recent federal legislation that affects children with disabilities, two new categories have been proposed, autism and traumatic brain injury, and there is debate about whether to include attention deficit disorders as yet another category.[4]

Comment

There has been considerable argument over how best to identify these various types of children. Dozens of task forces have grappled with these matters. Scores of articles, chapters, and monographs have dealt with the issue. In spite of all this effort, there is no more agreement now about how to identify children of certain types (e.g., learning disabilities and emotional disturbance) than there was twenty-five years ago.

But the upshot of all this—the need to identify children and youth for special services—is that a mammoth assessment industry has been created. A major component of this industry, the publishers—particularly those that market tests, surveys, inventories, and scales having to do with identification—has greatly profited from the need to "certify" certain types of youngsters. Publishers have also gained from this need to identify and separate by the many textbooks on assessment they have published.

Moreover, universities and colleges have benefited from this desire to assess in that most of them have a course or two on assessment. In addition, many of them have programs to prepare personnel who administer tests, which includes school psychologists, counselors, and therapists of many types.

In spite of the costs and the fact that so many professionals are involved, there is always a number of "false positive assessments," those from which youngsters were assessed but not found to qualify. In New York City, about 15 percent of those assessed are not identified as handicapped. In those cases there is a considerable waste of money, for the assessed children were not sent to another place for different instruction, and the information from the tests was not helpful in their current location.

In an effort to simplify the identification process for learning disabled youngsters in the state of Washington and to reduce the costs of those assessments, requests for proposals have been issued to all school districts. Districts have been asked to develop alternative ways to assess and qualify learning disabled students for services that are less expensive.

Delivery Systems

When special education students were identified for services many years ago, they were, as indicated earlier, sent to special schools apart from the public schools. Later, when special education youngsters were instructed in public schools, they were educated in self-contained classrooms. Youngsters of the same type, according to some sort of assessment, were gathered together and taught by a teacher who may have been trained specifically to deal with youngsters of that kind. Itinerant teachers were also engaged, several years ago, to provide assistance either to youngsters who had sensory or physical impairments or to teachers who were serving them. Later, a number of other service delivery models were arranged: resource rooms, consulting teachers, and special tracks.

Currently, several delivery options are available in most school districts. It is not unusual at the elementary level to have self-contained classrooms, resource rooms, and consulting or itinerant teachers. Moreover, great numbers of special education youngsters are, of course, mainstreamed into regular classes. At the high school level, it is common to have even more delivery systems: regular classes, resource rooms, self-contained classes, basic track classes, cotaught classes, vocational settings. Some youth are educated in the community, receiving training in such locations as hospitals, day care and recreational situations, and a variety of businesses.[5]

It is often difficult to determine why schools have chosen the types of delivery systems they have. When administrators, teachers, coordinators, parents, and others are asked about their choices, their responses are often vague. It seems that some schools operate the way they do because they have always carried out business that way or they have been influenced by the arrangements of other schools.

A few exemplary schools throughout the country are now making more thoughtful decisions when it comes to setting up various delivery systems. This is especially noted at the secondary level where educators are concerned about keeping youth in school and considering what it is they will do once they graduate. As more schools consider these matters of retention and outcome, their curricular options are being revised, and that, to some extent, dictates their delivery systems.

Many schools, particularly at the elementary level, are opting for prereferral delivery systems, an approach whereby teams of professionals determine the instructional plans for youngsters (see chaps. 4 and 6). When such a plan is in operation, youngsters who are a concern to teachers for one reason or another are evaluated by a team of teachers who offer suggestions to referring teachers for dealing with the problems in their classrooms. Traditionally, when a child becomes a "focus of concern," she or he is tested by a psychologist or other specialist, and if the results of those tests so indicate, the child is sent to a special room for instruction.

The primary motive behind the prereferral plan is to save money. As indicated in the preceding section, there is always a number of false positive assessments when traditional approaches are arranged. When youngsters are not evaluated by a corps of psychologists and other outsiders but are dealt with by teachers familiar with the child's surroundings, considerable money is saved. Beck,[6] who designed a prereferral program in Great Falls, Montana, and has since promoted it throughout the country,[7] shows data to indicate that prior to a prereferral process, 54 percent of those referred for special education in six elementary schools were eventually placed in special education. Following implementation of the prereferral teams, 80 percent of those referred were later placed in special programs. Whether or not the youngsters were better off academically or socially because they stayed put rather than packing up and moving to special rooms is unknown, but the district did save considerable money by changing their assessment approaches.

Not only is it difficult to discern, as indicated earlier, why schools have certain delivery systems as opposed to others, it is not clear, when interviewing school personnel, why some youngsters are sent to one situation and others to a different location. Explicit criteria for deciding about who will be placed in which setting are generally not available. According to Truesdell,[8] the majority of teachers do not list specific qualities for students who will be mainstreamed. Generally, they mainstream well-behaved students who they believe will "fit" in with the regular classes. She goes on to say that decisions about mainstreaming were made with insufficient information about programs and students, and as a result mainstreaming is inaccessible to some, inappropriately scheduled for others, and often arbitrary. Although the building principal in her study advocated mainstreaming, he neither initiated discussion to develop specific criteria for selecting students for mainstreaming nor instituted practices that increased access or equalized status for special education.

Delivery systems have stimulated intense and prolonged educational debates for several decades. Dozens of so-called "efficacy" studies have been published. Carlberg and Kavale[9] conducted a meta-analysis in which they analyzed the data from fifty of these studies, relying on "effect size" as a dependent variable to assess the impact of independent variables such as placement, type of outcome measure, internal validity, and other educational, personal, and methodological variables. Their data show that special class placement was significantly inferior to regular class placement for students with below-average IQs, but special classes were significantly superior to regular classes for children with behavioral disorders, emotional disturbance, and learning disabilities. Their analysis indicates that other independent variables bore little or no relationship to effect size.

Comment

When youngsters with handicaps are mainstreamed into the general system, they are not always integrated into *all* the school's curricular offerings, particularly at the secondary level. Whereas youth with disabilities are often mainstreamed into vocal music, English, physical education, industrial arts, and arts and crafts classes, they are not mainstreamed as often into science, foreign language, and instrumental music situations. The same can be said for the integration of individuals with disabilities into the extracurricular features of schools, many of which are the primary reason that many youth remain in school (e.g., athletic teams, clubs, music and drama groups). And not infrequently, children with handicaps who are integrated with others at school are isolated from their peers once the school bell rings and they go home. Dorris laments in *The Broken Cord* that Adam "never once received so much as a telephone call or an invitation from a 'friend.'"[10] This, in spite of the fact that he was mainstreamed and yearly report cards claimed that he was making a great number of friends.

Curriculum

The matter of curricular options available to youngsters and youth is directly related to the preceding two matters: identification and delivery systems. This is particularly true for students with handicaps at the secondary level.

For regular education youngsters in elementary schools, there is generally one curricular track: they move from first grade to second, to third, and so forth. In some instances there are ability groups at the primary or intermediate level into which youngsters are separated from their age-mates and associated with those who match up with them in a subject such as reading or mathematics.

At the secondary level, particularly in high school, there are often two or three curricular tracks. They are referred to by various names, but often there is a basic track for the slowest youth; a general track for the bulk of the students, those who may go on to college; and an advanced track for the top 25 or 30 percent of the students, the ones who will go on to universities and colleges.

As for special education students, there is generally one option available at the elementary level, the same as that for the general education students. Although some of them may be educated in self-contained classes or resource rooms, assisted by itinerant or consulting teachers, their curriculum is much like that offered their general education mates.

At the secondary level, several curricular options are available. A few of the special education students might be in the top track along with general education pupils, several of them would be involved in the regular or middle track, and many would be instructed in the lowest or basic track. In addition to those three paths, great numbers of youth with disabilities are provided a functional or community-relevant curriculum, and several are placed in a vocational curriculum.

Numbers of educators maintain that most youngsters with mild disabilities should be offered the same curriculum as that provided their non-handicapped peers—that is, large doses of science, social studies, math, and English, plus the usual electives. Some suggest that support from resource or consulting teachers be provided;[11] others, that aspects of their programs should be modified.[12] Yet others suggest that study skills instruction[13] be provided to support them in the regular curriculum.

Brolin has recommended a career education model for special education and other youth. Following that approach, referred to as "Life-Centered Career Education," students are assisted to acquire twenty-two major competencies in three major curriculum areas: daily living, personal-social, and occupational skills. According to Kokaska and Brolin, "these competencies represent what research, practitioner experience, and expert opinion have deemed essential for successful career development."[14]

Gill and Edgar[15] take a more radical position on curriculum and recommend four options for handicapped adolescents, each of which specifies a desired outcome.

Option 1: Direct or indirect instructional support is provided in the general education environment; the desired outcome is postsecondary education resulting in competitive employment.

Option 2: Direct instructional support is offered in the regular vocational education environment; the desired outcome is competitive employment immediately after leaving school.

Option 3: Community-based academic and vocational skills are offered; the desired outcome is competitive employment.

Option 4: This option expands the supported employment initiative; the outcome is supported employment and supported living.

Comment

Although educators and researchers have suggested that aspects of instruction be modified or study skills instruction be provided as ways of assisting handicapped youngsters to stay with the regular curriculum, these practices are not widespread. Many teachers are unable or unwilling to modify and supplement their practices. Goodlad[16] notes that one of the most disturbing findings in their study of schooling was the narrow range of instructional techniques they observed, particularly at the secondary level.

One of the problems with setting up proper and accommodating situations for students with disabilities (and others, for that matter) is the fact that teachers generally do not communicate with one another, and this is especially true across the two systems, general and special education. Special teachers are generally not trained to interact with either general teachers or vocational teachers. And the same could be said for general teachers and vocational teachers. Certainly, that same criticism could be leveled at school psychologists and building principals. Although psychologists might be trained to work with special education students, they ordinarily do not receive instruction in dealing with teachers of any type. And although principals might be required to learn about working with regular students, they receive little training in dealing with vocational or special education students or their teachers.

It will be interesting to see how the many plans for restructuring unfold with respect to curriculum and how they affect students, those with and without handicaps. Moreover, it will be of considerable interest to observe the effects of such highly publicized projects as President Bush's America 2,000 and Theodore Sizer's Coalition of Essential Schools, neither of which speaks to students with special needs.

Evaluation

With respect to individuals with handicaps, two aspects of evaluation have troubled educators for some time; one pertains to program evaluation and the other to individual evaluation. As for the former, a standardized achievement test of one form or another is ordinarily administered to youngsters across the land at some time during the year (see chap. 7). In Washington state, for example, students at three grade levels—fourth, eighth, and tenth—are tested each October. The reason for giving the tests is to determine how well students are getting along in various subjects.

Numbers of individuals look at the results of these tests, some more seriously than others. In numerous locales, the results are published in newspapers by district and by specific school; the scores are there for all to see. Understandably, there is a good deal of pressure on administrators, teachers, and children to do well on the tests—so much pressure, in fact, that district personnel have been known to cheat. According to an article in the *New York Times*,[17] folks in Staten Island allegedly changed dozens of answers to test items so that their "scholars" looked better than they actually were.

In most schools, youngsters with disabilities are either "excused" from taking these tests, or if they do take them, their scores are not included with those of the nonhandicapped students. The obvious reason for not including the test scores of the children with disabilities in the general analysis is that they will probably lower the school's or district's average and cause them to look bad. According to data from the National Longitudinal Transition Study, 38 percent of the handicapped were exempted from taking minimum competency tests.[18]

The federal initiative, America 2000, calls for the administration of national tests. The contention is that nationwide testing will hold all students to "New World Standards" and will spur public interest in education and better instruction from teachers. The arguments, pro and con, for such tests are heated and relate to several points, but the following appear to be the three main topics: What kind of test should be administered? How many tests should be given nationally? For what purpose are the tests given?[19] Whether or not politicians decide to administer nationwide tests, it is doubtful that special education youngsters will be involved, at least not in the overall and final analyses.

If special education students are not to be included in the mainstream when it comes to these general assessments, how are they and their programs to be evaluated? Several alternatives are available, one of which was proposed by Halpern, Benz, and Lindstrom,[20] who developed a method for evaluating secondary special education, transition, and adult service programs. Using his approach, reviewers score programs on seventy-one items from six categories: curriculum and instruction, coordination and mainstreaming, transition, documentation, administrative support, and adult services.

Another way to evaluate special education programs or individuals in special or regular education programs is to rely on *individualized education programs* (IEPs)—that is, to determine the number of objectives on those forms that have been achieved and the extent to which they have been accomplished. A number of educators have recommended this approach.[21]

Still a different approach for evaluating special education programs or the progress of individuals is to depend on *curriculum-based measures*.[22] For that form of evaluation, teachers obtain data on activities that are actually being taught. If, for example, students are instructed in reading from Lippincott textbooks, their performances from those materials would be evaluated; they would, in other words, be measured directly. Furthermore, when that form of assessment is involved, teachers obtain useful data quite often, sometimes daily.

Another option for assessing special students is the *portfolio method*.[23] When that type of appraisal is adopted, teachers provide students with folders, and periodically they or the students place materials in them. If the papers and other items are organized properly, it is easy to tell over time whether or not progress has been made in specific areas.

Yet another assessment alternative is referred to as the *dynamic assessment approach*.[24] With that method, students are assessed on a certain skill, then given instruction on carrying it out, and tested once again on performing that skill. The idea is to determine the effects of short-term instruction.

One of the issues involved with the evaluation of students with disabilities has to do with grading: Should they be graded on the same bases as other students, whatever that might be, or should different approaches be used? This issue has perplexed teachers for years, particularly at the secondary level. Rojewski, Pollard, and Meers[25] surveyed secondary vocational educators to determine how they evaluated mainstreamed special needs students. In the process, they identified six different approaches:

1. *Traditional grading,* where either a letter or number was given
2. *Pass/fail grading,* to demonstrate whether a student met predetermined standards
3. *Checklists,* to monitor progress against predetermined standards
4. *Contract grading,* as an agreement between student and teacher on whether or not a specified task had been completed
5. *Letters/conferences* with parents, to describe student's activities and accomplishments
6. *Blanket grades,* regardless of a student's performance

Most educators believe that students with disabilities are given a break when it comes to grades, regardless of the method. Calhoun and Beattie[26] report from their survey that twenty-five out of twenty-six general and vocational teachers indicated that they have different grading criteria for exceptional students. Although daily grades are handled in a standard manner, the course grade is "bumped" upward at report card time.

Comment

Recently, when I was discussing matters of publishing, marketing, and research with personnel from a local publishing company, I learned of a new twist on assessment. One of their staff informed me that she had received a few calls from teachers in the area asking about the correspondence between the words taught from one of their reading programs and the words included on an achievement test given in their district. They wanted to know that if they taught youngsters to read from that program, would the learning of those particular words be reflected on the test. Those inquiring teachers wanted to get credit for what they taught; they did not necessarily want to teach something about which their youngsters would not be tested and for which they would not be given credit. This is just another case of test makers "driving" the curriculum, or at least the procedures that articulate the curriculum.

Funding

Related to funding, Sapon-Shevin[27] has asked how the resources could be distributed within school buildings in a way that responds to a wide range of student needs rather than in response to categorical labels. Others have asked that question, but not all agree that a redistribution of monies would be in the best interest of students with handicaps. Many of those who believe that funds should be earmarked especially for individuals with handicaps are of the opinion that too much is siphoned off these allocations for youth with special needs as it is. They maintain that it is best to have standard categories, with stipulations that designated amounts of money go directly to them rather than into a common fund.

No question about it, special education programs are expensive. Since passage of PL 94-142 in 1975 until 1986, special education funding from all sources has been $16 billion.[28]

Although federal dollars for special education have always been disbursed in accordance with a flat, student-based formula (e.g., each child served in special education was given an equal number of dollars regardless of type), the states have developed alternative reimbursement patterns to allocate the monies that must be generated to support programs (see chap. 5). Two common formulas are the flat rate and the weighted-pupil calculation. When the former is used, a fixed amount of funds per child, teacher, or classroom unit is provided. This method is relatively simple to administer and does not require labeling of students by handicapping condition. Weighted-pupil calculations are based on types of specific children multiplied by an average per-pupil cost or on a type of weighted formula tied to the type of service or degree of disability.

Washington state, for example, distributes its state funds to school districts on a weighted basis; the most severe youngsters, or those who require the most service, generate the most money. The range of money that districts receive is about $10,000 for deaf-blind students to about $900 for those with communication disorders. Districts are given approximately $2,750 for each student with learning disabilities, the largest population.

Dempsey and Fuchs[29] have compared those two student-based formulas for funding disbursement in Tennessee. From 1979–80 through 1982–83, the flat rate was used, and between 1983–84 and 1987–88 a weighted formula was implemented. Their results indicate a dramatic shift in placement from lower-funded (less expensive) to higher-funded (more costly) service options concurrent with the change from a flat to a weighted reimbursement formula. In other words, as funding shifted from a flat to a weighted rate, many students were moved from partial to comprehensive resource programs, or from less to more financially rewarding, and to school programs that were more restrictive in terms of pupil placement. When Dempsey and Fuchs inquired of the special education directors' motives for these shifts, nearly 80 percent of them believed that placement changes were based on legitimate service needs.

Comment

There has been considerable concern about the appropriation of funds and the allocation of services for categories of youth—those in handicapped or

Chapter I programs and those in other remedial and compensatory programs—because services must be separate and rigidly detailed. Although they are to some extent correct, a few districts are "creative" when it comes to allocating funds and services, and the rules and regulations for many of the programs are not quite as rigid as they appear to be. To a great extent these concerns can be dealt with rather smoothly if the director of special education is administratively responsible for Chapter I, ESL, remedial, and other such programs. Along with the request for proposals regarding the identification of children with learning disabilities, Washington state has requested proposals from districts, asking them to come up with plans for serving the various related populations of children together. According to Schrag (see chap. 9), other states are willing to waive certain requirements in efforts to better serve students and perhaps save money in the process.

Responsibilities and Relationships

A question related to responsibilities is, *Who* is responsible to *whom* for what? Another question, this having to do with relationships, is, To what extent, and about what, should individuals from the two systems interact with one another?

Early on, when special youngsters were sent to self-contained classes, special education teachers were totally responsible for them. Once those youngsters were away from their general education classes, those teachers lost interest in them. We cannot be too critical of that attitude, for classroom teachers have their hands full.

When resource programs were established, although the responsibilities of special and general teachers were sometimes shared, they were not always clearly stated. As a result, when either set of teachers is asked to comment on the attitudes, roles, responsibilities of the other set, they are often unimpressed. Among other things, special education teachers express disappointment with the attitudes of general education teachers regarding students with handicaps. General education teachers make known their dissatisfaction with the assistance they receive from special education staff.

Davis[30] published a list of thirty-two competencies and skills required of resource teachers; only four are noted here:

- Knowledge of and skill in employing a variety of methods for teaching reading
- Ability to deal effectively with personal and professional frustrations related to the position
- Ability to communicate with parents
- Knowledge of and skill in employing a variety of pupil behavior management techniques

According to his survey, resource teachers are expected to know a great deal about instructional materials and procedures, about classroom management and assessment, and about legislation and communication. A heavy assignment—no wonder the resource teachers disappoint others now and then.

Friend[31] has proposed another list of competencies, many of which were similar to the ones noted by Davis. Although the special and regular teachers she surveyed were in close agreement as to the expected abilities and responsibilities of resource teachers, they disagreed as to the extent resource teachers carried out the various tasks. Classroom teachers rated the resource teachers significantly low on four items: systematically evaluating interventions, consistently seeing teachers as partners when planning programs, regularly scheduling conferences with teachers, and precisely explaining their perceptions of problems to teachers.

One of the difficulties with the resource room arrangement is that the two sets of teachers—general and special—are not in agreement about the role of special teachers, whether they will serve in a supporting role or actually take over certain instructional responsibilities. When special education teachers support the instruction of general teachers, they are informed by the general teachers as to what the objectives are for the children. Special teachers learn about the books, methods, or procedures that their general teachers use and involve them as they set out to reinforce the general teachers' efforts. When special education teachers assume full responsibility for teaching certain skills (e.g., math and reading), *they* decide on the objectives and on the processes and procedures for attaining them. Either arrangement, supplementing or supplanting, will work as long as everyone understands and agrees with the plan.

Several teachers, administrators, observers, and others who are involved with schools have commented that special and general education teachers communicate more when the two sets of teachers share responsibilities for youngsters' development. Certainly one of the reasons for setting up collaborative situations, not only among teachers but between teachers and parents, school people and university folks, is that it is a tough assignment to educate children, especially those identified as remedial, at risk, and handicapped. Everyone needs all the help they can get. Prereferral teams have done a great deal toward fostering collaborations across the two camps.[32] For that approach, as described earlier, a team of three or four teachers is formed who react to teachers' referrals and suggest several techniques for dealing with social or academic behaviors. From those suggestions, referring teachers select tactics and try them out with children of concern. If successful, that's that; but if not, it is back to the team. With those prereferral arrangements, and knowing that pupils who are of concern will probably remain in referring teachers' classes, teachers are motivated to work together and come up with solutions to the problems.

Meyers, Gelzheiser, and Yelich[33] have compared the extent to which teachers involved in "pullout" and "come-in" programs collaborated. For the latter programs, special education teachers actually went into regular classrooms and instructed groups of pupils there. Their data show that there was considerably more collaboration among teachers when the latter model was installed. Those data indicate that close proximity, shared responsibility notwithstanding, stimulated collaboration.

Johnson and Pugach[34] list a number of social and academic behaviors and asked teachers to identify the ones for which they might seek assistance from other teachers. Their data reveal that teachers were more apt to ask one another for help for academic matters than for social concerns. This is interesting yet discouraging when one considers that about 67 percent of teachers' concerns about their students have to do with social or management matters.

Comment

From my experiences in working in various schools, I note three circumstances that stand in the way of establishing good relationships among general and special education teachers.

1. Not a few special education teachers serve as advocates for their students, and, according to some regular teachers, they occasionally overplay their role. A situation of this type was a teacher of developmentally delayed, autistic-type youngsters at an elementary school. Because she had worked with many of her boys and girls for two or three years, knew them so well, and wanted so much for them, including the opportunities available in regular classes, she demanded that the staff and administration integrate her charges. She was relentless, never missing an opportunity to speak up for her citizens.

One could argue that she was doing right by her students, using the laws and her pressures to open doors for them. But one could argue too that if her goals were to facilitate the integration of her youngsters into regular classes over time and in several circumstances, she should have taken a more collaborative approach.

2. In some schools, the special education teacher seeks to control all information and knowledge that has to do with special education. This causes problems. To illustrate this type of situation, I am reminded of a junior high school at which I worked, assisting the administration and teachers to come up with a plan for mainstreaming.

To carry out this assignment, I spent several days visiting special and general classes, interviewing teachers, and chatting with students. From those visits and interactions, the following picture emerged: some general teachers had special education youngsters in their classes and were getting along fine, others had special education pupils in their classes and did not want them there, and a few had never had special education students in their classes and they wanted it that way. Although a disappointing appraisal, it was quite the ordinary.

But the feature of that school that fascinated me was the way in which one of the resource teachers acted. She wanted, and apparently had gained, a corner on all matters that dealt with special education. She made all the decisions: about assessment, placement (which included mainstreaming), curriculum (whether or not it should be different, modified, or whatever), grading, and all other aspects of special education. Although most of the general teachers did not mind her autocratic control (for they did not want to know any more about students with handicaps than they had to), she neither encouraged them to learn more about those students nor collaborated with them in planning those youngsters' programs. I referred to her as "Madam Mainstreamer."

3. Some special education teachers start up their classes several days after the opening day of school and gradually add pupils to them. Although this is a relaxed and leisurely way to begin the year, the practice does nothing for establishing positive relationships between special and general teachers. The rationale for the graduated involvement plan is that if teachers take time and are deliberate as they diagnose students, they will identify their precise problems and be able to hone in with the most concordant interventions. That is well and good, but general teachers cannot do it that way. They have more children in their classes and just as many problems, and they have to begin diagnosing and instructing from day one with the entire cast. Those teachers are greatly put off by the gradual expansion model.

Homogeneity and Heterogeneity

As I indicated at the outset of this chapter, I will give more attention to the issue of homogeneity and heterogeneity than I have the others because it has played a central part in the forming of classes and the designing of instruction for students with handicaps. Two parts comprise this section. In the first, I summarize data from four research studies colleagues and I have carried out that deal with this issue. In the second section, I note and comment on the seven justifications and steps that are often given for being involved with grouping and tracking.

Summary of Studies

In our earliest study of this type, we obtained data in four prereading skills (i.e., see-to-say names of letters, see-to-say sounds of letters, see-to-say initial sounds of pictures, and hear-to-say initial consonants of three-letter words) from twenty-four students in a first-grade class. In another study, we gathered oral reading and comprehension rates from eighteen high school students (learning disabled and nondisabled) as they read text of six types: from a TV guide, a recipe, instructions on a bleach bottle, a manual on fire prevention, a bus schedule, and a want ad. For our third project, about 200 secondary-level students (learning disabled and nondisabled) were involved. Data in that study were pupils' scores on teacher-made tests that covered their assigned materials in a variety of content area classes (e.g., science, language, social studies). For our fourth study, one class of children from each grade level (kindergarten through six) was involved. Data were obtained from those children in from four to six skill areas (e.g., oral reading, comprehension, vocabulary, arithmetic, writing).

Following are four summary statements from those studies:

1. There is considerable variability at all levels, kindergarten through twelfth grade, even though the classes were homogeneously formed and even when the scores of special education students were not considered in the class ranges.
2. There was considerable variability across all subjects (prereading skills, reading at all levels, arithmetic from first to sixth grade, responding to content materials of various types).
3. There was considerable variability of scores for the students with learning disabilities when their data were analyzed separately. In fact, there was just as much variability in their scores as there was in the scores of the youngsters with no disabilities.
4. When the scores of students with and without disabilities were plotted alongside one another for the same attributes, there was always some overlap. Some scores of the children with learning disabilities fit within the range of the youngsters with no disabilities, and some scores of the youngsters with no disabilities fit in with those of the students with disabilities.

Rationale for Grouping and Tracking

Following are seven questionable reasons that are often given for becoming involved with tracking or grouping, most of which are paraphrased from the book *Keeping Track: How Schools Structure Inequality* by Oakes:[35]

1. Tracking will reduce, if not eliminate, the variability among students. This assumption appears to be the very foundation of tracking: if a behavior such as reading is identified for students of a given age (e.g., third-grade level) and if youngsters can somehow be sorted out with respect to their ability on that skill, that group will be reasonably homogeneous.

According to our data, there is a tremendous amount of variability in classes that are ostensibly homogeneous. This was true at every grade level, for every subject, and for several types of youngsters.

2. When homogeneous groups are formed, the task of instruction will be simplified. The idea behind this assumption is that if youth can be homogeneously grouped, then teachers can rely primarily on the same teaching and management techniques with all students.

Because there is so much variability in classes at the elementary and secondary levels, it would be quite inappropriate to arrange the same instructional practices for all children and expect all of them to thrive. Our data show that when a single technique is arranged for all youngsters in a class—one proclaimed by others as "effective"—some students improve dramatically, some slightly, some not at all, and the scores of a few students actually deteriorate because of the practice.

3. Slow, average, and fast students (intellectually speaking) learn best when they are grouped separately.

Good and Marshall[36] conclude from their analyses that the overall gains of children were higher in heterogeneous classes than they were in homogeneous classes, and this was particularly true for low-achieving students. In our studies, particularly from the third one to which I referred, about as many lower-functioning students improved, as a function of arranged practices, as higher-functioning students. This would seem to indicate that students of all types, in the same class, can achieve at acceptable rates.

4. Not only are slow students better off when educated with those of their kind, but they will develop better self-esteem if they are grouped together and will make more friends.

According to Oakes,[37] tracking seems to foster low self-esteem among lower-functioning students and, furthermore, promotes school misbehavior and dropping out. The large data bank from which she drew her conclusions also indicates that students in low-track classes, far more than those in the high track, believed that other students in their classes were unfriendly to them.

5. Students can be properly sorted into groups with some type of test, interview, survey, or a combination of those approaches. The related assumption is that youngsters' past academic achievements and attitudes toward education are strong predictors of those abilities and traits in the future. This was definitely not the case in the second study I summarized earlier; there was overlap between the ranges of students with and without learning disabilities.

If youth are grouped on the basis of any single trait or even on a collection of related traits, they may all be much alike on that set of attributes, but chances are they will differ widely on the many other skills, traits, behaviors, or whatever that have not been assessed and have not played a part in the grouping process. Furthermore, although it might be possible to identify a collection of youngsters who are much alike on certain behaviors on one day, that does not mean that they will be alike on those measures the next month, or even the next week or day. It is quite likely that if a group of youngsters started out at about the same level on a skill or two on one day, a few of them would improve dramatically, some gradually, and some not at all. So one might say that even if we can achieve a sort of *static* homogeneity, it is doubtful than we could attain a *dynamic* homogeneity, one that held constant over time.

6. Schools have established policies regarding grouping and tracking. Many parents, students, and others assume that schools have carefully detailed policies about tracking that, among other things, specify the condi-

tions for sending students into one situation or another and explain the process for shifting pupils from one group to another.

According to Oakes,[38] only two of the twenty-five schools in their sample provided them with documents that outlined the structure of their tracking systems. Of those, only one document was a formal policy statement; the other was simply a letter of explanation to teachers about the criteria to use when placing students. With respect to shifting tracks, Oakes remarks that the school administrators in the study estimated that fewer than 30 percent of the pupils would be shifted from one track to another in a year. Berger[39] claims that in New York, only 5 percent of the city's children assigned to special education ever rejoined the mainstream. It appears that once on a track there is not much switching.

7. It is acceptable to establish a hierarchy of tracks or groups in schools—college preparatory, regular, basic, and vocational—and it is acceptable to label students who are placed in those tracks as "college prep students" and so forth.

According to Good and Marshall,[40] tracking shows a consistent pattern of deprivation for low students. Teachers make fewer demands and hold lower standards for low-track classes and prepare less for low-ability students. And consider this quote from Oakes:[41]

> We have seen that these differences [between instruction in high- and low-track classes] taken together form a cycle of conditions that enhance opportunities for high-track students—more time set aside for learning by teachers, more actual class time observed to be taken up with learning activity, more time expected to be spent on homework, fewer students observed off-task, students' perceptions of learning as the thing they do most in class, and more of the kind of instructional practice that is likely to motivate students to learn and decrease the time needed to do so. We have also seen that conditions were such that low-track students' opportunities were more restricted in all these ways.

Comments

If there are so many negative outcomes from grouping and tracking and if there appear to be so few positive outcomes, then how do we break the habit? What do we do instead? Recently, I have given thought to the positive features of the one-room or country schools that were so prevalent in the Midwest a century ago. Although there were some grim tales about education in those austere situations, there were some pluses, ones that I have considered in coming up with a different arrangement.[42] The first part of my plan would be to have many more elementary schools than we now have, all of which would be small and located near the homes of children or the workplaces of their parents. There would be, for example, several of these schools in the downtown areas of cities.

I recommend that there be from 50 to 150 children in each school, staffed by three to ten teachers. In these schools, groups of from ten to fifteen heterogeneous youngsters would be loosely formed. Children could be assigned to teachers at random, by drawing names from a hat. In this way, a teacher might have under his charge a couple of twelve-year-olds, a ten-year-old, three seven-year-olds, and an assortment of others. Among that teacher's group might be an orthopedically handicapped girl, a boy with learning disabilities, and another boy with developmental disabilities.

With those highly variable arrangements, teachers would have to recognize differences among and between their students because they would be so extreme, and as a possible consequence, they might not rely on the common lecture-discussion-review-test type of teaching. Moreover, there is a chance that teachers, in recognizing each youngster's abilities and needs, would attempt to develop them, regardless of ages, sizes, or labels.

The probability is increased with such arrangements that teachers would interact a great deal with one another, for they would have to. Teachers would of necessity learn about the strengths and interests of their fellow teachers and seek them out when they needed help. To accommodate those collaborations, teachers would need and be provided with time to talk to one another. Truesdell is of the opinion, and I am in complete agreement, that "teachers must be supported in their efforts to instruct a wider range of students not only with small classes, but also with more flexible time scheduling, time within the school day to meet with other teachers and support personnel, and supervisors that expect and reward curriculum adaptation and individualized instruction."[43] Teachers in the type of "school" I have envisioned would have more time for preparation and collegiality than they do now because they would not be required to keep all the children at school all day every day. Some students would be given assignments and told about resources in the community, to go off on their own and come back at a scheduled time to review what they had done and to pick up another assignment.

These schools would be located in temporary facilities: in houses, apartments, shopping malls, and office buildings. They would be formed as needed and would not be loaded up with a great deal of equipment. They would, however, have the most up-to-date microcomputer and other technological equipment available, particularly that which has to do with telecommunications. With that equipment, students and teachers could tap into libraries throughout the country, interact with dozens of computer networks, and communicate with other schools in their district and perhaps others.

CONCLUDING REMARKS

In my opinion, educators have spent too much time musing and "researching" the issue of identification, particularly as it relates to providing labels such as learning disabilities. There is, however, a great need to come up with creative ways to identify individuals' needs and to pinpoint areas about which to begin instruction.

As for delivery systems, an issue identified here, researchers have devoted too much energy to comparing one with another, trying to find the best one for children of a certain type. Those efforts should be curtailed. Instead, there is a need to identify new and different service delivery models and to come up with ways to evaluate the development of individual students when provided experiences in several environments.

Curriculum, as an issue, should command a great deal more time and energy. There is a critical need to study the curricular offerings of students with and without handicaps with respect to outcomes. We must consider just what it is that youth are able to do once they pass through a particular curriculum.

With respect to evaluation, educators should be encouraged to adopt one or several of the options now available for assessing performances of groups or individuals. Many teachers and researchers have become disenchanted with standardized tests, for one reason or another, and are exploring the options now available and attempting to develop yet others.

As for the funding of educational programs, special or regular, we need to consider alternate ways to allocate monies. One approach would be to provide certain funds to districts, schools, or even specific classrooms for improving the abilities of youngsters in least restrictive environments. As it is now, most funding patterns reinforce systems for serving students in restrictive situations, ones in which they do not necessarily prosper.

What with the most recent move toward mainstreaming prompted by the regular education initiative and, more generally, the efforts to restructure schools, it is imperative that schools more clearly identify the roles and responsibilities of teachers who serve youngsters with disabilities. Representatives from both camps must meet over extended periods and at various levels—local, state, and national—to discuss and iron out these matters.

And then we have the issue of homogeneity and heterogeneity. It will indeed be a tough assignment to break through the many beliefs that have to do with homogeneous grouping. Ideas stemming from those beliefs have formed the very bases of our educational system: the age-level classes, the tracks, the subdivisions within special education, the related curricular and service delivery models, the expectations of teachers, parents, administrators, and the students themselves. Whether or not a radical approach to dealing with the issue such as the one I recommended is needed to jar educators into breaking loose from the traditional system is debatable, but somehow we must restructure the current system toward assuring educational services designed to accommodate the diversity of students now in schools.

NOTES

1. John W. Lloyd, Nirbhay N. Singh, and Alan C. Repp, *The Regular Education Initiative: Alternative Perspectives on Concepts, Issues, and Models* (Sycamore, IL: Sycamore Press, 1991).

2. Mara Sapon-Shevin, "Special Education and the Holmes Agenda for Teacher Education Reform," *Theory into Practice* 24 (1990): 55–60.
3. Joseph Berger, "Costly Special Classes Serve Many with Minimal Needs," *New York Times*, 30 April 1991, pp. A1, A12.
4. Education of the Handicapped Act Amendments, PL 101-476, 1990.
5. Thomas C. Lovitt, *Introduction to Learning Disabilities* (Boston: Allyn & Bacon, 1989).
6. Raymond Beck, personal communication, 1990.
7. Jerry Weast, Raymond Beck, Suellen Gabriel, Phillip Bornstein, Thomas Lovitt, and Denise Conrad, "Project RIDE [Responding to Individual Differences in Education]" (elementary version) (Longmont, CO: Sopris West, 1986); and Jerry Weast, Larry Williams, Raymond Beck, Suellen Gabriel, and Thomas Lovitt, "Project RIDE [Responding to Individual Differences in Education]" (secondary version) (Longmont, CO: Sopris West, 1987).
8. Lee Ann Truesdell, "Mainstreaming in an Urban Middle School: Effects of School Organization and Climate," *The Urban Review* 20, no. 1 (1988): 42–58.
9. Conrad Carlberg and Kenneth Kavale, "The Efficacy of Special versus Regular Class Placement for Exceptional Children: A Meta-analysis," *The Journal of Special Education* 14 (1980): 295–309.
10. Michael Dorris, *The Broken Cord* (New York: Harper Perennial, 1989), 110.
11. J. Frederick West and Lorna Idol, "Collaborative Consultation in the Education of Mildly Handicapped and At-risk Students," *Remedial and Special Education* 11 (1990): 22–31.
12. Thomas C. Lovitt and Steven V. Horton, "Adapting Textbooks for Mildly Handicapped Adolescents" in *Interventions for Achievement and Behavior Problems*, ed. Gary Stoner, Mark R. Shinn, and Hill M. Walker (Washington, D.C.: National Association of School Psychologists, 1991), 439–71.
13. Donald D. Deshler, Jean B. Schumaker, and B. Keith Lenz, "Academic and Cognitive Interventions for LD Adolescents. Part 1," *Journal of Learning Disabilities* 17 (1984): 108–17.
14. Charles J. Kokaska and Donn E. Brolin, *Career Education for Handicapped Individuals*, 2d ed. (Columbus, OH: Merrill/Macmillan, 1985).
15. Douglas H. Gill and E. Eugene Edgar, "Secondary Special Education/ Transition in Washington: A Framework for Improving Outcomes" (unpublished manuscript; Seattle: Experimental Education Unit, University of Washington, 1991).
16. John I. Goodlad, *A Place Called School* (New York: McGraw-Hill, 1984).
17. Evelyn Nieves, "A School's Tests Are Investigated for Tampering," *New York Times*, 3 July 1991, p. A13.
18. Mary Wagner, *Youth with Disabilities during Transition: An Overview of Descriptive Findings from the National Longitudinal Transition Study* (Menlo Park, CA: SRI International, 1989).
19. Nolan Walters, "True or False? National Tests Are Good for America," *Seattle Times*, 9 July 1991, p. A3.
20. Andrew S. Halpern, Michael R. Benz, and Lauren Lindstrom, "A Systems Change Approach to Improving Secondary Special Education and Transition Programs at the Local Community Level" (unpublished manuscript; Eugene: University of Oregon, 1991).
21. Joseph R. Jenkins, Stanley L. Deno, and Phyllis K. Mirkin, "Measuring Pupil Progress toward the Least Restrictive Alternative," *Learning Disability Quarterly* 2 (1979): 81–91.

22. Thomas C. Lovitt, "Behavioral Assessment of Learning Disabilities" in *Handbook on the Assessment of Learning Disabilities: Theory, Research, and Practice*, ed. H. Lee Swanson (Austin: Pro-Ed, 1991), 95–119.

23. Sheila W. Valencia, "Alternative Assessment: Separating the Wheat from the Chaff," *The Reading Teacher* 44 (1990): 60–61.

24. Annemarie Sullivan Palincsar, Ann L. Brown, and Joseph C. Campione, "Dynamic Assessment" in *Handbook on the Assessment of Learning Disabilities*, 75–94.

25. Jay W. Rojewski, Richard R. Pollard, and Gary D. Meers, "Grading Mainstreamed Special Needs Students: Determining Practices and Attitudes of Secondary Vocational Educators Using a Qualitative Approach," *Remedial and Special Education* 12 (1990): 7–15.

26. Mary Lynne Calhoun and John Beattie, "Assigning Grades in the High School Mainstream: Perceptions of Teachers and Students," *Diagnostique* 9 (1984): 218–25.

27. Sapon-Shevin, "Special Education and the Holmes Agenda," 55–60.

28. *Thirteenth Annual Report to Congress on the Implementation of the Individuals with Disabilities Education Act* (Washington, D.C.: U.S. Department of Education, 1991).

29. Samuel Dempsey and Douglas Fuchs, "'Flat' versus 'Weighted' Reimbursement Formulas: A Longitudinal Analysis of State-wide Special Education Funding Practices" (unpublished manuscript; Nashville: Vanderbilt University, 1992).

30. William E. Davis, "Competencies and Skills Required to Be an Effective Resource Teacher," *Journal of Learning Disabilities* 16 (1983): 596–98.

31. Marilyn Friend, "Consultation Skills for Resource Teachers," *Learning Disability Quarterly* 7 (1984): 246–50.

32. Douglas Fuchs and Lynn S. Fuchs, "Exploring Effective and Efficient Prereferral Interventions: A Component Analysis of Behavioral Consultation," *School Psychology Review* 18 (1989): 260–83.

33. Joel Meyers, Lynn M. Gelzheiser, and Glenn Yelich, "Do Pull-in Programs Foster Teacher Collaboration?" *Remedial and Special Education* 12 (1991): 7–15.

34. Lawrence J. Johnson and Marleen C. Pugach, "Classroom Teachers' Views of Intervention Strategies for Learning and Behavior Problems: Which Are Reasonable and How Frequently Are They Used?" *The Journal of Special Education* 24 (1990): 69–84.

35. Jeannie Oakes, *Keeping Track: How Schools Structure Inequality* (New Haven, CT: Yale University Press, 1985).

36. Thomas L. Good, and Susan Marshall, "Do Students Learn More in Heterogeneous or Homogeneous Groups?" in *The Social Context of Instruction*, ed. Penelope L. Peterson, Louise C. Wilkinson, and Maureen Hallinan (New York: Academic Press, 1984), 15–38.

37. Oakes, *Keeping Track*.

38. Ibid.

39. Berger, "Costly Special Classes Serve."

40. Good and Marshall, "Do Students Learn More?"

41. Oakes, *Keeping Track*, 111.

42. Wayne E. Fuller, *The Old Country School* (Chicago: University of Chicago Press, 1982).

43. Truesdell, "Mainstreaming in an Urban Middle School," 56.

4

Toward a Comprehensive Delivery System for Special Education

James M. Kauffman and Daniel P. Hallahan

"Your design must be directed primarily at helping all students meet world class standards in five core subjects."[1] This constraint on designs for a "new generation of American schools" was proposed by the chief executive officer and the chairman of the board of the New American Schools Development Corporation (NASDC). The NASDC was created in response to President Bush's unveiling in April 1991 of his new strategy for American education. Its emphasis on the achievement of world-class standards by all students follows a spate of "system-wide 'crisis rhetoric'"[2] and a rush of calls for "radical reform," "restructuring," and "transformation" of American public education, including appeals for integrating general and special education.[3]

Much of the current language of education reform consists of disparaging commentaries on the failure of American education and calls for inclusiveness (all students) and unity of service delivery structures (integrated, merged). Some researchers have observed that American education does not appear by objective standards to be the miserable failure portrayed by its contemporary critics.[4] In appeals for integration of general and special education the two are frequently described as separate systems, yet one might note the ways in which special education already exists as an integral component of public general education. In this context, we must consider carefully the implications of key concepts in reform rhetoric and the ways in which general and special education have been, are, and should be integrated in a comprehensive delivery system.

Authors' note: Preparation of this manuscript was supported in part by the Commonwealth Center for the Education of Teachers, Curry School of Education, 405 Emmet Street, University of Virginia, Charlottesville, VA 22903. We are grateful to Doug Fuchs for his helpful comments on an earlier version of this chapter.

Special education evolved as an integral part of public general education in the early twentieth century, as MacMillan and Hendrick explain in chapter 2.[5] In conception, special education was—and we argue that it remains—a necessary and integral part of a comprehensive general education delivery system. A comprehensive education delivery system addresses the educational needs, but not all the needs, of all children, not merely most. Special education originated because the education designed for most children was not having the desired effect on some. Educators saw that the appropriate education of all children required different instruction (i.e., special education) for a minority.

A central issue in designing a comprehensive education delivery system is the definition of *all*, a word with desultory meanings. More than the rhetorical meaning of *all* is at stake in designing a comprehensive delivery system. What is at stake is (1) whether general education will have a special-purpose branch to serve the exceptional needs of some children and (2) how that branch will be articulated with the trunk program of education. Thus, the varied meanings of *all* in controversies regarding special and general education, and the implications of these meanings for a comprehensive delivery system, are central issues in our discussion.

THE VARIED MEANINGS OF *ALL*

The implicit and explicit meanings of *all* are critical for understanding political and educational dialogue because one typically assumes that the freedoms, rights, and responsibilities addressed in these exchanges are limited, not absolute. The user of the word *all* does not usually intend that it be interpreted literally because either tradition or rational discourse (or both) suggests exceptions, meaning that *all* usually represents only an approximation (and sometimes not a very close approximation) of every individual. *All*, then, is frequently understood to exclude certain individuals, sometimes for reasons that are justifiable and sometimes for reasons that are not. The varied meanings of *all* are therefore of considerable consequence to those who may be tacitly excluded.

Impoverished and Exclusionary Meanings of *All*

The meaning of *all* can be impoverished, either by unintelligible exclusions or by extreme literalness. In today's political rhetoric regarding education, and too often in the speaking and writing of educators, we encounter the cliché "all children can learn" proffered without clarifications that might make it more than a hint of an allusion. One must ask for answers to follow-up questions to this slogan: What can all children learn? At what rate? With what allocation of instructional resources? To what degree of proficiency or mastery? For what purpose? These are particularly important questions when we are considering students who are exceptional—markedly different from their typical age-mates in ways that are directly related to learning and instruction (thinking, communicating, or moving).

One might interpret the hackneyed "all children can learn" to mean that most children can learn what most teachers are supposed to teach at about an average rate and to a generally acceptable degree of mastery. Perhaps it is intended as a reminder that students differ in some ways that are very seldom inherent constraints on teaching and learning (e.g., color, gender, or socioeconomic status) and that teachers have sometimes been guilty of lowered expectations based on these differences that have relatively trivial implications for instruction. But "all children can learn" is a hollow slogan when we consider the full range of child characteristics. It is devoid of meaning because it merely reifies two facts: (1) many students, but not literally all, can learn what we expect of the typical student, and (2) most children, but not literally all, can learn something worthwhile. Historically, users of this slogan have not meant it to include all children with disabilities because some of them cannot learn that which, presumably, "all children" can.

Until the 1970s, many children with disabilities were routinely excluded from public schools. Educating "all children" once meant, in the common parlance of many state legislators and local school officials, something considerably less than teaching every youngster who can learn useful skills. Since enactment in 1975 of the federal legislation known commonly as PL 94-142 (now the Individuals with Disabilities Education Act, or IDEA), the courts have interpreted the education of "all handicapped children" to mean the inclusion of literally all, regardless of the nature or severity of their handicaps. The blunt literalness of high court interpretations of federal special education law apparently allows no living child to be found ineducable, meaning that schools must provide a free appropriate public "education" to children with scant cortical function and even to those with no cerebral cortex and no possibility of consciousness.[6] Whether attempting to educate children who are permanently unconscious is a moral imperative or a mockery is an open question for philosophical debate, but legislation and litigation have left no room for educators' clinical judgment on the matter.

We are unable to describe educational needs of permanently unconscious and semicomatose children, although these children have obvious needs for humane treatment. We realize, nonetheless, that what constitutes a sufficient state of consciousness or cortical function to create an educational need is a matter of informed judgment in the individual case. Our point is that *all* can be impoverished of meaning in discussions of education in either of two ways: when it is used glibly and insidiously to exclude children who are not typical in what they can learn or, on the other hand, as a cudgel of literalness that equates inability to learn only with total brain death.

The most extreme cases of cognitive disability and their deliberate inclusion in "all handicapped children" in federal mandates are not merely distracting aberrations for two reasons: (1) they demand that any serious discussion of the inclusion of all children in general education confront the full range of disability without implicit exclusions, and (2) they force us to consider the careless use of *all* and the implications for designing a service delivery system that includes children whose special educational needs are tacitly ignored. The excluded and ignored children often are not only those with such profound intellectual impairments that they arguably have no educational needs but many who have impairments of a far milder form and who can clearly be educated, including children with mild or moderate mental retardation, emotional or behavioral disorders, and learning disabilities.

As efforts to reform, restructure, or "reinvent" American schools have gained momentum, many educators have suggested that schools must become more inclusive of children with diverse educational needs—that schools must serve the needs of all children. Thus we must consider carefully the meanings of *all* in discussions of education reform.

Meanings of *All* in Education Reform

In the language of current education reform, *all* often does not mean literally every student. In fact, it clearly must be interpreted to exclude many students who do not have profound cognitive impairments. The educational goals for the year 2000 set by President Bush and the states' governors are a case in point. We recognize that many students with disabilities are fully capable of meeting or exceeding the expectations set by the nation's leaders if they are provided appropriate education. Yet the goal that by 2000 "all children will start school ready to learn," for example, is vague in its implications for gifted and handicapped children. To say that "all" students will be ready to learn and be literate is appealing rhetoric, but it renders actual achievement of these goals impossible. We believe that President Bush and the governors are serious in their hope that public education will be improved, but we do not believe that they have considered the ramifications of their goal statements for students with disabilities.

We interpret such goal statements as indicating a lack of awareness of the full range of children's abilities, with the implicit assumption that *all* means, in actuality, "most" or "a somewhat greater percentage." What will children be ready to learn when they start school? What is the meaning of "ready"? At what age will children start school? Clearly, we might expect very dissimilar answers for children with severely limited cognitive abilities, those of near average intelligence, and those with extremely high intellectual abilities. Without answers to these questions, we see *all* in most of the goal statements of education reform as implicitly excluding many exceptional children.

Special education and the problem of constructing a service delivery system that includes exceptional children have been ignored or mentioned only in passing in discussions of general education reform. "The silence about the needs of, or outcomes for, handicapped children in the current reform movement is deafening."[7] The omission may be interpreted in at least two ways. One interpretation is that the needs of exceptional children are considered by most educators not to merit special attention. Accordingly, *all* in the language of reform means those children who are not so different from the norm that the goals established for "all students" are reasonable. Thus, for example, when the president and governors established the goal "By the year 2000 every adult American will be literate and possess the knowledge and skills necessary to compete in a global economy and exercise the rights and responsibilities of citizenship," they were apparently unconcerned about students whose cognitive disabilities preclude their learning to read or to understand concepts such as rights and citizenship and those who can only acquire rudimentary knowledge and skills that will neither make them competitive in a global economy nor enable them to exercise responsibilities of citizenship in meaningful ways. The implication is that special education will be necessary to address the needs of those forgotten in the press to restructure general education.

An alternative interpretation is that the reforms proposed for general education will be (or can be) so sweeping and revolutionary that the need for special education as such will be obviated. In essence, the trunk program of general education should assimilate its special education branch; general education must become special for all students, such that all students are treated with the same care for meeting individual differences, hence without marking any person or service as extraordinary. Special education will, in effect, become "normal" or standard educational practice. Special and general education will be merged into a single entity described in the language of reform as "supple," "flexible,"[8] and even as intended to provide "*an elite education for everyone.*"[9] The implication is that restructured general education will provide sufficient safeguards for meeting the needs of exceptional children, an assumption that, we shall show, is untenable.

Even when special education is specifically at issue in discussions of reform, however, *all* is sometimes apparently used with the tacit assumption that no one will ask whether *all* is meant to be taken literally. One widely cited education reform program, known as Success for All[10] and commonly offered by its author as an alternative to special education, clearly does not address the needs of all students.[11] It might more candidly be called "Higher Achievement for Most." Another program widely lauded in the special education reform literature is the Adaptive Learning Environments Model (ALEM) of Wang and her colleagues.[12] Some have stated, "All types of students can be accommodated in ALEM classrooms,"[13] yet it is clear that ALEM has not been demonstrated to meet the needs of all students, particularly not all students with mild or moderate disabilities.[14]

Claims of success for all students in any given program said to be an alternative to special education as it is currently structured are sometimes qualified by explicit exclusions, for example, "those who are retarded or severely emotionally disturbed, as well as those with physical, speech, or language deficits and those with severe learning disabilities."[15] Excluded students are sometimes described as those who are not "judgmentally" handicapped.[16] These exclusions are logical contradictions, namely, that success must be defined as impossible for some students in programs claiming success for all or, on the other hand, that the success of some students must be judged by a different standard from that presumably applicable to all students. We shall return to the problem of these lacunae in the logic of reform.

Candor and prudence in stating goals and making claims for the inclusiveness of educational programs might make innovations and reform proposals less beguiling and create less confusion about what is possible and desirable in public education. Unfortunately, the relentless hyperbole regarding programs said to be alternatives to special education, combined with current political and economic pressures for the reform of both special and general education, have led to much confusion regarding the nature of special programs and their roles in a comprehensive service delivery system designed to meet the educational needs of all students.

THE PRESS FOR SPECIAL EDUCATION REFORM

Extreme unhappiness with American public education is today de rigueur, although many of the bases for its condemnation are questionable.[17] Perhaps dissatisfaction with special education is an indication of the degree to which it is now seen as an integral part of the public education system. Before discussing how we might work toward a comprehensive service delivery system, we examine problems created by current reform rhetoric. Although we recognize that education—special education included—needs substantial improvement, we believe that much of the current press for radical restructuring is based on misrepresentations, tortured ideologies, and conceptual confusion.

Misrepresentations

Part of the press for special education reform and the integration of special with general education has been created by scathing commentaries on educational outcomes for children with disabilities who have received special education and by ardent claims that alternatives to special education are known to produce superior outcomes for all children. Critics of the current system of special and general education charge bluntly that it does not work, provides no benefit, and therefore cannot be justified, whereas restructured programs are highly successful and serve all children well.[18]

Space does not allow us to review the findings here. Suffice to say that research has yielded mixed findings for both prevalent service delivery models and restructured programs. We believe that the conclusions that special education has failed and that restructured programs have not are overgeneralizations. They can be reached only by ignoring substantial findings to the contrary, and they can be maintained only by assiduously avoiding critical analysis of both rhetoric and research.[19] In our view, they are dangerous exaggerations that distort perceptions and create a climate in which research data are devalued in favor of ideologies that, although otherwise defensible, have been twisted into parodies.

Tortured Ideologies

Special education is accurately portrayed as justified in part by two ideologies: civil rights and normalization. Both ideologies have been of considerable value to special education, but both have been invoked inappropriately in attempts to justify proposals that undermine its conceptual foundations.

Civil Rights

Equal protection of law and equal educational opportunity are concepts supporting special education for exceptional students. These same concepts support the integration of diverse ethnic groups in public schools. The educational rights of exceptional children and those of ethnic minorities rest on the same foundation, namely, that children's characteristics must not be used as a justification for unfair treatment (i.e., treatment that denies them equal opportunity to learn). Nevertheless, unfairness in education has historically had very different meanings for ethnic minorities and exceptional children. In the case of ethnic minorities, providing different education for children with the same needs has been seen as creating unfairness; in the case of exceptional children, however, providing the same education for children whose needs are significantly different from others' has been viewed as unfair. When one disregards these differences in the nature of unfairness and applies the same criteria for judging discrimination to exceptionality and ethnicity, civil rights arguments become non sequiturs.

Some calls for radically restructured special and general education assume an isomorphism of ethnicity and disability, which yields the conclusion that separating exceptional children for instruction is as unfairly discriminatory as maintaining schools segregated by ethnicity.[20] Some have used the argument that separate education is inherently and unfairly unequal when children are segregated by skin color or ancestry to justify the conclusion that grouping children for instruction based on their performance is inherently and unfairly unequal, particularly when children differing in performance are instructed in different classrooms. This line of reasoning ignores the fact that racial segregation was the total separation of children for instruction according to the dichotomous and, presumably, instructionally irrelevant variable of skin color, whereas schools separate children into groups for special education for varying amounts of time (a relatively small amount of the school day for most) based on assessment of their academic performance and instructional needs.[21]

Those who have recently proposed to establish special academies for Black male students have reversed the argument that separate education is inherently and unfairly unequal when the basis for separation is ethnic identity or gender. In our view, these proposals have merit precisely to the extent that one can make the case that ethnic identity and gender are characteristics determining what or how students can best be taught. Our interpretation of equal educational opportunity is that students must not be grouped for instruction by caprice or by criteria that are irrelevant to their learning and social development but that they must be grouped by criteria directly related to what they are to learn and how they can be taught most effectively.

Normalization

Normalization, the concept on which landmark legislation and litigation in special education has been built, has lost much of its meaning. Rather than a guiding principle for developing services for persons with disabilities, it has become codified as a rule requiring that all students with disabilities be educated in general education classrooms. It has been reduced to a slogan standing for the politically correct position of total integration or inclusion, but it is a much more complex notion than many realize.

Some proponents of educational reform have misconstrued the normalization principle as a rationale for abolishing pullout programs.[22] Wolfensberger has addressed this misconception, stating that normalization and mainstreaming should not be considered synonymous.[23] Today's advocates of total integration have fashioned the meaning of "normalization" for their own purposes. They would certainly have a difficult time reconciling their push for total integration with Wolfensberger's position on the subject. Regarding the misconception that normalization means that people with retardation should *always* work in culturally normative settings, for instance, Wolfensberger has stated, "In fact, I do not recall meeting a single normalization advocate or even zealot who has not recognized the need for at least some type of sheltered work conditions and circumstances for at least some retarded persons."[24]

Furthermore, although favoring small residential arrangements, Wolfensberger is a strong proponent of a variety of different options. For those requiring psychiatric services, for example, he has proposed no less than fifteen different types of models varying in separateness as a function of the characteristics of the clients. Currently, public school programming for students with disabilities appears to be headed in the opposite direction. Instead of multiple service delivery options, the rush toward total integration is reducing the number of alternatives for educational placement.

Although Wolfensberger was not clear on the subject in his earliest formulation of the normalization principle, he later clarified that he did not

mean to equate normalization with the statistical norm.[25] His later concep-
tualization places more importance on the *perceived* value of the means to
achieving normalization. Even so, however, one can argue that the most
effective treatment methods may not always be those that are most culturally normal or valued. Mulick and Kedesdy, for example, contend that in the
case of self-injurious behavior in persons with autism, culturally normative
responses worsen the behavior, and some of the most efficacious treatment
techniques for self-injurious behavior in persons with autism run counter to
normalization principles.[26] The culturally normative response to someone
who injures him- or herself is consolation or a response that draws attention
to the injured person. Social attention to self-injurious behavior, however,
actually leads to increases in self-injury. Techniques that would not be high
on a list of cultural normality, such as restraint and punishment, are the
ones that researchers have found most effective in reducing self-injury.

A less dramatic, but more common, example of how the best educational techniques are not always culturally normative pertains to the learning problems of children. Placing students in small groups and using a
highly teacher-directed, drill-and-practice approach is not the way most
children are taught to read, nor is it consistent with current trends in educational reform. Research has documented, however, that just such an
approach is the most successful for students with learning disabilities.[27]
Such an approach, however, would meet Wolfensberger's later conceptual-
ization of perceived value.

To us, it seems that the almost obsessive concern for normalization
promulgated by some advocates of mainstreaming and deinstitutionalization promotes a demeaning attitude toward those with disabilities. There
needs to be a balance between focusing on changing the person with a disability to be more "normal," by attending regular schools and classes and
being included in the standard curriculum, versus changing society to
accept people who have disabilities. As Hauerwas notes,

> We usually associate movements toward justice in our society with the
> language of equality. We assume to be treated equally is to be treated
> justly, but on reflection we may discover that is not the case. Often the
> language of equality only works by reducing us to a common denomina-
> tor that can be repressive or disrespectful.[28]

Because the originators of the principle of normalization— Bank-Mikkelsen,
Nirje, and Wolfensberger—have often written passionately about the validity
of the concept, they have probably given present-day normalization proponents justification for imbuing it with status equivalent to one of the Ten
Commandments.[29] We note that Wolfensberger describes normalization on
the societal level, meaning that society should be more tolerant of the differences of people with disabilities, and that he has stated, "Normalization does
not mean that only normative human management tools and methods are
used—merely that these be as normal *as feasible*" [italics added].[30]

Advocates of total integration have unfortunately twisted the original intent of the principle of normalization. As a guiding principle, it provides an appropriate rationale for much of what we should be trying to do in educating children with disabilities; as a pretext for total integration or a rationale for wholesale mainstreaming and deinstitutionalization, its meaning is distorted to such an extent that it is in danger of becoming an empty slogan.

Conceptual Confusion

Proposals for integrating special and general education have reflected considerable confusion about basic concepts, including as they do the juxtaposition of incongruous meanings, the use of self-contradictory lines of argument, and antipathy toward critical analysis of purposes and means to achieve them. Such confusion leads inevitably to a circularity of reasoning that thwarts the good intentions of reformers.

Incongruities of Meaning

Much of the language of radical restructuring is peculiarly oxymoronic, containing appeals for common specialness, excellence without exception, and the normalization of exceptionality. Lipsky and Gartner conclude that "it is time to move on to the struggle of changing the educational system to make it both one and special for all students,"[31] ignoring the inherent contradiction of the concepts *same* and *special*. Another example of puzzling disregard of meanings in the reform literature is the statement of the National Center on Education and the Economy that "the challenge is to provide *an elite education for everyone*."[32] These nonsensical "struggles" and "challenges" are similar to others one might construct from combinations of opposite meanings, such as "The challenge is to foster democracy without involving ordinary citizens" or "It is time to move on to the struggle for standards of excellence not derived from comparisons." Perhaps such language has become the norm in the sound bites associated with advertising and political campaigns in which success is based on the assumption that the public will not think critically and analytically, but we hope for a higher level of discourse about educational reform—at least among educators. Language of this type belies any intent to bring intellectual integrity to the tasks of educating children and their teachers,[33] and it carries a peculiar irony when the avowed intent of reform is to promote critical thinking, prepare students to "render critical judgment," and produce students "whose understanding runs deep."[34]

Self-contradictory Arguments

Lines of argument offered in support of radical restructuring are often incoherent. One commonly finds self-contradictions in stated assumptions about why special and general education have failed and how their failures can be reversed.

In a paper circulated by the National Center on Education and the Economy, Gartner and Lipsky state that we must abandon the notion that learning problems are inherent in children: "The current practice of special education operates on a deficit model; that is, it identifies something as wrong or missing in the student."[35] Yet one of their recommendations for improving student productivity is "Do not waste time on 'teaching,'" and they go on to say that "the outcome of an education is student learning, [and] it is only the student who can do that learning."[36] On the one hand, they fault special education for identifying something wrong with the student; on the other hand, they argue that students, including those who have failed, hold the keys to their own failure and success.

Criticism of special education is occurring in the larger context of criticism of public education. General education, critics claim, is failing to reach its goals with many students, including those identified as handicapped and many who are not. We agree with Keogh that "it is a strange logic that calls for the regular system to take over responsibility for pupils it has already demonstrated it has failed."[37] MacMillan and Hendrick[38] buttress Singer's observation that "special education was the solution to the regular educator's thorny problem of how to provide supplemental resources to children in need while not shortchanging other students in the class. Nothing else has happened within regular education to solve this problem."[39] We note also that many of the instructional reforms so far implemented in general education and widely favored among general educators (e.g., less explicit, more child-directed, more "developmental" instruction) are those that researchers have found most likely to lead to failure for handicapped and at-risk students.[40]

Critics have characterized special education as a failure,[41] as segregationist,[42] as a way of diminishing children,[43] and as a second-rate system.[44] Yet the same writers have suggested that special education provides a model of what general education should become and that, were special education merged with general education, all students would benefit, none would be diminished, and general education could become first-rate. We do not understand how the alleged failures—general and special education—will be transformed by this fusion, particularly how losing its separate identity will turn special education from evil to good. We understand that reformers propose that purportedly nefarious aspects of special education (e.g., special identities called labels, students taught in places other than their home school or regular classroom) will not be parts of restructured education. But special programs present dilemmas, not the least of which is that when special identities of students are lost, so is the capacity to provide special services,[45] and that stigma and separation can be greater problems in home schools and regular classes than in alternative schools and classes.

Antipathy toward Analyzing Purposes and Means

As Fuchs and Fuchs have noted, some have presented the goals of restructured general and special education in impressionistic, nonempirical terms.[46] Reformers say that special and general education as they currently exist have failed, and often we read and hear that neither "works."[47] Yet we are not told, except in impressionistic and even surrealistic language, how we should judge that either is "working."[48] The aversion to logical analysis of purposes and means is particularly evident in discussions of performance outcomes and policy (i.e., structure and regulation of access to programs).

What would characterize the distribution of outcomes if general or special education, or both, worked? If all students received an appropriate education, if not the best education possible, would we have fewer or more children who compare unfavorably to the majority on important outcomes? Would the disparities between the achievement of high and low performers become smaller or greater? That is, would we expect education that works to increase or decrease population variance? To us, it is apparent that these and other questions that must be addressed in careful analyses of performance goals have been sidestepped in appeals for reform. If they are not addressed, however, reform proposals are merely bravado, which leaves all of us confused about just what is intended.

Reformers also skirt questions regarding the relationship between special and general education. If special and general education are to become a unitary system, as some suggest,[49] what are the criteria for judging that they are unitary, not separate? What makes a program special or separate? Designated personnel? Special personnel training? Budget lines? Separate professional organizations? What percentage of time must a student be taught in a different curriculum to make a program separate or segregated from that received by others? What physical distance from another group of students constitutes segregation? If a unitary system is to be "supple" and "flexible," what are the criteria for judging that these characteristics have been achieved? Should it contain no option for special classes or schools, no different curricula or goals for different types of students, no "standard" expectations for any group of students? What would a supple, flexible system allow, and what would it disallow? Who will be the arbiters of what is acceptable and what is prohibited in a flexible system?

Given that certain components of a service delivery system are deemed essential, how does one create and maintain the policy structures necessary for their inclusion? Some reform advocates propose a unitary system of service delivery in which current federal regulations are reduced or eliminated.[50] We can think of no case in which important rights and protections are safeguarded without legislation and regulation, human nature being what it is. As Fuchs and Fuchs conclude, the appeal for a unitary, deregulated system is more than an ahistorical, nonempirical perspective; its naiveté invites the neglect of students with disabilities whenever there are competing interests, and there are always competing interests.[51] That a particular school or community appears, at least temporarily, to have gone beyond current regulations in the care of its students must not be interpreted to mean that public policy can be based on the assumption of public goodwill toward children with disabilities or that what is possible in one school is possible in any.

SPECIAL EDUCATION AS PART OF A COMPREHENSIVE SERVICE DELIVERY SYSTEM

To this point we have discussed only problems with the revisionist critique of special education. We acknowledge that special education is beset by substantial problems that must be addressed in any serious effort to improve it. We believe that these problems are primarily a result of inept professional practice and misunderstanding of what special education is. Contrary to the assertion that special education is flawed in its basic conception,[52] we maintain that the basic idea of special education is as sound as the very notion of public education. What is needed is not the reconceptualization or reinvention of special education but a sober look at the postulates on which a comprehensive service delivery system might be based and a careful examination of the extent to which the practice of special education so conceptualized falls short of the ideal. To this end we propose eight postulates and corollaries that might provide the framework for making special education an effective branch of a comprehensive service delivery system.

Postulate 1: Public schooling must serve equitably the educational needs of all children by helping them achieve a level of academic, social, and vocational competence commensurate with their potential.

This postulate reaffirms our belief that public schools must serve more than academic needs and that it must address the full range of students' educational needs, from those of the most talented or intellectually gifted to those of students with such severe intellectual impairments that they will be able to learn only simple self-care skills. It recognizes that students have needs that are not educational and acknowledges that some children, though a very few in number, may have no educational needs.

Corollary 1a: Because public education must serve all children who have educational needs, the largest part of general education must be designed for the modal characteristics of students and teachers.

Public education by definition must serve the masses. Like any product or service designed for the public, most of public education must be designed to fit the most common (modal, "standard") characteristics of consumers. Economies of scale require that products and services designed for the general public be structured by the size, shape, and abilities of citizens falling within a limited band of variability around a mean. This does not mean that individuals with characteristics very different from the average cannot be accommodated by services or product lines designed and produced by public agencies; it does mean, however, that the needs of exceptional individuals will not be met by the standard products and services that are appropriate for most persons.

Likewise, education must be structured so that the modal teacher is capable of accomplishing the tasks of education with most students. This does not mean that the performance capability of the average teacher cannot be raised through better training; it does mean, however, that expectations for the performance of most teachers must not outstrip what the average teacher can do with appropriate training.

> *Corollary 1b:* Because public education must address all children's educational needs, it must include explicit structures ensuring the accommodation of exceptional students.

Explicit structures creating differentiation of public services are required to meet extraordinary needs. Exceptional children by definition require extraordinary education—that which is different from the standard education that serves most students well. The structure of education includes goals, lines of authority, roles and responsibilities of personnel, budgets and purchases, allocation of time and space, curriculum, selection and assignment of students to classes, and evaluation. Failure to create and maintain explicit structures accommodating exceptional individuals inevitably results in the neglect of those for whom the core services are inadequate. The necessary explicit structures may become a predictable or required part (a "normal" part) of public services, but without these structures we can predict that exceptional individuals will be ill served.

Dramatic changes in certain school structures—lowering the typical class size to twelve or fewer students or placing two competent teachers in every class of twenty-five students, for example—would allow teachers to accommodate greater variability in student characteristics. Even assuming these desirable (but highly improbable) changes in standard school structures, however, teachers will not be able to accommodate every student within the new, standard structure. No single teaching arrangement is infinitely flexible.

> *Postulate 2:* Exceptional students differ significantly from the modal or typical student in instructionally relevant ways that result in their inevitable failure, given standard educational goals and programs.

Abilities to access and process specific information are directly relevant to instruction. The extreme differences in such abilities of some students preclude their attainment of certain educational goals that are appropriate for most students. Moreover, standard instructional programs that are successful with most students cannot accommodate extreme differences in students' abilities to perceive, organize, store, retrieve, and apply information to the solution of specific problems. Thus, some exceptional students will fail to meet standard educational goals regardless of the instructional program that is provided; others will be able to meet standard educational goals but not with standard instructional programs.

Teachers must not be led down a path of fantasy or intellectual duplicity regarding what is possible and what their moral responsibility is when confronted by students whose needs they have not the resources to meet. Goodlad suggests, "For teacher education programs not to be models of educating is indefensible."[53] He notes, further, that teacher education programs have a moral responsibility to confront their limitations:

> Even supposing it could be argued that all traits are amenable to education, teacher education programs possess neither the resources nor the time to redress severe personality disorders; and they appear ill-equipped to perform much lesser tasks. Consequently, the moral and ethical imperatives of selection require that applicants be counseled out if they fall seriously short in characteristics that are deemed important but for which there are no programmatic provisions. Failure to so counsel is morally wrong, and the consequences are costly.[54]

We believe that the same moral responsibility applies to teachers in our public schools who are aware that they are ill equipped to redress the limitations of their students' ability to learn.

Corollary 2a: The requirement of alternative educational goals and programs must be made explicit for exceptional students.

When standard goals or instructional methods are inappropriate for a student, appropriate alternatives must be available. These alternatives will not be available in all school systems unless they are explicitly required by law and regulation, as public attention and economies of scale are inevitably centered on meeting modal needs. The implicit or explicit assumption that standard educational goals and programs will accommodate the educational needs of all students is not only logically untenable but places the onus of proof on the student when questions regarding an individual student arise. The explicit requirement of alternatives to meet the needs of exceptional students places the burden of proof on the school's service delivery system.

Corollary 2b: Alternative goals and programs must be expressed as alternative curricula and methods for exceptional students.

Educational goals and programs entail instructional materials, teaching procedures, and an array of activities designed to result in the acquisition of specific skills, attitudes, and values. Thus, goals and programs for exceptional students involve alternative curricula or methods, beyond the range of the standard materials, procedures, and activities that produce acceptable outcomes for most students.

Corollary 2c: Alternative curricula and methods sometimes require alternative grouping of students.

It is axiomatic that a teacher cannot teach all things to all students at the same time. Students are necessarily grouped for instruction in specific content according to the teachers' instructional capabilities and the germane pupil characteristics. Moreover, the greater the variability in a group of the students in their characteristics germane to instruction (beyond a base level of manageable variability), the smaller the number of students a teacher is able to instruct successfully. Efficient and effective instruction of nonexceptional students can best be accomplished by forming standard patterns of grouping (i.e., groups designed for instruction of students falling within a band of teachability in specific skills). Effective and efficient instruction of exceptional students sometimes requires nonstandard groupings to facilitate the use of alternative curricula and methods.

Both general and special educators teach heterogeneous groups of students. Teachers observe variability between students on specific characteristics and within individual students in various domains such as academic, social, and vocational skills. Instructional grouping must be designed to limit the heterogeneity of students to facilitate effective and efficient instruction.

We recognize that some categorical groupings do not achieve their intent of substantially reducing the variability among students to be instructed. Moreover, we recognize that it is neither possible nor desirable to reduce the variance of instructionally relevant characteristics in groups of students to near zero. Effective teaching demands the ability to accommodate a tolerable level of student variance. Nevertheless, we assert that, as Goodlad argues for teacher education, a moral commitment to educating children and youth carries with it the clear implication that teachers must recognize the limitations of their ability to accommodate student variance and seek alternative instruction for those whom they are not equipped to serve competently.[55] A further implication is that in a comprehensive service delivery system, the student whose characteristics are judged to be incompatible with those of an instructional group must be included in an alternative group of students for whom alternative instruction is offered. A final implication is that individual instruction in one or more areas of the curriculum may be required for some students.

We note that alternative grouping of students for special education may sometimes be necessary to avoid significant deleterious effects for nonhandicapped students. At times, students with disabilities may be so disruptive or otherwise require so great a proportion of the teacher's resources that the educational needs of other members of the class suffer to a significant degree. We recognize that the degree of interference with the education of other students is a matter of professional judgment, but we think it better that the issue be addressed rather than ignored. We believe that it is the moral responsibility of the teacher to see that all students are receiving a fair chance to succeed. The consequences of failure to make such judgments in education are, as Goodlad points out, costly.[56]

> *Postulate 3:* Exceptional students must have open to them the full range of options for instructional grouping and environments for delivery of educational services. No single curriculum, instructional approach, grouping plan, or learning environment is appropriate for all students.

Given the extreme differences in the instructionally relevant characteristics of children and youth, a very wide range of options for instructional grouping and learning environments is required. It is self-evident that not all kinds of instruction and environmental conditions can be present in one classroom or school at the same time. Recognition of variance in instructional needs, beyond lip service to designing individualized programs, demands recognition of the need for variance in service delivery options. Restriction to one or a few service delivery options increases the rate of poor fits between students and the curricula and methods employed in their instruction.[57]

> *Corollary 3a:* The full range of grouping options ranges from full-time placement in standard educational curricula and groups with special assistance to special residential schools.

We may assume that for educational purposes students are not exceptional if their needs are adequately met in standard educational groups and by standard curricula and methods without supplementary services. Some exceptional students' appropriate education is possible without alternative grouping, so long as they are provided supplementary services (e.g., alternative instructional strategies) not required by modal students. Thus, not all exceptional students need alternative grouping for instruction. Other students, however, are exceedingly unlikely to receive appropriate education without placement in alternative instructional groups or alternative learning environments. The relevant characteristics of some students are so different from those of most students that they require substantially different environments for learning in one or more areas of their curriculum. These different environments may be best constructed in part-time or full-time special classes, alternative day schools, or residential schools.

> *Corollary 3b:* Selection of instructional and grouping options should be guided by the policies and procedures established in IDEA (PL 94-142); parents and teachers must together select the least restrictive appropriate option from a full range of alternatives.

In 1975, PL 94-142 (now IDEA) established the expectation that appropriate education of children with disabilities will be a part of all schools' service delivery system. The policy represented in this law is that decisions regarding appropriate education and the least restrictive environment will be made jointly by educators and parents of students with disabilities on an individual basis. Procedural protections in the law are designed to ensure that a full range of instructional and grouping options is available and that the environment (placement) option judged least restrictive is chosen from those that are first judged appropriate.

Postulate 4: Alternative goals and instruction needed by exceptional students will not be ensured without explicit, permanent structures that include them in a comprehensive system of public education.

Public education itself was established by explicit, permanent structures, first those creating public schools, then those involving mandatory school attendance, later those granting equal access to schooling by students of color, and more recently those ensuring accommodation of students with disabilities. In each case, explicit and permanent structures were required to produce the intended benefits to students and the larger society. In the case of special education, the basic structures were provided by IDEA.

Corollary 4a: These structures must include special education as an integral but clearly differentiated part of a comprehensive service delivery system; the structures must include special teachers, administrators, funding mechanisms, and procedures.

IDEA established, within the larger structure of general education, mechanisms designed to require attention to the needs of students with disabilities. These mechanisms include fiscal, administrative, procedural, and instructional requirements that are necessary to ensure the inclusion of special education in school systems' service delivery. Without identifiable special personnel, specific funding channels, and procedural requirements, school systems are unlikely to be held accountable for their accommodation of students with disabilities; without these structures, the burden of proof of failure to accommodate is on the student and parents.

Corollary 4b: Special education structures must be ongoing; they must not be viewed as temporary measures that can be eliminated once their objectives have been achieved and special education is ensconced in public education.

The structures that created public schools, required student attendance, demanded equal access by students regardless of color, and required accommodation of students with disabilities cannot be abandoned under the assumption that once they have accomplished their purpose they are superfluous. Without constant attention to their preservation and maintenance, these structures and the practices they support will inevitably deteriorate and collapse. Special education has become an integral part of public education service delivery, but it will be maintained as such only if its supportive structures are maintained.

Postulate 5: The structures needed to ensure appropriate education of exceptional students require carefully regulated decisions regarding which students shall receive specific educational options.

Special provisions for at least some students with special needs have been "normal" components of the public education service delivery system of most state and local education agencies for two decades or more. Only since 1975, however, has federal education policy set the expectation that special education for all students with disabilities will be a part of the total symmetry of schools. Prior to the enactment of IDEA, the designation of students as having special needs, and therefore as needing special education programs, was not carefully regulated in most states. Consequently, decisions regarding the selection of individual students for specific instructional options were often capricious, and parents were often excluded from participation in the processes of identification and placement of their children.

Students cannot be provided educational options that are substantially different from the standard program without someone's making the decisions regarding which students should receive such options and which students should not. If one argues that no student should receive a "standard" program—that all students' programs should be individualized, and therefore "special"—we can predict that the vast majority of students' programs will be highly similar and hence "special" only in name. That is, it is predictable that a limited range of variability will define what is typical, expected, or unremarkable for students of a given age. Some students, however, will need programs that are remarkable outliers (i.e., very different from most).

The question remains, should the decision that a student needs a substantially different program from that appropriate for most students be regulated, such that special consideration and parental participation are required? One might argue that the same level of care and parental participation should be required in decisions regarding all students' programs. We question whether this argument can be grounded in the realities of public schooling and understanding of the responsibilities of teachers. Moreover, we see this argument as reducing all students' needs to unity, not merely to a common denominator. It is based on the denial of difference, not its recognition. The consequences of educators treating decisions regarding all students' programs with the same level of scrutiny would be predictably disastrous for students with special needs, much as the failure of professionals in other fields (law and medicine come immediately to mind) to discriminate cases requiring a special level of scrutiny would predictably result in grotesque malpractice.

Corollary 5a: Selection of educational options is unavoidably judgmental, requiring informed professional and parental judgment of the individual student's abilities and needs.

There are two ways for educators to avoid making difficult judgments about which students should be granted special options. One is to treat all cases the same, which, as we have discussed, is tantamount to malpractice. The other is to set forth criteria based on psychometric data and to make these criteria the sole basis for decisions, which may seem to remove subjectivity from the decision-making process but also leads inevitably to abrogation of professional responsibility.

Education, like every other profession, is inherently judgmental. To speak of the "judgmentally handicapped" is as trite as to speak of the "judgmentally guilty," the "judgmentally ill," or an automobile that is "judgmentally unsafe." When disability or guilt or danger is said to be "obvious," we must ask, "Obvious to whom?" When the consequences are significant for the individual about whom a decision is made, society imposes regulatory mechanisms for making judgments, including procedural and authority structures.

True, there are cases in which most or all casual observers might judge an individual to have a disability—the "obvious" cases. Nevertheless, the great majority of cases of disability are not "obvious" to the casual observer. Moreover, the suggestion that special education should serve only the "obvious" cases or those whose disabilities are "severe" does not make special education nonjudgmental. "Obvious" and "severe" are themselves judgments about which well-informed persons may disagree. A structure is needed, therefore, for decision making in the case of students who may need nonstandard educational options. IDEA and attendant regulations set forth such a structure, which requires that the informed and combined judgment of educators and parents be the basis for the identification of handicapped students and for designing their programs.

Corollary 5b: The procedures for making judgments regarding educational options must be explicit, not covert.

As we have seen, judgments regarding the educational options students are eligible to receive cannot be avoided. All options should be available to all students who need them, but it is obvious that not all students will need all options. How, then, are decisions regarding options to be made? Asserting that general education should be sufficiently "flexible" or "supple" to accommodate all students begs the question; it is a ruse for driving the decision-making process underground, unless the regulatory mechanisms for decision making are explicated. IDEA was enacted in large measure because identification and placement decisions regarding handicapped children were not aboveboard. Moreover, the law was designed precisely to require that public education be flexible, supple, and accommodating of special needs.

When explicit structures for making decisions are not present, decisions regarding selection of curriculum and programming options cannot be monitored effectively.[58] Appeals to deregulate special education eligibility decisions are a direct appeal to abandon the structures—the procedural protections—that are necessary to maintain open and accountable decision making.

> ***Corollary 5c:*** Judgments regarding educational options must not be made solely on the basis of psychometric data; teachers and parents must be the primary decision makers.

Psychometric assessments may yield useful information for decision making, but they are not sufficient in themselves for determining students' educational needs. Parents and those who are responsible for teaching the student must be the primary decision makers. Their decisions may be imperfect, but they are nevertheless the best equipped to make decisions regarding individual pupils when their judgment is informed by the best available data.[59] This principle is embodied in IDEA.

> ***Corollary 5d:*** Selection of specific educational options unavoidably results in labeling.

Individuals who receive educational programs (or any other treatment or recognition that others do not) are labeled by whatever language we use to describe them. The labels may not be the traditional ones associated with special education, but they are labels nonetheless.[60] Care must be taken to avoid letting labels turn into abusive epithets, but our choice is clear: Either we label students with disabilities by speaking of their special needs, or we label them only as students, thereby denying the possibility of providing special programs for them.

Furthermore, the suggestion that programs but not students should be labeled[61] is gratuitous, as IDEA requires special education labels only for reporting purposes. The law does not require that students themselves be given labels, nor does it require that students be grouped by traditional special education categories. With regard to labels, the law requires only that programs for students with specific handicapping conditions be available and that students with disabilities be placed in programs designed to meet their special individual needs. The appeal for restructuring that eliminates labeling, then, must be seen for what it is—an appeal based on misrepresentation of the law and one not cognizant of the consequences of ignoring differences.

> ***Postulate 6:*** Appropriate education of exceptional students depends on adequate preparation of professional personnel.

Teaching exceptional students well requires specialized training as surely as specialized training is required for other professionals who deal with unusual cases. We recognize that basic professional training must prepare the teacher to respond appropriately to a wide range of students. All professions see the need for a core of common training as well as the need for specialized training for those who will serve clients with particular needs.

Corollary 6a: All professional educators must be prepared to accommodate diversity among students and to recognize the need of some students for alternative instruction.

All teachers must be prepared to deal with diversity among the students they teach. It is also axiomatic that all teachers have limitations in the diversity they are able to accommodate. A critical aspect of ethical practice in any profession is recognition of one's limitations of training and expertise. Teachers who are unprepared or unwilling to request consultation from others and to refer a student for possible alternative placement when they are not able to meet the student's needs are in violation of federal special education policy as stated in IDEA. Moreover, they are violating standards of professional conduct.

Corollary 6b: Special educators must be prepared first as general educators and, following a period of successful practice as general educators, receive additional extensive training in specialized instruction.

One of the most substantial problems faced by special education is improving the competence of its classroom practitioners. Our belief is that special education has erred in its preparation of preservice teachers. Special education teachers must have prior training and experience as general educators if their training is to be truly specialized and if they are to collaborate effectively with teachers in general education classrooms. More than a cursory textbook understanding of the conditions and rigors of teaching in general education is required of special teachers who are to be collaborators with general educators.

Corollary 6c: Optimum accommodation of exceptional students depends on preparation of general and special educators to collaborate with other professionals and parents.

Teachers will become effective collaborators only if they are taught the procedures and skills involved in working with professional colleagues. Both general and special educators must receive training in how to work with each other for the benefit of exceptional students, how to work with noneducation professionals whose related services are required for their students, and how to work with parents as partners. The neglect of these procedures and skills in teacher training programs is a serious problem limiting the effectiveness of special education as part of a comprehensive service delivery system.

Postulate 7: The outcomes used to judge the effectiveness of general education are not always appropriate as criteria for judging the effectiveness of special education.

Special education is sometimes assessed by noting discrepancies between the performance of students with disabilities and that of the general population of students. Predictably, special education so weighed is found wanting, as the measure of success is inappropriate. Many students with disabilities can, if they are provided appropriate education, be expected to achieve outcomes similar to those of their nondisabled peers. It is predictable, however, that the rate of failure by those standards (e.g., graduation rate, number of passing grades, transition to higher education, successful employment) will be higher for students with disabilities than among students without disabilities, given equally appropriate education for the two groups. Special education must be conceptualized as a continuing support system for students who cannot be enabled to participate in programs appropriate for modal students as well as a means of addressing academic and social deficits that are remediable.

Corollary 7a: Appropriate education for exceptional students will not necessarily result in their performance within the range deemed adequate, expected, or "normal" for nonexceptional students.

The expectation of a "cure" for educational disabilities—enabling all disabled students to function as if their disabilities no longer existed—is not realistic. If appropriate education is assumed to be only that which allows the student to achieve "normal" educational progress, then many exceptional students, their teachers, their parents, and the public face uninterrupted failure and censure.

Corollary 7b: The informed, ethical behavior of practitioners is an important criterion for evaluating the appropriateness of special education and evaluating its practices.

The extent to which special education improves students' performance over what they would otherwise achieve is an important criterion for evaluating its practice, but it must not be the sole criterion. As is the case in other professions, the outcome of individual cases must be evaluated in the light of the best professional practices under the circumstances. The extent to which procedures designed to protect the interests of the involved parties were followed and the extent to which the behavior of professional practitioners was informed and ethical must be weighed in the balance.

Postulate 8: Special education may not be the only special compensatory program serving students who have difficulty in school, but it must be maintained as a branch of general education having special identity and articulation with other programs.

It is a truism that many students have difficulty in school. Nevertheless, we can safely assume that the effective education of all students will not eliminate variance in the desired performance outcomes of the student population. In fact, we venture that a uniform degree of improvement in the education offered every student would increase the population variance in such outcomes, which would make the educationally "disadvantaged" even more so. This is one of the reasons we believe compensatory education programs are necessary for students who perform poorly; such programs are a means of "leveling the playing field" somewhat in the interests of fairness and human compassion as well as the eventual economic benefits of the habilitation of those who are given special assistance.

All compensatory programs are by definition failure-driven; they are intended to compensate for conditions producing actual or predicted failure of individuals. Access to compensatory programs is knowingly granted only to individuals judged to be in jeopardy, and for good reason: Access by all squanders the resources intended for those "at risk" and, predictably, quickly bankrupts the program. When the risk factors that predict failure are complex, poorly understood, and pandemic, as they are in many schools, extraordinary care must be taken to protect the interests of specific groups through special allocations of compensatory resources. Attention to either prevention or remediation alone is insufficient; special resources must be allocated both to programs designed to avoid failure and to those designed to cope with the reality of failure.

> *Corollary 8a:* An array of special programs with specific eligibility criteria for participation is an appropriate means of creating a comprehensive service delivery of general education.

Given the range of educational needs in most school systems, it is not reasonable to believe that one compensatory program will be sufficient to provide the comprehensive services necessary. Even those who argue passionately for restructuring to eliminate separate program authority recognize the need for an array of special programs for selected students. One can imagine a school situation that has programs such as the following (Reynolds's list includes five more):[62]

- The Braille Reading Program
- The Reading Recovery Program
- The Intensive Basic Skills Program
- The Social Skills Program
- The White Cane and Mobility Program

As we have seen, the issue of eligibility for special programs cannot be avoided. The criteria and procedures for determining individual students' eligibility for specific programs must be regulated explicitly. Otherwise, eligibility will be covertly determined, the reasons and processes for program selection being matters one cannot monitor effectively.

> *Corollary 8b:* Efforts to marginalize or disable special education by obscuring its identity through its assimilation into general education must be resisted.

To flourish, a program of education must enjoy visibility, status, budget, and personnel—those things that give it borders and identity. Without these, the program inevitably becomes increasingly derelict in both intent and accomplishment. Goodlad describes the unhappy situation of teacher education:

> First, the farther down in a university's organizational structure teacher education finds itself, the less chance it has to obtain the conditions necessary to a healthy, dynamic existence. Second, the farther down in the hierarchy teacher education finds itself, the less likely it is that it will enjoy the tender loving care of those tenure-line faculty members universities strive so hard to recruit. Who, then, speaks for teacher education? Who speaks for those who would become teachers?[63]

We might substitute *special education* for *teacher education* in this statement. Goodlad goes on to suggest the minimum essentials for making teacher education "[fit] comfortably into the context of a college or university":

1. A school or center of pedagogy with a sole commitment to teaching
2. "Its own budget, determined in negotiation at the highest level of budget approvals, and this budget must be immune to erosion by competing interests"
3. Authority and responsibility for student selection and personnel
4. A full complement of faculty
5. Control over specification of prerequisites for admission[64]

We suggest that the same minimum essentials are necessary for special education to fit comfortably into the context of the public school. Those who encourage general education to assimilate special education fully or urge special education to merge with general education cannot be both aware of the realities of educational organizations and concerned for special education's viability.

CONCLUSION

The capacity of American public education to respond humanely and effectively to variance among students should be expanded, but this can be accomplished only by maintaining and strengthening the essential structures on which a comprehensive delivery system is based. Although general and special education are now distinctive parts of an integrated system, their interface needs more attention.

Many of the suggestions for restructuring or integrating special and general education, however, are based on notions that have a highly charming surface appeal but are the antitheses of a reflective, analytical approach to the problems of designing a comprehensive service delivery system of education to serve an extremely diverse student body. They suppose a world in which one never need take a hard look at realities, one in which inspirational rhetoric and the callousness of policymakers in the Reagan-Bush era to the plight of the socially, economically, and educationally disinherited will carry the day. We return to Goodlad's observations on the conditions of renewal in teacher education. He calls for substantially increased resources to conduct the enterprise.

> And these resources must be made secure for the purposes intended. That is, they must be earmarked for and assigned to a unit with clear borders, a specified number of students with a common purpose, and a roster of largely full-time faculty requisite to the formal and informal socialization of these students into teaching. Put negatively, these resources must not go to the larger, multipurpose unit of which teacher education is a part; there they run the danger of being impounded by entrepreneurial program heads and faculty members.[65]

The people responsible for teacher education, suggests Goodlad, must have clear focus, identity, and authority. His prediction of the alternative: "Otherwise, teacher education will remain an orphan, dependent on charity and goodwill."[66] We believe that the same is true for special education if its mission is to be taken seriously. Special education once was what Goodlad describes as the inevitable consequence of lack of focus, identity, and authority—an orphan, dependent on charity and goodwill in a larger, multipurpose unit, its resources constantly in danger of impoundment by competing interests. The interests now competing most overtly for special education's resources are (1) concern for underachieving students who are at risk for greater failure and (2) pursuit of the higher performance of "all" students out of concern for America's economic competitiveness. These interests will, of course, seek to attach special education's resources by arguing that these assets must not be protected from infringement because their reallocation or redistribution can serve not only children with disabilities but the common good as well.

After a long period of struggle, special education has finally achieved the status of a normal part of public general education and been integrated into the fabric of our thinking about students' special needs. It has done so only by recognizing the realities of which Goodlad speaks, and it will remain such only if it is successful in fending off the entrepreneurial interests and irresponsible attacks that threaten its hard-won position.

NOTES

1. William F. Blount and Thomas. H. Kean, *Designs for a New Generation of American Schools: A Request for Proposals* (Arlington, VA: New American Schools Development Corporation, 1991), 3.
2. C. C. Carson, R. M. Huelskamp, and T. D. Woodall, *Perspectives on Education in America: Annotated Briefing—Third Draft* (Albuquerque: Systems Analysis Department, Sandia National Laboratories, 1991), p. 172.
3. See also John W. Lloyd, Alan C. Repp, and Nirbhay N. Singh, eds., *The Regular Education Initiative: Alternative Perspectives on Concepts, Issues, and Models* (Sycamore, IL: Sycamore, 1991).

4. Gerald W. Bracey, "Why Can't They Be Like We Were?" *Phi Delta Kappan* 73 (1991): 104–17. See also Carson et al., *Perspectives on Education*.

5. See also Irving G. Hendrick and Donald L. MacMillan, "Selecting Children for Special Education in New York City: William Maxwell, Elizabeth Farrell, and the Development of Ungraded Classes, 1900–1920," *Journal of Special Education* 22 (1989): 395–417.

6. *Timothy W. v. Rochester, New Hampshire School District*, 875 F.2d 954 (1st Cir. 1989), cert. denied, 110 S. Ct. 519 (1989). See also Martha M. McCarthy, "Severely Disabled Children: Who Pays?" *Phi Delta Kappan* 73, no. 1 (Sept. 1991): 66–71.

7. Anne M. Hocutt, Edwin W. Martin, and James D. McKinney, "Historical and Legal Context of Mainstreaming" in *The Regular Education Initiative*, 24.

8. Dorothy K. Lipsky and Alan Gartner, "Capable of Achievement and Worthy of Respect: Education for Handicapped Students as If They Were Full-fledged Human Beings," *Exceptional Children* 54 (1987): 69–74.

9. National Center on Education and the Economy (NCEE), *To Secure Our Future* (Rochester, NY: National Center on Education and the Economy, 1989), 9.

10. See Robert E. Slavin, "General Education under the Regular Education Initiative: How Must It Change?" *Remedial and Special Education* 11, no. 3 (1990): 40–50; Robert E. Slavin et al., "Neverstreaming: Prevention and Early Intervention as an Alternative to Special Education," *Journal of Learning Disabilities* 24 (1991): 373–78.

11. See Melvyn I. Semmel and Michael M. Gerber, "If at First You Don't Succeed, Bye, Bye Again: A Response to General Educators' Views on the REI," *Remedial and Special Education* 11, no. 4 (1990): 53–59; Robert E. Slavin, "On Success for All: Defining 'Success,' Defining 'All,'" *Remedial and Special Education* 11, no. 4 (1990): 60–61.

12. For example, see Margaret C. Wang, Maynard C. Reynolds, and Herbert J. Walberg, "Rethinking Special Education," *Educational Leadership* 44, no. 1 (1986): 26–31; Margaret C. Wang, Maynard C. Reynolds, and Herbert J. Walberg, "Integrating the Children of the Second System," *Phi Delta Kappan* 70 (1988): 248–51; Margaret C. Wang and Nancy J. Zollers, "Adaptive Instruction: An Alternative Service Delivery Approach," *Remedial and Special Education* 11, no. 1 (1990): 7–21.

13. Douglas Biklen and Nancy Zollers, "The Focus of Advocacy in the LD Field," *Journal of Learning Disabilities* 19 (1986): 583.

14. James H. Bryan and Tanis H. Bryan, "Where's the Beef? A Review of Published Research on the Adaptive Learning Environment Model," *Learning Disabilities Focus* 4, no. 1 (1988): 9–14; Douglas Fuchs and Lynn S. Fuchs, "An Evaluation of the Adaptive Learning Environments Model," *Exceptional Children* 55 (1988): 115–27.

15. Slavin et al., "Neverstreaming," 377.

16. Maynard C. Reynolds, Margaret C. Wang, and Herbert J. Walberg, "The Necessary Restructuring of Special and Regular Education," *Exceptional Children* 53 (1987): 391–98.

17. Carson et al., *Perspectives on Education*.

18. Biklen and Zollers, "The Focus of Advocacy"; Alan Gartner and Dorothy K. Lipsky, *The Yoke of Special Education: How to Break It* (Rochester, NY: National Center on Education and the Economy, 1989); Dorothy K. Lipsky and Alan Gartner, "Restructuring for Quality" in *The Regular Education Initiative*, 43–57; Maynard

C. Reynolds, "An Historical Perspective: The Delivery of Special Education to Mildly Disabled and At-risk Students," *Remedial and Special Education* 10, no. 6 (1989): 7–11.

19. Douglas Fuchs and Lynn S. Fuchs, "Framing the REI Debate: Abolitionists Versus Conservationists" in *The Regular Education Initiative*, 241–55; Daniel P. Hallahan, James M. Kauffman, John W. Lloyd, and James D. McKinney, eds., "Questions about the Regular Education Initiative," *Journal of Learning Disabilities* 21, no. 1, special issue (1988); James M. Kauffman, "The Regular Education Initiative as Reagan-Bush Education Policy: A Trickle-Down Theory of Education of the Hard-to-Teach," *Journal of Special Education* 23 (1989): 256–78; James M. Kauffman, "Restructuring in Sociopolitical Context: Reservations about the Effects of Current Reform Proposals on Students with Disabilities" in *The Regular Education Initiative*, 57–66; James M. Kauffman and Daniel P. Hallahan, "What We Want for Children: A Rejoinder to REI Proponents," *Journal of Special Education* 24 (1990): 340–45; James M. Kauffman and Patricia L. Pullen, "An Historical Perspective: A Personal Perspective on Our History of Service to Mildly Handicapped and At-risk Students," *Remedial and Special Education* 10, no. 6 (1989): 12–14.

20. Lipsky and Gartner, "Capable of Achievement"; William Stainback and Susan Stainback, "A Rationale for Integration and Restructuring: A Synopsis" in *The Regular Education Initiative*, 225–39; Madeleine C. Will, "Let Us Pause and Reflect—But Not Too Long," *Exceptional Children* 51 (1984): 11–16.

21. Kauffman, "The Regular Education Initiative"; Kauffman and Hallahan, "What We Want for Children."

22. For example, Alan Gartner and Dorothy K. Lipsky, "Beyond Special Education: Toward a Quality System for All Students," *Harvard Educational Review* 57 (1987): 367–95.

23. Wolf Wolfensberger, "The Definition of Normalization: Update, Problems, Disagreements, and Misunderstandings" in *Normalization, Social Integration, and Community Services,* ed. R. J. Flynn and K. E. Nitsch (Baltimore: University Park Press, 1980), 71–115.

24. Ibid., 98.

25. Ibid.

26. James A. Mulick, and Jurgen H. Kedesdy, "Self-injurious Behavior, Its Treatment, and Normalization," *Mental Retardation* 26, no. 4 (1988): 223–29.

27. W. A. T. White, "A Meta-analysis of the Effects of Direct Instruction in Special Education," *Education and Treatment of Children* 11, no. 4 (1988): 364–74.

28. Stanley Hauerwas, *Suffering Presence: Theological Reflections on Medicine, the Mentally Handicapped, and the Church* (Notre Dame, IN: University of Notre Dame Press, 1986), 213.

29. See N. E. Bank-Mikkelsen, "A Metropolitan Area in Denmark: Copenhagen" in *Changing Patterns of Residential Services for the Mentally Retarded,* ed. Robert B. Kugel and Wolf Wolfensberger (Washington, D.C.: President's Committee on Mental Retardation, 1969), 227–54; B. Nirje, "The Normalization Principle and Its Human Management Implications" in *Changing Patterns in Residential Services,* 179–95; Wolfensberger, "The Definition of Normalization."

30. Wolf Wolfensberger, *Normalization* (Toronto: National Institute on Mental Retardation, 1972), 238.

31. Lipsky and Gartner, "Capable of Achievement," 73.

32. NCEE, *To Secure Our Future*, 9.
33. See John I. Goodlad, *Teachers for Our Nation's Schools* (San Francisco: Jossey-Bass, 1990).
34. Carnegie Forum on Education and the Economy, *A Nation Prepared: Teachers for the 21st Century* (New York: Carnegie Foundation, 1986), 20.
35. Gartner and Lipsky, *The Yoke of Special Education*, 20.
36. Ibid., 28.
37. Barbara K. Keogh, "Improving Services for Problem Learners: Rethinking and Restructuring," *Journal of Learning Disabilities* 21 (1988): 20.
38. Chap. 2 in this book; see also Hendrick and MacMillan, "Selecting Children for Special Education."
39. Judith D. Singer, "Should Special Education Merge with Regular Education?" *Educational Policy* 2 (1988): 416.
40. Douglas Carnine, "Increasing the Amount and Quality of Learning through Direct Instruction: Implications for Mathematics" in *The Regular Education Initiative*, 163–75; Douglas Carnine and Edward Kameenui, "The Regular Education Initiative and Children with Special Needs: A False Dilemma in the Face of True Problems," *Journal of Learning Disabilities* 23 (1990): 141–44.
41. Lipsky and Gartner, "Restructuring for Quality."
42. Stainback and Stainback, "A Rationale for Integration and Restructuring."
43. Lipsky and Gartner, "Capable of Achievement."
44. Wang et al., "Rethinking Special Education"; Wang et al., "Integrating the Children of the Second System."
45. See Martha Minow, "Learning to Live with the Dilemma of Difference: Bilingual and Special Education" in *Children with Special Needs*, ed. Katharine T. Bartlett and Judith W. Wenger (New Brunswick, NJ: Transaction Books, 1987), 375–429.
46. Fuchs and Fuchs, "Framing the REI Debate."
47. For example, Lipsky and Gartner, "Restructuring for Quality."
48. James M. Kauffman, "What Happens When Special Education Works? The Sociopolitical Context of Special Education Research in the 1990s," invited address, Special Interest Group: Special Education Research (Boston: Annual Meeting of the American Educational Research Association, April 1990).
49. For example, Dorothy K. Lipsky and Alan Gartner, "Restructuring for Quality"; Stainback and Stainback, "A Rationale for Integration and Restructuring."
50. For example, Gartner and Lipsky, *The Yoke of Special Education;* NCEE, *To Secure Our Future*.
51. Fuchs and Fuchs, "Framing the REI Debate." See also Hocutt et al., "Historical and Legal Context of Mainstreaming."
52. Lipsky and Gartner, "Restructuring for Quality."
53. Goodlad, *Teachers for Our Nation's Schools*, 59.
54. Ibid., 284.
55. Ibid.
56. Ibid.
57. See James M. Kauffman and Stanley C. Trent, "Issues in Service Delivery for Students with Learning Disabilities" in *Learning about Learning Disabilities*, ed. Bernice Y. L. Wong (New York: Academic Press, 1991), 465–81, for comments regarding learning disabilities.
58. Catherine A. Feniak, "Labelling in Special Education: A Problematic Issue in England and Wales," *International Journal of Special Education* 3 (1988): 117–24.

59. Michael M. Gerber and Melvyn I. Semmel, "Teacher as Imperfect Test: Reconceptualizing the Referral Process," *Educational Psychologist* 19 (1984): 137–48.

60. See Feniak, "Labelling in Special Education"; Martha Minow, "Learning to Live with the Dilemma of Difference."

61. Maynard C. Reynolds, "Classification and Labeling" in *The Regular Education Initiative*, 29–41; see also Stainback and Stainback, "A Rationale for Integration and Restructuring."

62. Reynolds, "Classification and Labeling," 35.

63. Goodlad, *Teachers for Our Nation's Schools*, 277.

64. Ibid., 278.

65. Ibid., 152.

66. Ibid., 153.

5

Financing the
Educational Delivery System

Charles D. Bernstein

The goal of this chapter is to provide the reader with a theoretical and practical introduction to special education finance. The theory will focus on what a financial system can and should do, complemented by real-life examples that will illustrate how financial systems actually function. The chapter significantly reflects my perspective, derived from a diverse array of experiences.

The chapter begins with a description of what a special education financial system should accomplish and how it should function. The limitations of finance as a rational discipline are described, along with examples of the irrationalities that are responsible for many of the problems generated by the financial system. The heart of the chapter is made up of discussions of the four big questions addressed by a special education financial system: What does special education cost? Who pays? Who provides the services? How is the money distributed?[1] Finally, the chapter concludes with a description of an ideal system and a tale of how a proposed introduction of such a model system was torpedoed.

A CAVEAT

It is appropriate to address an aside to those who might consider skipping this chapter to focus on programs rather than numbers. One of the most disquieting aspects of the field of special education is the deference that is offered, even by the most outspoken of advocates, to "financial experts" in the determination of educational policy. Finance becomes the secret language spoken only by the initiated and through which any change or reform must pass to become manifest. What is ostensibly a technical subject is actually one that can easily become political and subject to the same differences of opinion that affect policy in general. When program experts defer to financial experts, they cede to them important, sometimes invisible but no less powerful control over the implementation of policy. The result is that we have developed special education delivery systems in which the tail wags the dog and the cart pushes the horse.

It is therefore essential that individuals involved in programs approach finance as an accessible subject that they can master. Better still, they should approach finance people with the imperative that they *must* understand the financial considerations before policy can proceed. Part of their hesitation, undoubtedly, is a residual of "math phobia" that may have encouraged them at a relatively young age to choose a "people-oriented" profession rather than an economic one. Part of their hesitation also is because of the fact that finance can be excruciatingly boring.

Finance in general, and education and special education finance in particular, are for the most part commonsense disciplines. The data and the formulas can be understood, given a reasonable level of attention and assuming a willingness and determination to understand. The purpose of this chapter is to give an overview of how special education finance works. It should be a sufficient primer to assist anyone in the field to better understand a financial expert making a presentation.

If, after completing this chapter, a reader cannot understand the fundamentals of what is presented by a financial expert, then it is the fault of the expert. If confused by a presentation, the determined reader should demand clarification. If still confused, the reader should ask him- or herself the reason that he or she is meant *not* to understand. A handy rule of thumb regarding finance (and it must be kept in mind even in the too frequent face of scornful contempt) is that incomprehensible financial presentations occur because the expert is confused or intentionally seeks to confuse.

PURPOSE OF THE SPECIAL EDUCATION FINANCIAL SYSTEM

One of the reasons that finance is sometimes a confusing topic is that it is not always clear what its goals are and what it is supposed to accomplish. Typically, a special education financial system serves a number of goals.

Above all, a financial system *distributes funds* to support educational programs. At a minimum, the system should funnel funds to educational agencies in accordance with legislative and administrative mandates. Such a function implies a high degree of accountability to ensure that funds are used for the purposes for which they were intended.

To the extent that funding is based on objective factors, the financial system *collects data* pertaining to those factors. For example, systems that distribute money according to the numbers of children served or, alternatively, the numbers of staff employed will generate data on the numbers of children or staff. Those data can be used to project future needs, plot trends, measure cost effectiveness, and in general manage special education programs.[2]

The financial system *monitors results.* To the extent that goals exist, especially if they pertain to the objective factors cited earlier, it becomes possible to track progress. For example, the same forms that are used to request money may be used to measure changes in the numbers of children identified, served, and even remediated.

The financial system *supports and enforces policies.* Funding mechanisms can serve to emphasize political mandates such as mainstreaming or regionalization. In some cases, the policy is implicit in the funding itself; for example, funds that can only go to fund consortia-provided services will serve to stimulate the formation of consortia.[3]

The criteria of a funding system should reflect the social goals of those creating the system. Thus, anyone who was opposed philosophically to the labeling of children by handicapping condition would not support a funding system that distributes funds according to the handicapping conditions of the children served. Similarly, a system that provides a flat reimbursement per child for all children identified regardless of handicapping condition, which serves, nonetheless, to promote the identification of children with mild disabilities, does not serve the interests of anyone desiring to focus resources on the children who are most seriously disabled. As we will see subsequently, various funding mechanisms, if not managed appropriately, will tend to promote some unintended outcomes; one is better than another to the extent that it is better at encouraging a particular policy agenda.

Notwithstanding these points, to the extent that most people share some common values such as democracy and efficiency, it is possible to list criteria that most people agree are desirable. Thus, a special education system should be as follows:

- *Comprehensive*—supporting the full range of programs deemed desirable
- *Flexible*—permitting programs to adapt to changing needs, encourage efficiencies whenever possible, and incorporate new programs and changing prices without requiring a reformulation of the entire system
- *Equitable*—providing funds so that resources are allocated according to needs
- *Simple*—helping to permit everyone to understand what is being funded and why, as well as minimizing the costs of implementing the system
- *Compatible*—complementing the regular education financial system so that special programs can be integrated with regular education programs

For the most part, then, the better a funding system manifests the criteria listed above, the better it is. We will return to these criteria when describing a model system.

FINANCE AS A GAME

In theory, finance is a rational discipline. In practice, it can become a tool of manipulation. As stated earlier, one of the reasons that finance matters often are so inaccessible is because some practitioners intend for them to be inscrutable. While their reasons range from the noble to the ignoble, it is invariably true that such efforts serve to limit the effectiveness of the democratic process. So that we all may become equal participants, it is essential that we understand the games that financial specialists play and their motivations for playing them.

Profit

The primary financial practitioner is the district business manager who is charged with maintaining the balancing act in which seemingly unlimited needs compete with each other for limited and often uncertain resources. Since under law school districts cannot engage in deficit financing, the business manager—at the risk of a career—manages expenditures so that they do not exceed revenues. The already difficult and political task of balancing needs and resources is exacerbated by uncertainty. Revenues may be less than anticipated and almost never exceed expectations. Expenditures are always more than expected because of unanticipated events: a shortfall in state funding or tax revenues, a successful parent lawsuit, an expensive disability claim, or several new children requiring intensive services not available in the district.

The result is a search for the antidote to uncertainty—"profit" that can serve as a reserve. The motivation for a not-for-profit agency to identify and exploit potential profits is neither the traditional one of a return to shareholders nor any dishonest inclination toward personal gain. It is, however, no less powerful as a buffer to cushion the vicissitudes of risk resulting from uncertainty. In short, the business manager has a strong interest in creating "profits" from one program to offset the real or potential losses in other programs.

Although special education programs can be a burden to a local agency, they can also be a boon to districts, providing more revenue than the actual costs of their operation and resulting in a "profit." The plea for funding that can be made on behalf of special programs is compelling and dramatic; it is not uncommon to find educators who are outspoken advocates for the dignity of the handicapped unabashedly parading persons with disabilities through the halls of the legislature during budget hearings. Profit usually derives from generating funding while limiting services. Obviously, it is not in the business manager's interest for this to become known to advocates, who are intent on maximizing expenditures, or legislators, who are trying to minimize them.

Freedom and Control

District administrators invariably are fiercely protective of their own way of accomplishing things and tend to resist any financial system or reporting system that purports to direct or change their behavior. "Just give us the money and let us figure out how to spend it; we know what we need" is their frequently heard battle cry.

On the other side of the argument are the advocates who fear that districts have more interest in their bank statements than in serving children with disabilities appropriately. They agitate for more legal safeguards, more planning, more oversight, more parental or specialist involvement, all of which tend to drive up the costs of providing services and reduce the discretion of administrators.

The advocates are by no means a monolithic bloc. Some argue for stronger direction of the process by psychologists, others by teachers. Yet others prefer the integration of children into the regular programs almost exclusively, whereas some prefer segregation when appropriate. There are individuals who emphasize primary services, and others promote support services. Some argue for regional services, others for local providers with an option for regional consortia. These battles are typically fought by lobbyists at the state level, but their outcomes have a major impact on the requirements of programming established at the local level.

Specific financial systems by their very construction may favor one philosophy or approach over another and thereby reduce the freedom of district business managers to implement their own approach. Although it is possible to make financial systems neutral with respect to philosophy, they rarely are. To be successful, therefore, a financial system must either be as neutral as possible or reflect the prevailing consensus of opinion. Better still, that consensus should be expressed explicitly so that debate focuses on real issues and differences rather than on indirect and often arcane technical matters that exclude everyone but the financial experts even though the outcome has immense programmatic implications.

Cost Containment

Complex financial systems involving poorly understood regulations or difficult paperwork may serve, intentionally or otherwise, as a brake on the provision of appropriate services. In other words, awkward systems may be created or may be allowed to continue because they serve a political agenda.

For example, one state maintains a reimbursement formula in which the sums of money provided may be reduced if funding is insufficient to cover claims. The result is an incentive for districts to delay creating additional classes or services, despite an expected need, to reduce the risk of coming up short of funds. The mere threat of insufficient funding is, therefore, enough to reduce services and, ironically, to ensure that the available funds are sufficient after all.

Cost "Games"

The most significant games pertain to *average* cost versus *marginal* cost. An example will illustrate the point. If a classroom of twenty children costs a total of $60,000 (teacher's salary and benefits, room materials, and prorated portion of administration, maintenance and utilities, etc.), the *average* cost is $3,000 per child. That is simply the arithmetic product of the total cost divided by the number of children ($60,000/20). To add ten children might cost an additional $3,000 for additional materials, but it would not require additional classroom or administrative staffing, additional maintenance, or additional utilities. The *marginal* cost, or incremental cost, of those ten children is, therefore, $300 per child, or the additional cost divided by the number of additional children served ($3,000/10). The *average* cost for all thirty children is then $2,100 per child ($63,000/30).

When school enrollments were increasing in the 1950s and 1960s, business managers argued for funding schools using the average cost of services. (In the illustration above, that would be $3,000 per child using old data and $2,100 per child using the newer data, resulting in a "profit" of revenue over actual costs of $2,700 or $1,800, depending on which figure is used to determine the average cost.)

Using average cost for reimbursements is a clear and simple approach. Yet, it is conceptually wrong because it serves to collect an excess amount to cover the costs of overhead (e.g., the school principal), which has already been paid for from the first twenty children. Thus, a profit is created, which, as already pointed out, is a prime motivator for business managers. However, when enrollments begin to decline, a serious problem results. A reduction of one child eliminates a reimbursement of $3,000 or $2,100 when, in fact, the actual costs decline by the marginal cost of only $300.

Reducing enrollments during the 1970s and 1980s meant that districts experienced funding losses that were greater than their ability to reduce costs, which created a "loss" in the program. Suddenly, average costing was viewed for what it is: an unstable economic concept that, when incorporated into a school financial system, produces profits for local agencies during growth and losses during declines.

COSTS

To a large extent, the determination of special education costs is a policy question, not an analytical one. The first issue involves the definition of "special education." Does it include, for example, the assessment of all children in regular programs who may be handicapped? Alternatively, does it include only the assessment costs of those ultimately identified and exclude the assessment costs of those for whom special education was not indicated?[5] For example, in some districts and states, all psychologists are assigned to special education; in others, they are all charged to the regular program, and a flat fee per assessment is assigned to the special education program. Does special education include the regular classroom for the mainstreamed child or only the special services necessary to support the mainstreamed child? Is speech a special service, a regular service, or does classification depend on the intensity of the services? These are the types of questions that must be answered before it is possible to examine the costs of special education. Yet, there is no objective answer to the questions; they are matters to be resolved by policymakers.

Costs are frequently confused with other concepts. *Cost* pertains to the sum of the market values of the components that comprise the thing to which costs are being attributed. For example, the charges for components and labor to produce a scanner that enlarges print for the visually impaired might be $250. What is actually paid for the combination of those components may be more or less than what it costs and is referred to as its *price;* for example, an organization might sell the scanner to a district for $1,000 or lease it for $50 per month, figures that represent prices. A sum of money provided to cover the costs but that may or may not be equal to the cost is referred to as an *allocation* or *reimbursement.* For example, a state might reimburse local agencies 75 percent of their out-of-pocket expenditures for equipment, whether purchased or leased. A *limit* is a ceiling that a cost, price, allocation, or reimbursement may not exceed but that may become identical with the elements that it constrains. For example, because a state limits the reimbursement for a visual scanner to $750 and reimburses only 75 percent of the cost, the selling organization may decide that an appropriate price should not exceed $1,000.

The time perspective is an essential ingredient of cost. Last year's cost is not likely to be the same as this year's. To the extent that allocations are based on prior-period costs without adjustments for time, they are out of date and, typically, insufficient to cover costs.

At first glance cost data would seem to be a factual representation, but they are not. Accounting costs are heavily dependent on the definitions of special education and the assumptions made, which are typically not obvious to either the collector or the user of accounting data. Although the total income and expenditures for school programs are probably accurate because they are documented by invoices and checks, the distribution of these incomes and expenditures among various programs involves artificial manipulations that are heavily dependent on the assumptions made and the skills and consistency of the people doing the manipulations.

The notion of *full cost* pertains to the equitable sharing of all school costs by special education programs. Yet, how do we determine what is equitable? Should children in wheelchairs assume their fair share of the costs of the playground? Should a deaf child bear a portion of the cost of a music teacher? Should a learning-disabled child bear a full-day burden for the maintenance of the regular classroom even though he or she spends half a day in a resource room that also is burdened with either a full or half day of maintenance costs? Does full cost include the cost of the regular classroom for the child who is fully mainstreamed and requires only the support of a consulting teacher? The answer is that it depends on the particular definitions and policies as well as the accounting conventions and procedures that have been established. These are determined according to administrative requirements such as the need for data and the cost of collecting it. In the end, the answer does not really matter, as long as the answer is consistent for everyone.

In referring to special education costs, some people prefer to talk about *direct costs,* which are those costs that can be specifically attributable to the existence of the special education program. Such a notion excludes the cost of the playground or the music teacher or maintenance or the regular classroom. Instead, it includes the special class, resource, and consulting teachers from the examples above.

Marginal costs refer to the additional cost of providing a single individual with service. The marginal cost of providing a special class for the first and only child in the room might be $40,000. The additional, or marginal, cost for a second child might only be $300 for materials. A financial system that provides $3,000 per child would be an insufficient incentive for the creation of the special class in an area in which an insufficient number of children is likely to lead to an underutilization of services. This is particularly true in rural areas. In fact, many states provide for additional allocations, sometimes known as a "sparsity factor," in rural areas to adjust for the underutilization that typically occurs.

Allowable costs typically refer to costs that are approved by a state agency for reimbursement. To the extent that some costs are not approved, they are less likely to be reported, which results in cost figures that fairly represent the expenditures for which reimbursement is generated but that are not indicative of what is actually being spent. In other words, the cost to the reimbursing agency may be less than the cost to the service provider.

In the late 1960s and early 1970s, the National Education Finance Project (NEFP)[6] collected and published cost data for a variety of state agencies. To eliminate the effect of differential price levels and special local conditions, NEFP researchers developed a cost index that compared the per-pupil expenditures for special services with the per-pupil expenditures for regular education programs. These *relative costs* were typically expressed by handicapping condition and were based on historical costs that did not reflect the change over time in the mix of the severity of the handicaps or the change in programming options. They also had the tendency to become self-fulfilling prophecies: since all funds provided are usually spent, programs that were funded at some multiple of regular education were likely to end up "costing" that same multiple. Moreover, since special education represents only the numerator of the equation, two districts with equal special education costs might generate differing amounts of support for special education solely because the costs of their regular programs differ for some reason. The NEFP studies produced widely differing cost indices within and among districts. Nevertheless, they were averaged and then used by legislators as the basis for developing statewide financial systems.

Cost studies frequently have serious methodological problems, yet these limitations are often ignored by legislators eager to use the data to support a new or revised financial system. Financial systems are also subject to a number of biases, some of which are unsupported by reality. One common myth, for example, is that the severity of a child's handicapping condition is an indicator of the level of funding required for service to support it. In fact, it is not uncommon for a child with mild handicaps who is almost able to function independently in a regular classroom to benefit not only from the regular program but also from a variety of expensive support services, while a child with severe disabilities might be served appropriately by a segregated special class only.[7]

The point of this discussion of costs is to point out that displays of data, though appearing to be objective and factual representations, are subject to errors, omissions, faulty assumptions, historical oddities, improper interpretations and manipulations, and outright bias. Issues pertaining to the costs of special education can be illustrated by a discussion of mobility training. For someone who receives assistance from a fellow participant in a support group and who already owns a cane, the cost might be nothing. For someone who attends ten sessions at a nonprofit clinic, the cost of attending might be $300. If a cane were needed, the price might be an additional $100. For someone who requires the assistance of a guide dog, the entire fee for the animal and the training might be $3,000. One's assumptions about depreciation schedules for the cane or the dog and the distances one travels to attend are factors that preclude a simple response to the question, "What is the cost of mobility training?" In this sample situation, the answer is, From nothing to $3,000. If a government agency were to reimburse this service, it would be difficult, if not impossible, to set up a formula. Would it reimburse everyone according to actual costs, or would it reimburse at an average rate of, say, $500 that would overreimburse the person in a support group while underreimbursing the owner of the guide dog? Would the agency use last year's costs or adjust to account for current fees? Would it make allowances for the individual who had a more difficult time and needed additional assistance? Would the formula favor certain public policies, such as a desire to reduce dependence on animals?

In sum, the answer to the question "What is cost?" is that it depends on who is asking the question and why. Ultimately, the answer is political, not analytical.

SOURCES OF FUNDING

A financial system may include funding from a number of sources including the federal government, state government, and local agencies as well as multiple sources within those agencies. The relative roles that each of these agencies should play is, again, a political issue.

Historically, schools were funded primarily by local property taxes. With the advent of equalization initiatives in the courts and in legislatures, the burden of funding has shifted to the states. The passage of PL 94-142 in 1975 and the significant interventions of the federal government into special education policy and programming have tilted the burden of funding toward the federal government, although state funding remains the most significant source.[8]

Decision making inevitably follows funding. With the move toward more state and federal funding came a reduction in local control over special education programs. Federal monies carried with them, for example, federal concerns regarding the racial balances of the enrollments in special services. Specifically, the result of federal reporting forms that compared the racial balance of total school populations with special program populations has been to establish de facto racial quotas. Similarly, reporting forms that ignore the mandate of appropriate programming and instead focus on the mandate of least restrictive environment have resulted in quotas on segregated services.

Federal and even state control is a major source of frustration to educators at the local level. Efforts to separate funding from control have resulted in proposals to fund special programs by means of block grants in which lump sums of monies are provided to state or local agencies without specific directions for expending them. However, typically, special education advocates are not willing to see special education funding lumped with funds for compensatory or health programs, with local administrators being permitted to decide which needs are more deserving of being funded.

Major federal and state mandates coincided with declining enrollments in the schools and, therefore, declining funding. The reduction in funding was exacerbated by tax reduction efforts in the early 1980s. The result today is a substantially increased requirement for funds and insufficient funding from all levels of government, which has led to a high level of resentment among advocates of regular and other compensatory programs.

SERVICE PROVIDERS

We now move our focus to questions of which agencies are paid and what services they provide. Up to the mid-1960s, educational services were primarily the province of local school districts in conjunction, occasionally, with one or more state-operated schools serving severe needs. More recently, a number of trends have come together to alter the nature and mission of service providers. Today, services are provided by a much broader variety of agencies, including local, regional, state, as well as private vendors.

The first trend was the consolidation of small school districts that occurred in, and was even encouraged by, states in the 1960s and 1970s. The idea was that larger units could more economically provide specialized instructional and support services that were mandatory but could not be justified for small populations. Even if smaller local agencies did not merge officially, the same efficiency rationale was used to encourage the formation of special purpose "consortia," or combinations of local agencies in a region, in order to promote a more optimal use of resources.

The second trend was the emphasis, encouraged by many parental and professional groups, on the integration of special needs children into more "regular" school settings.[9] At the milder end of the special needs continuum, this became known as "mainstreaming"; at the more severe end of the continuum, it manifested itself as "deinstitutionalization," or the removal of children from large, typically state-run facilities and their placement in local facilities such as small-group homes.

The third trend that affected the providers of special services was the change in revenue sources that occurred. The tax revolt of the late 1970s was a major factor in limiting the amounts of money that could be raised and creating competition for limited funds with other social needs. At the same time, courts were limiting the financial inequalities in school funding caused by the great variations in local property values. The result was that states and the federal government became substantially more important sources of the funding of services and, sometimes, the provision of services.[10]

A fourth trend was the federal emphasis on making available a variety of support services that were necessary for education but not educational in themselves. Traditional school systems were typically not prepared to provide such services, which required a new focus on cooperation with other public agencies, especially those dealing with health services, and other private agencies that specialized in these "related" services.

What we have today is a range of services offered by a variety of providers. Although the nature of these services is to a large extent prescribed by federal and state regulations, the coordinator is the local school district. In general, the majority of services are still provided by the local agency. Services necessitated by the less frequently occurring handicapping conditions and the expertise that is traditionally outside the educational realm are provided by regional agencies, consortia of local, private, and state agencies. The local school district remains the primary provider of educational services; the other organizations are important providers of both educational and related services.

The locus of control and coordination has become the IEP—the individualized education program that is required of all children displaying or at some risk of developing special needs. The whole assessment and IEP formulation process is managed at the local level although, as we have seen, various services may be provided by a range of service providers. In some cases, special interagency agreements or compacts (broad frameworks describing the basic working arrangements by which two or more agencies cooperate) will have been negotiated with other public or private agencies serving as a general framework for cooperation in the provision of services as they become necessary on a case-by-case basis.

The immediate goal is that special needs children have access to a comprehensive range of services appropriate to their needs. The long-range goal, both for reasons of effectiveness and efficiency, is to coordinate special education programs with other categorical programs—especially those that serve the same population such as health programs, vocational education, and compensatory programs—so as to eliminate duplication and to ensure necessary coordination among programs.

DISTRIBUTION SYSTEM

Though it is really the last component of a funding system, the mechanism by which funds are distributed receives most of the attention in discussions of funding. That is because the actual behavior of teachers and administrators, and thus the quality of services provided, are influenced by these mechanisms that, in theory, should be neutral in their impact.

An important aspect of the distribution system is the timing of payments. When special needs programs were smaller, it was not unusual for service providers to be reimbursed by a state for providing services as much as a year or more after the service had been provided. As the number of children served grew, the practice of providing services in advance of reimbursement became a serious burden for providers, especially when programs were growing quickly. Despite the fact that payments to providers may be based on historical costs, most local agencies provide some sort of advance or "forward funding" of some or all of their costs so that the timing of payments approximates the timing of expenditures.

The most visible aspect of the distribution system involves the "formulas," or bases, by which the amounts paid to providing agencies are calculated. These formulas are of the various types described next.

Unit

A *unit* is typically synonymous with *classroom* or *teacher,* although it is also applied to other services. A unit of service, therefore, would generally consist of all the resources (e.g., a person, an office, supplies and materials, janitorial service, utilities) necessary to create a bundle of services designed to serve a group of children (e.g., 25:1 for instruction, 200:1 for administration, 80:1 for transportation). Ohio, for example, uses a unit formula in which the number of units is calculated using pupil-teacher ratios that are prescribed for each category of handicapping condition. Every unit calculated generates a specified level of funding.

A unit system works well in regular education where the typical grouping of services is a classroom or classroom teacher. It worked originally in special education where the special classroom was virtually the only service offered. It was adaptable to the resource teacher and even the psychologist, social worker, or occupational therapist. However, it did not work as well for individualized, lower-incidence services such as service contracts for individual students or for related services in which children were being counted a second time for the support service.

In the past, some financial specialists felt that unit formulas were too limiting to accommodate a continuum of services that was required as part of the federal government's increasing participation in funding in the mid-1970s. They believed that these formulas favored special classes to the detriment of the newer services that were being offered, especially those for children with mild disabilities.

Weight

Weighted formulas derive from a series of financial studies done in the late 1960s and early 1970s by the National Educational Finance Project (NEFP). At a time of high inflation when figures using actual dollars quickly became outdated, the researchers created a methodology by which an index specified the cost of special education as a multiple of the cost of regular education. For example, the research in a particular state might show that the cost of a child with a certain handicap or in a special setting might be twice that of a child in the regular school setting; in that case, the weight for that child would be 2.0, and he or she would be counted twice for the sake of determining reimbursements.

Florida reimburses local agencies using a weighted formula. In that state, children with handicaps are provided various weights according to the handicapping category in which they are placed. Each agency then submits a census of children showing the number of children in regular education, each counted as 1.0, and those requiring special education or other compensatory services with their associated weights. The numbers of children in each category are multiplied by their corresponding weight to produce a weighted total of children. That total is then multiplied by the dollar value associated with a single child without handicaps to compute the grand total to be reimbursed.

Weighted formulas make a major assumption that the various components of the costs of each type of service will maintain a linear relationship with each other. Since they are composed primarily of personnel-related expenses, the assumption is perhaps reasonable. However, to the extent that the cost of a service might be based more on the price of equipment that is declining over time, the relationship between it and the costs of regular education might not be stable.

Another problem with weighted formulas is that they tend to take a specific type of special education service, a specific mix of services for a specific handicap, and even accounting aberrations in a particular period and fix them permanently into formulas to be used indefinitely. A review of NEFP and NEFP-type studies shows substantial variations in the indices that were established in various states. Obviously, that could be a reflection of differing regular education programs, differing special programs, or a combination of both, but common sense would suggest that the degree of variability in programming is not great enough to account for the variation in the indexes. Furthermore, if the variability from state to state were that great, it could be inferred that there would also be great variability from district to district within a state and that the specific state indices would not apply to all areas.

Finally, most weighted formulas are tied to handicapping labels that professionals view as potentially stigmatizing. Worse, when the diagnoses of children are tied directly to funding, this creates a strong incentive to choose one diagnosis over another. Of course, this problem could be eliminated if the weighting were done by service option (e.g., special class, itinerant specialist, OT/PT) and the weights reflected actual costs so that there was no "profit" to be made by referring a child to one type of service over another.[11]

Actual Cost

Under an actual cost system, part or all of the actual costs for educating children with disabilities is reimbursed to the providing agency following the submission of a complete accounting of these costs. Typically, the state defines "allowable" costs (e.g., salaries, benefits, transportation, books, equipment) that may be included for reimbursement. Occasionally, ceilings for certain types of expenditures are also specified.

In Wisconsin, local agencies are reimbursed for 70 percent of the actual costs of special education. Certain types of costs are specified as "approved," and there is a ceiling on expenditures for books and equipment.

One of the main problems of an actual cost system is that it is by nature an after-the-fact system: the money has to be spent for reimbursement to be requested. Even if state funds are advanced based on an estimate of future need, school districts tend to be wary of spending money that is not in hand or guaranteed and that may not be adequately reimbursed if state funds are insufficient. An actual cost system also requires an elaborate set of accounting standards, a reasonable level of accounting oversight, and an extraordinary amount of expensive record keeping.

Personnel

Under a personnel formula, agencies are provided funds to hire specific types of special education personnel, both certified (professional) and classified (clerical and support). To ensure that enough funds are available, local agencies may be required to obtain advance approval for their hiring levels.

Illinois reimburses agencies a flat dollar amount for each special education teacher, psychologist, director, and other professionals. The state also pays half the salary or a flat amount, whichever is less, for each noncertified person in special education programs.

Personnel formulas, like unit formulas, are seen by policymakers as a throwback to older days when the only educational service was a classroom with a teacher. In concept, they ignore the cost of contracts with other agencies and individuals, especially those providing private programs and related services, and they exclude labor-saving technology and equipment. Legislators view them as possible budget-breakers that encourage unnecessary hiring and discourage the use of nonpersonnel services that might be more effective, less expensive, or both.

Fixed Sum

Fixed sum formulas establish a dollar amount to be reimbursed for each child. These sums typically differ according to type of handicap, severity of handicap, or type of service provided.

Arizona employs a fixed sum formula. That state reimburses local districts a specified amount for each special education child according to his or her handicapping category.

Fixed sum formulas share a number of the drawbacks cited above. They are typically based on historical data, updated according to some cost-of-living adjustment that may not be related to costs, and distribute funds according to handicapping labels. Thus, implicitly, they assume that the services offered do not change in composition and that the same services are prescribed for specific handicapping conditions. In addition to fixing past practices, they also memorialize accounting errors and inconsistencies. Again, there is an incentive to diagnose children according to labels that provide higher reimbursements without regard to the services actually provided.

Excess Cost

The notion of excess cost derives from an underlying philosophy that local agencies have a certain level of responsibility for educating all children in their area but that higher levels of government, state or federal, have the responsibility to cover the additional costs incurred for children who have handicaps. These additional costs are considered "excess." Pennsylvania reimburses local agencies fully for their excess costs. However, the costs subject to reimbursement are limited to certain approved categories and limits.

Some policy analysts have objected to the word *excess* and its negative connotation that the costs for special education are somehow unnecessary or excessive. Others have objected to the underlying philosophy that every child is entitled to a basic foundational support and that everything over and above that is to be handled differently (even if supported more fully), as opposed to the notion that every child is entitled to whatever it takes to provide equal access to education. It certainly is true that the notion of excess cost harkens back to a day when it was expected that state funds would fund special education more fully than general education. Today, however, with the greater participation of states and the federal government and a diminishing reliance on local property taxes, states are providing a higher proportion of all education funds, general and special. Consequently, the notion of excess cost is somewhat outdated. Ultimately, it remains more of a philosophical concept than an actual distribution mechanism.

Block Grant

Under a block grant, the state provides a sum of money to cover a variety of needs, including special, compensatory, and other programs. The allocation of these funds to serve the various needs most effectively is left up to each local agency.

Washington lumps its reimbursement for children with learning disabilities into a block grant with funds for vocational, migrant, Native American, and pregnant minors programs. The other special education programs in that state are funded from a different formula.[12]

Although a block grant is a lump sum of money that bears no relationship to any single child or category of children, it should nevertheless bear some relationship to need. To establish the level of need, one could look backward at historical data or forward to a projection of resources needed at some estimated market price. To adjust the funding to meet current needs, it would then be necessary to continue to monitor historical information or to project future needs. If one were going to all this trouble, it would then make sense to tie the reimbursements to the data of the projections, as we see in the aforementioned formulas.

In other words, a block grant is really more of an administrative posture that encourages local agencies to spend their funds as they best see fit rather than an actual computational mechanism for funding. If a block grant is to meet needs, it must be calculated according to some formula that specifies a level of money per classroom, per teacher, per condition of child, or per type of service provided.

Formulas are rarely pure forms; more often they are hybrids of the previously described formulas. A state might use one of the formulas for the authorization and another for the actual reimbursement. For example, hiring levels might be authorized in advance using a personnel formula, but reimbursements could be based on actual costs, not exceeding authorized levels.

The drawbacks of any of the formulas can be overcome by administrative measures: a unit formula, for example, could be modified to provide partial units for related services; a weighted formula could be based on the type of service provided rather than the handicapping category; actual costs could be reimbursed in advance by using estimates based on approved projections rather than on complex accounting data; personnel formulas could be modified to establish "personnel equivalents" for contracted services or equipment; fixed sums could be generated for specific services offered rather than handicapping conditions served; and so forth. It is true that some formulas contain biases by virtue of their very structure, but these biases can be eliminated by building in administrative controls where necessary.

Thus, a state could provide $30,000 for a special class serving ten children in the following ways:

1. *Unit*—A unit reimbursement of $30,000 for a classroom is provided.
2. *Weight*—A child in a special class generates a weight of 3.0. A regular education child generates $1,000 per year, so a special education child generates $3,000 per year. A class of ten children would generate $30,000.
3. *Actual Cost*—The state reimburses 75 percent of total expenditures. A special class involves a teacher salary of $25,000, a part-time aide salary of $5,000, total benefits of $5,000, a books and materials allowance of $1,500, janitorial and utilities of $1,500, and administrative overhead of $2,000, for a total of $40,000. The state would then reimburse three-quarters of that, or a total of $30,000.
4. *Personnel*—The state reimburses the full cost of a teacher at $25,000 per year and an aide at $5,000 per year, for a total of $30,000.
5. *Fixed Sum*—The state reimburses $3,000 per child in a special class or $30,000 for the whole class.
6. *Excess Cost*—A regular education child generates $1,000 per year in state reimbursements. A special class, containing ten children, costs $40,000. The state pays the difference between the total cost of the classroom ($40,000) and the income it generates ($10,000), or a total "excess cost" of $30,000.
7. *Block Grant*—The state provides $30,000 as part of an overall grant to a local agency to cover all special and compensatory programs.

In short, it is possible to use any one of the formulas outlined here to generate the same level of local income. Any one of them can be used to create a comprehensive, appropriate, flexible, fair, and administratively simple system. Still, it is important to understand the inherent theoretical weaknesses of the various formulas so that controls may be established in advance that will eliminate or reduce the impact of their respective weaknesses in practice.

An important factor in the selection of a formula is the degree to which it permits special education finance to be integrated with the funding system for general education and other special programs. This has become especially important as states have become a more important source of local school finance and with the increasing emphasis on mainstreaming. All of the funding formulas (with the exception of excess cost and, possibly, the block grant) have been used to finance general education as well as special education. As states move toward financing the majority of local education, it makes little sense to think of separate financial systems for special and general education.

MODEL FOR THE FUTURE

In creating a vision of what a model special education financial system should be, we must begin with the essential criteria for such a system. A model financial system should encompass the following traits:

- *Rational*—The system should be transparent so that the underlying policy assumptions are clear, which would thereby permit decisions to be based on an open debate of the issues in which all parties may participate rather than *sub rosa* through financial intricacies that only experts can understand.
- *Comprehensive*—It should accommodate the full range of services, service providers, and handicapping conditions, including other special services such as vocational education.
- *Flexible*—It should facilitate changes in services and the creation of new services as well as be adaptable to differing local conditions within a state and changing price levels resulting from inflation.
- *Equitable*—It should treat equally urban and rural agencies, large and small agencies, rich and poor agencies so that all children, regardless of condition, have access to special services without undue stress and stigma.
- *Simple*—The system should be compatible with, if not identical to, the system used for general education, should be comprehensible to staff and parents alike, and should facilitate accountability without massive amounts of expensive paperwork.

There is an approach that meets all of the preceding criteria and yet, for a variety of reasons, has met with little success. That approach focuses on funding *services*, not children. For example, rather than funding an educably mentally retarded (EMR) child with $3,000 a year, a state would provide $30,000 per year in funding for a special class serving ten children. All ten of those children might have been diagnosed as being mentally retarded, but some might just as easily be considered, for example, emotionally handicapped. The decision to group or segregate children would be based on the ability of the setting and the particular staff to serve a child's individual needs.

In other words, for funding purposes it does not really matter what a child "is" but what services a child *needs*. The IEP becomes the basis for determining funding needs. Such a system reduces the incentive to label a child as EMR because it generates more funding than the more appropriate label of emotionally handicapped. If the child needs a special class, that is the service that would be provided, regardless of the label. Of course, for federal and state reporting purposes, labels would still be used, but they could be a notation on the child's file rather than, metaphorically speaking, a sign on the classroom door.

Still, someone might argue, EMR children do cost more because they need other services. That could be true. Some might need some other services; others might need even more services; still others might need none at all. Whatever the needs are, assuming they were specified on the IEP, the service would be funded if it were required and not funded if it were not. A child requiring occupational therapy, for example, might generate an additional $500 per year to fund a weekly visit of an outside contractor. A child requiring counseling might generate $800 more for semiweekly assistance, regardless of whether he was EMR or emotionally handicapped and regardless of whether or not he was also receiving occupational therapy.

The system could be managed on an a posteriori basis, by which local agencies would be reimbursed for services already provided, or on an a priori basis, by which they would be approved in advance for providing services based on their historical incidence rates and programming or simply on a projection of their needs based on population and an expert projection of the needs. An after-the-fact accounting could then be used to require a return of some or all of the unexpended funds, if any. The expert opinion method of projecting needs consists of a review of the type and severity of special needs by an interdisciplinary panel of special education experts. This method has been used frequently to build a consensus of opinion regarding the services needed to serve a specific population of children, which is then used for creating budgets and for monitoring actual results.

When confronted by such a system, the financial department would likely respond, Run on the treasury! Of course, limits and controls would have to be established. Regulations would have to be written that would ensure, for example, that special classes would serve an average of ten children or that special classes were being used appropriately by establishing some projection of the number of special classes that would be expected to be used by a local agency and then creating some oversight mechanisms to review variances. Peer review could be used to ensure that related services were not being overused and that local programming is appropriate.

Once the programming needs were established, it would be a relatively simple matter to attach costs to services. Each service is composed of a group of resources, each of which has costs associated with it. In fact, the universe of resources in education is somewhat limited: salaries and wages for people, benefits, materials, equipment, support services, administrative services, and transportation are the main ones, with people and people-related costs representing the vast majority of the dollars. As we saw in the "actual cost" reimbursement formula earlier, a special class might cost a total of $40,000 composed of the following: a teacher salary of $25,000, a part-time aide salary of $5,000, total benefits of $5,000, a books and materials allowance of $1,500, janitorial and utilities of $1,500, and administrative overhead of $2,000.

That figure, someone might argue, only includes a part-time aide, and we need a full-time aide for our special classes serving students with mental retardation and other intellectual disabilities. Again, the proposed system accommodates the needs perfectly. A special class with a full-time aide might, for example, generate funding of $45,000, whereas a special class with no aide might only generate $35,000. It would be possible to simply reimburse agencies for what they actually provided by having them specify the number of special classes offered with no aide, a half-time aide, and a full-time aide. Similarly, it would be possible to specify what would be normal practices: for example, 25 percent with no aide, 50 percent with a half-time aide, and 25 percent with a full-time aide, for an *average* special class with a half-time aide or, stated differently, an average cost of $40,000 per special class, consisting of 25 percent at $35,000, 50 percent at $40,000, and 25 percent at $45,000.

One of the most powerful features of such a system is that it transforms budget discussions into discussions of tangible services. A 10 percent cut in the $40,000 funding for a special class is not an abstract concept: it literally means a $4,000 cut in the teacher's salary, a $4,000 cut in benefits, a $4,000 cut in the books and materials allowance, the elimination of the part-time aide, or a change in ratios so that each class serves an average of eleven children, which results in a 10 percent reduction in the number of classes needed. It is relatively easy for legislators to cut dollars but very hard for them to reduce the more tangible resources such as staff, benefits, or books and materials.

So we have a seemingly ideal system—one that is based on services specified in the IEP—that minimizes the need for labeling, that can be used to anticipate actual resource needs for both projections and controls, and that makes budget negotiations a rational procedure. Why has such a system not been proposed? In fact, such a system did become, under the sponsorship of the state advisory board, a legislative proposal in California in 1982. However, it failed to clear key committees and finally died without reaching the legislature.

The reasons for the proposal's failure echo the discussion at the beginning of this chapter on the games that are played with school finance. A grassroots proposal from members of the state advisory board had not been invented by any of the major state policymakers, the state superintendent, the speaker of the assembly, or the governor. Moreover, it challenged the vested interests of the politicians; there was more concern about the "winners and losers" than about the correctness of the approach. In fact, because of some grandfathering of old provisions of the state's patchwork financial system, some large, politically powerful local educational agencies were actually being overfunded for special education services and were unwilling to give up those extra funds.

Thus, the barriers to a coherent, comprehensive, and equitable approach to financing special education services are not technical. We have the knowledge to create such a system. We have a variety of alternative methods for creating such a system so that it meshes with the general education financial system. We typically have historical data that can be used to project needs and determine the adequacy of available resources. We probably even have sufficient resources to fund such a system. What we lack is the political will to challenge the entrenched interests, including the politicians themselves, who, perhaps unwittingly, have become our most influential educational administrators. It is up to parents, teachers, school administrators, and concerned citizens to sharpen their financial skills so as to be prepared to regain their roles in the determination and implementation of educational policy.

NOTES

1. Charles D. Bernstein, William T. Hartman, Michael W. Kirst, and Rudolph S. Marshall, *Financing Educational Services for the Handicapped: An Analysis of Current Research and Practices* (Reston, VA: Council for Exceptional Children, 1976).
2. See, for example, M. T. Moore, E. W. Strand, M. Schwartz, and M. Braddock, "Patterns in Special Education Service Delivery and Cost," Contract 300-84-0257 (Washington, D.C.: Decision Resources Corporation, 1988); and Richard A. Rossmiller, James A. Hale, and Lloyd E. Frohreich, *Educational Programs for Exceptional Children: Resource Configurations and Costs* (Madison: University of Wisconsin, 1970); and Leigh S. Marriner, "The Cost of Educating Handicapped Pupils in New York City," *Journal of Education Finance* 3 (Summer 1977): 82–97.
3. Henry M. Levin, "Some Methodological Problems in Economic Policy Research: Determining How Much Should Be Spent on Compensatory Education," *Education and Urban Society* 7, no. 3 (1975): 303–33; William J. Hartman, "Policy Effects of Special Education Funding Formulas," *Journal of Education Finance* 6, no. 2 (1980): 135–39; and Martha F. McCarthy and Daniel Sage, "State Special Education Fiscal Policy: The Quest For Equity," *Exceptional Children* 48, no. 5 (1982): 414–19.
4. See, for example, Kenneth Strike, "The Ethics of Resource Allocation in Education: Questions of Democracy and Justice" in *Microlevel School Finance: Issues and Implications for Policy*, ed. David H. Monk and Julie Underwood (Cambridge, MA: Ballinger, 1988), 143–80.
5. Henry M. Levin, "Financing the Education of At-risk Students," *Educational Evaluation and Policy Analysis* 11, no. 1 (1989): 47–60.
6. Richard A. Rossmiller, James A. Hale, and Lloyd E. Frohreich, *Educational Programs for Exceptional Children: Resource Configurations and Costs*, National Educational Finance Project Special Study 2 (Madison: University of Wisconsin, 1970; out of print).

7. Ellen S. Raphael, Judith D. Singer, and Deborah Klein Walker, "Per Pupil Expenditures on Special Education in Three Metropolitan School Districts," *Journal of Education Finance* 11 (Summer 1985): 69–88.

8. Kay Forbis Jordan and Mary P. McKeown, "Equity in Financing Public Elementary and Secondary Schools," in *Finance Policies and Practices*, ed. James W. Guthrie (Cambridge, MA: Ballinger 1980).

9. See, for example, John W. Lloyd, Nirbhay N. Singh, and Alan C. Repp, eds., *The Regular Education Initiative: Alternative Perspectives on Concepts, Issues, and Models* (Sycamore, IL: Sycamore, 1991).

10. *Serrano v. Priest*, 5 Cal. 3d 584, 96 Cal. Rptr. 601, 487 P. 2d 1241 (1971); *San Antonio Independent School District v. Rodriguez*, 411 U.S. 1 (1973); *Robinson v. Cahill*, 62 N.J. 473, 303 A.2d 273 (1973); *Seattle School District v. State*, no. 81-2-1713-1 (Thurston County Superior Court, 7 Sept. 1983) (i.e., *Doran II*).

11. Samuel Dempsey and Douglas Fuchs, "'Flat' versus 'Weighted' Reimbursement Formulas: A Longitudinal Analyses of Statewide Special Education Funding Practices" (unpublished manuscript; Nashville: George Peabody College of Vanderbilt University, 1991).

12. John S. Pearson, "Special Education Funding in Washington: An Overview and Explanation of the State's Funding System and Distribution Formula for Special Education," paper presented at the Eighth Annual Pacific Northwest Institute on Special Education and Law (Tacoma, WA: Tacoma Convention Center, 23–25 Sept. 1991), sponsored by the Law Division Institute for the Study of Educational Policy, College of Education, University of Washington, 173–81.

6

Curriculum Considerations

Marleen C. Pugach and Cynthia L. Warger

Curriculum decisions involve what students should learn and what schools should teach. The curriculum unifies school experience and reflects the educational goals that school districts expect their students to achieve. In this chapter, we use *curriculum* to denote the plans made for guiding learning in schools. It usually is represented in retrievable documents containing several levels of generality. Since experiences in the particular learning environment are a central influence on what is learned, *curriculum* also refers to the implementation of those plans in the classroom.[1]

In an inclusionary model of education, one that promotes educating students with disabilities in general education classrooms with same-aged peers, curriculum takes on major significance, particularly since the principal rationale for removing students with disabilities from general education classrooms is their inability to succeed in the standard academic curriculum. Any consideration of integrating special and general education must be well grounded in an analysis of curriculum issues and the expectations that various approaches to curriculum create for learners.

Our purpose in this chapter is to clarify the position that curriculum plays in the ongoing debate on integration as a goal for students with disabilities and to foster discussion among special and general educators alike on the curriculum issues that need to be addressed. In the absence of a curriculum framework, discussions of integration are incomplete.

We have based our analysis on three assumptions. First, curriculum issues, broadly interpreted, deserve (and have always deserved) a central place in school improvement debates as they relate to educating all children, especially those targeted for special education programs. The general education curriculum poses problems for students with disabilities and thus affects the ease and success with which integration can take place. Second, curriculum problems exist within special and general education, but the difficulties in each area are different, and neither area has succeeded in creating a positive educational situation for students with disabilities. Third, efforts to reform curriculum generally must proceed with special education explicitly in mind to assure that the particular needs of students with enduring disabilities are considered and those of students whose disabilities are functions of the existing curriculum are not ignored. In order to focus the discussion squarely on curriculum, this chapter is limited to a consideration of integration as it relates to the amount of a standard core curriculum that students with disabilities may be expected to master, not to proximity issues that arise when students with disabilities learn different content side by side with their same-aged peers.

FRAMING CURRICULUM ISSUES

The curriculum question that surrounds the issue of integration is not whether a single academic curriculum can be constructed to accommodate all learners, no matter how diverse. Clearly, there is a point at which curriculum content must diverge if our schools are to be inclusive of children and youth with the full range of disabilities. Instead, we see the appropriate question as, What conception of curriculum maximizes the likelihood that most students will have successful school experiences? Consequently, we view integration or full inclusion primarily as a social aim that in and of itself does not depend on the existence of a unitary academic curriculum. Yet it is only in the context of curriculum that we can begin to clarify the questions with which special education has been grappling for the past several years: What are reasonable educational goals for students designated as requiring special education? Should these goals differ from those set for non–special education students in the mainstream?

In order to clarify the integration goal as it relates to all categories of disability, one must know how special education students interact with the curriculum. Some students, chiefly those with severe and profound disabilities, are not expected to learn the core academic curriculum. Over the past decade, there have been major advancements in the design of functional and community-referenced curricula for students whose disabilities range from severe to profound. A similar situation exists with respect to students with moderate disabilities. For these students, the challenge of integration is to define and provide the kinds of social interactions they will have with their able-bodied peers and in what contexts. Because the outcomes of integration in this sense tend to reflect social goals rather than academic learning, the curriculum may or may not be targeted as an appropriate context in which to achieve the educational goal of integration.

Another group of students, those with sensory or physical disabilities, requires adaptations in order to negotiate the existing curriculum, however it is conceptualized. For them, the content of the curriculum itself is not typically at issue; rather, the issue is how to gain access to it—through instructional modification, material adaptation, and technological advances.

Finally, other students, chiefly those with mild disabilities, usually have been removed from general classrooms only after they have come into contact with the core curriculum, on a part- or full-time basis. For them, instruction in the core curriculum has failed to provide motivation and/or successful learning experiences. Special education is meant to provide both and, as much as is feasible, ensure their interaction with their general education peers. What is unclear is the degree to which the core curriculum in general education still represents the desired educational outcomes for these students and how the aim of integration might be balanced with academic outcomes. It is for students with mild disabilities, who comprise the largest and fastest-growing number of students in special education,[2] that curriculum and, more specifically, integration into the general education curriculum pose the most thorny issues.

Since the late 1960s, the special education field has actively supported policies that favor educating students with disabilities in the "least restrictive environment." In fact, the explicit goal of many special education programs is to return students to the general education setting for as much of their school day as possible. Although special educators hold different views of how much integration should be advocated for students,[3] there is general agreement on the broad goal of fostering and maintaining successful integration in general education programs for students with disabilities. Our intent here is not to enter into this debate (see chap. 4) but rather to consider the implications of advocating a general education core curriculum when integration for students with disabilities is in fact deemed justifiable.

WHY THE TRADITIONAL CURRICULUM POSES A DILEMMA FOR INTEGRATION

General education focuses on the common needs, problems, interests, and concerns of young people and society.[4] Through the development of curriculum, educators decide what is commonly taught and learned. As Tyler puts it in his now classic monograph on curriculum development, common curriculum concerns grow out of a consideration of three competing but not contradicting elements: the learners themselves, society's needs, and the major functions the subject areas can play in advancing education.[5] According to Dewey, the interaction of all three elements is paramount;[6] in the absence of such interaction, one element is likely to be pursued and defended in opposition to the other two. Contemporary critics have noted that, as Dewey predicted, today's common curriculum typically is interpreted in terms of academic subjects alone.[7] In this conception of curriculum, it is assumed that what is important to know is limited to what can be found in the content of the various subject areas. The other two elements—namely, the learners and the needs of society—are relegated to diminished importance relative to academic content. Notwithstanding the fact that the academic content taught is often dull, it nevertheless dominates.

Typically, subject-area curriculum content is learned within a school organizational structure called the "graded school."[8] In graded schools, the curriculum is delivered to groups of students by a single teacher. The content is organized sequentially so that students of the same chronological age progress through or learn the same material at the same pace. Tests and assessments sort out those students who cannot learn at the same rate as their peers. The graded school requires an organizational scaffolding in which the curriculum is divided into equal segments, instruction proceeds along a predetermined scope and sequence arrangement based on the acquisition of isolated academic skills, tests determine whether the knowledge and skills have been learned, and promotion is allowed only for those students who have attained the minimal levels set for each grade.

As Paris and Oka point out, when achievement standards are used to measure children's learning and performance, it is inevitable that some children will fail more often than others.[9] Aptitudes, whether measured through academic learning or through other abilities, are normally distributed, and thus measures that compare relative achievement among students usually will identify an unsuccessful group (see chap. 7). When successful achievement is defined by academic subject mastery alone, schools become active participants in the sort-and-select process, a process that is based on predictions of future paths individual students may follow in their lives.[10] There is little leeway for students who learn at a different pace, who require a different style of teaching, or who bring different ways of reacting and behaving into the classroom. Seen from this vantage point, an unavoidable outgrowth of the graded school system is special education. Those students who cannot achieve in the general education classroom are identified and sorted into programs that, it is said, better address their specialized needs.[11]

But students identified as having disabilities are not the only ones who are unable to keep up with the standard, lock-step curriculum. Many others also have difficulty achieving basic literacy and numeracy. Large numbers of students who are members of racial, ethnic, or linguistic minorities and students who are termed at-risk for reasons such as lower socioeconomic status or socioemotional lability are included in the growing list of those for whom the mainstream educational system is failing.[12] The dominant approach to curriculum is not meeting the educational needs of large numbers of low-achieving students who do not fall under the aegis of special education but for whom a pullout or separate system of remedial education is proposed and carried out under the rubric of compensatory education. A curriculum based on the assumption that most children come to school ready to learn, with some rudimentary knowledge of the alphabet and prereading skills like knowing how to hold a book and employing left-to-right progression, is not easily absorbed by the large numbers of students who may not, in fact, come to school with these skills. Given the pressure to succeed in each grade level in a lock-step fashion, students who fail to demonstrate these skills early on rarely catch up. To reduce the pressure on teachers, and ostensibly to better meet the needs of various ability groups, tracking has become a near universal but highly ineffective feature of schooling.[13] Additionally, retention as early as kindergarten is a common yet inappropriate outgrowth of the current approach to curriculum and to the graded school as a means of its transmission.[14]

Despite the many acknowledged problems with the standard, graded-school curriculum, the proliferation of the graded school as the predominant organizing structure for delivering the curriculum has most often led to school reform proposals that are focused on increasing subject-area achievement through adherence to a common core curriculum. In the early wave of reforms, Adler's Paideia Proposal[15] and Boyer's analysis of high schools[16] both advocated this approach to curriculum reform. These were followed by more recent critics who have argued that what is needed is a common core curriculum, one that ensures that all students learn a common body of knowledge that is essential for living in this society.[17]

These discussions have been fueled by results from national assessments suggesting that students in the United States are lagging behind students in other industrial countries with regard to higher-level knowledge in math and science[18] and from employability studies that point to a growing undereducated work force that increasingly jeopardizes the country's economic security.[19] Reforms in general education have attempted to reverse these trends by toughening academic standards and graduation requirements,[20] and a common theme is "more rigorous content for all students."[21]

Adherence to academic content alone as the approach to the organization and delivery of the curriculum has serious implications not only for the education of students with disabilities but for the ever increasing percentage of students who are unsuccessful in meeting academic expectations of schooling. If the previous curriculum was too much for them, then the direction in which general education is moving—toward that of higher standards, more content depth, as well as increased expectations for higher-order thinking skills—may indeed compound potential difficulties for integration. Given that most school systems still use the graded structure, students with mild learning or behavioral differences, including those who have never left and those who may be returned to the mainstream, must be able to fit into that structure if they are to succeed.

The assumptions on which the graded structure is built ensure that adaptation for individuals is difficult, if not impossible, to achieve. The graded structure assumes that all students of the same chronological age are ready to be taught the same objectives, that all students require the same amount of time to master the predesignated objectives, and that all students can master the predesignated objectives for the grade level across all curriculum areas during the same year.[22] Unfortunately, these assumptions are not founded in either research or in the practices observed in schools.[23]

In response to the limitations of the lock-step system, many general education teachers have made efforts over the past decade to individualize instruction and to introduce instructional strategies that attempt to meet a wider range of learner variance.[24] However, a study of general education practices as they pertain to facilitating inclusion of students with disabilities indicates that flexibility is difficult to accomplish within a lock-step structure:

> Teachers did not make professional decisions about what to teach their students; for all subjects they followed the sequence of lessons outlined in teachers' manuals, deviating only if required by district mandates. This meant that students often missed learning some important skills that were covered in units late in their books. The teachers did not seem insensitive to the needs of the slowest or the fastest student; but they were more committed to routine than to addressing individual difference.[25]

Thus, the structure of the curriculum itself exerts a profound influence on the actions teachers take in their classrooms and, driven by a uniform conception of curriculum as the routine acquisition of subject matter, impedes even the best-intentioned efforts to provide for individualization. Rather than attempting to adapt a curriculum and school structure that appear to be fundamentally ill suited to the increasingly diverse nature of the student population, it seems wise to accept the condition that it probably is impossible to encompass these differences within the educational expectations and specifications of a strictly graded system.[26]

But problems with the dominant curriculum structure are not new; indeed, they have been recognized by professionals in special and general education alike. Shifting demographics and the unyielding data, year after year, indicating an unacceptable rate of school failure, particularly for students who hold minority status, make ever more pressing the question of what constitutes an appropriate, effective conception of curriculum for today's children and youth. In this light, special educators' concerns about integration can provide an expanded context for the consideration of curriculum limitations and can represent a potential source of support for reform of the curriculum.

CURRICULUM TRADITIONS IN SPECIAL EDUCATION

Since the enactment of PL 94-142, special educators have struggled to balance two sometimes competing requirements: providing an individualized education program (IEP) and doing so in an educational setting that is deemed to be the least restrictive one. In general education, what a student learns and where he or she learns it are inseparable; in special education, this has not been the case. To understand curriculum traditions in special education fully, both the location of the education, or placement, and the individualized program, must be considered.

The IEP as Curriculum

Because the IEP is required by law, in practice it has often become the curriculum for students with disabilities. In theory, for students in special education, the curriculum should be adapted to meet their unique needs through the IEP. The development of the IEP is intended to be the major activity by which special education intersects with the general education curriculum, although in practice this is not typically the case.[27] The IEP is meant to identify not only the specific curriculum needs of each student but also the concomitant instructional approaches to be used. As such, it is a tool developed specifically to protect individual difference as an educational reality within the schools, the vehicle by which the common curriculum is to be tailored to allow success for students with disabilities. It is the IEP that should protect special education students from sameness in instruction. Likewise, it is also the vehicle by which professionals enter into formal agreement that the standard curriculum may not be at all appropriate for some students.

Goldstein suggests that knowledge of curriculum is the basis on which all individualized instructional planning for special education should take place.[28] Curriculum knowledge, she argues, is the "keystone" from which differentiation should emanate. Simultaneously, however, Goldstein observes that curriculum knowledge is effectively absent from the world of special education. As a result, the selection of curriculum by special educators represented in the development and implementation of IEPs is idiosyncratic at best and lacks continuity either with the general curriculum or with subsequent experiences within special education. Goldstein's early admonitions regarding curriculum are borne out in recent research on the content of special education and other forms of remedial instruction. As stated earlier, these studies have documented the absence of a coherent relationship between curriculum choices in special education or remedial pullout programs and the curriculum in general education classrooms, specifically in the area of literacy instruction.[29] Rather than providing instructional support to increase the likelihood that students obtain the core curriculum, special and remedial education teachers define their own curricula and use a variety of materials to attain them, often without adequate regard for what goes on in the general classroom.

In addition to the fragmented nature of the content that is presented in special and remedial education relative to the general curriculum, the degree of individualized planning based on specific curriculum adaptations that takes place within special education is unclear. Wesson and Deno, in an analysis of IEPs in reading, have found little if any differentiation among plans for mildly handicapped students in resource rooms.[30] Similarly, Ysseldyke and his colleagues have noticed little difference in actual instruction across three categories of mild disability.[31] The promise of individual curriculum adaptation does not seem to have come to pass, or, as Smith concludes after reviewing a decade of research on IEPs, "as practitioners, perhaps we should acknowledge the IEP as nonviable and impractical and pursue other methods that show evidence of 'specially designed instruction.'"[32]

In the presence of a standard, general curriculum that has failed students identified as having disabilities, special education seems to have provided little in the way of meeting individual needs in relationship to adapting the common curriculum. This state of affairs is particularly troublesome given the undue amount of time special education teachers report spending on paperwork (which often includes IEPs), a requirement that contributes heavily to teachers' decisions to leave special education.[33]

PROVIDING THE CURRICULUM IN
THE LEAST RESTRICTIVE ENVIRONMENT

The IEP dictates not only what a student should learn but also where that student will learn. Inclusion has long been a goal to which special educators aspire, and the general classroom is the setting in which special educators have wanted their students to be included. This preference for the general classroom is operationalized in the least restrictive environment clause of PL 94-142 and denotes, in essence, an acceptance of the core curriculum as a suitable goal for most special education students and definitely for students with mild disabilities. In fact, as some special educators point out, those who argue in favor of integration assume that the curriculum in general education is developmentally appropriate and that students will receive a curriculum matched to their individual needs.[34] Consequently, when students with disabilities are assigned to a general education setting, the general education curriculum comes with the package.

Without support, few students with disabilities can easily make the transition into both a general education setting and a general education curriculum. This support has often taken the form of alternative programming, with the focus on "getting the student back into the mainstream" rather than on learning the core curriculum.

Special education professionals have not generally been interested in the form and content of the core curriculum.[35] Rather, in their own practice, special educators have looked to these alternative orientations toward curriculum as a basis for programming with students who have mild disabilities. According to Polloway and his colleagues, these orientations include (1) remediation of academic skills and development of social competency, (2) maintenance of general education skills through such approaches as tutoring and learning strategies, and (3) functional focus as it relates to vocational and/or adult outcomes.[36]

Note that both the remediation and maintenance orientations hold mastery over the core curriculum, however it is structured, to be an acceptable goal; they offer assistance to students in acquiring competence in discrete skills and strategies as a means of enabling a speedy return to the curriculum of the general classroom. Decisions about curriculum content and form are left to general education colleagues, with efforts focused on aligning special education instruction to the core curriculum as exemplified in the recent reform efforts in California.[37]

Observational studies have questioned the assumption that effective instructional practices in the pullout component are aligned with the core curriculum.[38] These conclusions are based on findings that the curriculum materials students most often use in their pullout programs are not linked to the core curriculum and that virtually no attempt is made to help students integrate what is learned in resource rooms with what is taught in general education classrooms. Further, special educators tend to treat the standard curriculum as a collection of academic activities that their students will tap into whenever they are ready to spend time in general education classes, which leads to fragmentation of content learning and denies students a consistent exposure to the scope and sequence of the curriculum area.

The implications of this pullout system tend to surface when grades must be given. Students with disabilities enrolled in general education classes are more likely than other students to receive failing grades, apparently because general education standards are more difficult to attain than those used in special classes.[39] In response to this dilemma, some districts have lowered graduation requirements and made available separate diplomas for special education students, practices that some consider further evidence that special education students do not receive education commensurate with students in general education programs. A long-standing issue for all educators has been determining the meaning of grades, deciding whether educators should evaluate students with special needs by the same standards as other students, and selecting equitable forms of student evaluation, particularly when students have not met the course objectives.[40]

As a means of establishing standards for students who are formally identified as having disabilities, special educators develop individual standards for every student through the IEP. Thus, the position special educators take is that students receiving their services should be evaluated according to how they have progressed on their IEPs, not to the standards of the general education curriculum. Given the current educational system, in which the practice of individualization seems to run counter to the prevailing curriculum structure, implementing the IEP has met with confusion, and limitations have surfaced. Because individualization is not easily provided in the context of general education, more specialized programming takes place within special education. Special educators spend more and more time in basic skill remediation, preparing students to return to the general program, and devote less and less time to the study of subject domains.

DEFINING THE CURRICULUM ORIENTATION
OF SPECIAL EDUCATION

Given that the general curriculum has not been the focus of special education practice and that achieving individualized instruction has not occurred through the IEP, what is the curriculum that special education students actually do experience in school? What content do they encounter, and in what ways does it differ from approaches to the core curriculum?

Typically, the curriculum in special education classes is limited to basic literacy and numeracy;[41] access to content is restricted to low-level curriculum texts, particularly in reading. Exposure to social studies, science, and the arts occurs in the context of a mainstreamed classroom or not at all. Scheduling problems associated with the prevalent pullout model often preclude special education students from participating in subjects other than reading and mathematics.[42] As a result of the prevailing practice of teaching basic skills in special education classes, the curriculum is clearly differentiated from that of general education; there is less of it, fewer subjects are valued as important to study, and consequently, children's educational experience is severely limited. In relationship to the age-old curriculum question "What's worth knowing?" the curriculum as it is enacted within special education reflects a set of skills that are believed to form the foundation for the acquisition of an academic curriculum in the tradition of academic rationalism, but the set in itself is narrowly conceived. Clearly, there is more worth knowing.

Within special education, preparation for the academic curriculum is grounded in a concern for organizing and packaging instructional material for efficient learning.[43] Eisner and Vallance classify philosophies of education that favor efficiency of instructional means over ends as "technological" approaches to schooling.[44] In the quest for efficiency, content is subordinated to process in many instructional programs in special education. Programs like DISTAR, for example, are concerned primarily with the efficient acquisition of basic skills.[45] Related to this concern for efficiency is the widespread use of extrinsic reinforcement, which is also based in a technological mode of schooling. Centrally concerned with the efficient acquisition of measurable skills as an educational end, special educators have relied on various forms of behavioral management that have long accompanied the practice of special education. It is not uncommon for the implementation of behavioral management programs to overshadow academic content in special education classrooms.[46]

Similarly, even some of the recent attempts to foster cognitive-mediational, or strategic, learning within special education isolate the strategies themselves from meaningful instruction and teach them as a rigid set of efficient prescriptions.[47] Although the trend toward strategy instruction is generally quite promising because it provides teachers with approaches to enhance their students' involvement in complex, independent thinking and problem solving, the teaching and learning of strategies has to be linked to curriculum content in order to be effective.[48] Strategies themselves, taught in isolation and devoid of linkages to academic content, do not constitute a curriculum.

Pairing a technological curriculum orientation with a truncated view of the role of subject-matter content has resulted in a narrow view of schooling for students in special education classes. Meaningful, child-centered experi-

ences in school do not characterize the curriculum choices that special educators have made. Special education has been slow to respond to the construc-
tivist paradigm,[49] which suggests that the most powerful approach to learning is based in meaningful literacy and numeracy experiences. What is most
striking within special education classes seems to be the homogeneity of a
curriculum grounded in a remarkably similar set of curriculum practices—
namely, the study of isolated skills and strategies—taken to an extreme in
relationship to similar curriculum practices within general education.

In short, the curriculum that special education has enacted over the
years, and the whole school context in which special education takes place,
have interacted to disenfranchise students from access to a broad, rich, and
meaningful education. A similar disenfranchisement takes place with
respect to low-achieving minority students in urban schools.[50] Not only has
the curriculum itself been narrow, but it is implemented in a context that
deprives special education students of the opportunity to participate in a
unified learning community in the classroom. Simply put, there is little
opportunity to be engaged in a community of learners when the student is
either working on individual, skill-driven remediation in a segregated special education setting or else spending part of the day in one classroom and
part in another but unavailable to be part of the group for much of the
time. With community lacking in both settings, the chance for meaningful
school experiences is further limited.

As a result of these curriculum dynamics, special education seems to
function more like another curriculum track, similar to those described in
the work of Oakes.[51] The curriculum itself is highly differentiated from the
intent of the general education curriculum, but instructional differentiation
within special education classes (between as well as within categories of mild
disability, especially) is limited.[52] Curriculum differentiation is the signal
difference in the way special education typically accommodates for individual difference. But for most special education students, namely those with
mild disabilities, this role as a separate track is not a legitimate one. Special
education is meant to be a temporary intervention to enable students to
"catch up" and return to the general curriculum or to support students in
their participation in the general school curriculum. However, because only
a small percentage of special education students ever exit from their special
education programs,[53] the tracking analogy holds. The classic problems
with tracking, which are seen as "fragmenting students' educational experiences and as denying large numbers of students access to knowledge and in
effect, denying access to an education of quality,"[54] are precisely the kinds
of problems that characterize the curriculum of special education.

THE SEARCH FOR A BALANCED CURRICULUM

Given the inherent difficulties in the prevailing general curriculum structure, as well as the limitations on curriculum as it is enacted within special

education, the task of ensuring that most students will master a core curriculum is formidable. The dominant educational practices in this country—tracking, age-graded classes, and a content-driven curriculum—function, after all, under the assumption that large groups of students, including many children and youth with disabilities, are not worthy of access to high-status subjects or meaningful school experiences. Although the structural features that have been created to absorb the high rates of failure resulting from this system appear not to foster student achievement, these structural features are well entrenched and often supported by bureaucracies designed to maintain their status.

For special education, the challenge goes far beyond the logistics of physical proximity to general education classrooms and raises the basic question of how access to the curriculum can be made equitable. Even with years of attention to the task, integration of students with varying degrees of readiness has remained an elusive goal for the schools. At its most fundamental level, the structure of the general education curriculum poses problems for students with disabilities, and these problems affect the ease and success with which integration can occur at the classroom level. Special education as the large, separate system we know it to be today came about for a particular set of reasons anchored in the structure of the general education curriculum. The specific challenge now is whether a core curriculum can be developed and delivered that gives students access not only to the classroom but to the acquisition of knowledge as well.

But providing equity is not a simple matter. Goodlad and Oakes state that at the root of a school organization that supports limited access to knowledge for certain groups of students is a limited conception of what intellectual and character development actually mean.[55] At a minimum, they argue, these misconceptions about learning and individual difference (and the educational structure that these misconceptions have led educators to create) must be rejected and replaced with a new, more equitable structure.

Precedence for an inclusive, equity-oriented approach to schooling exists in a landmark court ruling in Kentucky.[56] The court found that although universal education has historically meant universal opportunity—and not all children were expected to master the entire curriculum—this practice would no longer be tolerated. Schools in Kentucky are now charged with providing equal access to knowledge, which implies the acquisition of knowledge itself. How this will be achieved and whether it will be successful are precisely the sorts of challenges facing those who promote equitable results of access to knowledge for greater numbers of children in schools, including those who are currently in special education.

Despite these well-intentioned directives for equity in access to knowledge, nobody has yet developed curriculum arrangements that best create and sustain the expectation that most students can, in fact, be successful in school. In what currently exists, we face a general education tradition in which individual difference has held little importance and a special education tradition in which curriculum content is watered down at best. Reconciling these two disparate traditions is not likely to be an easy task. But, as Goodlad points out, "if knowledge is to be increasingly democratized—that is, extended to larger percentages of the population for longer periods of time—then it simultaneously must be increasingly humanized—that is, rendered in such way as to be learnable."[57] The challenge to create a school structure that promotes the right of all children to acquire knowledge pertains not only to students with disabilities but to the student population in general.

Notwithstanding problems with the curriculum as it is currently conceptualized and enacted in general and special education alike, both sides bring strengths to curriculum reform efforts. Glatthorn suggests that special and general educators form interdisciplinary teams to share perspectives in curriculum reform discussions.[58] As part of joint professional development efforts, Glatthorn envisions cooperative teams composed of special and general education teachers operationalizing, adapting, and enriching the curriculum to serve all students better. What specific strengths would be brought to such a set of discussions?

For its part, special education has always expressed concern for meeting the individual needs of students. Special education has consistently voiced the position that children and youth do not all learn the same way and that a single approach to learning is not likely to suffice.[59] A second strength special education brings to discussions of curriculum reform is its concern for societal acceptance of differences among students in the schools. Because concerns for societal acceptance of difference certainly do not rest with special education alone, special educators have the opportunity to forge new alliances with like-minded general educators. Finally, special education has kept at the forefront of its work, especially in the area of moderate, severe, and profound disabilities, a concern for the quality of life of its graduates.

General education brings important complementary strengths to the reform efforts. Clearly, it is the general education constituency that is concerned for identifying what is most worth teaching and learning in school; content and its place in the realm of education are at the forefront of the general education enterprise. Also, general education tends to focus more on the classroom as a group and, at its best, as a community of learners. The tendency to be concerned for the place of the individual within the group and its community is an important aspect of curriculum reform, particularly as it relates to the notion of curriculum as the total experience of schooling.

Curriculum reform that needs to be achieved through discussions among special and general educators should attend to the balance between their relative strengths. Balancing those strengths hails back to the three sources of curriculum goals noted by Tyler but identified earlier by Dewey—namely, the learner, the society, and the subject matter. Combining the strengths of special and general education and the singular concerns each field seems to express might do much to help us begin developing a curriculum that does not simply treat each of these three separately, as Tyler did, but also leads to their real integration.[60]

COMPLEMENTARY, NOT COMPETING, CURRICULUM ORIENTATIONS

In embarking on joint discussions of curriculum and its place vis-à-vis integration, it is important also to understand the underlying philosophies that have driven the various educational commitments we see in special and general education today. One classic schema for analyzing philosophies of curriculum is Eisner and Vallance's enumeration of five competing conceptions of curriculum.[61] Each conception places differing emphasis on curriculum content, goals, and organization as a means of fostering different educational goals. This schema provides a heuristic by which to describe the goals and content of the special and education curriculum. Further, it highlights the familiar fact that educators hold varying views regarding the purpose of education—and the way curriculum should be organized to achieve it—varying views that derive from deeply held convictions about what is best for children. Let us take a closer look at these competing conceptions of curriculum.

1. *Curriculum as the development of cognitive processes.* This conception of curriculum is based on the belief that the goal of education is to provide students with "a repertoire of essentially content-independent cognitive skills applicable to a variety of situations."[62] These generalizable psychological processes can then be applied to any situation. This curriculum orientation is not concerned with content per se.

2. *Curriculum as the technical organization of material.* This conception of curriculum is derived from the belief that the goal of education is to provide students with the most efficient means of learning whatever content they are expected to know. Similar to the cognitive processes approach, this orientation is not concerned with content either but instead sees the technological processes of learning as primary.

3. *Curriculum as self-actualization.* This conception of curriculum is "child centered, autonomy and growth oriented, and education is seen as an enabling process that would provide the means to personal liberation and development."[63] The choice of content is directly related to how it promotes self-growth, and it is the whole experience of schooling and the results of that experience in terms of personal development that constitute the curriculum. The purpose of curriculum is to provide an integrated educational experience in the context of a community of learners. This orientation to curriculum stands in clear contrast to the first two, in which content is a means to an end. In this conception of curriculum, content and process interact as mutual supports for the goal of personal autonomy.

4. *Curriculum as social reconstruction.* This conception of curriculum is closely related to curriculum as self-actualization, but the goal of schooling extends beyond personal growth to its function as a means to social reform. Curriculum in this conception is also a total experience; "it is the traditional view of schooling as the bootstrap by which society can change itself."[64] Social issues and the values that are most supportive of societal change are explicit in this curriculum tradition.

5. *Curriculum as academic rationalism.* In this view, the purpose of curriculum is to transmit the common cultural knowledge of the society as a means of fostering a democracy. It stresses the acquisition of classic information and concepts stemming from what is thought to be the best thinking of humankind. It encompasses the study of the traditional disciplines, although how those are defined is changing as we approach the twenty-first century. Current approaches to the general education curriculum, based as they are in subject-matter content, most often represent an academic rationalist perspective.

Eisner and Vallance recognize that no approach to curriculum is as pure as their conceptions would suggest, and setting these five as competing conceptions would be inappropriate given the curriculum reform effort we envision for schools of the future. What may be a more fruitful approach is to talk about complementary conceptions of curriculum, in which Eisner and Vallance's specific orientations are integrated as needed to form a balanced curriculum. Each conception then might act as a screen against which curriculum decisions could be measured, in the way that Tyler's philosophical and psychological screens were meant to provide a check against academic rationalism alone.[65]

How might each conception be part of the picture of curriculum reform? As noted previously, for example, academic content has not been a primary concern for special education professionals (see chap. 2), but it needs to be, especially for the large number of students labeled as having mild disabilities. Students should be learning meaningful academic content; moreover, they are capable of learning a higher order of content than has previously been thought appropriate.[66] The cognitive approach, which is supported by research on social constructivism, continues to show the importance of acquiring powerful strategies to foster independent learning.[67] One of the important tenets of this approach to curriculum is that strategies are acquired in the context of meaningful content, which links it with the concerns for curriculum content within the academic rationalism tradition.

The concern for personal relevance is one that has been lacking in both special and general education, where the acquisition of skills, basic or otherwise, in the absence of meaningful context has been the norm. The trend toward more interdisciplinary curriculum at the elementary, middle, and secondary level is also an attempt to reintroduce personal relevance into the curriculum.[68] Perhaps more important, redesigning the structure of schools—away from age-graded classes and toward multiage teams, smaller schools, and schools within schools—should provide a sense of school as generally a meaningful place.

A concern for curriculum as social reconstruction might include two dimensions of reform: the social acceptance of disability and difference within the school (whether or not curriculum differentiation is needed) and efforts to make schools less competitive and more supportive through alternative organizational dynamics. Here, approaches like cooperative learning,[69] classwide peer tutoring,[70] and a revival of Goodlad and Anderson's nongraded primary school for four-, five-, six-, and seven-year-olds[71] hold promise for accommodating the diversity of learners in schools.

Finally, regarding curriculum as technology, there are without question places where efficiency in learning would be welcomed. For example, in *Becoming a Nation of Readers,* the Commission on Reading found that the teaching of phonics, which should be done early and simply, consistently lacked good instructional design.[72] Curriculum as technology, carefully used, would likely be a useful adjunct to the high-level content and process knowledge that people need to negotiate in today's complex world; however, it should always be seen as a means, not as a curriculum end.

If we see these five orientations to curriculum as competing, we focus more on their exclusivity than on the need for their complementarity as part of more inclusive curriculum practices in the schools. If we accept the idea that curriculum is the total experience of schooling,[73] then each conception of curriculum has a place in making school successful for all students.

The Persistent Issue of Individual Difference

According to Fenstermacher, there is "some doubt whether matters of individual difference are a red herring or a red flag when considering the feasibility of a common curriculum."[74] Yet the question of how to deal with individual difference within the framework of a common general curriculum is an enduring one, and it is clearly a red flag for special educators who are concerned about the capability of the curriculum to accommodate differences in students. The question is whether it is the curriculum that needs to be individualized, which thus violates the notion of a common core, or whether the instructional approaches to a core curriculum should be individualized.

Guided by a general adherence to academic rationalism, the existing common curriculum has failed to achieve the goal of accommodating individual difference through instructional variation.[75] Likewise, creating different curriculum tracks, through formal tracking or remedial/special education programs, has been equally ineffective. In conceptualizing an alternative curriculum orientation, one that is better able to capture and sustain the interest of children and youth in today's schools, it seems apparent that a successful curriculum philosophy will need to guide reform efforts such that (1) a single curriculum orientation is not adhered to exclusively and (2) instructional variation is built into the plan, reserving curriculum differentiation for cases of enduring disability that require such action. Hardwiring the curriculum to meet individual needs, accompanied by structural changes that support a more flexible orientation to schooling, will do much to preclude the necessity for the differentiated curriculum tracks that now begin as early as kindergarten.

Certainly there are profound individual differences among students; they exist in every classroom in every school in the United States. The problem of meeting them comes from assuming too quickly that some children are incapable of producing quality work, which results in either removing them from the general education classroom or relegating them to low tracks within general education. Pulling children out for compensatory and special education or tracking confuses the issue by assuming that the existence of individual differences is solved by separation. An opportunity exists to clear up this confusion and to make good use of special education's traditional worry about meeting individual needs. As equal participants in curriculum reform, special and general educators have the potential opportunity, by adopting a more accommodating approach to curriculum, to debunk the assumption that differentiated, separate curricula is the answer to student diversity. When the curriculum itself takes individual needs into account, the specter of individual difference as something that cannot be accommodated within the general education classroom recedes.

SUPPORTING THE CHALLENGE AHEAD

Succeeding at this curriculum transformation requires hard work. But such efforts stand to gain momentum and authority from an alignment of the resources and energy of all those for whom the current curriculum has posed difficulties. An important member of the necessary constituency is special education. The successful alignment of special and general education with respect to issues of curriculum will depend in part on establishing the belief that the curriculum needs to be structured such that most students, whether or not they are identified as needing special education, ought to be able to achieve it. It will also be necessary to continue to clarify that for some students with enduring disabilities, the core academic curriculum, no matter how it is conceptualized, will not be appropriate.

The distinction between curriculum goals for students with mild disabilities and social goals in integrated settings for students with more enduring disabilities is rarely addressed in the integration literature in special education, usually because of confusion between the legitimate social goal of integration and integration as a strictly academic pursuit. One of the obstacles to achieving integration arises when it is discussed outside of the context of curriculum, which then leaves unaddressed the question of the point at which individual difference leads to the need for radically different curricula. Only when the shortcomings of the general education curriculum are analyzed and mapped against a consideration of the special education curriculum does it become clear that for most students in special education, a restructuring of the curriculum itself—not the development of a series of different curricula—is probably the best means of creating the conditions for educational success.

As the general field of education struggles to gain acceptance for a new concept of curriculum, special educators have a central role to play. Special educators represent a constituency that can argue eloquently for a concept of curriculum that addresses diversity in the student population. When combined with the existing efforts of professionals in the subject areas who are already working toward this end, a coalition can be built to press for curriculum reform that benefits all children.

Special education stands to gain a great deal from becoming an active participant in the curriculum reform process; if such reform is successful, many of the students who are now in special education may be able to participate as full members of the general education communities in their schools. For students with enduring disabilities, those who cannot profit from the general education curriculum, however reformed, the social aim of integration must be recognized and held paramount as a social goal of schooling. When academic content diverges, it must do so in a context of acceptance for its purpose.

The social goal of integration brings to the forefront an age-old dilemma facing public schools: that of how to educate all the nation's children, no matter how diverse. Our country is one of the few in the world that holds that all children have a right to an education. In a democratic form of government, citizens are capable of carrying out their responsibilities of self-governance only when they are well educated. We cannot afford to let education for children and youth with mild disabilities dissolve or become diluted out of administrative convenience or out of confusion with the place of curriculum. We must, as Wiggins states, "undercut this utterly undemocratic myth that some students aren't capable of quality work."[76] What we can do is use the current discussion as a springboard to rethink curriculum and rechannel our energies into improving educational circumstances for all children. By modifying the ways in which we think about curriculum, we can intelligently discuss what is good for content, what is good for the learner, and, indeed, what is good for society.

NOTES

1. The term *curriculum* has many interpretations on many levels. In this chapter, we have used it generically to refer to Elliot Eisner's concept of the explicit curriculum (*The Educational Imagination*, 1979), or the goals and objectives for all of

the various content areas. However, the explicit curriculum is mediated by each teacher who teaches or interprets it so that what students actually learn as a result of schooling is rarely, if ever, an exact match with the explicit curriculum. To be sure, students also learn a great deal that is not explicit, namely, the "hidden" curriculum (see, for example, Phillip W. Jackson's *Life in Classrooms*, 1968). Therefore, it is important in any consideration of curriculum to realize that constructing a curriculum for others' use does not assure that it will be interpreted as developed. Miriam Ben-Peretz, in her book *The Teacher-Curriculum Encounter: Freeing Teachers from the Tyranny of Texts* (Albany: State University of New York Press, 1990) uses the term *curriculum potential* to indicate the relationship between curriculum materials themselves and how teachers embellish, or interpret, those materials in the act of teaching.

2. Office of Special Education Programs, *To Assure the Free Appropriate Public Education for All Handicapped Children: The Twelfth Annual Report to Congress on the Implementation of the Education of the Handicapped Act* (Washington, D.C.: U.S. Department of Education, 1990).

3. For discussions on what has been termed the "regular education initiative," see Bob Algozzine, Larry Maheady, Katherine C. Sacca, Larry O'Shea, and Doris O'Shea, "Sometimes Patent Medicine Works: A Reply to Braaten, Kauffman, Braaten, Polsgrove, and Nelson," *Exceptional Children* 56 (1990): 552–57; Sheldon Braaten, James M. Kauffman, Barbara Braaten, Lewis Polsgrove, and C. Michael Nelson, "The Regular Education Initiative: Patent Medicine for Behavioral Disorders," *Exceptional Children* 55 (1988): 21–27; William E. Davis, "The Regular Education Initiative Debate: Its Promises and Problems," *Exceptional Children* 55 (1989): 440–46; Alan Gartner and Dorothy K. Lipsky, *The Yoke of Special Education: How to Break It* (Rochester, NY: National Center on Education and the Economy, 1989); Alan Gartner and Dorothy K. Lipsky, "Beyond Special Education: Toward a Quality System for All Students," *Harvard Education Review* 57 (1987): 367–95; Joseph R. Jenkins, Constance G. Pious, and Mark Jewell, "Special Education and the Regular Education Initiative: Basic Assumptions," *Exceptional Children* 56 (1990): 479–91; James M. Kauffman, Sheldon Braaten, C. Michael Nelson, Lewis Polsgrove, and Barbara Braaten, "The Regular Education Initiative and Patent Medicine: A Rejoinder to Algozzine, Maheady, Sacca, O'Shea, and O'Shea," *Exceptional Children* 56 (1990): 558–60; Lawrence Lieberman, "REI: Revisited . . . Again," *Exceptional Children* 56 (1990): 561–62; Mara Sapon-Shevin, "Working towards Merger Together: Seeing Beyond Distrust and Fear," *Teacher Education and Special Education* 11, no. 3 (1988): 103–10; Maynard C. Reynolds, Margaret Wang, and Herbert J. Walberg, "The Necessary Restructuring of Special and Regular Education," *Exceptional Children* 53 (1987): 391–98; William Stainback, Susan Stainback, Lee Courtnage, and Twila Jaben, "Facilitating Mainstreaming by Modifying the Mainstream," *Exceptional Children* 52 (1985): 144–52; Glenn A. Vergason and M. L. Anderegg, "Save the Baby! A Response to 'Integrating the Children of the Second System,'" *Phi Delta Kappan* 71, no. 1 (1989): 61–63; Margaret C. Wang, Maynard Reynolds, and Herbert J. Walberg, "Integrating the Children of the Second System," *Phi Delta Kappan* 70 (1988): 248–51; Madeline C. Will, "Educating Children with Learning Problems: A Shared Responsibility," *Exceptional Children* 52 (1986): 411–15.

4. James A. Beane, *A Middle School Curriculum: From Rhetoric to Reality* (Columbus, OH: National Middle Schools Association, 1990).

5. Ralph Tyler, *Basic Principles of Curriculum and Instruction* (Chicago: University of Chicago Press, 1949).

6. John Dewey, *The Child and the Curriculum* (Chicago: University of Chicago, 1902).

7. Beane, *A Middle School Curriculum.*

8. Larry Cuban, "The 'At-Risk' Label and the Problem of Urban School Reform," *Phi Delta Kappan* 71 (1989): 780–801.

9. Scott G. Paris and Evelyn R. Oka, "Self-regulated Learning among Exceptional Children," *Exceptional Children* 35 (1986): 103–8.

10. Michael W. Apple, *Education and Power* (Boston: Routledge & Kegan Paul, 1982).

11. At the secondary level, it has been observed that many different, often unfocused curricula exist. Ernest Boyer makes this argument in *High School* (New York: Harper & Row, 1983). Nevertheless, the same kind of sorting of students takes place despite the fact that the pressure of the academic curriculum is mitigated by the existence of these differentiated and less rigorous curricula.

12. Thomas P. Lombardi, Kerry S. Odell, and Deborah E. Novotny, "Special Education and Students at Risk: Findings from a National Study," *Remedial and Special Education* 12, no. 1 (1990): 56–62; Research for Better Schools, *A Study of Special Education: Views from America's Cities* (Philadelphia: Research for Better Schools, 1986).

13. Jeannie Oakes, *Keeping Track: How Schools Structure Inequality* (New Haven, CT: Yale University Press, 1985).

14. Lorrie A. Shepard and Mary Lee Smith, "Synthesis of Research on Grade Retention," *Educational Leadership* 47, no. 8 (1990): 84–88.

15. Mortimer J. Adler, *The Paideia Proposal: An Educational Manifesto* (New York: Macmillan, 1982).

16. Ernest L. Boyer, *High School: A Report on Secondary Education in America* (New York: Harper & Row, 1983).   ·

17. These critics include Lynn Cheney, *American Memory: A Report on the Humanities in the Nation's Public Schools* (Washington, D.C.: National Endowment for the Humanities, 1987); E. D. Hirsh, *Cultural Literacy: What Every American Needs to Know* (Boston: Houghton Mifflin, 1987); Diane Ravitch and Chester E. Finn, *What Do Our 17-Year-Olds Know? A Report of the First National Assessment of History and Literature* (New York: Harper & Row, 1987).

18. See Gregory R. Anrig and Archie E. Lapointe, "What We Don't Know about What Students Don't Know," *Educational Leadership* 47, no. 3 (1989): 4–9.

19. See, for example, American Society for Training and Development, *Training for America: Learning to Work for the 21st Century* (Alexandria, VA: American Society for Training and Development, 1989); Anthony P. Carnevale, Leila J. Gainer, and Ann S. Meltzer, *Workplace Basics: The Skills Employers Want* (Alexandria, VA: American Society for Training and Development and U.S. Department of Labor, 1988).

20. Alan A. Glatthorn, *Curriculum Reform and At-risk Youth* (Philadelphia: Research for Better Schools, 1985); John O'Neil, "Drive for National Standards Picking Up Steam," *Educational Leadership* 48, no. 5 (1991): 4–8.

21. Michael Cohen, *Restructuring the Education System: Agenda for the 1990s* (Washington, D.C.: National Governor's Association, 1988); Anne C. Lewis, "Getting Unstuck: Curriculum as a Tool of Reform," *Phi Delta Kappan* 71 (1990): 534–38.

22. William Stainback, Susan Stainback, Lee Courtnage, and Twila Jaben, "Facilitating Mainstreaming by Modifying the Mainstream," *Exceptional Children* 52 (1985): 144–52.

23. Gary D. Fenstermacher, "Introduction" in *Individual Differences and the Common Curriculum: Eighty-Second Yearbook of the National Society for the Study of Education. Part I,* ed. Gary D. Fenstermacher and John I. Goodlad (Chicago: National Society for the Study of Education, 1983).

24. Joni Alberg, "Models for Integration" in *The Regular Education Initiative: Alternative Perspectives on Concepts, Issues, and Models,* ed. John W. Lloyd, Nirbhay N. Singh, and Alan C. Repp (Sycamore, IL: Sycamore Press, 1991).

25. Janice M. Baker and Naomi Zigmond, "Are Regular Classes Equipped to Accommodate Students with Learning Disabilities?" *Exceptional Children* 56 (1990): 525.

26. John I. Goodlad and Robert H. Anderson, *The Nongraded Elementary School,* rev. ed. (New York: Teachers College Press, 1987).

27. James E. Gilliam and Margaret C. Coleman, "Who Influences IEP Committee Decisions?" *Exceptional Children* 47 (1981): 642–44; Ann Nevin, Melvin I. Semmel, and S. McCann, "What Administrators Can Do to Facilitate the Regular Classroom Teacher's Role in Implementing Individual Educational Plans: An Empirical Analysis," *Planning and Changing* 14 (1983): 150–69; Marleen C. Pugach, "Regular Classroom Teacher Involvement in the Development and Utilization of IEPs," *Exceptional Children* 48 (1982): 371–74; James E. Ysseldyke, Bob Algozzine, and D. Allen, "Participation of Regular Education Teachers in Special Education Team Decision Making," *Exceptional Children* 48 (1982): 356–66.

28. Marjorie T. Goldstein, "Curriculum: The Keystone to Instructional Planning in Special Education," paper presented at the Annual Meeting of the Association for Educational Communications and Technology (Dallas, May 1982).

29. Richard L. Allington and Peter Johnston, "Coordination, Collaboration and Consistency: The Redesign of Compensatory and Special Education" in *Effective Programs for Students at Risk,* ed. R. E. Slavin, N. L. Karweit, and N. A. Madden (Boston: Allyn & Bacon, 1989); Lorin W. Anderson and Leonard O. Pellicer, "Synthesis of Research on Compensatory and Remedial Education," *Educational Leadership* 48, no. 1 (1990): 10–21; Ann McGill-Franzen and Richard L. Allington, "The Gridlock of Low Reading Achievement: Perspectives on Practice and Policy," *Remedial and Special Education* 12, no. 3 (1991): 20–30.

30. Caren L. Wesson and Stan L. Deno, "An Analysis of Long Term Instructional Plans in Reading for Elementary Resource Room Students," *Remedial and Special Education* 10, no. 1 (1989): 21–28.

31. James E. Ysseldyke, Patrick J. O'Sullivan, Martha L. Thurlow, and Sandra L. Christenson, "Qualitative Differences in Reading and Math Instruction Received by Handicapped Students," *Remedial and Special Education* 10, no. 1 (1989): 14–20.

32. Steven W. Smith, "Individualized Education Programs (IEPs) in Special Education—From Intent to Acquiescence," *Exceptional Children* 57 (1990): 12.

33. Bonnie S. Billingsley and Lawrence H. Cross, "Teachers' Decisions to Transfer from Special to General Education," *The Journal of Special Education* 24 (1991): 496–511.

34. Harold W. Heller and Jeff Schilit, "The Regular Education Initiative: A Concerned Response," *Focus on Exceptional Children* 20, no. 3 (1987): 1–11; Joseph R. Jenkins, Constance G. Pious, and Mark Jewell, "Special Education and the Regular Education Initiative: Basic Assumptions," *Exceptional Children* 56 (1990): 479–91.

35. John O'Neil, "How 'Special' Should the Special Ed Curriculum Be?" *Curriculum Update* (Sept. 1988): 1–8.

36. Edward A. Polloway, James R. Patton, Michael H. Epstein, and Thomas E. C. Smith, "Comprehensive Curriculum for Students with Mild Handicaps," *Focus on Exceptional Children* 21, no. 8 (1989): 1–12.

37. Patricia Winget, "Education Programs Must Integrate to Benefit All Students at Every School, Says Honig," *The Special Edge* 4, no. 7 (1990): 1–4.

38. Richard Allington and Ann McGill-Franzen, "School Response to Reading Failure: Instruction for Chapter I and Special Education Students in Grades Two, Four, and Eight," *Elementary School Journal* 89 (1989): 529–42.

39. Thomas P. Lombardi, Kerry S. Odell, and Deborah E. Novotny, "Special Education and Students At Risk: Findings from a National Study," *Remedial and Special Education* 12, no. 1 (1990): 56–62.

40. Joy W. Rojewski, Richard R. Pollard, and Gary Meers, "Grading Mainstreamed Special Needs Students: Determining Practices and Attitudes of Secondary Vocational Educators Using a Qualitative Approach," *Remedial and Special Education* 12, no. 1 (1990): 7-15, 28.

41. Catherine V. Morsink, Robert S. Soar, Ruth M. Soar, and Roberta Thomas, "Research on Teaching: Opening the Door to Special Education Classrooms," *Exceptional Children* 53 (1986): 32–40.

42. McGill-Franzen and Allington, "The Gridlock of Low Reading Achievement," 20–30.

43. Peter Clough and David Thompson, "Curriculum Approaches to Learning Disabilities: Problems for the Paradigm" in *Learning Disability: Dissenting Essays* ed. B. Franklin (New York: Falmer, 1987).

44. Elliot Eisner and Elizabeth Vallance, *Conflicting Conceptions of Curriculum* (Berkeley: McCutchan, 1974).

45. Russell Gersten, John Woodward, and Craig Darch, "Direct Instruction: A Research-based Approach to Curriculum Design and Teaching," *Exceptional Children* 53 (1986): 17–31.

46. Jane Knitzer, Zina Steinberg, and Brahm Fleisch, *At the Schoolhouse Door: An Examination of Programs and Policies for Children with Behavioral and Emotional Problems* (New York: Bank Street College of Education, 1990).

47. The problem of isolating instruction in strategies is addressed by Annemarie S. Palincsar, Yvonne David, Judith Winn, and Dannelle Stevens, "Examining the Contexts of Strategy Instruction," *Remedial and Special Education* 12, no. 3 (1991): 43–53; and Carole Sue Englert, Taffy E. Raphael, Linda M. Anderson, Helene Anthony, and Danelle D. Stevens, "Making Strategies and Self-talk Visible: Writing Instruction in Regular and Special Education Classrooms," *American Educational Research Journal* 28 (1991): 337–72.

48. Lauren B. Resnick and Leopold E. Klopfer, "Toward the Thinking Curriculum: An Overview" in *Toward the Thinking Curriculum: Current Cognitive Research,* ed. L. B. Resnick and L. E. Klopfer (Washington, D.C.: Association for Supervision and Curriculum Development, 1989).

49. McGill-Franzen and Allington, "The Gridlock of Low Reading Achievement," 20–30.

50. See Annemarie S. Palincsar, "The Roles of Teachers and Students in Literacy Learning," paper presented at the Annual Meeting of the International Reading Association (Las Vegas, May 1991), for discussion of instructional choices in learning disabilities classes; and Dennis L. Carlson, "Managing the Urban School Crisis: Recent Trends in Curriculum Reform," *Journal of Education* 171, no. 3 (1989): 89–108, for a discussion of the problems with basic-skills instruction as a reform strategy in urban schools.

51. Jeannie Oakes, *Keeping Track: How Schools Structure Inequality* (New Haven, CT: Yale University Press, 1985).

52. Bob Algozzine, Catherine V. Morsink, and Kate M. Algozzine, "What's Happening in Self-contained Special Education Classrooms?" *Exceptional Children* 55 (1988): 259–65; Wesson and Deno, "An Analysis of Long Term Instructional Plans."

53. Deborah K. Walker, Judith D. Singer, Judith S. Palfrey, Michelle Orza, Martha Wenger, and John A. Butler, "Who Leaves and Who Stays in Special Education: A 2-Year Follow-up Study," *Exceptional Children* 54 (1988): 393–402.

54. Lynne Miller, "The Regular Education Initiative and School Reform: Lessons from the Mainstream," *Remedial and Special Education* 11 (1990) 3: 19.

55. John I. Goodlad and Jeannie Oakes, "We Must Offer Equal Access to Knowledge," *Educational Leadership* 45, no. 5 (1988): 16–22.

56. Jack D. Foster, "The Role of Accountability in Kentucky's Education Reform Act of 1990," *Educational Leadership* 48, no. 5 (1991): 34–36.

57. John I. Goodlad, "Individuality, Commonality, and Curriculum Practice" in *Individual Differences and the Common Curriculum*, 304.

58. Alan A. Glatthorn, "Cooperative Professional Development: Facilitating the Growth of Special Education Teachers," *Remedial and Special Education* 11, no. 3 (1990): 29–34, 50.

59. Barbara K. Keogh, "Improving Services for Problem Learners: Rethinking and Restructuring," *Journal of Learning Disabilities* 21, no. 1 (1988): 19–22; Ann L. Brown and Joseph C. Campione, "Psychological Theory and the Study of Learning Disabilities," *American Psychologist* 14 (1986): 1059–68.

60. The relationship between Dewey and Tyler's treatment of these three cornerstones of curriculum goals is addressed in Daniel Tanner and Laurel N. Tanner, *Curriculum Development: Theory into Practice* (New York: Macmillan, 1980).

61. Elliot Eisner and Elizabeth Vallance, *Conflicting Conceptions of Curriculum* (Berkeley: McCutchan, 1974).

62. Ibid., 6.

63. Ibid., 9.

64. Ibid., 11.

65. Ralph Tyler, *Basic Principles of Curriculum and Instruction* (Chicago: University of Chicago Press, 1949).

66. Henry M. Levin, "Accelerated Schools for Disadvantaged Students," *Educational Leadership* 44, (1987): 20.

67. Resnick and Klopfer, "Toward the Thinking Curriculum."

68. James A. Beane, *A Middle School Curriculum: From Rhetoric to Reality* (Columbus, OH: National Middle Schools Association, 1990); Heidi Jacobs, ed., *Interdisciplinary Curriculum: Design and Implementation* (Alexandria, VA: Association for

Supervision and Curriculum Development, 1989); Floyd J. Rutherford and Andrew Ahlgren, *Science for All Americans* (New York: Oxford University Press, 1990); Judith Zorfass, Catherine C. Morocco, Shira Persky, Arlene R. Remz, and Cynthia L. Warger, *Make It Happen! Inquiry and Technology in the Middle School Curriculum* (Newton, MA: Education Development Center; Alexandria, VA: Association for Supervision and Curriculum Development, 1991).

69. Robert E. Slavin, "Synthesis of Research on Cooperative Learning," *Educational Leadership* 48, no. 5 (1991): 71–82; Robert E. Slavin and Robert J. Stevens, "Cooperative Learning and Mainstreaming" in *The Regular Education Initiative*.

70. Larry Maheady, M. Katherine Sacca, and Glen F. Harper, "Classwide Peer Tutoring with Mildly Handicapped High School Students," *Exceptional Children* 55 (1988): 52–59.

71. John I. Goodlad and Robert H. Anderson, *The Nongraded Elementary School*, rev. ed. (New York: Teachers College Press, 1987).

72. Commission on Reading, *Becoming a Nation of Readers* (Washington, D.C.: National Academy Press, 1985).

73. Elliot W. Eisner, *The Educational Imagination* (New York: Macmillan, 1979).

74. Fenstermacher, "Introduction," 6.

75. John I. Goodlad, *A Place Called School* (New York: McGraw-Hill, 1984); Goodlad, "Individuality, Commonality, and Curricular Practice"; and Fenstermacher, "Introduction."

76. Grant Wiggins, "Experts Examine Roadblocks to Curriculum Reform," *ASCD Update* 32, no. 6 (1990): 4.

Toward a Comprehensive Program of Evaluation

Mary Lee Smith and Audrey J. Noble

Ask a special educator what is meant by evaluation, and the response is likely to touch two points: (1) diagnosis—that is, psychometric assessment of individuals for selection and placement in special education categories and programs; and (2) the pupils' accomplishment of the objectives in individualized education programs (IEPs). This view of evaluation parallels the Tylerian or goal attainment model, in which one carefully examines "inputs" and "outputs" and judges the program as good or bad based on individuals' accomplishment of the stated objectives.

Although tradition and authority recommend this model of evaluation, it overlooks elements of the program and its contexts that may be critical for an adequate analysis of the merits of special education. Consider, for example, once the child is accurately assessed and placed, what transpires from day to day, what counts as teaching and learning, what materials and resources are available, what relationships and transactions occur, and whether the lot adds up to worthwhile educational, social, and psychological experience. If one is following the goal attainment model, these concerns are concealed in a black box and largely ignored by those who ought to judge. Furthermore, the dominant view of evaluation in special education reflects a single value perspective—that there is only one set of values that special education (and evaluation of its programs and policies) must address: free and appropriate education for all those who need it. Whether or not a school complies with this value is the primary standard by which one judges the worth of the program, according to this view.

Although the goal attainment model dominates practice in special education (and perhaps the typical general education organization as well), evaluation theory has matured. In this chapter, we aim to draw on contemporary theory and practice in evaluation and policy research, and we propose a model for evaluating the comprehensive system advocated elsewhere in this book.

This chapter is committed to the idea that evaluation ought to encompass the program as a whole, including the contents of the black box and what they mean to the people involved, which exists itself in larger institutional contexts and intellectual, political, and legal systems. The purview of evaluation ought to include empirical, moral, and rational analysis aimed at (1) understanding the everyday experience of students and teachers and (2) analyzing the enactment of policies and their effects.

From our previous experience and research, we have come to believe that special education is one structure in a two-structure educational system (a point of view that is largely shared in chap. 2). Special education advocates and caring professionals have accomplished much for pupils with disabilities, particularly in promoting educational rights and in integrating delivery of instruction. Yet separation, almost to the point of moiety,[1] exists between general and special education. Members of the two groups receive disparate training, occupy different roles and positions in the school organization, and identify with different professional groups with alternative norms and ideologies (i.e., special education offers services only to those with labeled deficits and thus must subscribe to an ideology of psychological and physiological defects rather than "deficits" of curriculum or instruction).

The legal and professional history of the field and the legal markers of pupils, teachers, administrators, and resources of special education all contribute to this separation.[2] Evidence for the existence of subcultural differences is most clear when members of the two groups meet to negotiate a change in a pupil's status, which signifies a potential shift in responsibility for the welfare of that pupil from one group to the other.[3] This duality has important implications for nearly every aspect of evaluation, including who evaluates and what methods and standards are employed.

Special education advocates argue that the organizational distinctions must be maintained, or the rights of the handicapped to a free and appropriate education will be lost (see chap. 4). Desire to protect the "specialness" of special education by legal means also implies to some people that it should be protected from the scrutiny of external evaluators. It is clear, for example, that policymakers make no demands for empirical tests of the efficacy of, say, resource rooms compared to "no treatment" of the learning disabled. According to federal law, all who are identified must be served. Recall the periodic and skeptical demands for empirical proofs of the comparative effectiveness of bilingual education,[4] and one understands how immune special education has been from critical scrutiny.

This chapter follows from the themes of this volume that with the proper safeguards and critical analysis, an integrated system of special education and regular education can better serve all pupils (see chap. 1).

EVALUATION DEFINED AND REFINED

What is evaluation? Following House,[5] we define evaluation as analysis that leads to judgments about the worth of something, using defensible criteria of merit. An evaluation asks whether a particular program such as the (hypothetical) Integrated General and Special Education Program (IGSEP) at Alpha School has merit. Is it effective, good in itself or better than its alternatives, efficient, fair, worth continuing, in need of reform, accomplishing its mission, satisfactory to its constituencies, in compliance with regulations? Evaluation also pursues questions of policy, both local and national: What are the implications of Alpha District's policy of serving all pupils with multiple disabilities at one school? What are the effects of adding attention deficit disorder to the categories of handicapped pupils that schools must serve?

To answer questions such as these involves two primary considerations. First, one must consider the problem of knowledge construction and knowledge claims: How do we know when Alpha's resource room provides an effective curriculum for pupils with learning disabilities? How does a parent or policymaker judge the claim that the program was beneficial? The second consideration is about values. By what standards and criteria do we judge the worth of the program or policy? Who should judge? At what time during the life of the program should judgment occur? How and by whom should such judgments be used to modify programs?

During the thirty years in which educators and social scientists have evaluated programs and policies according to modern conceptions of evaluation, they have discovered few simple answers.[6] Solving the two problems of knowledge claims and values claims became the impetus for the development of a variety of evaluation approaches, models, and theories. In the next section, we describe several theories of knowledge and method and values.

Knowledge Claims

One basis of judgment of program worth is an adequate account (descriptions and propositions) of it. What counts as an adequate account is itself a question with implications for ontology, epistemology, methodology, and social theory. That is, what is the nature of the world, what is the nature of knowledge about it, by what means and methods can it be known, and what is the nature of social action? Although these questions form the substance for lively debate among evaluation theorists,[7] members of the two systems of schooling may view them as unimportant or settled or presuppose answers without thoroughly examining the questions.

Positivism

In an intellectual tradition dominated by psychology and medicine, such as special education, questions about knowledge claims are taken for granted or answered emphatically by appeal to the scientific method. According to the positivist view, the social world is knowable and follows universal laws that can be discovered by the use of objective methods, carefully operationalized constructs, and properly controlled procedures. Reality can be accounted for by sets of simple variables and the causal connections among them. Valid knowledge is that which corresponds to the real world external to the observer and is capable of being verified and replicated. Valid knowledge claims are believed to emanate from scientifically correct research procedures.

Furthermore, this traditional view of science and knowledge makes no distinction between physical and social or human phenomena and, consequently, no distinction between the methods of natural and social sciences. Social theory is reduced to something similar to individual trait psychology. That is, to understand social life it is necessary to understand the individuals who make up the group and their constellation of physiological and psychological traits. Applied to the evaluation of programs for children with disabilities, this set of positivist assumptions focuses primarily on correct diagnosis of pupils' characteristics and needs. This process assumes that treatment plans follow logically from accurate diagnosis of traits (analogous to medical diagnosis and treatment) and definition of treatment objectives.

The evaluation theory identified with Tyler[8] is the simplest manifestation of positivist evaluation models and the one most consistent with current thinking about evaluation in special and much of general education. In this model, the evaluator takes the expressed goals and objectives of the program and translates them into outcome measures. The program staff designs instruction to meet the goals. At the end of the program cycle, the evaluator measures attainment and compares those measurements with the stated objectives. The worth of the program is determined by the discrepancy between the two. In special education, the objectives are determined in the IEP. The teachers translate these objectives into learning activities and report each child's progress in meeting the objectives at the end of the cycle. The percentages of individual accomplishment are then aggregated into percentage of objectives met at the school or district level.

The evaluation of IEPs is only one of myriad examples of the Tylerian or goal attainment model. The plan in 1991 for a state-by-state comparison of achievement on national tests of national goals is another. The model lends itself to accountability programs, wherein state agencies examine the attainment of goals for, to cite an example, school vaccination programs to determine if public money is being used efficaciously to prevent outbreaks of infectious diseases.

Knowledge claims for Tylerian models rest on precise specification of objectives and reliable measurement of outcomes. Contemporary evaluation theorists such as House[9] criticize the model because it fails to consider broadly enough many program consequences. That is, programs can have effects, both positive and negative, that are not reflected in goals. For example, a program of integrative movement may fail to achieve its prespecified degree of gain on achievement tests but may produce dramatic gains on the self-confidence of pupils with mental retardation. Evaluations that are based on measured gains on only those dimensions the goals address may undervalue the actual benefits of the program to the participants.

Programs can also be unfair to certain populations. For example, specialized schools for creative and talented pupils may accomplish their objectives but harm ordinary children who might have benefited from the presence of gifted children in their classrooms. Thus, the goal-based evaluation might be too narrow. In addition, programs can have effects that are no better than the effects of alternative programs or of no program whatsoever. For example, young children may stutter less after a program of tongue-thrust therapy, but the improvement may be no greater than what one would expect by the same children simply developing normally, with no therapy at all.

Furthermore, goal attainment models focus only on inputs and outputs. What actually transpired in the interval between the stating of objectives and the measuring of outcomes is not itself the object of scrutiny in the goal attainment model. After reading a negative evaluation report on a program for hearing-impaired junior high school pupils, the district special education director would not be able to determine whether the program was less than successful because the teacher was not well trained, the pupils were poorly motivated, expectations were too low, the curriculum was dull, the method of measurement was invalid, or a dozen other possibilities. Besides failing to examine the contents of the program's black box, goal attainment models fail to consider the influences of context or the transactions that characterize the program.

Applied social scientists have recommended the methods of comparative experimentation as a way to establish causal links between the program itself and its consequences. In the experimental model,[10] the evaluator not only measures the intended outcomes of the program but tries to rule out alternative explanations for the effects observed. For example, if a measured effect of a program of vocational training for persons with mental retardation is their employment in a related job, the evaluator tries to establish that the program itself was responsible and that the measured outcome did not result from something else, such as the passage of time alone.

Further, the experimental evaluation model employs statistical calculation of group effects and rules out alternative explanations by randomized assignment of subjects to treatment alternatives as a way of attaining internal validity. The outcomes of the comparative studies are simple manifestations of the program goals. Knowledge claims for evaluations using this model follow from precise measurement of outcomes and careful experimental technique. In other words, the best, most valid evaluation knowledge comes from studies with the most controlled and rigorous methods. Through the internal validity that experimental methods offer, the evaluator controls bias as well as causal claims.

Although the comparative-experimental model is an obvious advancement over the goal attainment model, it is not without its critics. Cronbach,[11] for example, argues that for every rigorous experimental control the evaluator exerts, there is greater potential for some other source of spuriousness, such as artificiality and reactivity, to intrude.

Interpretivism

Evaluators who are dissatisfied with positivist models look to interpretivist theories of reality and knowledge for rationales to support alternative ways of developing accounts of programs and their effects. Interpretivists deny that a social world exists independent of one's perceptions of it. Instead of one reality, they believe in multiple realities. All knowledge, they say, is screened through a filter of individual interpretations. Knowledge is not discovered; it is constructed by a knower in direct contact with the object of knowing. Evaluation, therefore, is unavoidably subjective and must account for personal meanings of both the program participants, constituents, and the evaluators. Not only is objectivity impossible, research is a human and social endeavor that is itself value laden.[12] According to this view, subjectivity colors every stage of the evaluation process from selecting appropriate questions to study, to selecting methods of measurement, to interpreting probability statements.

Interpretivists reject the positivist tendency to reduce complex reality to simple variable definition and claims about cause and effect. Instead they see the school holistically.[13] Educational programs are causally complex, and multiple organizational, linguistic, and cultural contexts must be taken into account in examining their worth.

Objective, technically adequate methods of design, analysis, and measurement may be desirable but do not guarantee validity. All methods are fallible and can never produce, singly or in combination, a correct god's eye view of reality; findings are always subject to interpretation, open to alternative hypotheses and new data.

Interpretivists such as Stake[14] believe that the social world is complex and that the social context in which a program exists influences the program itself and must be expressly accounted for in evaluation. Teachers and pupils act toward each other and in relation to the program according to the meanings they attach to it. Consider, for example, a child assigned to a pullout program for learning disabilities. The program may be state-of-the-art in curriculum and instruction, but classmates still describe her leaving as "going to the dummy class." Because of this social meaning and her accommodation to it, the child experiences a different "curriculum" than the one the program staff believes they deliver. Another child going to the same class may work out with the teacher a different definition of the situation that rejects the classmates' characterization. Because individuals act in a situation according to the meanings they assign to it, program results are less predictable than they seem to be by simply examining goals and test results.

Interpretivist evaluators, therefore, must get close to the social processes where such individual and collective meanings are constructed and must take intention and social context into account in searching for program effects. These evaluators directly observe everyday actions in natural settings and form relationships with participants so that their meanings can be revealed.

For evaluators of the interpretivist persuasion, understanding the meanings and actions of teachers, parents, and pupils is of primary importance. Teaching is not a technical or mechanical transmission of skills prescribed by experts and packaged in curricula. Instead, teachers act on the material, transform it, integrate it with personal, often unarticulated knowledge (as distinct from formal or propositional knowledge), and reconstruct it in transactions with pupils. The evaluator must be present to observe and record this process, or the evaluation will be incomplete. To ignore the teachers' perspective or to treat teachers as passive research "subjects" is to distort the evaluation. Qualitative, naturalistic, ethnographic, or illuminative approaches best reflect the genuine worth of an endeavor.[15]

The interpretivists' view of social life dictates that evaluations encompass not only the everyday actions of program participants but the processes of pupil identification and selection for special programs. The positivist views selection as the straightforward diagnosis of pupil traits. This view presupposes that individuals possess traits in certain amounts that are relatively stable over time and circumstances (e.g., a dyslexic in school is a dyslexic in his scout troop). Interpretivist social theory[16] presumes instead that categories such as dyslexia are not natural entities but are worked out in interactions within social contexts (the "six-hour, in-school, dyslexic"). Furthermore, there are political, organizational, and social influences on identification.[17] What one school defines as dyslexia is considered normal in other schools because of different selection dynamics.

Interpretivists reject internal validity as the standard for knowledge claims in evaluations. Instead, they look favorably on accounts that are authentic representations of the actions and meanings of participants within the social context of the program. The report must be coherent, credible, complete, recognizable to participants, and promote understanding in the reader.

Multiplism

Critical realists posit a real world separate from the observer yet believe that no single way of studying and portraying that reality is free of distortions. Each is fallible and offers at best a limited view of the phenomenon. Each research method has a characteristic error. But by looking for congruence in accounts across methods, operationalizations, and researchers, one can attain reliable knowledge.

According to this methodology, although comparative experiments narrow the range of evaluation outcomes, may not generalize to natural settings, and may produce reactive subject behavior, they do offer the only means of teasing out the effect of the program from the effect of extraneous variables. Qualitative approaches solve the problems of artificial experimental arrangements and narrow indicators, but they are limited in ability to sample cases broadly. Though the researcher may see effects as they emerge in context, he or she may not be able to attribute them unambiguously to the program. The results of representative surveys may be generalizable to populations but often gloss over meanings and leave attribution of cause to the respondents themselves.

Furthermore, according to this view, researchers bring particular perspectives to their analyses that color the results. Teachers-as-evaluators might choose to consider a different set of questions than evaluators trained in psychometrics and statistics; psychologists might choose a different set of questions and approaches from sociologists or economists.

Multiplists believe that the real effect of a program can be determined by examining the extent of convergence of findings across studies that employ a variety of definitions of effect, a variety of research methods, and multiple researchers with a variety of perspectives. Thus, the policymaker or decision maker must scrutinize the universe of studies on the topic (making sure that they have used multiple methods and perspectives), criticize the methods, interpret the collective results for convergence, and engage in debate with scholars and participants about the meaning of the whole.[18] The evaluator of multiplist persuasion might commission a set of studies to be done independently by multiple investigators using different methods and engage in the same kind of discourse over the collective results. According to this methodology, local circumstances constrain scientists' ability to arrive at general laws. Therefore, local conditions and variation in participant meanings are given serious attention in determining knowledge about programs and their effects.[19]

Consider the following example of an evaluation inspired by the methodology of multiplism. A district commissions a study of the relationship between special education placements and retentions in grade. The policy researcher, a multiplist, conducts a careful statistical study of the correlation between the two phenomena among schools in the district. She draws on archival records and closely examines how schools define placement and retention, count their instances, and control the quality of the data. She pays special attention to the variation among schools in how they define and count both placements and retentions. She conducts nonparticipant observations of placement meetings to make assertions about how the decisions are made and how procedures and implicit definitions vary. She interviews participants in the processes so that later she can triangulate across data sources and arrive at a picture of what happens, how it happens, how participants interpret it, and what effects it might have. She subjects her analysis to the scrutiny of experts and participants to round out and challenge her own understanding based on the evidence and subsequent discussion of its meaning. She finds a way to represent her understandings to participants and other stakeholders through narrative vignettes, general description, and those assertions that survived the scrutiny of confirmation and disconfirmation procedures.[20]

Critical Theory

Still another theory of social reality and methodology must be considered. Critical theorists reject positivist claims for objective knowledge of the world and technical methods of knowing it.[21] Critical theorists argue that the social and educational world can be known only through the filters of individual interpretations. Yet social and material circumstances influence these interpretations. In other words, individuals interpret the world in ways that reflect their positions in society—economic and social class, gender, ethnic group, and position (teacher vs. pupil vs. administrator) in the organization. Each position has special values and interests that must be taken into account in the process of knowledge construction and the evaluation of knowledge claims. Sometimes these interests amount to ideologies. Appeals to logic or technical research validity by one party or another may be simple expressions of self-interest or group interest. The evaluator herself also has group interests that may be reflected in selection of questions to ask or data to report.

Critical theorists design evaluations (or use results of existing studies) that encompass multiple methods and perspectives. They engage in deconstruction or criticism of not only the methods of the study but also the interests and ideologies of participants, administrators, and evaluators. For example, a critical analysis of the study of the relationship between special education placements and grade retentions would certainly examine the extent to which both sorts of decisions related to the ethnic group, economic class, and gender of pupils; would determine whether the ideology of special placement supports the interests of one group over those of another; and would seek to enlighten the participants about issues of interest and ideology that intrude on what many believe are straightforward and technical school organizational procedures.

In this section we have sketched four alternative knowledge claims underlying evaluation. One who seeks to evaluate the integrated general and special education program should engage in analysis of beliefs and assumptions about the nature of reality, knowledge, and method. Positivist knowledge claims rest on a belief in a single, materialistic reality that we can eventually come to know with precision and objectivity by using proper research procedures. Multiplists believe in an external reality that cannot be known perfectly and directly because research methods are fallible and researcher biases inevitable. However, reliable knowledge about social phenomena can be attained in the convergence of evidence across studies employing multiple methods and perspectives. Interpretivists believe in multiple realities and the context dependence of social action and reject objectivity as a standard of evaluation. Critical theorists agree that we live in an interpreted world for which apparently objective and standardized research procedures are inadequate, yet the interpretations and constructions we arrive at are themselves affected by economic and social structures.

Value Claims

Attention to the importance of values in evaluation has progressed with the growth of the profession itself. The first generation of evaluators largely ignored the issue, declaring their work to be value-free. Values were considered equivalent to bias, something that good scientific research ought to eliminate or control. As *value-neutral* scientists, evaluators relied on the accepted methods of social science to protect them against bias.[22] The evaluator's responsibility was to establish fact; it was the client's place to assign value to the findings. Values were to be sorted out by the citizenry. To the extent that different values for different interest groups were considered at all, utilitarianism dominated. That is, attaining the greatest good for the greatest number (as reflected, say, in average benefit produced by alternative treatments) was the standard of worth employed by value-neutral evaluators.

One would expect practitioners to be less than enthusiastic about value-neutral evaluations of their educational programs. The scope of such evaluations is narrow and the results of little use in planning or making adjustments to policies or practice. Yet educators seem to assume the value-neutral perspective when they use diagnostic testing to select pupils for special programs. The selection process ignores even such simple value issues as these: Whose values are served by categorizing a child as mentally retarded rather than as learning disabled? What is the fairness of retaining a child in a grade because his first language is not English?

The value-neutral approach has been soundly discredited in contemporary evaluation theory in favor of three alternatives: value relativism, value commitment, and value criticism.

Value Relativism

Value relativism holds that the task of the evaluator is to bring to the surface participants' values along with their beliefs, attributions of program effects, and their practices, none of which is to be judged by anything other than their own standards. This is similar to the stance taken by ethnographers toward the disparate cultural groups they study. The evaluator suspends judgment and avoids making comparisons.[23]

Yet a disproportionate distribution of power often undermines the practical application of a value-relative approach in the evaluation of educational programs. One can see several ways this happens in the case of special education. First, school reform initiatives frequently emphasize the values of certain groups, which lends credence and weight to specific concerns and overlooks those of others. The school choice movement, for example, is currently gaining momentum and, if successful, will assign low priority to concerns for disabled and other disadvantaged groups (see chap. 1).

Second, through regulation and financial incentives, the federal government makes some values less equal than others. Governmental agencies or the legal system can, for example, require that schools apply extraordinary resources for the education of pupils with multiple disabilities without regard to opportunity costs to the school district as a whole.

The Regular Education Initiative represents a third argument against value relativism. In their rebuttal of the traditional special education model, which focuses on the deficits in student learning and ability, Lipsky and Gartner propose building programs based on the strengths and capacities of all pupils and not on their identified handicapping conditions.[24] Each of these examples shows how viewpoints of dominant groups may overshadow those of the less powerful. Evaluation of programs cannot afford the luxury of value relativism.

Value Commitment

Those who are value committed define a reality and truth that fit their ideology and attempt to promote that definition in public discourse. This version of reality determines what values are deemed realizable and sets the evaluation agenda. For example, an evaluator committed to a utilitarian perspective would be driven by the belief that worth is based on the greatest good for the greatest number. Special attention to special populations, which would result in unequal funding, would thus be considered imprudent from this perspective. An evaluator who adheres to an egalitarian ideology would concentrate on issues of social justice. From the egalitarian perspective, a program's worth is based on its ability to minimize inequality. Value-committed evaluators attempt to reduce the scope of moral debate because their particular version of reality contains and is master of value choices.[25]

Public Law 94-142, the Education for All Handicapped Children Act of 1975, and PL 101-476, the Individuals with Disabilities Education Act of 1990, form the cornerstone of the value-committed perspective held by the special education profession. Most of its members promote the version of reality and value stance explicit in these laws and rarely make concessions to alternative value positions. Questions or criticisms are often met with the statement "It's the law, and that's that." Applying Rein's analysis of value claims,[26] the law has created the reality in which special educators exist and the values that are realizable: that "all handicapped children" have a "right to a free and appropriate public education," that the state must identify, locate, and evaluate all children in need of special education, that pupils with disabilities must be educated to the extent appropriate with their nondisabled peers. Debate about alternative positions is closed. The justification for such a stance is egalitarian rather than utilitarian. A program's worth is established by its ability to minimize inequality and promote social justice, to level the playing field in the interests of fairness and compassion.[27]

Value Criticism

Those who challenge the value-committed perspective of PL 94-142 question the separation of the systems and call for renegotiating relations with general education. They reject the claim that the law ties their hands and propose alternatives. Reynolds suggests that through such alternatives as performance waivers and grassroots innovations, special education can be built on a firmer foundation in research and evaluation than has been true in the past.[28] That is, the present "reality" of special education as a separate legal and organizational entity is not a fact of nature or a constitutional necessity. Instead it is a social construction that can be reanalyzed and renegotiated according to a variety of value stances and political compromises to meet the needs of constituencies.

Value-neutral, value-relative, and value-committed approaches all possess unique advantages as foundations for evaluation: pure science, pure suspension of judgment in favor of description, or pure moral commitment. Yet each stance precludes public scrutiny and debate and thus begs the question for evaluators. House has argued that at its best, the evaluation of educational and social programs aspires to be an institution for democratizing decisions by making programs and policies more open to public scrutiny and deliberation.[29] A pluralistic outlook to evaluation is most congruent with an educational system built on democratic principles.

A value-critical approach to evaluation affirms that attention to the multiple values of those who have a stake in the program is central to the process. The claims, concerns, and issues of stakeholders serve as organizational foci, the basis for determining what information is needed and how elements of the program should be judged.[30] The values of those invested in or affected by the program are not simply taken as given but are submitted to critical review. Since values are manifested as policies, goals, and procedures, they must be examined according to their consequences and implications. The value-critical approach tries to understand the logic, meaning, and consistency of ends and attempts to make a critique of values at every stage of the analysis.[31] Values are not arbitrary as the value-neutral approach may imply, nor are they assumed to be exclusive and morally correct, as the value-committed approach suggests. The values that influence a program should be subjected to careful debate and inquiry.

TOWARD AN EVALUATION MODEL

An evaluation model of an integrated special and general education program that is comprehensive in scope and adequate by contemporary evaluation standards ought to employ multiple methods and perspectives and take a critical view of a plurality of values; so goes our argument. With apologies and appropriate credit to Cronbach, House, and Rein, we offer an approximation of what such an evaluation model might be for a school district, an intermediate school district, or other consolidated unit.

We envision an evaluation plan characterized by panels and cycles. The panels set and advise on agendas, integrate and react to evidence. Cycles consist of sequential stages of activities. Although we have a medium-sized school district in mind, the size of panels could be adjusted upward in the case of larger units or downward in the case of single schools. However, even smaller panels need adequate representation of stakeholders. The sequences of activities in the cycles should be preserved even in districts that can afford fewer studies.

Panels

The design panel (DP) has primary responsibility for the evaluation as a whole. It consists of a chair or convener (with authority designated by the district superintendent), two or more evaluation specialists, two standard bearers of special education interests, two standard bearers for general education interests, and one standard bearer for the public interest. This panel establishes the membership of the other two panels.

The advisory panel (AP) consists of teachers and administrators of both special and general education, representatives of major stakeholding groups such as parents and pupils, an evaluation consultant, a curriculum consultant, a pupil personnel specialist (e.g., psychologist), and a legal counsel. Its responsibilities are to critique methods of study and interpret findings, to identify and represent the values and information needs of stakeholding groups, and to solicit public review.

The technical evaluation panel (TEP), made up of specialists in various research persuasions, advises on design, data collection, and analysis, and one member serves on the advisory panel.

Cycles

Stage 1

The initial challenge faced by the DP is to identify all the constituent groups. The evaluation should recognize three classes of constituencies: (1) primary interests are those focused on the educational system as a whole, that is, the integrated system; (2) secondary interests are those emerging from the separate general and special education structures; and (3) tertiary interests, that is, ethnic group advocates, professional groups associated with identifying educational needs, and the like. Such a distinction helps to ensure that the identification of stakeholding groups and evaluation questions will be balanced in any cycle and comprehensive over time. Stakeholding groups that have an interest in the programs or its outcomes would represent the school at which the evaluation is directed. At a minimum, these groups would include teachers of general and special education, administrators in both structures, community advocates, pupils, taxpayers, and personnel specialists such as psychologists.

Having listed the stakeholding groups, the AP should survey them and conduct hearings to catalog the goals and information needs of each one. The AP critically analyzes the goals, including those of special education, to ascertain those values inherent in the goals and asks, What does this goal mean? Why is it worthwhile? What are the consequences of pursuing these aims? The debate should probe the essence of the goals, not simply the methods for attaining them. A plurality of goals across stakeholding groups will yield conflicting values and perspectives. Without expecting a consensus, through dialogue and negotiation with these groups, the AP will complete a catalog of values and present it to the DP along with the evaluation issues and questions from the analysis of values. In addition, the AP attempts to locate new stakeholding groups to include in the process.

Stage 2

The DP then generates a set of evaluation issues and questions that pertain to each constituent group as well as core issues that cross special interests. The following questions are examples of issues that cross lines of special and general education and the integration of the two structures:

- What are the long-range effects on all pupils of pulling out children with disabilities into resource rooms with special education teachers versus teaming special education teachers and pupils in the regular classroom?
- What are the qualities of the educational experience received by children identified as disabled?
- How effective are the methods of teaching teachers how to teach more widely diverse groups of pupils?

An example of a question likely to emerge from the specialist constituency is this:

- Are the instruments and procedures used to identify pupils with disabilities adequate by psychometric standards, fair to minority pupils, and correctly used in this district?

This process will yield many more issues than can reasonably be managed in an evaluation cycle. The DP will need to coordinate the determination of priority of the various issues. Cronbach suggests that evaluation issues be analyzed according to leverage (issues considered central because many constituencies care about them) and uncertainty (issues considered central because little, or conflicting, knowledge exists regarding them). Issues with high leverage and high uncertainty should be given high priority.[32] The DP outlines the kinds of evidence necessary to answer these questions and the criteria for judging them.

The AP reviews progress so far, adds to and prioritizes questions and agenda, and conducts public hearings to make sure all stakeholding groups are given voice in the process.

Stage 3

On determining the priority of questions, the evidence needed to address these specific issues, and the appropriate criteria for judging both programs and studies, the DP decides on a constellation of studies. These are then commissioned through allocation to its own evaluators and requests for proposals from evaluation contractors. It is the responsibility of the DP to ensure that the entire constellation represents a variety of research perspectives (i.e., traditions, biases, status positions) and research methods and approaches.

To provide further assurance of pluralistic perspectives, during each cycle the DP will fund or otherwise make provision for one action research study to be conducted by teachers, parents, or pupils. Participatory action research aims at a partnership in which "insiders" (e.g., teachers, parents, pupils) become more theoretical about their practice and experience and "outsiders" (e.g., evaluators, researchers, university experts) become more practical about their theory.[33] Both insiders and outsiders are coequal inquirers in the process of evaluation. The focus of study should be on issues of practice, an example of which might be to address the trade-off teachers make between increasing pupil diversity and decreasing class size. In such a partnership between evaluators and practitioners, the outsiders introduce inquiry methods and standards for evidence, and the practitioners frame new information based on their own interests and standards.

The TEP provides advice on the design of the studies. The AP reviews progress and makes sure that interests and evaluation needs stemming from those interests are balanced.

To illustrate the kinds of studies that might make up an evaluation agenda in one cycle, we offer the following hypothetical case of Alpha School District.

> Alpha District's DP set seven priority issues for the first stage of its evaluation plan. The questions selected were those having both high leverage and uncertainty, as the AP had determined. In consultation with the TEP, the DP designed seven studies that incorporated the multiple views of its stakeholders and involved multiple methods and perspectives.
>
> Study 1 addresses the question, How effective are IEPs for reflecting and communicating the progress of pupils with disabilities? The

question is based on the need to match the internal record-keeping functions that IEPS usually serve with external information needs about the effectiveness of treatment programs. Members of the AP were concerned that IEP objectives were sometimes set unrealistically low, so that records would show success even when actual accomplishment was low, or that IEP objectives show little relationship with the content of the curriculum pupils receive.

The study has both qualitative and quantitative elements. Researchers from the central office conduct a secondary analysis of a representative sample of all IEPs filed over the past two years. They design a content analysis questionnaire that counts incidence of accomplishment of objectives, match of objectives with curriculum, and the extent of verification of accomplishment by independent measurements. They survey parents of sampled pupils, teachers in classes where pupils were mainstreamed, and special education teachers about their perception of progress on both IEP objectives and other indicators of progress.

For the qualitative elements of the study, researchers conduct semistructured interviews with a small group of special education and other staff who are directly involved in IEP development and evaluation. The agenda for the interviews will be to provide educational staff with the chance to reflect on particular cases and the mental constructs they were holding when they selected IEP objectives and determined whether they later were accomplished.

Study 2 addresses the question, Which of the available alternative treatment arrangements is most effective in meeting the needs of learning disabled pupils? Because learning disabilities are the most prevalent category of disabling conditions, this question has high priority. Because there is controversy in the profession about whether pullout programs are preferable to programs that place special education staff within regular classrooms, this question has salience among teachers in the district.

The DP commissions a consultant from the university to conduct the study. The researcher is to use a quasi-experimental design to compare three treatment arrangements: pullout (where children with learning disabilities leave their mainstream classroom for one hour per day for their program in the resource room), in-class (where the resource room teacher spends a specified amount of time in the mainstreamed class, paying primary attention to the learning disabled pupils but also helping the regular teacher), and self-contained class (where the children with learning disabilities receive all their educational programs in one class). The researcher attempts to control such extraneous variables as gender, age, and degree of impairment of pupils in the three groups. At the end of the experimental period, the researcher will measure the three groups on such variables as educational achievement, self-esteem, and social adjustment. The reaction of parents and staff will also be measured.

Study 3 addresses the adequacy of learning opportunities experienced by pupils in resource rooms. The AP recommended this study because general education teachers and administrators questioned whether curriculum and instruction received in the most prevalent organizational arrangement for special education students complements, supplants, or is inconsistent with what they receive in their mainstreamed classes.

District researchers design a systematic observation schedule for use in a representative sample of resource room placements to count academic engaged time, document learning opportunities, and judge the quality of materials, instruction, and interactions experienced by pupils in both resource room and mainstreamed classes. A measure of consistency of curriculum will also be used. To corroborate findings from this analysis, lesson plans will be used and teachers asked to complete journals.

Study 4 consists of a longitudinal analysis of the occupational, educational, and independent living status of pupils with disabilities after they graduate from secondary school or otherwise leave special education. This recommendation is taken directly from the section on evaluation and program information of PL 101-476.

Researchers from a sociological research institute are asked to conduct the study, which will consist of standard survey research procedures in which the population of pupils is defined, a representative sample is selected, interview protocols are developed, data are collected and analyzed, and a report is written. Besides documenting the status of these former pupils, the researchers will ask them to rate the quality of the school experiences they had and the contribution of the educational programs to their present lives.

Study 5 considers the meanings of pupil diversity among general and special education teachers. Clinical interviews will be conducted with teachers to determine their beliefs about the nature of pupil diversity (abilities, handicapping conditions, gender, ethnic, socioeconomic status, and the like), about the potential contribution of various educational arrangements for these pupil categories, and about the teachers' self-assessments of their competency to deal effectively with pupil diversity.

Study 6 consists of a review of special education identification procedures. A committee of psychologists, speech-language specialists, and special education diagnosticians document the instruments and measures used in identification and placement. For the measures listed, the committee gathers information from the psychometric literature about the validity of each one and its fairness with respect to special populations. The committee samples the files of pupils previously placed and determines how effectively test scores were used to arrive at accurate diagnoses and treatment prescriptions. In particular, they look for whether assessment evidence was systematically overlooked or conflicting data were ignored in the interests of confirming the teacher referrals.

Study 7 consists of an action research study involving general and special education teachers and students that examines the issue of vocational expectations and needs (i.e., what level of employment do regular and special education teachers expect pupils with disabilities to reach?).

Stage 4

The studies are conducted, more or less independently of each other. The TEP periodically reviews progress on the studies.

Stage 5

On completion, the evaluators of the various studies provide the findings, conclusions, and preliminary judgments and recommendations to the DP. The DP then reviews and criticizes the studies themselves, integrates results across studies, and prepares reports for presentation and review.

The AP reviews documents and writes reactions, addressing the overall evaluation issues defined earlier and conducting public hearings to incorporate reactions of stakeholding groups. The DP then incorporates reactions into a culminating report.

Stage 6

After completion of the report, the DP addresses the next level of concern. The constellation of studies has likely produced conflicting data or accounts or left some critical questions unanswered. The DP moves into the next cycle by identifying information needs, lower-priority questions or emerging questions, or stakeholding groups whose needs for information have not been met in the current cycle. These become grist for the mill in setting the evaluation agenda in the next cycle.

DISCUSSION

A comprehensive program of evaluation should deepen our understanding of the meaning of a free and appropriate education. Our responsibility and our struggle as educators is to interpret, create, and promote appropriate learning experiences for all students. This mandate compels us to reexamine our current separatist design of general and special education. The prevailing Tylerian, value-committed model of evaluation maintains the focus on two things—organizational compliance and pupil achievement of objectives—and blinds us to questions of value in the transactions that make up programs. A focus such as this raises legitimate concerns from anyone outside the special education community of the worth of special education programs and creates conflict.

We see the Regular Education Initiative as a manifestation of this conflict. In his analysis of dominant ideologies, Rein[34] might be describing the conflict when he argues that mistrust of a dominant ideology does not arise from a fear that it is nonadaptive but that it may be too adaptive and thus perpetuate injustice. Looking another way, we can imagine a set of political events in which the hard-won rights for educating the disabled are overturned by the failure of the special education community to coalesce its interests with those of education as a whole. The latter might happen more readily through open discourse and mutual reflection. If evaluation is to serve a purpose for the system as a whole, perhaps it is in promoting such deliberation.

To develop a better understanding of what actually occurs in the name of learning, we have proposed a multiplistic, value-critical model of evaluation. The purpose is to examine a wider range of issues from multiple perspectives and to uncover unanticipated consequences of current practices. Even an evaluation, however, should not evade the critical scrutiny usually reserved for programs and policies. Such scrutiny comes under the heading of metaevaluation.[35]

Metaevaluation standards (i.e., for judging the merits of the evaluation itself) for a comprehensive evaluation for an integrated general and special education program should not be set in advance. At the end of a cycle one should examine several features.

First, one must examine whether the evaluation illuminated the program itself, its context, and program effects, broadly conceived. Although we have argued for a multiplist evaluation model, we acknowledge that close description of the participants' everyday life is the bedrock on which effects can be built. No amount of experimentation will make up for an analysis of the meanings of those most closely involved. We accept the interpretivists' premise that actions depend on context and that people act in relation to educational programs according to the meanings they hold.

Second, we accept Cronbach's notion that evaluation should enlighten the citizenry and stakeholding groups so that they may participate more effectively in the political process that shapes education.[36] It is the firsthand accounts of program activities and their social contexts that these groups can effectively use to form judgments, through what Stake and Trumbull refer to as naturalistic generalizations.[37] Enlightenment of participants as a standard for judging evaluations follows from the idea that program policies and decisions are incremental. The "instrumental view" of evaluation results; that is, that particular findings from evaluations directly transfer to actions of policymakers and decision makers is an inappropriate standard for judging the merits of the evaluation we outlined here.[38] Nor should the evaluation be solely symbolic. The model should not be implemented for the sake of evaluation, merely to placate the public that the district is taking a hard look at its programs but not necessarily doing so with purpose.

Third, one must judge after the cycle whether multiple methods were used, whether the model functioned as intended, and whether it addressed multiple values of multiple constituencies. In particular, one must access, perhaps through an evaluation audit, that the legally established rights of the disabled population have not been suborned to the interests of the majority. This standard follows the idea that the effects of a program on the least advantaged groups must be judged as fair.[39]

Fourth, the evaluation must be examined to determine whether the "subjects" of the study were treated ethically. Greene recognizes that evaluation is a moral activity and evaluators moral actors.[40] Evaluators, no less than teachers, should scrutinize themselves and solicit the scrutiny of others so that their day-to-day practice and the consequences of their studies can be judged. One important aspect of this analysis is the dissolution of status barriers between evaluators and those subject to evaluation. We must recognize that those whom evaluators study are actively constructing their worlds and engaging in educational and emotional transactions with pupils, and therefore they ought to be equally involved in the construction and critique of knowledge and value claims.

NOTES

1. Harry F. Wolcott, *Teachers versus Technocrats* (Eugene: Center for Educational Policy and Management, University of Oregon, 1977), 116.
2. Gillian Fulcher, "Students with Special Needs: Lessons from Comparisons," *Journal of Education Policy* 5, no. 4 (1990): 347–58.
3. Mary Lee Smith, *How Educators Decide Who Is Learning Disabled: Challenge to Psychology and Public Policy in the Schools* (Springfield, IL: Thomas, 1982), 147–49.
4. Ursula Casanova and Sheila Chavez, "Sociopolitical Influences on Federal Government Funding of Gifted and Talented and Bilingual Education Programs" (unpublished manuscript; Tempe: Arizona State University, College of Education, 1991), 18–20.
5. Ernest R. House, "Trends in Evaluation," *Educational Researcher* 19 (1990): 24.
6. Ibid., 24–25.
7. William R. Shadish, Jr., Thomas D. Cook, and Laura C. Leviton, *Foundations of Program Evaluation* (Newbury Park, CA: Sage Publications, 1991), 36–64.
8. Ralph W. Tyler, "The Objectives and Plans for a National Assessment of Educational Progress," *Journal of Educational Measurement*, 3 (Spring 1966): 1–10.
9. Ernest R. House, *Evaluating with Validity* (Beverly Hills: Sage Publications, 1980), 228.
10. Thomas D. Cook and Donald T. Campbell, *Quasi-experimentation: Design and Analysis Issues for Field Settings* (Chicago: Rand McNally, 1979), 50–54.
11. Lee J. Cronbach et al., *Toward Reform of Program Evaluation: Aims, Methods, and Institutional Arrangements* (San Francisco: Jossey-Bass, 1980), 295–313.
12. J. Habermas, *Knowledge and Human Interests* (London: Heinemann, 1972), 5–26.
13. Harry F. Wolcott, "Criteria for an Ethnographic Approach to Research in Schools," *Human Organization* 34 (Summer 1975): 103–24.
14. Robert E. Stake, retrospective on "The Countenance of Educational Evaluation" in *Evaluation and Education: At Quarter Century*, ed. Milbrey W. McLaughlin and D. C. Phillips (Chicago: National Society for the Study of Evaluation, 1991), 74–76.
15. David M. Fetterman, *Ethnography in Educational Evaluation* (Beverly Hills: Sage Publications, 1984), 13; Yvonna S. Lincoln and Egon G. Guba, *Naturalistic Inquiry* (Beverly Hills: Sage Publications, 1985), 187–95; Malcolm Parlett and David Hamilton, "Evaluation as Illumination: A New Approach to the Study of Innovatory Programs" in *Evaluation Studies Review Annual*, vol. 1, ed. Gene V.

Glass (Beverly Hills: Sage Publications, 1976), 140–57; and Michael Quinn Patton, *Qualitative Evaluation Methods* (Beverly Hills: Sage Publications, 1980), 19.

16. Peter L. Berger and Thomas Luckman, *The Social Construction of Reality* (New York: Anchor Books), 104–16.

17. Hugh Mehan, "Language and Schooling" in *Interpretive Ethnography of Education*, ed. George Spindler and Louise Spindler (Hillsdale, NJ: Erlbaum, 1987), 109–17; Smith, *How Educators Decide Who Is Learning Disabled*, 99–101; James E. Ysseldyke, "Current Practices in Making Psychoeducational Decisions about Learning Disabled Students," *Journal of Learning Disabilities* 16 (Summer 1983): 226–33.

18. Donald T. Campbell, "Science's Social System of Validity-enhancing Collective Belief Change and the Problems of the Social Sciences" in *Meta-theory in Social Science: Pluralisms and Subjectivities*, ed. D. W. Fiske and R.A. Shweder (Chicago: University of Chicago Press, 1986), 108–35.

19. Lee J. Cronbach, "Beyond the Two Disciplines of Scientific Psychology," *American Psychologist* 30 (Feb. 1975): 116–27.

20. Mary Lee Smith, "The Whole Is Greater: Combining Qualitative and Quantitative Approaches in Evaluation Studies" in *Naturalistic Evaluation: New Directions for Program Evaluation*, ed. David D. Williams (San Francisco: Jossey-Bass, 1986), 37–54.

21. Wilfred Carr and Stephen Kemmis, *Becoming Critical* (Philadelphia: Falmer Press, 1986), 129–52.

22. House, "Trends in Evaluation," 25.

23. Harry F. Wolcott, "Mirrors, Models, and Monitors: Educator Adaptations of the Ethnographic Innovation" in *Doing the Ethnography of Schooling*, ed. G. Spindler (New York: Holt, Rinehart, & Winston, 1982), 68–95.

24. Dorothy K. Lipsky and Alan Gartner, "Restructuring for Quality" in *The Regular Education Initiative: Alternative Perspectives on Concepts, Issues, and Models*, ed. John W. Lloyd, Nirbhay N. Singh, and Alan C. Repp (Sycamore, IL: Sycamore, 1990), 43–56.

25. Martin Rein, *Social Science and Public Policy* (Middlesex: Penguin Books, 1976), 254.

26. Ibid., 254.

27. House, *Evaluating with Validity*, 127–29.

28. M. C. Reynolds, "Classification and Labeling" in *The Regular Education Initiative*, 21–42.

29. House, "Trends in Evaluation," 24.

30. Lee J. Cronbach, *Designing Evaluations of Educational and Social Programs* (San Francisco: Jossey-Bass, 1982), 240; Egon G. Guba and Yvonna S. Lincoln, *Fourth Generation Evaluation* (Newbury Park, CA: Sage Publications, 1989), 50.

31. Rein, *Social Science and Public Policy*, 74.

32. Cronbach, *Designing Evaluations*, 240.

33. M. Elden and M. Levin, "Cogenerative Learning" in *Participatory Action Research*, ed. W. F. Whyte (Newbury Park, CA: Sage Publications, 1991), 57–65.

34. Rein, *Social Science and Public Policy*, 258.

35. Michael Scriven, "An Introduction to Meta-evaluation," *Educational Product Report* 2 (1969): 36–38.

36. Cronbach, *Designing Evaluations*, 4–22.

37. Robert E. Stake and Deborah J. Trumbull, "Naturalistic Generalizations," *Review Journal of Philosophy and Social Science* 7 (1982): 1–12.
38. Carol H. Weiss and Michael J. Bucuvalas, "The Challenge of Social Research to Decision Making" in *Using Social Research in Public Policy Making,* ed. Carol H. Weiss (Lexington, MA: Lexington, 1977), 213–34.
39. House, *Evaluating with Validity,* 160.
40. Jennifer C. Greene, "Responding to Evaluation's Moral Challenge," paper presented at the Annual Meeting of the American Educational Research Association (Chicago, April 1991), 1–2.

8

Putting It All Together at the School Level: A Principal's Perspective

Lynn Baker Murray

This chapter presents a vision embracing the optimistic belief that we can provide productive learning for all students in our school and that classroom teachers are responsible for and capable of assuring each child's success. Diversity is honored, and individual differences are provided for as teachers adapt their pedagogy to a wider range of learning styles and performance levels. School staff members are committed to a team approach in the belief that students' needs are best met when professionals collaborate and share their knowledge and skills. The school district is committed to providing adequate resources, materials, time, support services, personnel, and staff development. With practices and procedures logically connected to enact this vision, program coherence with equitable access for all students becomes an attainable goal.[1]

Equitable access means that students with disabilities have the same access to knowledge, growth, achievement, success, and belonging as do students without handicaps. It means that we eliminate practices and conditions that restrict the learning environment, conditions that put certain students at risk and structure inequality.[2] It means an end to a system that ignores children with critical needs or warehouses others in separate schools or classes. It embraces many of the practices being promoted in the name of mainstreaming. Educational opportunities and activities are relevant and developmentally appropriate for all students. The educational environment is flexible enough to accommodate a variety of performance levels and learning styles simultaneously. No student's opportunity to learn is hampered or limited by the activities and needs of other students.

Simple inclusion in classes with age-mates, however, is not enough. Is it appropriate for a fourteen-year-old with a learning impairment to be sitting in a math class with her age-mates listening to a lecture and completing practice worksheets on multiplying and dividing fractions, when she has yet to understand the basic concepts of fractions? Situations such as this occur too often for mainstreamed students. While her age-mates are studying fractions, perhaps this student would be better served by providing individualized community living skills, such as measuring and following directions for making simple meals.

While meeting the special needs of students with disabilities, the quality of education must not be significantly impaired for the general education students. Consider the second grade student with emotional disturbance who refuses to engage in an assigned task, who instead talks out frequently, tips over his desk, drops papers and books, and sings tonelessly while the teacher gives the class instructions. Unless swift and effective management techniques channel this student's behavior toward more productive and acceptable pursuits, other class members are likely to experience a reduction in the quantity and quality of their educational opportunities.

Inclusion of students with handicaps, particularly those with severe behavioral problems, significantly complicates instruction and classroom management.[3] The challenge is to structure educational environments and provide adequate training and resources so that students with handicaps do not drain teachers' attention from the majority of the class so that all students can perform at their best at all times.

WHO ARE OUR SPECIAL STUDENTS?

We envision a school where students are in regular attendance with age-mates who are traditionally attached with special education labels such as mentally retarded, emotionally disturbed, learning disabled, hyperactive, hearing impaired, vision impaired, and speech impaired. Yet, our schools are becoming increasingly populated by students with special needs who have not been labeled as special as states tighten their eligibility requirements for special education in efforts to contain costs. Evans[4] remarks that students with handicaps typically display motivational and behavioral problems such as the following: attention seeking, passive refusal, fluctuations in attention, and difficulty sustaining previous gains. Many students without handicaps also display these characteristics. We are seeing a more widespread deterioration in motivation and behavior of students and in the support and responsiveness of their families.

The nature of our society, families, and children is changing rapidly. The social service demands on the schools are mounting as we see the impact of divorce, single-parent families, two-wage-earner families, substance abuse, and poverty on our youngsters. The changes in our world and workplace are raising expectations for today's school graduates, yet students have a deteriorating personal and social support system. We must address the motivation and behavior of all our students, more and more of whom are tuned out and left out by schools that continue to overemphasize large-group instruction, teacher-centered lectures, drill-and-practice routines, and testing of unconnected skills and content.

> Study after study reveals the dominance of telling, lecturing, questioning the class, and monitoring seat work. The inquiring, questioning, probing, hypothesizing kind of intellectual endeavor often associated with learning is not usually found in classrooms.[5]

Our general education system must be revised. Too many schools persist with practices that have not changed over the past fifty years or even more. "Perhaps the last real structural change occurred when the desks were unbolted."[6] Our classrooms must take on a new look. We need to remove the teacher from the front of the room and provide more opportunities for student-directed, small-group work, longer-term projects, experiential learning, and authentic products.

We cannot expect to successfully include youngsters with handicaps in regular classrooms if those classrooms are unable to accommodate greater diversity. Teachers cannot be expected to handle the diversity alone, isolated behind their closed door, as they have been in the past. Teachers need opportunities and time to talk with one another, solve problems, share expertise and resources, and coach and support one another. As general and special education systems become more integrated, the characteristics of general education will need to change radically. We can no longer count on special education to fix the special students that general education did not manage.

There are simply too many students with too many needs. Fewer and fewer students fit neatly into the traditional teacher-centered classrooms of the past. Teachers who overemphasize large-group activities and teach to the middle are reaching fewer and fewer students. Teachers of this type are leaving out more students than just those with disabilities. Many changes that are made to accommodate students with handicaps in the general classes will probably benefit other students as well. As Maheady and his colleagues point out, "Improving the overall effectiveness of regular class instruction may take precedence over the development of procedures to help learners with mental retardation compensate for the lack of quality instruction in the first place."[7]

The remainder of this chapter presents several key characteristics and practices found in the general education system that enable students with handicaps to have equitable learning opportunities in the mainstream. It also characterizes key elements of an integrated special education support system to augment the mainstream. Lastly, it offers some suggestions for effective staff development as a necessary ingredient to support the system change required to enact this vision.

SOME ESSENTIAL CHARACTERISTICS OF
THE GENERAL EDUCATION SYSTEM

A school that provides for students with special needs also provides a rich environment for their classmates without handicaps. We can release ourselves from teacher-centered instruction and deliver more child-centered instruction, focusing on active learning and microteaching (i.e., specific individual or small-group skill building as required by student performance and task demands). Skill development can be individualized to specific students within any given instructional context. Picture a classroom teacher working with a group of youngsters with a two- to three-year age span, various ethnic and economic backgrounds, and considerable diversity in academic, motivational, and social levels. Teachers would experience more success and more students would be engaged if teachers utilized student-centered, experiential, cooperative learning, peer tutoring, and other such teaching strategies. To be effective with a diverse group of youngsters, teachers should avoid lecture-oriented, large-group activities where everyone does the same thing at the same time. Instead, the teacher could work with smaller groups of youngsters for brief times during the week for building specific skills, conferring, assessing, redirecting, and sending them out on their own the rest of the time. Resnick[8] argues that skill building tends to take care of itself for most students when teachers provide authentic learning activities.

We can establish cooperative classroom communities where students are actively involved in activities that are connected to their own families and communities. To do this, teachers must adopt a more flexible approach to instruction and the delivery of curriculum.

First, the curriculum must be relevant and challenging, guaranteeing skill development as well as interest. In delivering that curriculum, teachers need to reduce their reliance on lectures in the upper grades and on lock-stepped instruction from basal readers and workbooks in the lower grades. Too often, we see classrooms where all the pupils are doing the same thing in the same way, engaged in learning activities that are generally disconnected from their outside lives and contexts.

Consider a class of middle school students studying the geography of the Middle East, where the teacher lectures, students take notes, and then follow up with an application exercise such as labeling and coloring a map. How engaged is a turned-off student likely to be? What happens to the student who cannot write fast enough or spell accurately while taking notes? Can we think of student-directed, engaging activities that would more likely deliver the same intended outcomes—developing familiarity with the geography, characteristics, culture, and politics of Middle Eastern countries?

Contrast this approach with a mathematics lesson intended to teach such basic geometric principles as area, perimeter, and height, in which each student designs, draws, and furnishes his or her own dream house. In that example, students become actively engaged in a project that has personal meaning. They can design a house that looks much like the one they live in, or they can create one that is entirely different, depending on their skill level and understanding. What matters is that students are active and make decisions as they wrestle constantly with the objectives of the lesson, thus stretching themselves to the edge of their competence.

Consider the primary classroom where the teacher reviews the morning seatwork for the day, and students work diligently on their phonics practice sheets. Later, the teacher meets with one group after another for the lesson in the basal reader, carefully guided by the teacher's manual, followed by more workbook practice. What happens to the student who has trouble sitting still, working alone for long periods of time? What happens to the student who can whiz through the seatwork without thinking about what he does because he reads several grade levels beyond that he is in? Could this class be organized in another way? Might reading instruction be carried out as effectively with all students engaged in more active learning? Students could be tutoring one another, pairing up and reading to each other from favorite books, taking turns predicting what is going to happen next, rewriting stories written by others, writing journals, writing stories to be edited and read by other students, and being involved in other activities more engaging and important than completing worksheets. Students who need more supervised reading instruction could spend more time with teachers, aides, volunteers, older students working in small groups on specific decoding and comprehension skills.

When the learning environment is structured so that youngsters are engaged in active, participatory learning, youngsters with handicaps tend to disappear. The classroom environment honors and nurtures diversity, allowing for different roles and talents. It is a worthwhile goal to structure lessons so that students with handicaps fit in to the extent that if you did not know who they were ahead of time, you could not find them amid the group of actively involved learners.

To create and maintain a flexible and engaging classroom like those just portrayed, certain pedagogical elements, practices, and services are essential. In the remainder of this section, several of them are considered in more detail:

- Multiage grouping
- Authentic products and projects
- Integrated assessment strategies
- Collaborative learning groups
- Peer and cross-age tutoring
- Classroom management and disciplinary strategies
- Guidance and counseling services

Multiage Grouping Practices*

Schools are establishing multiage classrooms as a more sensible approach to addressing the wide range of diversity in our students. Multiage classrooms dispel the sense of gradedness and nurture a spirit of family; they create a learning community. Students stay with the same peer group for more than one year. The group is an intentional blend of ages, grades, skill levels, and talents, heterogeneously assembled in order to maximize peer uniqueness and interaction and the potential for peer modeling and coaching.

Such classrooms adopt a child-centered perspective where students' needs influence the curriculum. Student assessment is embedded in learning and is more formative, as opposed to the traditional end-of-chapter tests or basic competency, outcomes-based tests. There is less pressure to race through the curriculum. Instead, teachers adopt a flexible approach to curriculum that allows greater depth, with an active learning, experiential orientation. Peer models provide motivation and sometimes assistance for the less able students. Students with a variety of learning styles and levels can be accommodated with small groupings for skill development. Students with large differences are less isolated, because it is natural for everyone to be working at their own level and pace. Children become accustomed to seeing their peers learn at different rates and in different ways, which results in a growing comfort with their own learning styles.

Students gain from the extended relationships with their teacher, staying with him or her for more than one year. They learn to work comfortably and effectively together. The fall lag, when students appear to have forgotten everything over the summer, is greatly shortened. Students and teachers are better able to pick up where they left off in June because they do not have to work out a new set of classroom rules and instructional procedures. New students to the classroom also settle in more quickly because they have older peers to show them the ropes. They are blended in, with a lot less teacher attention required for classroom management and establishment of routines.

Authentic Products and Projects

It is often said that instruction for students with disabilities is most effective when it is practical, set in a familiar context so that skills can be applied in a way that students see as useful. The same applies for all students. Youngsters will become more attentive when activities focus on authentic projects and products connected with their real world and community. Eliot Wigginton, developer of the *Foxfire* books[9] argues that we need to develop ways in which curriculum

---

*Information in the section on multiage grouping practices is based on personal communication with a number of Vermont teachers, primarily Linda Smith, of Fairfield, Vermont; Molly McClosky, of Charlotte, Vermont; and Peg Dorta, of Underhill, Vermont.

objectives are used to design the work so that what the students do is actually put those objectives to work in a real way, instead of endless practice against the day when they might be able to do something useful with them.[10]

Students show significant performance gains in achievement and motivation when given real projects, real problems, and real discussions.[11] We need to integrate skills and curriculum objectives into authentic learning activities. Wigginton comments that teachers

can talk till they're hoarse, and nobody will hear what they're saying. The point is to have students themselves identify why all this stuff exists, and why it's in school curriculums, and what they might be able to do with it.[12]

Students need to be involved, but in doing things for real consumption by the outside world, with each project building in scale. Wigginton's work builds on Dewey's belief that we should help students develop "thicker" experiences so that their experiences will eventually play out into something that resembles wisdom, judgment, and sophistication.

Why not rethink the English class with an authentic product focus instead of the time-worn practice of writing themes or research papers that are turned in to teachers, graded, and then forgotten or at best put into portfolios? Consider instead the learning opportunities described in the *Foxfire* books,[13] in which students capture the oral history, stories, and traditions to be preserved and shared with an entire community of readers over a number of years. With a flexible project such as this, all students, regardless of their ability and interest level, are likely to find productive roles. It may be that not all students will write stories, essays, or poetry. Some of them may draw cartoons, and others may focus on layout and design. These kinds of authentic projects require students to plan the overall production of their magazine, from deciding the contents, researching, and writing the stories, to carrying out the logistics of production and distribution.

While this kind of activity clearly emphasizes communication skills (because it is an English class), it also stresses planning, problem solving, decision making, taking responsibility, and carrying out a complicated project to its completion. And, when it is done, students will have something to show for their efforts that has meaning and worth beyond the classroom. The grade does not matter as much as the students' sense of accomplishment and ownership.

Integrated Assessment Strategies

A stronger focus on authentic products also has significant implications for our methods of assessment. In recent years, much has been said about the shortcomings of standardized, objective assessment strategies commonly used in schools. Wiggins[14] remarks that the United States is the only major country that relies so heavily on norm-referenced, short-answer tests, with little use of performance or classroom-based assessments. Such testing practices are grossly inadequate for preparing students for the world in which they will live.[15]

> Never do we stop to ask how we could make our evaluative gatekeeping model the kind of self-observation and informed critique that separates ball tossers from fine pitchers, doodlers from artists, or instrumentalists from musicians. Yet virtually every student walks out of school into years of long-term projects: raising children, building a house, running a farm, writing a novel, or becoming a better lab technician. All of these projects require moment-to-moment monitoring, Monday morning quarterbacking, and countless judgements of errors and worth. Unfortunately, very little in the way we now structure assessment names or encourages those lifelong skills.[16]

Standardized and short-answer tests that so dominate assessment practices are primarily measures of factual and declarative information. They have little to do with more complex cognitive outcomes that are so essential in our complex society.[17]

We can adopt a more context-embedded assessment process, as opposed to the traditional method of postunit testing and grading. Wiggins[18] argues that we should pay more attention to the criteria for assessment as a part of the teaching and learning process. We can expect students to pay as much attention to those criteria as do teachers. Self-assessment can be more prominent than is typical in conventional testing practices. Students can become more involved in their own assessment, identifying the specific characteristics of their own performance and improvement as they progress from month to month, from project to project, as measured against their own thorough understanding of the criteria for excellent performance. Students and teachers can negotiate specific intended outcomes and expected performance. As students develop more skills, expectations can become more ambitious and complex. They can go beyond the simplistic, observable, and measurable behavioral objectives one sees much of in most curriculum packages.

Rather than using tests as after-the-fact devices for checking up on what students have learned, we can make assessment strategies an integrated part of instruction. Assessment, or "exhibitions of mastery,"[19] can be a central vehicle for clarifying and setting intellectual standards. The performance "is not a check-up, but at the very heart of the matter."[20]

> Students can organize portfolios of their products that are carried from year to year. While achievement tests offer outcomes in units that can be counted and accounted, portfolio assessment offers the opportunity to observe students in the broader context: taking risks, developing creative solutions and learning to make judgements about their own performances.[21]

Portfolios provide a complex and comprehensive view of students' performance in context. They allow students to be participants in rather than the mere objects of assessment and encourage the development of more complex cognitive skills, independence, and self-direction.[22] For example, within a writing portfolio, expectations can go beyond typical expectations in grammar, punctuation, and spelling. Subjective criteria such as voice, interest, and coherence can take on more importance. One can see greater emphasis on thinking skills, creativity, and maintenance of high interest for one's audience. Portfolios capture the student's process in context. Teachers and students alike can assess the evolution of any piece of writing,

> starting with incubation, changing into notes, undergoing revision, settling into its near-final form, and zigzagging between these different moments as well. In fact, knowing how to pursue the work of writing is as much a part of what is learned as is the sense for where a semicolon goes or how dialogue ought to sound.[23]

Within a mathematics portfolio one can also expect to see emphasis on thinking, reasoning, problem-solving skills, and connections to real-world situations and other curricular areas. Within these portfolios we can see development of the language of mathematics, generation of multiple strategies of problem solving, self-assessment, and a sense of math empowerment.[24] On a day-to-day basis, teachers can rely more on careful observation, narrative recording, and frequent journal entries describing student performance, instructional needs, and next challenges. They can adopt strategies similar to Goodman's[25] "kid-watching" procedures for reading, which involve observing, interacting, documenting, and interpreting. Teachers can observe and interact with students performing in natural settings, gathering clues to their use of specific cognitive operations. They can record strengths, weaknesses, and demonstrations of skill mastery. Assessment need not occur only at testing times but as an ongoing part of the teaching and learning process. Report cards and test grades can take on less significance, being supplemented by portfolio products, self-assessments, and narrative descriptions of student performance.

Collaborative Learning Groups

Collaborative, or cooperative, learning groups are being successfully implemented in more and more classrooms at all age levels. Slavin's[26] synthesis of the research cites cooperative learning

> as a means of emphasizing thinking skills and increasing higher level learning; as an alternative to ability grouping, remediation, or special education; as a means of improving race relations and acceptance of mainstreamed students; and as a way to prepare students for an increasingly collaborative work force.[27]

Although there are many cooperative learning models, they all have in common the principle that students share common goals, work together to learn, and are responsible for one another's learning as well as their own. Cooperative learning models range from the Johnsons' Learning Together model,[28] to the various forms of team learning,[29] to the jigsaw model,[30] to the group investigation model.[31]

The Johnsons' cooperative learning model involves five basic elements: (1) positive interdependence, (2) face-to-face interaction, (3) individual accountability, (4) social skills, and (5) group processing.[32] Slavin's team learning models rely on three central concepts: (1) team rewards, (2) individual accountability, and (3) equal opportunity for success.[33]

Collaborative learning groups provide opportunities for students to find roles where they can be contributing members. The Johnsons' Learning Together model provides students with assigned roles, such as time-keeper, encourager, facilitator, recorder, and so on.[34] The jigsaw model[35] assigns students dual roles through membership in "expert" and "home" groups. Students first attain familiarity and mastery of material in the former groups and later teach their assigned material to other members of their "home group."

Collaborative groups can be very effective in improving basic skills. Learning team models, such as Cooperative Integrated Reading and Composition (CIRC) and Team Assisted Individualization (TAI) developed by Slavin and his colleagues[36] incorporate structured learning materials in basic skills areas. The majority of group work takes place in pairs, but each student is also a member of a larger team. Students work in pairs on highly structured, individualized learning materials appropriate to their own skill levels. They practice together, quiz, and give feedback to each other. Students earn points, while working in pairs, for both correct responses and effective tutoring and teaching behaviors. Larger teams collect member points earned during study periods as well as points earned on tests and exams. These team approaches to learning basic skills provide a means for combining cooperative learning strategies with programmed instruction, while allowing students to carry out most of the data keeping and management functions themselves.[37]

Collaborative groups are also effective for practicing and building inquiry and problem-solving skills throughout the curriculum. Sharan and Sharan[38] have developed the group investigation process for cooperative groups, in which students investigate their chosen subtopic within a broader topic such as Native Americans. Within this broad topic a student group might investigate the variety of dwellings used by different tribes in different areas across the United States. Student groups plan and carry out detailed investigations of their subtopics, which culminate in a final presentation of their most significant learning for the entire class. Final presentations may be delivered in a variety of forms, including exhibits, models, learning centers, written reports, dramatic presentations, guided tours, and slide presentations. While students are carrying out their investigations and preparing their final presentations, the teacher is constantly making judgments and suggestions based on frequent conversations and observations of each student's academic and social activity. Sharan and Sharan[39] maintain that these procedures ensure development of a wide range of skills. The projects "give students more control over their learning than other teaching methods. They raise questions that reflect their different interests, backgrounds, values, and abilities."[40]

Alternatively, consider a less complex collaborative learning activity to building thinking skills—a mathematics and English metacognitive writing task, carried out in student pairs. Students are asked to think about a particular problem that they had previously solved in cooperative groups in a mathematics class. They are paired with one another and take turns coaching their partner through an oral description of how they solved the problem. They are expected to talk about their own thinking processes. Each student talks while the partner listens and takes notes. Note takers record their partners' steps for solving the problem and reflect on whether it makes sense to them. Once partners have a complete set of notes, they write down their own problem-solving descriptions, continuing to receive feedback from their partners. This activity surely results in deeper metacognition, greater understanding of the problem-solving strategies employed, and more stretching of one's competence, as a result of the encouragement and challenge received as part of the collaborative process.

Collaborative group work can provide opportunities for each student and encourage high levels of student involvement and engagement. We have found that regular debriefing of group process and outcomes results in greater commitment to group outcomes and higher participation rates, as well as a sense of competence and accomplishment on the part of students with all levels of ability and interests. Group tasks can be structured to be within each child's ability to succeed and contribute, and yet they are stretching. Tasks, roles, and expectations can be structured so that students rise to the occasion, performing at levels of sophistication and competence that surprise themselves as well as their teachers.

We find that collaborative group work results in special students being more active and involved than when they participate in a traditional teacher-centered mode. They fit in; their eyes sparkle; they are engaged. Over time, the general education students become more tolerant, accepting, and eventually respectful of less able students. The former students learn that just because Sam cannot read very well, that does not mean that he cannot talk, think, and solve problems. Students begin to be appreciated for their other talents as well, such as their sense of humor, their ability to draw, or their willingness to encourage others. Teachers report that as a result of working in cooperative groups, special students become less hesitant to offer ideas in larger group discussions. They develop more confidence in their ability to think and contribute.

On a broader level, collaborative work reinforces the importance of developing cooperative skills for the workplace, beginning as early as the first grade. Students learn to work in concert toward goal accomplishment, taking advantage of the strengths of each member of the group—all important competencies in the workplace.

Peer and Cross-age Tutoring

Tutoring can occur in many different ways and at varying levels of formality throughout the school system. Same-age students can assist each other in paired learning tasks, similar to the metacognitive interviewing and writing exercise described earlier. Or they can help one other by sharing special skills or by following more formalized procedures whereby students drill each other for skill building in spelling or mathematics or for retaining content in social studies.

Tutoring strategies can take advantage of the concept of "opportunity to respond" discussed by Delquadri and his coauthors.[41] Increasing students' rate of responding, along with corrective feedback, will result in significant gains in achievement and performance in areas in which it is applied. Many children fail because of a lack of opportunities to respond, and many classroom environments provide too few opportunities for students, which results in too many students engaged in off-task behaviors. Tutoring strategies can greatly increase opportunities to respond in almost any subject area. Delquadri and his colleagues[42] provide detailed descriptions of classwide tutoring applied to the development of reading, mathematics, and spelling. Maheady and his coworkers[43] provide another example of similar procedures applied in a high school social studies classroom.

These approaches are similar to Slavin and his colleagues' Paired and Team Cooperative Learning model[44] discussed earlier. In these examples, students are paired up for a while as tutors, then for a period of equal length as tutees. Students earn individual and team points for correct responses, effective tutoring behaviors, and quiz and test scores. Structured tutorial or paired-learning situations show reduced spelling errors, increased reading accuracy and rates, greater comprehension, more on-task and academic behaviors, and higher test scores in all content areas where they were implemented.[45]

On a less formal basis, older students may work with younger students on specific skills or on project-oriented activities. Students can be of assistance in other ways; for example, rewriting textbooks in their own language to be used by reluctant readers or listening to the stories of young writers. Tutoring models can provide for a multitude of benefits for students involved. Not only do students who are being tutored receive special assistance, but the tutors gain as well by experiencing a boost in confidence, strengthening their skill level, and increasing sensitivity to the needs of others.

Classroom Management and Disciplinary Strategies

A disciplinary system that provides clear expectations and a support system is essential to help students adjust and succeed. Every school must have a system to maintain order, assure basic human consideration, and resolve conflict. Coherent, consistent, and clear expectations are especially important to compensate for some youngsters' chaotic, confusing, and inadequate personal support systems.

Many children come to school with complex needs and weak personal and social support systems. Every classroom includes a number of children who are attempting to cope with the impact of divorce, abuse, neglect, drugs and alcohol, poverty, and family economic crisis. These children need clear expectations and a support program to help them fit into what is happening at school. Middle school students especially display an overpowering emphasis on peer expectations and norms, many of which may conflict with school expectations and goals.

Our schools need clear behavioral expectations and support structures to respond to "adjustment" problems as they occur. Failure to respond effectively brings on behavior that can result in rapid deterioration of the quality of the educational environment for all students and their teachers. We see students acting out, disrupting classes, displaying disinterest, refusing to participate in projects, and engaging in conflict with other students. Although more interesting and engaging learning activities would probably reduce the number of youngsters who are disruptive or turned off, some students will struggle in the face of the most relevant activities.

Teachers can anticipate these struggles by providing a clear set of expectations for conduct. They can negotiate contracts with their students that specify rules and expectations that students wish to hold for teachers as well as for students. These contracts clearly indicate predictable consequences for negative or destructive conduct. When classroom rules and agreements are clearly displayed in classrooms, they can be consulted and referred to as reminders whenever a student's conduct must be addressed. Contracts highlight individual responsibility and choice, emphasizing that each person is responsible and will be held accountable for their choices.[46]

Inevitably, some students will challenge classroom contracts, consistently pushing beyond their limits. We can expect our general behavioral system to work effectively with approximately 90 percent of the students, but we need additional strategies for dealing with the remaining 10 percent.[47] Often all that is needed is a more specific and individualized behavioral contract developed between teacher and student. On occasion, the principal, guidance counselor, and parents are included in developing and carrying out these contracts.[48] While the guidance counselor and principal may be involved in negotiating individual contingency contracts for more extreme behavioral problems, the principal often plays the role of the "enforcer" when necessary, enacting suspension and other, more severe consequences when students engage in destructive or harmful behavior.

Guidance and Counseling Services

An effective counseling and advising service needs to be available for students. Most students need some support and intervention at some point in their school careers. The guidance counselor can meet with troubled students one-on-one or in small focus groups directed toward enhancing problem solving, decision making, personal planning, and social skills.

For instance, the guidance counselor may form a small group of students (nominated by teachers) who are notorious for disrupting classroom activities with troublesome arguments and disputes involving fellow students and teachers. These students are gathered together for regular training and practice sessions where they practice social skills, such as following directions, giving and receiving positive and negative feedback, and negotiating with peers and adults. We find that after practicing these social skills in a variety of school environments, with a variety of school personnel, the negative and argumentative behaviors are often replaced by more effective communication, problem-solving, and negotiating behaviors. Students are not born knowing these acceptable skills, nor are they modeled for them in many of their homes. We know, however, that they can learn and practice good social skills.

Another common guidance group involves children of divorce. As many as half of the children in many classrooms may have recently experienced or are currently in the midst of a family divorce. School performance and behavior is almost always negatively affected by family marital problems.[49] Divorce groups provide children with an opportunity to talk about their fears, generate solutions and strategies for coping with the situation at home, realize that the divorce or separation is not their fault, and, perhaps most importantly, find out that they are not alone with their feelings and fears. These discussion groups can lead students toward taking charge, developing a sense of control over their own lives and enhancing their self-esteem.

The guidance counselor also offers prevention services for all students, working with whole classrooms and often teaming with classroom teachers. These whole-class sessions provide a nonthreatening forum for group discussions on important themes and pressures, such as drug and alcohol abuse, sex, divorce, and self-confidence.

The goal is to develop an integrated support system for students that includes general education, special education, guidance, and the family and outside agency personnel. For more severe adjustment problems, students and their families can be referred to outside agencies for counseling and other support. School personnel may confer and coordinate with outside service personnel to attempt parallel practices within the school when appropriate.

CHARACTERISTICS OF THE SPECIAL EDUCATION SYSTEM

What is conventionally viewed as special must begin to be viewed as a necessary component of normal. The special education system needs to become an integrated support structure, so entwined with the general system that it may be difficult to identify it as a separate structure. This will require some significant changes in the way we do business, in the ways general classrooms operate, and in the ways we provide support services for learners with special needs. Such changes must be granted special status until they receive the attention and support necessary for general inclusion.[50]

As we work toward a more integrated general and special education system, we must change some of the emphasis in special education. We need to spend less time categorizing and counting students. This overreliance on diagnosis and categorization encourages the unrealistic notion that if we can name it, we can fix it. We need to preserve the energy necessary to assure a wide range of meaningful learning opportunities and accommodations. With our limited resources, we cannot afford to waste energy implementing and monitoring legalistic procedures for evaluating, identifying, classifying, developing IEPs, and assuring parental rights.

While these procedures were developed with great expectations and promise, they have been disappointing in practice. They have encouraged adversarial relationships between parents and professionals, as parents make increasingly unrealistic demands for special services and miraculous cures for their children. They have resulted in procedures that overshadow the needs of youngsters. They have resulted in paperwork and procedural burdens on professionals, effectively robbing students of the scarcest resource in schools–teacher time. Today, most special educators estimate that 50 percent of their time is spent on paperwork and other procedural and bureaucratic activities. Every minute that educators spend on complicated diagnostic procedures and reports is time not spent collaborating with other educators and providing direct services to students.

The goal that every student will have an IEP will never be realized as long as we remain burdened with such formalized documentation, restrictive identification and categorization rules, mechanistic procedures for parent involvement, and measurement of discrete IEP objectives. Rarely do these procedures connect in meaningful ways with the curriculum-in-practice and instructional strategies in classrooms where students spend most of their time.

We need more collaborative teamwork between special and general educators. Educators from a variety of disciplines can pool their expertise in ways that can produce continuous appraisal of each child's current personal, social, physical, and intellectual performance and needs. Their programming can become more dynamic and holistic, integrating activities and interventions, with far more effectiveness than the fragmented and compartmentalized interventions produced by overspecialized, separate delivery systems. Specialists such as the school psychologists, consulting teachers, and speech and language pathologists can redefine their roles to take on consulting, collaborative partnerships with general classroom teachers. At the simplest level, ancillary staff can consult with general educators, providing specific suggestions and strategies to enhance growth and development of students with disabilities in the general class. At a more intense level of intervention, for students with greater needs and deficits, specialists can roll up their sleeves, put away their tests, and join with classroom teachers in their classrooms, working side by side to devise accommodations that enable special students to experience success along with their peers.

On a systemwide basis, all educators (not just the specialists) need a mechanism to join together and share expertise. They need a forum through which they can develop strategies to best meet the wide range of student needs that confront them on a daily basis in classrooms. This forum can be provided by building-based teams (often referred to as teacher support teams) that encourage collaborative sharing and problem solving.

The Teacher Support Team

A teacher support team consists of special and general educators working collaboratively to solve learning problems, difficulties, and challenges as they appear. Adjustment and learning problems can be addressed through a collaborative problem-solving model that provides for a range of accommodations and strategies to improve student performance and meet individual needs. Involvement in teacher support teams strengthens teacher competence and ownership in addressing a wide range of learning problems and challenges.[51] Special educators join their general education colleagues in rearranging the learning environment to enable all students to improve their performance and to experience more success. When students first begin to struggle with their learning or behavior, specialists join with the principal and classroom teachers to carefully explore individual needs. Student needs are matched with different, promising instructional strategies. As new strategies are tried, members of the teacher support team monitor student performance, adjusting their strategies as needed to ensure student success.

We need to resort to a formal special education diagnosis and classification only after a number of accommodations and adjustments have been tried without obtaining the desired results. Even when a child is officially classified as a special education student with a designated handicapping condition that significantly impairs his or her ability to learn, special education services can be provided within general classrooms to a great extent. As student needs become more complex, special and general educators can continue to work together as a team, while increasingly intense (costly or specialized) supports are added to the student's learning environment.[52]

The Supports—A Continuum of Services

Special education has long relied on a model that provides for a continuum of services[53] that become increasingly costly, individualized, and specialized based on the degree of severity and complexity of learning and behavioral problems. The traditional special education continuum need not be dismantled but should use the general classroom as the site for delivery of most of those special services. We do not need to remove students with learning disabilities to resource rooms to deliver specially tailored instructional methods in small groups. Those special instructional methods and even special personnel can be brought to the classrooms.

When we bring the special services to the classrooms, we inevitably find other children who are not labeled as handicapped who can benefit from the special instruction being offered. Those children are included in the group as well. When we do this, we are forced to acknowledge that the special education continuum looks the same whether we take time out for the lengthy special education identification, diagnosis, classification process, or not. We need to discover ways to deregulate and "de-bureaucratize" these processes and procedures if we are to make the best use of the energy, expertise, and training of our specialists and ancillary staff. (See chap. 9 for a discussion of current state waivers.)

Family Contact and Coordination

As soon as a child begins to present learning problems, the teacher support team initiates coordination and problem solving with the family. We hope to find the family available and able to work in concert with school personnel to redesign and rethink the child's program to encourage a higher success rate.

Individual contracts with at-home consequences for acceptable performance are often our first line of defense. For example, family members and teachers jointly develop performance contracts for students who are not engaged in classroom activities or who are engaged in disruptive behaviors. If students meet contract expectations, they are provided with in-class consequences, such as individual computer time with an older student, and home consequences as well. Popular home consequences are time playing with their mothers or fathers for older students and reading time with a parent or older sibling for younger students. Family coordination plans often include simple forms of instructional intervention, such as paired reading time, homework checking, or even tutorial sessions for drill and practice of basic skills. Often, key family members are provided with support and training to enable them to carry out the at-home intervention procedures effectively.

If family intervention does not provide enough support to result in the desired performance, or when the family is unavailable or unable to work with their child, we move to the next step in the continuum, increasing the intensity of our intervention. If the family is involved, however, and able to work effectively with their child, family support is maintained as we intensify our supports.

Consultation between Ancillary Staff and Teachers

If initial teacher support, team problem solving, and experimentation with adjustments to the learning environment do not result in the desired results, specially trained staff (assigned based on a match between the student's needs and specialists' areas of expertise) become more intensely involved. They provide more focused consultation with the classroom teacher, adjusting, redesigning, and monitoring educational interventions for individual children.

Specialists often provide classroom observations, detailed data collection, analysis, diagnostic teaching, and coaching as part of the collaboration with classroom teachers at this stage. Teacher and specialist(s) continue to modify the learning environment and instructional strategies until the child in question performs successfully.

Direct Intervention by Specialists

If success is not forthcoming, if special needs are so demanding that still more resources are required in the classroom, the specialist may team teach with classroom teachers. Classroom teachers and specialists team to provide direct instruction and assistance for students with highly specialized needs or performance levels so low that supports are required to enable functioning with dignity and competence among their age-mates. Specialists work with teachers to rethink and implement instructional activities that will successfully accommodate children with special needs.

Specialists are also available to assist in carrying out accommodations with small groups of children. Specialists may provide specific small-group instruction (often including other children in addition to the students with disabilities), while the classroom teacher engages in specific small-group instruction for others. At other times, specialists may team with the classroom teacher, assisting in the wide range of group management, individual evaluation, and feedback responses required in an active classroom.

Providing Paraprofessional Support

Students with highly specific or particularly disadvantageous handicaps, such as significant mental retardation, severe emotional disturbance, vision, hearing or other physical impairment, may need additional personnel to assist them in the general learning environment. In such cases, paraprofessionals (aides), supervised jointly by special and general educators, may be assigned to students. While aides may officially be assigned to individual students, they provide an enriching resource to the entire classroom from which all students benefit.

Consider an aide assigned to a student with learning impairments who functions academically two to three years behind most of her age-mates. The aide acts as a translator and simplifier of the curriculum as the special student interacts with the activities set before her. The aide's support activities are guided by the classroom teacher and specialists based on their best sense of what the student needs to be successful.

The aide might read aloud to compensate for delayed reading performance. He might discuss a reading assignment in detail to ensure comprehension before the student attempts an application activity. He might write an essay as the student dictates it, in preparation for editing. He might work closely with a collaborative group that includes the special student, intervening when necessary to ensure smooth group process among all group members, social appropriateness, and coaching the special learner to bolster her confidence or competence as needed. Or, the aide might take over other student groupings to enable the classroom teacher to work individually or in small groups with the special learner. The possibilities are endless, but what counts is the extra assistance for the classroom teacher and the special relationship that inevitably develops between the aide, the special learner, and her classmates.

Another example might involve a sign language interpreter assisting a student with a severe hearing impairment. The interpreter would assist the student to communicate with others and understand what is being said in the classroom through the use of sign language while simultaneously building oral language and lipreading skills. The interpreter can also assist other children in learning to adjust their position and body movements to facilitate the youngster with hearing-impairment's lipreading, as well as to heighten everyone's sensitivity to the importance and function of visual, tactile, and kinesthetic cues and prompts. It is quite likely that the aide would begin teaching classmates sign language, thus encouraging and facilitating more direct communication between hearing and nonhearing children. The hearing children are bound to be curious and captivated by this beautiful, special language.

When an aide is provided for a classroom that includes children with more intense special needs, the environment is always enhanced. One can expect to see greater tolerance for diversity, heightened appreciation for special talents, and other benefits derived from the additional energy added by another caring and committed adult.

Pullout Services

Some services, such as specialized remedial reading and mathematics programs, study and tutorial sessions, counseling, community and survival skills, and related services (e.g., speech, occupational, and physical therapy) are sometimes most effectively provided in small-group or one-on-one settings, apart from the large group. With the emphasis on mainstreaming, opportunities for specialized instruction to remediate the disadvantages of particular handicaps have fallen into disfavor. But specialized learning opportunities are necessary for some students to build the skills they need to enable them to perform successfully in other activities with their age-mates and peers. Often such services are necessary to enable students to build necessary skills in nonschool environments such as the community, workplace, and home.

We need to maintain such pullout services, however, and they have to be important for all students. Schools can be organized so that there are times in the day when most students have opportunities to participate in specialized sessions, at which time they pursue special talents and interests. Our educational system needs to be organized in such a way that pullout services do not restrict youngsters from otherwise beneficial experiences, while at the same time guaranteeing that pullout opportunities do not stigmatize them as less good or able.

Referral to Specialized and Intense Community Services

A detailed discussion of the characteristics and arrangements of specialized separate settings is beyond the scope of this chapter. Yet we need to recognize that the continuum of services for special needs children includes separate, specialized settings and services. We cannot ignore or deny the existence of students with needs so specialized that the regular classroom environment cannot be staffed with sufficiently specialized expertise to provide adequate accommodations or guarantee that the educational opportunities of the other students will not be compromised.

JUST HOW FAR CAN WE GO WITH MAINSTREAMING?

This is a controversial issue; there are no clear guidelines on which everyone agrees. Each child's needs—physical, emotional, and intellectual—need to be taken into account and weighed against a number of environmental factors. Brown and his colleagues[54] have made a significant contribution to the debate surrounding how far we can go with mainstreaming, particularly with respect to students with severe intellectual disabilities.

Brown and his coauthors argue that children with severe disabilities should be based in the general education environment—the same classrooms in which they would have been placed if they were not disabled—and their removal from that environment should occur only in ways that relate to their educational goals and needs. These children should be "insiders" who go out for short periods of time rather than "outsiders" who come to visit. Brown and his colleagues point out,

> The future leaders, tax payers, service providers, and parents of children with disabilities are in those regular classrooms. They need direct experience with the kinds of children they will produce and the diversity of citizens with whom they will associate.[55]

Brown and his coauthors suggest a number of opportunities that must be provided for the most severely impaired students.

Opportunities to Build Social Relationships

Building social relationships and skills that can be exercised both in and out of school are of paramount importance for all people, including individuals with severe handicaps. We know that large amounts of time spent in the same environments and in a variety of activities are necessary for such social relationships to develop.[56] The fewer environments and activities, and the less time in each environment, the less likely that any student will develop a well-rounded social existence. Thus, substantial amounts of time should be available for the development of social skills and relationships, especially in the younger years.

Opportunities to Respond to the Priorities of Parents and Students

The priorities of parents and students themselves when making decisions about where students will spend their instructional time must be considered. Decisions will vary depending on whether priorities are the development of social skills, home-living skills, or workplace skills.

Opportunities to Maximize Acquisition of Meaningful Skills

Another important factor to consider is the probability of acquiring meaningful skills and content being taught in general education classrooms. If the skill being taught is likely to carry little meaning for the student's functional needs or is unlikely to be acquired without large investments of time and energy, then the student would probably spend his or her time working on other goals in other settings. For instance,

> While non-disabled peers are dissecting frogs and dividing decimals, it may be more appropriate for a student with severe intellectual disabilities to (spend his/her time) [sic] learning to communicate to a store clerk, participating in the preparation of a meal at home, and functioning in an integrated worksite.[57]

Students need to develop skills and strategies that enable them to function in a number of different environments. As individuals with severe disabilities grow older, building necessary skills to successfully function in the community and integrated workplace should take precedence over other, more school-related goals. One might expect to see them spend substantial amounts of time in general classrooms during the elementary years, with decreasing amounts during middle and high school years. It is important that these students develop functional and social skills in nonschool environments as well.

We should ask, Will a particular objective and the associated expenditures of resources enhance function in an increased number of environments?[58] If the answer is no, then it may be more appropriate to trade off classroom time for time in other environments in order to assure that the student has access to the maximum variety of environments that will enhance his or her independence, quality of life, and successful functioning.

Opportunities to Be Educated by the Most Competent Personnel

Brown and his colleagues address the qualities of personnel that the youngsters with severe disabilities will encounter in the general classrooms, suggesting that "time spent with competent persons should be maximized and time spent with incompetent persons should be minimized, regardless of degrees, certifications, years of experience, or management-labor agreements."[59]

Few would debate the necessity of all of these opportunities for all children. We want *all* of these opportunities for *all* of our children. Decisions to pull students out of the mainstream will become less and less necessary as schools progress toward developing and integrating those essential characteristics of the general education system, especially active, collegial learning and authentic products and projects. Brown and his coauthors summarize their position on mainstreaming this way:

> How much time should be spent in regular classes? Enough to ensure that the student is a member, not a visitor. A lot, if the student is engaged in meaningful activities. Quite a bit if she is young, but less as she approaches 21.[60]

While the foregoing discussions provide key considerations for deciding which environment is most appropriate for students with intellectual disabilities, the considerations may be somewhat different for students with severe emotional disturbances. With students who are extremely disruptive, destructive, or dangerous, we must consider their impact on others, as well as consider their own needs. We need to balance the needs of all of the children in the classroom with the needs of the special child. When the behavior of one child endangers others or destroys their opportunity to learn because the classroom is thrown into chaos, then removal from the general classroom may be necessary. Such removal need not be considered permanent, however, and efforts to bring the disruptive or destructive behaviors under control should remain a priority in order to enable the return to the general classroom as soon as and as much as possible.

In summary, there are no hard and fast rules to guide our determination of the best learning environment for any child. Instead there are numerous and complex considerations that must be balanced across environments, people, activities, learning objectives, attitudes, values, and priorities. The challenge is to strike a balance and not let a few considerations dominate the involvement of others. A basic question to ask when deciding the most appropriate learning environment for any student is, Will this choice enhance his or her options and opportunities, or will it restrict them? Answering this question should guide our balancing act for individuals and groups of children, and related, we will more likely meet the challenges successfully.

Specialized settings are still required. But we have to assure ourselves and our students that every resource available in the general system has been exercised, that every option has been considered and given a fair trial. The choice to remove a child from a classroom should be made with convincing evidence that the most important learning cannot be accomplished in the regular school environment, given our present knowledge and resources. It is likely that the more inclusive and flexible we become, the more our fund of knowledge and structural arrangements will improve, which will thereby increase our capacity to effectively accommodate greater and greater diversity into our educational environments.

THE ROLE OF STAFF DEVELOPMENT

Schools are undergoing massive restructuring in order to enact many of the options discussed above. They are relying more on school-based decision making, increased collaboration directed at meeting individual student needs, and achieving high performance for all students. A coherent and comprehensive staff development program must be available to support teachers in envisioning and enacting system change, as well as in expanding their instructional repertoire to address the wide diversity of student needs and interests. This is where the role of the central office becomes important. While the principal sets the expectation that teachers are responsible for each child's success, the central office reinforces that by bringing teaching resources, staff development, and insights to schools from research and practice.[61]

Comprehensive staff development programs must be designed and enacted at the school building level. Training programs must be identified and delivered in ways that involve the entire staff, often by staff members themselves. Research on staff development indicates several key attributes that must be included in effective comprehensive staff development programs:

1. A climate and culture that supports collegiality and collaboration encouraging experimentation and risk taking
2. Use of knowledge, including research and models for effective teaching, and principles of adult learning and change
3. Participation and leadership, involving teachers and administrators sharing responsibility for leadership
4. Resources and opportunities ensuring sufficient time and appropriate incentives and rewards
5. Integration and coherence between visions, directions, goals, and support structures[62]

Staff development must provide teachers access to effective practices and strategies that enable them to respond to the demands of student diversity. Teachers will need to add a wide range of accommodations to their instructional repertoire. They need to develop authentic and integrated methods to assess student performance. They need to rearrange their classroom routines to introduce more flexibility, active learning, collaborative groups, and authentic projects. School personnel must learn to work collaboratively, share expertise and tend to special needs, carry out multi-age grouping and tutoring programs, and redesign the school day and other structures necessary to enact their visions for improvement.

In order to carry out systemwide changes, teachers need to take a collaborative, leadership role in making decisions. Yet, we too often expect change without expense, without providing the necessary resources. We make a big mistake if we simply assume that teachers can form teams, assess the current state of affairs, and plan and implement significant systemic changes without providing them with the tools and techniques to do so. In the absence of training and information about strategies for change, adult learning, and promising practices, teacher teams will, at best, produce changes that amount to tinkering with the system, or, at worst, bog down in unfocused and uninformed planning processes and give up in frustration.

Teachers need training and support to assess and analyze overall school effectiveness, as well as detailed information regarding promising practices to meet specific needs and changes as they are identified by the assessment processes. They need to acquire the techniques necessary to create and enact visions for sweeping change. They need to learn strategies for change and ways to monitor their progress during their improvement process.

We cannot underestimate the challenge involved in enacting sweeping change while still keeping the old system running. This requires a higher tolerance for chaos and ambiguity than many teachers possess. Evans[63] characterizes teachers as a veteran, aging group, with an average age of fifty, with twenty years of experience, lacking in flexibility, and opposed to change or a desire to make their job more demanding. Thus, our schools need to adopt an aggressive approach to change, with an insistent demand for high performance from all, teachers and students alike. Staff development, the latest research, ingredients for vision building, time for coaching, teaming, and collaborative problem solving must be made sufficiently available for schools to meet the demands for high performance for all students.

CONCLUSION

What, then, should our school look and feel like when the vision, practices, and directions discussed in this chapter are in place? Glickman[64] has coined the concept of "elite schools," describing them this way:

The decentralization, deregulation, site-based, empowerment movement is on the right track because it uses what we know. . . . By elite, I don't mean schools that are necessarily rich or poor, suburban, urban, or rural. I don't mean schools where all students have high IQs or all teachers have advanced degrees. Instead, elite schools are places where central office people, building administrators, and teachers trust each other to share in decisions about teaching and learning. . . . Elite schools are those where the faculty wants to share in the choice and responsibilities of schoolwide decisions and where administrators and supervisors likewise want them to share.[65]

We know a lot about how to organize and carry out good teaching; we know how to work effectively with the diversity that greets us in classrooms. We can envision a school that is dedicated to and capable of honoring, even capitalizing on, diversity, which thus enables high performance and success for all students.

It is a school staffed by teachers who provide for student-directed, experiential learning opportunities. Its routines are flexible, and learning products are authentic, with intrinsic interest for students and community alike, because they are connected to the daily lives and interests of students and their families. The special education system is not separate but is an integral part of the whole. Special educators focus on sharing their expertise, providing direct services to children, and teaming with general educators, without being overburdened by regulations, classifications, and procedural safeguards. School personnel recognize that no one teacher knows enough to deliver a constantly challenging, relevant program, making all necessary accommodations required by the diverse needs of his or her group of students. Teachers rely on one another, sharing expertise in order to enhance the learning opportunities for students, to add to the knowledge base available to them and to solve problems and provide for special needs as they arise. A continuum of progressively more intense support is available, through adding personnel with specialized expertise, as student needs become more complicated. A comprehensive staff development program provides for the continual growth and development of all staff, featuring best practices and strategies in pursuit of school improvement and an expanding repertoire of classroom instructional practices.

With these elements in place, provided with adequate resources and time, we will have created a school with program coherence and equity, staffed by educators who have the confidence and competence to provide for the productive learning and success for all students.

EPILOGUE: A SCHOOL IN TRANSITION

Now consider a snapshot of a school in transition, one that is currently providing for high performance for all students and that hopes to do even more.

Fairfield Elementary School serves students in grades kindergarten through eight. Grades kindergarten through five encompass 185 students attending self-contained classrooms, staffed by ten classroom teachers and five instructional aides. Grades six through eight serve ninety students, staffed by four content teachers and three instructional aides, with a typical departmental structure. In addition, a principal, consulting teacher (special educator), speech and language pathologist, Chapter I teacher, guidance counselor, librarian, and part-time music, art, nurse, and physical education staff serve all the grades. Psychological and therapeutic services are purchased on an as-needed basis on a slim budget.

Our Special Education System

Our special education delivery system looks much like that discussed in this chapter. Instructional staff recognize and embrace their responsibility to provide for the productive learning of all students with all ranges of ability and style. We provide the full continuum of services as described in this chapter. These services are not provided not only for the thirty-five special education students but for all students. Special services personnel come into contact with all students in a variety of ways almost daily. They are a part of every school team, from grade-level teams, to student-focused planning teams, to interdisciplinary teams, to staff development teams.

All but one of our 275 students are educated within our school, with the vast majority of special education instruction taking place within the regular classroom. In the elementary grades, most instruction is delivered in the general classroom by special services personnel while the teacher (often assisted by community volunteers and older students) works with other small groups engaged in activities appropriate to their current needs and performance levels. In the middle grades, remedial, direct instruction occurs during study periods. Remedial and supportive instruction is carefully coordinated with the classroom teachers' instructional program.

The Teacher Support Team is the linchpin of special services. The principal, support services personnel, and a general classroom teacher are permanent members of the team. Teachers who want to improve classroom accommodations and interventions are ad hoc members of the team. Classroom teachers bring their challenges to the team, which then joins with them in problem solving and developing accommodations and interventions.

Once plans are devised, team members assist classroom teachers to implement them, encouraging follow-up discussions and revisions, especially when results appear to be falling short of the mark. More time has been allotted to meetings, and training sessions have been provided to support our skill-building efforts. We expect this focus to continue into the future, with additional attention to expanding our repertoire of promising interventions and our capacity for parental involvement.

Our General Education System

In my earlier description of the general education system, I have taken more liberties, envisioning that which might or could be, stretching what we have actually been able to accomplish within our school. While we are well on the way to developing structures, activities, and attitudes that match those envisioned, we are prey to the limitations created by keeping the whole system running smoothly while simultaneously enacting sweeping change.

Our counseling program and classroom management strategies are fairly well developed and in tune with the characteristics described in this chapter. Our counselor joins with other staff members to provide large-group instruction for all ages on a variety of adjustment concerns, including drug and alcohol abuse, personal planning, social skills, self-esteem, and other topics.

The counselor and the principal are intimately involved in classroom management and disciplinary practices in all classrooms. They develop and carry out individual behavioral contracts with students and families, and they frequently team with teachers in the negotiation of classroom rules, expectations, and consequences. The entire staff has spent considerable time developing consensus on student expectations and appropriate, pre-dictable consequences for student behavior. Students of all ages have a clear understanding of behavioral expectations and likely consequences for their actions.

Less well developed but well under way are our collaborative and active and authentic learning and alternative, integrated assessment strategies. All teachers use these strategies some of the time. In fact, many of the examples and illustrations offered in this chapter are drawn from our own classrooms. At the most basic level, all of our classrooms have forsaken the physical arrangement of lining all desks in rows, with the teacher perma-nently installed in the front of the room. It is not at all uncommon to see students scattered about in industrious little working groups, planning, problem solving, and creating interesting products in a variety of content and interest areas.

All of our classrooms include collaborative group activities several times a week. Teachers have integrated aspects of the Johnsons' Learning Together model, the group investigation process, and the jigsaw model into their group activities. We have spent considerable time on developing and implementing self-evaluation, group monitoring, and group goal-setting approaches. Special education students are always integrated into these activities.

We make frequent use of peer and cross-age tutoring during large-group instruction, individual skill building, and collaborative group work time. Many middle school students have regular "jobs" in the elementary classrooms where they work with younger students in a variety of ways, including participating in structured reading-aloud programs to build accuracy, drilling for math facts, conferencing with young writers on editing their written work, rewriting primary students' poems and chants, practicing spelling in structured ways, and just being a "buddy."

Teachers are grappling with alternative and more integrated assessment strategies. At least a third of the staff is involved in training programs, skill building, experimenting, and problem solving. As a result of a state-initiated movement, fourth and eighth grade language arts and math teachers have been involved in a multiyear staff development program focused on the development of portfolios for mathematics and writing. Connected to this ongoing effort, several teachers have experimented with student self-assessment, narrative evaluation, and development of more integrated, interdisciplinary, and authentic projects and learning activities.

We have begun to develop multiage classrooms in Fairfield. This year we have three classrooms in the elementary grades with plans to add two more next year. The middle school will also be rearranged into multiage groups next year. In addition to the designated multiage classes, most teachers are experimenting with multisession, cross-age units of instruction whereby older and younger students work together in a given curricular area. For example, our fourth and eighth grade students worked together for several days developing mathematics problems and puzzles for each other to solve.

Our Challenges

The more we change and restructure the way we do things, the more we become aware of the challenge embedded in keeping the "old" system running while enacting sweeping changes. As we attempt to integrate and establish these promising practices, we are confronted with contradictions within our system, most of which we simply have to live with until we have enough time to work our way through the necessary changes. Our traditional curriculum structure and assessment practices create the most pressing challenge. They are like vestigial organs, but far more troubling because they get in our way; they conflict with many of our emerging practices. We need to reshape our curriculum in ways that go beyond our present level of understanding and expertise.

While we tackle these daunting curricular and assessment challenges, we also will need to maintain a portion of our attention on the change efforts reported earlier. For these changes do not happen overnight. It takes constant practice, encouragement, coaching, and problem solving to fully integrate new practices. Thus, while tackling new challenges, we know we must hold some energy in reserve to expand our special and regular education teaming and our instructional repertoire to constantly improve our ability to actively engage each and every learner in his or her own growth and success, to achieve the highest performance possible.

NOTES

1. John I. Goodlad, *A Place Called School* (New York: McGraw-Hill, 1984); Robert Evans, "Making Mainstreaming Work through Pre-Referral Consultation," *Educational Leadership* 48, no. 1 (Sept. 1990): 73–77.
2. John I. Goodlad and Jeannie Oakes, "We Must Offer Equal Access to Knowledge," *Educational Leadership* 45, no. 5 (Feb. 1988): 16–22; Goodlad, *A Place Called School.*
3. Evans, "Making Mainstreaming Work," 73–77.
4. Ibid.
5. Goodlad and Oakes, "We Must Offer Equal Access," 17.
6. Carl Glickman, "Pretending Not to Know What We Know," *Educational Leadership* 48, no. 8 (May 1991): 5.
7. Larry M. Maheady, Katherine Sacca, and Gregory F. Harper, "Classwide Peer Tutoring with Mildly Handicapped High School Students," *Exceptional Children* 55, no. 1 (Sept. 1988): 58.
8. Lauren Resnick, comments made in presentation at Educational Futures Conference sponsored by the Association for Supervision and Curriculum Development, Alexandria, Virginia, October 1991.
9. Eliot Wigginton, *Sometimes a Shining Moment: The Foxfire Experience* (New York: Doubleday, 1985).
10. Anne Meek, "On 25 Years of Foxfire: A Conversation with Eliot Wigginton," *Educational Leadership* 47, no. 6 (March 1990): 30.
11. Glickman, "Pretending Not to Know," 4–9.
12. Meek, "On 25 Years of Foxfire," 33.
13. Wigginton, *Sometimes a Shining Moment.*
14. Grant Wiggins, "Teaching to the (Authentic) Test," *Educational Leadership* 46, no. 7 (April 1989): 41–47.
15. Dennie Wolf, "Portfolio Assessment: Sampling Student Work," *Educational Leadership* 46, no. 7 (April 1989): 35–39; Robert J. Marzano and Arthur L. Costa, "Question: Do Standardized Tests Measure General Cognitive Skills? Answer: No," *Educational Leadership* 45, no. 8 (May 1988): 66–71; Glickman, "Pretending Not to Know," 4–9.
16. Wolf, "Portfolio Assessment," 35.
17. Marzano and Costa, "Question: Do Standardized Tests," 66–71.
18. Wiggins, "Teaching to the (Authentic) Test," 41–47.
19. Theodore Sizer, "Changing Schools and Testing: An Uneasy Proposal," in *The Redesigning of Testing for the 21st Century: ETS Invitational Conference Proceedings* (Princeton, NJ: ETS, 1985).
20. Wiggins, "Teaching to the (Authentic) Test," 42.
21. F. Leon Paulson, Pearl R. Paulson, and Carol A. Meyer, "What Makes a Portfolio a Portfolio?" *Educational Leadership* 48, no. 5 (Feb. 1991): 63.
22. Ibid.
23. Wolf, "Portfolio Assessment," 38.
24. *Vermont Mathematics Portfolio Resource Book* (Montpelier, VT: State Department of Education, 1991).
25. Yetta Goodman, "Kid Watching: An Alternative to Testing," *National Elementary Principal* 57 (1978): 41–45.

26. Robert E. Slavin, "Synthesis of Research on Cooperative Learning," *Educational Leadership* 48 (Feb. 1991) 5: 71–81.
27. Ibid., 71.
28. David W. Johnson and Roger T. Johnson, *Learning Together and Alone*, 2d ed. (Englewood Cliffs, NJ: Prentice-Hall, 1987).
29. Robert E. Slavin, *Using Student Team Learning*, 3d ed. (Baltimore, MD: Center for Research on Elementary and Middle Schools, Johns Hopkins University, 1986); Slavin, "Synthesis of Research on Cooperative Learning"; Robert Stevens, Nancy A. Madden, Robert E. Slavin, and A. M. Farnish, "Cooperative Integrated Reading and Composition: Two Field Experiments," *Reading Research Quarterly* 22 (1987): 433–54.
30. Elliot Aronson, N. Blaney, C. Stephan, J. Sikes, and M. Snapp, *The Jigsaw Classroom* (Beverly Hills: Sage, 1978).
31. Shlomo Sharan and Yael Sharan, *Small Group Teaching* (Englewood Cliffs, NJ: Educational Technology Publications, 1976).
32. Ron Brandt, "On Cooperation in Schools: A Conversation with David and Roger Johnson," *Educational Leadership* 45, no.3 (Nov. 1987): 14–19.
33. Slavin, "Synthesis of Research on Cooperative Learning," 71–81.
34. Johnson and Johnson, *Learning Together and Alone*.
35. Aronson et al., *The Jigsaw Classroom*.
36. Slavin, "Synthesis of Research on Cooperative Learning."
37. Ibid.
38. Shlomo Sharan and Yael Sharan, "Group Investigation Expands Cooperative Learning," *Educational Leadership* 47, no. 4 (Dec. 1989–Jan. 1990): 17–20.
39. Sharan and Sharan, *Small Group Teaching*.
40. Ibid., 20.
41. Joseph Delquadri, Charles R. Greenwood, Debra Whorton, Judith J. Carta, and R. Vance Hall, "Classwide Peer Tutoring," *Exceptional Children* 52, no. 6 (April 1986): 535–42.
42. Ibid.
43. Maheady et al., "Classwide Peer Tutoring."
44. Slavin, "Synthesis of Research on Cooperative Learning."
45. Delquadri et al., "Classwide Peer Tutoring"; Maheady et al., "Classwide Peer Tutoring with Mildly Handicapped High School Students"; and Slavin, "Synthesis of Research on Cooperative Learning."
46. William Glasser, *Control Theory in the Classroom* (New York: Harper & Row, 1986); William Glasser, *Schools without Failure* (New York: Harper & Row, 1969). For more information on a process for developing classroom contracts with groups of students, see Richard L. Curwin and Allen N. Mendler, *Discipline with Dignity* (Alexandria, VA: Association for Supervision and Curriculum Development, 1988).
47. Curwin and Mendler, *Discipline with Dignity*.
48. For more information on individual, contingency contracting, see William Jenson, Howard Sloane, and Richard Young, *Applied Behavior Analysis in Education: A Structured Teaching Approach* (Englewood Cliffs, NJ: Prentice-Hall, 1988): 220–26; or Beth Sulzer and Roy Mayer, *Behavior Modification Procedures for School Personnel* (Hinsdale, IL: Dryden Press, 1972).
49. Judith S. Wallerstein and Sandra S. Blakeslee, *Second Chances: Men, Women, and Children a Decade after Divorce* (New York: Ticknor & Fields, 1990).

50. John I. Goodlad and Thomas C. Lovitt, "Preface" in this book.
51. Evans, "Making Mainstreaming Work."
52. For more details on the formation and operation of teacher support and consultation arrangements, see Evans, "Making Mainstreaming Work;" and Joseph E. Zins, Michael J. Curtis, J. L. Garden, and C. R. Ponti, *Helping Students Succeed in the Regular Classroom: A Guide for Developing Intervention Assistance Programs* (San Francisco: Jossey-Bass, 1988).
53. Evelyn N. Deno, *Educating Children with Emotional, Learning, and Behavior Problems* (Minneapolis: University of Minnesota, 1978).
54. Lou Brown, Patrick Schwartz, Alice Udvari-Solner, Elise F. Kampschroer, Fran Johnson, Jack Jorgensen, and Lee Gruenewald, "How Much Time Should Students with Severe Intellectual Disabilities Spend in Regular Education Classrooms and Elsewhere?" *Journal of the Association for Persons with Severe Handicaps* 16, no. 1 (1991): 39–47.
55. Brown et al., "How Much Time Should Students . . .?" 40.
56. Douglas D. Biklen, "Making Difference Ordinary" in *Educating All Students in the Mainstream of Regular Education*, ed. Susan Stainback, William Stainback, and Marsha Forest (Baltimore: Paul H. Brooks, 1989), 235–48; Susan Stainback, William Stainback, and Robert Slavin, "Classroom Organization for Diversity among Students" in *Educating All Students*, 131–42; and Jeffrey Strully and Cindy Strully, "Friendship as an Educational Goal" in *Educating All Students*, 59–68.
57. Brown et al., "How Much Time Should Students . . .?" 43.
58. Ibid., 44.
59. Ibid.
60. Ibid., 46.
61. John I. Goodlad, "Access to Knowledge" in this book.
62. For more detailed information on research and strategies to implement effective building-based staff development, see Margaret A. Arbuckle and Lynn B. Murray, *Building Systems for Professional Growth: An Action Guide* (Andover, MA: The Regional Laboratory for Educational Improvement of the Northeast and Islands, 1989); Susan Loucks-Horsley, Cathy K. Harding, Margaret A. Arbuckle, Lynn B. Murray, Cynthia Dubae, and Martha K. Williams, *Continuing to Learn: A Guidebook for Teacher Development* (Andover, MA: The Regional Laboratory for Educational Improvement of the Northeast and Islands, 1987).
63. Evans, "Making Mainstreaming Work," 73–77.
64. Glickman, "Pretending Not to Know What We Know."
65. Ibid., 9.

9

Restructuring Schools for Better Alignment of General and Special Education

Judy A. Schrag

THE CONTEXT FOR CHANGE

In 1975, the U.S. Congress passed one of the most comprehensive education laws in the history of this country, the Education for All Handicapped Children Act, or PL 94-142. This act was a set of amendments to the Education of the Handicapped Act, which brought together various features of state and federal legislation into one national public law, making available to every eligible student with a disability a free and appropriate public education within the least restrictive environment. This law established a set of procedural safeguards and protections for children and their parents, as well as educational planning within the framework of an individualized education program (IEP) and the full involvement of the parents in the educational process.

Further amendments of PL 94-142 in 1978 emphasized the importance of a smooth transition of students from high schools to the world of work and community living. In addition, Part H was added, which initiated the Infant and Toddler Program with a four-year phase-in prior to implementation of a statewide, comprehensive interagency system of services. Congress also established 1991 as the deadline for preschool (ages three to five) mandates within each state as a condition for continued receipt of federal funds for these children with developmental delays and disabilities.

In 1990, Congress passed the Individuals with Disabilities Education Act (IDEA) with further amendments, refinements, and emphases, including improved services for children with disabilities from various cultural and minority groups, assistive technology as a related service, support for students with serious emotional disturbance, as well as continued improvements in transition and cooperative programming across special education,

203

vocational rehabilitation, mental health, and other social service agencies. In 1991, amendments to IDEA reauthorized the Part H, Infant and Toddler Program, as well as made further refinements in the Part B program.

The provisions and protections of this federal legislation as well as the various state laws in special education have served as the impetus and framework for tremendous improvements in programs and services for infants, toddlers, children, and youth with disabilities. During the 1989–90 school year, special education and related services were provided for 4,687,620 school-age children with disabilities. In addition, 250,000 infants and toddlers and 388,615 children ages three through five with disabilities and developmental delays were served in early intervention programs.[1]

Oliver Wendell Holmes once said, "The greatest thing in the world is not so much where we are, but where we are going." Despite the tremendous improvements in our progress toward full services, we are challenged to continue evolving our systems and services forward and to bring special education more in line with general education and other categorical or support programs.

Ongoing changes in special education could be seen as a needed paradigm shift; however, this suggests that one system has to be disposed for another. Our challenge, rather, is to look at special education as an evolving and developing system. The 1970s represented an era in which the emphasis was on access to education for children with disabilities. A separate body of knowledge emerged about working with specific handicaps and disabilities. Special education programs were often developed separately from and uncoordinated with general education.

In the 1970s, the emphasis for students with disabilities was on access to the same physical space as that given to students without handicaps or disabilities. Many children with disabilities were out of school and unserved. Programs that were developed were often separate and segregated. A separate agenda emerged in the form of a separate curriculum for children and youth with disabilities (e.g., Frostig developmental programs, SRA kits, Sullivan programmed materials, and DISTAR programs). Rather than content and curriculum, the emphasis in special education was on skill development and behavioral management. Mainstreaming efforts explored the parameters of common access to physical space within school buildings for students with disabilities.

The 1980s saw the emergence of curriculum access and a more holistic approach to the integration of programs. The body of knowledge and practice expanded to explore adaptation of general education curricula for students with disabilities, as well as intervention strategies that focused on peer tutoring, collaborative instruction, and cooperative learning.

The evolution of special education continues in the 1990s with exploration of program boundary issues among and between special education, Chapter 1, migrant education, bilingual education, other support programs, and general education. Efforts are being made to coordinate these educational programs as well as the broader programs of health, mental health, developmental disabilities, vocational rehabilitation, and other social service programs. The focus on service integration to serve the "whole child" will continue to the year 2000 within the context of educational reform. Parental involvement will continue to be a critical focus as programs and services continue to evolve.

One unintended outcome of the implementation of federal and state special education laws during the 1970s and 1980s is that special education has often been viewed as a separate system not effectively coordinated and aligned with general education. Special education has often been viewed as a "place" rather than as curriculum and instructional support. We are challenged by the need to balance the emphasis of the 1970s and 1980s on access, compliance, and the procedural construct of special education and related services with that of innovation, experimentation, and procedural and content fine-tuning in order to achieve an expanded emphasis on improved student outcomes. Special education must be viewed not as a "place" but rather as a set of instructional and curricular supports intended to provide a broad array of better student outcomes. A more coordinated and interfaced educational system that focuses on the "whole child" and curricular and instructional improvements is needed to assure better outcomes for our students with disabilities and their families.

As the balance between and emphasis on process and outcomes is explored, it will be necessary to maintain the rights of students with disabilities and their families (see Figure 1). The use of a "deficit" model in special

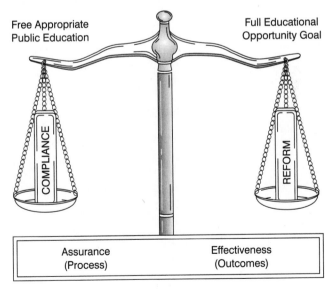

Figure 1
Challenge of the 1990s

education and the emphasis on skill development has also unintentionally communicated lower expectations for students with disabilities as compared to their peers without disabilities. Outcomes for students with disabilities must include a wide array of skills and other outcomes for all students as well as those unique to the disability (see Figure 2).

At least three reasons or forces prompt the need for further evolution of our special education programs and related services. First, the changing population of students in our classrooms is resulting in the continued blurring of special and general education programs as well as the social and health services needed to meet their complex needs. Second, outcome data support the need for improved results for students with disabilities. Finally, there is a growing body of knowledge from both research and practice regarding organizational, instructional and curricular strategies that work.

The timing is right for change. Educational reform is occurring across the country. A number of additional changes at the local level are being influenced by the America 2000 strategy proposed by President Bush and Secretary of Education Lamar Alexander. Current restructuring efforts within the states are stimulated by a focus on student performance, based on the premise that all students can and must learn at higher levels. In addition, current restructuring efforts within the states are based on a long-term commitment to fundamental, systemic change. This systemic change must deal with all the components within the educational system, including special education, with the goal of an interfaced, coordinated system of restructured service delivery that deals more effectively with complex student diversity.

The remainder of this chapter explores four questions for special education refinement and change within the context of overall educational change:

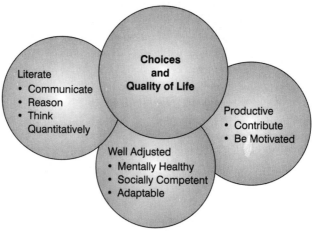

Figure 2
Outcome Framework

1. What do we want students with disabilities to know and be able to do?
2. What kinds of learning experiences, instructional strategies, and service delivery options produce these outcomes?
3. What considerations are needed in order to make special education more aligned and coordinated with general education and to assure that appropriate refinements and change will occur?
4. What type of accountability is needed to assure a positive relationship between our services and interventions with improved student outcomes and other desired results?

In addition to a discussion of these questions, examples of education reform occurring across the country that both indirectly and directly impact students with disabilities within the states related to these questions are highlighted. It should be noted that state examples of refinements, reform, and restructuring efforts involving special and general education are taken from a report that was developed by the Regional Resource and Federal Centers Program at my request as a resource document[2] for a Leadership Conference for State Directors of Special Education sponsored by the Office of Special Education Programs (OSEP). Other examples used throughout the chapter are taken from national reports produced by the National Governors Association[3] and the Council of Chief States School Officers.[4] Specific caveats of data gathering, analysis, and conclusions included within these reports are reemphasized here since I did not contact individual states personally to confirm the accuracy of information cited. It is also important to note that school restructuring and reform efforts within the states are at various stages of initiation, development, and implementation.

Throughout this chapter, specific issues are raised that must be resolved in order to better align special education with general education within the context of educational reform. For example, the role of the school principal will be emphasized as the instructional leader responsible for change at the school building level. The need for maintaining existing student rights will continually be stressed within the context of needed change. The generic term *students* will be used throughout to refer to infants, toddlers, children, and youth with disabilities and developmental delays who are eligible for early intervention or special education and related services.

REASONS FOR CHANGE AND REFINEMENTS IN SERVICES FOR STUDENTS WITH DISABILITIES

As stated earlier, tremendous growth and positive benefits have been made for students with disabilities and their families during the past ten to fifteen years. There are, however, several factors that stimulate continued refinements and improvements in our programs and services in order to achieve better outcomes for our students.

A Changing Student Population

The population of students being served within special education programs today and in the future is changing, which requires closer integration and coordination of services within the educational system and with a broader array of health and social services. For example, figures from the National Institute for Drug Abuse estimate the number of infants prenatally exposed to illicit drugs (cocaine, marijuana, and alcohol) to be 554,000 to 739,000—14 to 18 percent of all newborns.[5] Research and experience are insufficient to predict the number of children within this emerging population who will require special education and related services, with estimates varying from 5 to 52 percent.[6]

Other changes in the population of students include increased numbers of children who suffer from fetal alcohol syndrome, medically fragile conditions, Fragile X, and other syndromes such as Trisomy 13 and 18; who are premature with an increased likelihood of learning problems; who are culturally and linguistically diverse with learning problems; who are head injured; and who have other physical impairments as a result of child abuse. These changes will require use of the existing as well as an expanded knowledge base, differential intervention approaches, and parents trained and informed about available services for their children. The complex needs of these children are resulting in a further blurring of the responsibilities of special and general education as well as other categorical programs within the educational system. In addition, expanded interagency linkages between education, health and social services are critical to meeting the needs of these children.

Documented Outcomes of Special Education

Various studies tell us that students with disabilities continue to drop out of school at a rate of between 1.5 to 2 times greater than students without disabilities in general education.[7] Data from the National Longitudinal Study, mandated by Congress in 1983, found that 31.3 percent of all special education students within the sample of 6,000 students with disabilities between the ages of thirteen to twenty-one were failing in one or more classes. Of these, 20.5 percent were failing in six or more classes. In addition, less than 50 percent of special education graduates sampled were fully employed after leaving high school. Nineteen percent of youth with serious emotional disturbance were arrested. Of this total, 17.4 percent had been out of school less than one year, and 42.8 percent had been out of school for more than one year.[8]

Data also show that special education students are significantly more likely than students as a whole to come from low-income families, single-parent families, and families with heads of households with relatively little education. These economic and family structure factors present their own obstacles to educational achievement and later outcomes. Lower socioeconomic status contributes to the likelihood of youth dropping out of school, becoming involved with the criminal justice system, and doing poorly in the competitive job market.[9]

These data challenge us to double our efforts in transition; integration; curriculum adaptation; alignment of technology, media, and materials with curriculum and instruction; and implementation of a more dynamic continuum of educational options that emphasize greater continuity, fluidity, coordination, and availability. Our educational system simply must be a more integrated and coordinated system of education.

The Strategies Highlighted by Current Research and Practice

The third reason for greater collaboration and integration of the educational components, including special education, is that there is less need for gathering new information about what we do not know and more need for implementing what we know works, based on our existing and growing body of knowledge, research, and practice.

OSEP has had a five-year research agenda to help states investigate instructional, organizational, and administrative issues related to educating children with disabilities in the general classroom environment. Research competitions have resulted in forty-one projects funded within eight priority areas. The first ten projects, funded in 1985, investigated prereferral programs for providing instructional and evaluative services in general education settings before referral to special education become necessary (e.g., early identification systems, collaborative consultation models, and social skills training).

Beginning in 1986, the focus of research shifted to instructional and organizational designs developed in general education, building explicitly on the teacher and school effectiveness literature developed over the last three decades. In 1987, research projects were funded to identify instructional, administrative, and organizational strategies for delivering special education services within the regular classroom using teacher assistance teams, in-classroom assistance models, and teacher consultation strategies. A research synthesis project was also funded in 1987 to gather information regarding specific variables related to effective education of students with mild disabilities in general education settings.

In 1988, research projects supported the design of a school building model for educating all children with disabilities in general education. A center was also funded at Research Triangle Institute in North Carolina to engage in research synthesis, analysis, and information support for implementing services for students with disabilities in general education. During the next two years, 1989 and 1990, research projects examined general education curricula for kindergarten through grade eight in the areas of mathematics, science, social studies, and language arts. These projects analyzed the design of textbooks, teacher-delivery procedures, and scope and sequences of widely adopted K–8 curricula and selected alternative curricula. The pedagogical alignment of the curricular features with the learning characteristics and needs of students with disabilities was specifically studied. In addition, projects were funded to investigate the planning, adaptation, and individualization of instruction in mainstream settings containing students with disabilities. In 1992, research projects were funded to continue exploring the dimensions of high school curricula and adaptations needed for students with disabilities.[10]

OSEP has also funded system change grants in eleven states that are supporting efforts to restructure services for students with severe handicaps in least restrictive settings. In addition to this and other research and training and demonstration programs supported by the federal government, state education agencies have funded and carried out additional research and demonstration efforts to explore instructional, administrative, and organizational alternatives for students with disabilities and for other low-performing students.

Compendiums and other individual research cited later in this chapter also reflect a growing body of knowledge and practice about what works. Much of this research and practice is not unique to special education but represents effective school and teaching research in education and is directly applicable to special education.

RESTRUCTURING

Prior to 1985, the word *restructuring* was virtually unheard of in education discussions. Today, restructuring is occurring everywhere. In November 1989, the Council of Chief State School Officers published a report on the status of restructuring efforts within the states.[11] In addition, the National Governors Association completed a 1991 update of reform efforts within the states.[12] In 1991, the National Education Goals Panel released its first annual report on the progress of the nation toward reaching the National Education Goals.[13]

In April 1991, President Bush called for a renaissance in education, stating that we have been too timid and not bold enough in our efforts to restructure the schools. The president's educational strategy, America 2000, proposes ways to move the nation toward achieving the national education goals and educational excellence and to restructure and revitalize America's educational system by the year 2000. America 2000 builds on four related themes:

- *For today's students:* Better and more accountable schools
- *For tomorrow's students:* New generation of American schools
- *For the rest of us* (yesterday's student's/today's work force): A "nation of students"
- *For everyone:* Communities where learning can happen[14]

To date, thirty-seven states, one territory (American Samoa), and the District of Columbia have launched America 2000 initiatives. In addition, more than 1,000 cities have been designated America 2000 communities. America 2000 is a framework intended to support and expand school reform and restructuring efforts already under way throughout the states and to encourage a network of new American schools and communities. All of these reform efforts need to be inclusionary; that is, they must focus on "breaking the mold" to deal more effectively with the needs of all students, including those with disabilities.

There are at least two key features that distinguish current restructuring from previous educational change. First, current policies focus on student performance, with the premise that all students can and must learn at higher levels. Second, current restructuring policy is a long-term commitment to fundamental, systemic change. In the past, reforms have tried to change one piece at a time in a system of many interlocking and dependent pieces.

Following is a discussion of questions presented earlier in this chapter that frame the challenges of continued refinement in special education during the 1990s. Examples of restructuring and reform within the states that are directly or indirectly benefiting special education are provided.

What Outcomes Do We Want for Our Students with Disabilities?

Although school districts and states may choose different words to describe desired student outcomes for the general school-age population, the listing that is often found in various reports, articles, and educational discussions overlaps considerably, reflecting much agreement among educators and the public. These outcomes include literacy, thinking and problem-solving ability, personal responsibility, communication skills, the ability to demonstrate mastery beyond paper-and-pencil exercises, numeracy skills and their application, and the ability to locate, retrieve, and synthesize information.[15]

Students with disabilities should also achieve these outcomes. In addition, it is critical that persons with disabilities have effective interpersonal skills, personal and community living skills, and job skills so that they can make the same choices as persons without disabilities with full social participation in society and an opportunity for an enhanced quality of life. Persons with disabilities need to become productive, contribute to society, and be motivated. We want persons with disabilities to be well adjusted, mentally healthy and socially competent, and adaptable to circumstances of life (refer again to Figure 2).

OSEP has provided support to several states, including New Hampshire, Connecticut, Utah, Colorado, Arizona, and Michigan, within the State Agency and Federal Evaluation Studies Program to explore the impact of special education on specific student outcomes. OSEP has also recently funded a National Outcomes Center at the University of Minnesota. This center was established to work with states and other policy groups to develop a conceptual model of educational outcomes for students with disabilities and to generate a list of indicators of these outcomes as well as measures for evaluating students' progress toward them. As the work of the center progresses, technical assistance will be provided to states initiating school reform activities directed at improving outcomes for students with disabilities. This center has completed a synthesis report of information available in the current literature that pertains to the educational outcomes of students with disabilities, as well as the current status of outcome indicator activities within the states.[16]

Following is a selected list of state restructuring activities that involve special education within broader initiatives focused on student outcomes:

- In Alaska, a state curriculum initiative entitled "Student Outcomes" began in 1990 based on the philosophy that the purpose of public education is to ensure that each student has the knowledge, skills, and attitudes required for responsible citizenship, economic productivity, and personal fulfillment. Student Outcomes will be articulated in all academic disciplines for all students, including those with disabilities.
- California is initiating a reform activity, "Every Student Succeeds," that is intended to improve the educational, psychological, and social outcomes of students who are currently failing in school or who are at risk of failing in the future. Data are collected on over forty performance indicators. Within special education, an outcome survey instrument has been developed and field-tested for students within resource specialist programs.
- The Connecticut Mastery Test program was initiated in 1984 to measure learning outcomes that most students can reasonably be expected to attain. Students with disabilities are participating in this program.
- The Kentucky Education Reform Act of 1990 established a Council on School Performance Standards to frame outcomes for all students that is intended to become the basis for a model curricular framework, a comprehensive and performance-based assessment, and an accountability system. A task force has been formed to advise this council on how outcomes can be stated to address the needs of students with disabilities. Outcomes are to be inclusive and avoid a parallel curricular framework.
- Minnesota is implementing an outcome-based educational system on a pilot, research, or district choice basis that is designed to assure alignment among learner outcomes, the assessment and feedback process, and the instructional process. Special education is an integral part of this system.
- Within the Missouri Excellence of Education Act enacted in 1985, there is an emphasis on learner outcome-based instruction, including outcomes for higher thinking levels in reading and language arts,

mathematics, science, and social studies. Special education is actively involved in these efforts.

- Special education in Nebraska is focusing on performance-based instruction with outcomes including skills in basic skills and literacies, higher-order thinking, creative thinking expression, problem solving, lifelong learning, work entry skills, motivation and disposition to learn, citizenship, and social and democratic values and skills.

- In New Hampshire, a State Education Agency–sponsored task force on performance outcomes has been formed with the goal of outlining the essential skills required of all high school graduates, including students with disabilities, in such areas as critical and creative thinking, decision making, problem solving, communication, initiative, and leadership. New Hampshire has implemented a student outcome information system to assess the progress and performance of special education students along several outcome indicators.

- In Utah, special education has been an active partner in an outcome-driven developmental model that is currently being utilized in several school districts throughout the state.

- Educational reform legislation in West Virginia includes a focus on improved educational outcomes and benefit for all students. "Goals for the Year 2000" include readiness for first grade, equal educational opportunity, competitive scores on national tests, increasing the number of ninth graders continuing through graduation, graduates ready for postsecondary education or employment, and literacy in the working-age population. Special education is included as an integral component within this reform.

What Kinds of Learning Experiences and
Other Options Improve Student Outcomes?

There is a growing body of knowledge and agreement among educators about the kinds of learning experiences that achieve these goals. "Teaching by telling" and "learning as recall" are now being replaced with individual and team learning opportunities that engage students, provide challenging tasks, offer choices and multiple answers, include flexible grouping and scheduling, and stress exploratory learning. Classrooms that are focusing on better outcomes view students as active learners engaged in project-oriented activities and not simply as receivers of knowledge.

We have learned much from research and practice over the past fifteen years regarding the instructional process. Ysseldyke and Christenson[17] have summarized twelve important components of an effective instructional environment that are based on research and positively correlate with student achievement:

1. *Instructional Presentation.* The nature of instruction highly affects student achievement. Lesson development may be the single most

important aspect of instruction including the components of an overview, explanation, demonstration, guided practice, feedback, use of cues, clear communication of instructional goals, high degree of teacher-student interaction, clarity of task directions, and frequency of monitoring of student understanding.[18] Clarity of presentation is critical for presentation of new curricular content.[19]

2. *Classroom Environment.* Classroom management is essential for achieving an academic focus for behavioral rules and organizational routines and for increasing student engagement rates. Clear behavioral rules and expectations should be provided. It is also important that students be taught critical instructional routines so that interruptions during teaching are reduced and time between instructional activities is brief. A cooperative, pleasant, accepting, and supportive atmosphere is conducive to learning. The positive effect of these characteristics on student achievement has been empirically documented.[20]

3. *High Teacher Expectations.* Several researchers have emphasized the importance of setting high yet realistic expectations for all students, particularly for low-performing students.[21]

4. *Importance of a Cognitive Emphasis.* Students who are able to solve problems and cognitively approach a task achieve more in school.[22] Students with disabilities do not always have sufficient problem-solving skills; therefore, Weinstein and Mayer[23] have suggested direct teaching of learning strategies.

5. *Motivational Strategies.* The implementation of motivation for learning is undisputed in the literature as a positive impact on student achievement.[24] Contingent reinforcement is positively related to achievement, whereas noncontingent reinforcement is unrelated in most instances. Younger and low-ability children, however, benefit from noncontingent, socially motivated praise.[25] Cotton[26] also noted that instructional reinforcement alone is as powerful to enhanced achievement as a combination of instructional and behavioral reinforcement.

6. *Relevant Practice.* A student's success rate is an important measure of task appropriateness. During guided or initial practice, a student's success rate should be at least 70 to 80 percent. Later, in independent activities, the student should demonstrate a 90 to 100 percent success rate. Active student monitoring is critical.[27]

7. *Academic Engaged Time.* Increases in direct instruction are highly related to increasing student engagement in learning.[28]

8. *Informed Feedback.* Feedback must be specific and explicit. Effective feedback provides students with increased opportunities to respond. A high rate of student response is needed for effective learning. A number of researchers have stressed the importance of

academic feedback as being strongly and consistently related to student achievement.[29]

9. *Adaptive Instruction.* Adaptive instruction involves clearly communicated instructional goals at an appropriate level of difficulty, monitoring, thorough feedback, and student responsibility for task completion.[30]

10. *Progress Evaluation.* It is important to monitor student progress to provide corrections and allow students time to achieve mastery. Monitoring student performance during seatwork activities is essential to ensure success.[31]

11. *Appropriate Match between Student Characteristics and Instruction.* Marliave and Filby[32] found that effective teachers are those who have achieved the best curricular and instructional match for a student engaged in diagnosis and prescription.

12. *Student Understanding.* The student must have a keen understanding and perception of tasks and directives for increasing engaged time and achievement. Research has shown that students' perception of teacher intentions is not always that intended by the teacher.[33]

Hofmeister and Lubke[34] have written an excellent book, *Research into Practice: Implementing Effective Teaching Strategies,* that provides practical suggestions in six distinct areas for translating findings from research to practice: planning for instructional improvement, time management, teaching functions, academic feedback, academic monitoring, and classroom management.

The Northwest Regional Educational Laboratory[35] has completed a synthesis of existing literature on the effects of alternative instructional interventions, broad educational policies and directions, program strategies, classroom grouping schemes, and teaching methods and procedures. The study explored the effectiveness of alternative instructional interventions for Washington state students with mild learning disabilities and other low-performing students. Literature is summarized on four program strategies: prereferral interventions, teacher assistance and consultation teams, curriculum adaptation, and curriculum-based assessment. Four classroom grouping schemes are identified in the research synthesis: peer and cross-age tutoring, cooperative learning, ability grouping and reduction of class size. Literature regarding three teaching methods and practices are reviewed: reciprocal teaching, social skills training, and study skills training. Finally, this research synthesis explores broad educational policies such as early intervention, effective teaching strategies, building-based decision making, and location of services.

Another research resource about teaching and learning is the document *What Works: Research about Teaching and Learning.*[36] Gaylord-Ross[37] has edited an excellent book that incudes many strategies for integrating students with disabilities into schools and communities; research-based findings and effective field experience are emphasized. Finally, the American Association of School Administrators has recently released a report of the application of research and common sense regarding learning styles in practice.[38]

Following is a selected list of state restructuring activities that involve special education within broader teaching, organizational, and administrative change initiatives:

- New Jersey has been restructuring special education for about five years with a focus on coordination with general education and other categorical programs.
- California has 150 experiments or pilots that implement a number of strategies, including cooperative learning, collaborative instruction, and curriculum-based instruction, all with an emphasis on coordinating general and special education.
- The Washington State Department of Education has been conducting research with the Association of Washington School Principals for the past six years to support building-based change for low-performing students.
- Alaska is seeking to determine how supplemental services such as migrant, Chapter I, bilingual, and early childhood services can be more effectively provided in integrated regular classrooms.
- In American Samoa, special education has initiated a screening and remediation system so that children can receive intervention early within the general education system.
- School-based collaborative team models are being studied in the District of Columbia.
- Collaborative consultation, based on the West and Idol model,[39] is being implemented in approximately 500 school districts throughout the United States and Canada. This special education service delivery model provides for enhanced collaboration among classroom teachers, special educators, and support staff in educational programming for students with disabilities.
- In Georgia, a "principal's academy" is planned in order to focus on the roles and responsibilities of the building principal in the integration of special education into the total school program.
- Illinois is implementing initiatives that encourage special education and standard curriculum personnel to work closely to provide the best education for all students.
- Iowa has initiated a renewed service delivery system. Fourteen of its fifteen area education agencies are currently involved in this statewide effort. An important feature of these initiatives is the integration of general and special education, with site-based changes and less reliance on pullout programs with an emphasis on provision of special

education programs and services in conjunction with the regular classroom.

- A number of states, including Maryland, Minnesota, New Jersey, and Washington, are implementing school-level committees to provide support to classroom teachers for students with varying special needs, different site-based management strategies, collaborative management, and alternative instructional strategies for low-performing students.

What Is Needed to Better Align Special and General Education and to Stimulate Change?

Earlier sections of this chapter have discussed several changes needed during the remainder of the 1990s that can facilitate the better alignment of special education with general education. These changes include focus on outcomes, implementation of effective school research regarding curricular and effective instructional strategies, and use of models of service delivery that are better aligned with general education and other social and health services in order to deal with the complex needs of a changing population. These and other changes must be made within the context of overall education reform and school restructuring, with the school principal playing a key role in effecting systemic change at the building level.

Changing Roles and Responsibilities

Restructured schools are changing in a number of ways. Educators are rethinking the ways that teachers teach and students learn, reorganizing to share decision making, changing the ways classrooms and schools look, and making structural changes that are intended to produce better outcomes for all students. Schools focusing on long-term systemic change offer significant potential benefits to students with disabilities to the extent that such restructuring creates a learning environment within which *all* students can learn at higher levels.

Continuing and expanded school reform activities called for through America 2000 and ongoing state restructuring initiatives are requiring new roles and responsibilities for administrators and educators at all levels—federal, state and local. Teaching students to think and make informed judgments is much more difficult than teaching isolated facts. Providing guidance and assistance and empowering teachers to change are more difficult for school and central office administrators than generating and overseeing the implementation of school district policy. For administrators at the state and federal levels, it is also more difficult to provide technical assistance and information than it is to carry out enforcement activities.

As school systems move to restructure their schools, the type of assistance they are requesting from state education agencies (SEAs) is changing. School districts want both vision and practical assistance as they work to improve instructional delivery systems. They want information that is more user friendly, practical, and likely to cause systems change. School districts want SEAs to focus less on process and more on outcomes; support innovation; and be networkers, disseminators, and resilient negotiators.[40]

Increasingly, state officials are realizing that as SEAs carry out these changing roles, they cannot run the same kind of SEA. These departments are changing in nearly a dozen states, including Oklahoma, Kansas, Arizona, and California. Organizational changes in the Virginia SEA are emphasizing increased field consultation, staff development, and other services to local school districts such as dissemination of research and practice. Layers of bureaucracy are being reduced. SEAs such as that in Massachusetts are moving away from an emphasis on regulation and more toward a focus on service and technical assistance. The Vermont SEA has changed its mission from a regulatory approach to a technical assistance role to help and facilitate efforts at the local level that focus on improving student performance. The New Jersey commissioner of education has launched a two-year plan to change the way the SEA works with school districts with an increased technical assistance role. A report card is also being implemented to allow school districts to evaluate the SEA. North Carolina is also considering report cards for school districts to evaluate SEA performance.

Within these organizational changes, several states including Kentucky, South Carolina, and New Mexico have infused special education personnel or entire units within broader educational units as a method of assuring increased collaboration between general and special education as well as coordinated services to the field. Other states are maintaining separate special education units but are increasing cross-unit collaboration and involvement in service and technical assistance. In New York, the commissioner of education has put together a "New Compact for Learning" that will allow local leaders to initiate strategies to pursue statewide goals.

Likewise, roles at the federal level are changing. Within the Department of Education, new and/or expanded linkages and coordination are occurring across units, including special education, Chapter I, migrant education, bilingual education, and general education. The department is reexamining ways to streamline procedures and functions to increase its efficiency and service to the field.

Mary Jean LeTendre, director of compensatory education programs within the U.S. Department of Education, and I are working to establish a national work group on Chapter 1 and special education. This work group is exploring program boundary issues related to coordination of Chapter I and special education. It is also identifying effective Chapter I and special education coordinated programs across the country as well as policy and other barriers that are complicating and preventing program coordination.

Access to Knowledge

Access to existing knowledge and current practice is a challenge within school restructuring efforts across the country. In fact, lack of access may be a greater barrier to change than rules, regulations, traditions, myths, and mind-sets.

States are implementing long-distance learning and other teleconference networking as vehicles for teachers and administrators to increase their access to knowledge. Principal and teacher academies are being implemented in several states. University and school faculties are also collaborating to create professional development or professional practice schools. School district professional development opportunities are changing, with emphasis on peer assistance and coaching. Through computer-based conferencing, educators around the country are helping one another in the restructuring process. For example, IRIS, a national telecommunications network, offers a variety of on-line forums for teachers and administrators including the "Technology and Restructuring Roundtable" conference that allows educators who are involved in restructuring efforts a vehicle for exchanging ideas, information, frustrations, and visions. Special Net and other electronic communication networks are being utilized for sharing knowledge and practice.

Time

Time is needed to change schools into productive learning environments—time to learn, plan, test new ideas, maintain lines of communication. Change must match the values, preferences, and capabilities of each building, school district, community, and state. Sufficient time at the local level is needed to involve those who will implement change (i.e., classroom teachers and other service providers) and those who will be affected by change (i.e., the parents, students, and the community).

School reform efforts within a number of states are looking at ways to structure time in schools such as the number of school days in a year, the number of hours in a school day, the proportion of a school day allotted for a single course or subject matter, and the improvement in the quality of time spent in the classroom by all students. For example, Missouri is expanding a program for slower students who are left in general education classrooms but tutored by a consortium of teachers and parents. Other states identified earlier are implementing teacher assistance teams or other building-based, problem-solving models in which time is allowed for teachers and other service providers to resolve issues and share expertise and solutions for enhanced student learning. Rhode Island provides peer coaching and team teaching within its "extra help" literacy program for children in grade four. Illinois has initiated building-based teams to assist teachers in making more appropriate referrals to special education. Teacher assistance teams are being implemented within demonstration sites in Missouri. Massachusetts is employing various strategies to provide additional time for general and special educators to work with students who have disabilities and other special needs.

Technology

Technology-rich environments can help children learn in a variety of ways through guided discovery. Sensory enhancers, keyboard adaptations and emulators, and environmental controls and manipulators can increase student access to curriculum and instruction. Multimedia environments are offering cooperative learning and other integrated learning opportunities for many students with disabilities and other special needs. For the past seven years, the Council for Exceptional Children has operated a Center for Special Education Technology funded by OSEP to influence the quality and availability of technology used for students with disabilities.

What Accountability Is Needed?

Accountability is a central aspect of education reform. The essence of accountability is to provide assurances to those inside and outside the system that the schools are moving in the right direction and providing quality outcomes. There are several aspects of accountability within the context of reform.

Changes in how authority is distributed, how decisions are decentralized, how accountability systems operate, the extent to which flexibility can be provided in return for more accountability, and the type of incentives included are all aspects of program accountability that connect the structural features of the system to each other, to the content of the program, and to student outcomes.

Assessment

Traditionally, states and school districts have relied on standardized testing to determine the linkage between curriculum and instructional content and student outcomes. Within reform efforts, various states are implementing new methods of assessment such as portfolio assessment, curriculum-based assessment, and cluster assessment. Assessment tools are being designed that are not limited to measuring only the specific content that students know but what they can do with what they know—to go beyond measuring knowledge to measuring performance and providing feedback for improving teaching and learning. For example, Vermont is involved in a unique experiment to create alternative assessment tools involving development of performance criteria that encourage critical thinking and higher-order thinking. Missouri has implemented Mastery of Achievement tests. In California, every public school student is provided a School Improvement Report. Other states including South Carolina, Minnesota, and Washington are exploring the use of curriculum-based assessment. Utah special education is an active partner in an outcome model with accountability performance assessment.

America 2000 endorses voluntary national assessment to challenge students to meet world-class standards. The National Council on Educational Standards and Testing is proposing that portfolio and cluster testing be utilized rather than relying on one standardized national test. These modified testing approaches should benefit students with disabilities who have typically failed on standardized tests. The work of the National Outcomes Center discussed earlier will also be valuable in looking at additional ways to measure outcomes for students with disabilities.

Teacher Assessment

Efforts to improve teacher assessment is another accountability variable. In addition to teacher assessment involving passing minimal competencies, meeting increased certification standards, or taking additional course work, some states are exploring modified teacher support systems that provide incentives for teachers to pursue professional knowledge, experiment with new approaches, seek collaboration with peers, and raise the quality of instruction. At least a dozen states currently participate in the National Network for Educational Renewal that provides partnerships between colleges and universities and school districts for the purpose of supporting teachers' ability to effect school renewal.[41]

Some states are also providing statewide incentives for improved achievement that reward schools and districts for progress. These strategies include providing extra discretionary funds, sharing and other networking opportunities, teacher and administrator academies, and showcasing good practices. North Carolina has made provisions to provide additional salary increments in school districts that achieve specific goals. Utah awards $10,000 for some schools each year in its Schools for Excellence Program.

Flexibility from Rules

A number of states are also experimenting with statutory and regulatory waivers that allow schools and districts to be exempted from particular rules or regulations. For example, Washington state has implemented waiver authority in selected pilot school districts using alternative strategies for low-performing students. The South Carolina Board of Education has approved a sweeping deregulation plan under which schools with a history of superior academic achievement will automatically be released from numerous state regulations governing staffing, class scheduling, and class structure. The Illinois State Board of Education has adopted recommendations for a new system of regulating and recognizing local schools as an effort to emphasize educational results, increase flexibility, and improve accountability of schools. Mississippi has relaxed some state regulations for schools showing improvements in specified areas. Colorado has announced the development of "educational creativity schools" that will give each of twenty to thirty schools a $5,000 grant and waivers from state regulations identified as barriers to improvement. The Maryland Board of Education has approved an education improvement program that will hold schools accountable for what their students have learned and will waive selected state regulations that stand in the way of improvement. The New Mexico legislature has passed a bill allowing the State Board of Education to waive regulations for innovative educational reforms. The Texas legislature has passed a similar bill that exempts school districts from numerous state regulations in return for improved student achievement. Florida provides grants to school districts to restructure elementary education, including upgraded classrooms. Waivers from some state regulations are also provided. Kentucky reform legislation replaces a highly regulated system with one that focuses on student outcomes. Tennessee has passed legislation that creates a three-year deregulation program while proposing numerous educational reforms.

Even though the majority of waiver or deregulation strategies occurring within states are within general education, this greater flexibility has the potential to benefit many students with disabilities who spend the majority of their day in general education if the result of such increased flexibility is program and curricular changes that value and effectively deal with student diversity. As stated earlier, it is important that the rights of students with disabilities and their families be preserved as change occurs.

Federal legislation has also been introduced in Congress that, if passed, would allow federal rule waivers for selected states and school systems in areas other than those that guarantee student rights such as IDEA and Part H, Infant and Toddler programs.

Decentralization

Decentralization (often in the form of site-based management) has also been seen as an important accountability variable of school reform. Decentralization allows decisions to be made at multiple levels. Decentralization works best when school faculties have additional time and training to carry out their new responsibilities. Therefore, some states are adding additional days for new management and decision-making tasks. In others, stipends and release time are provided for increased responsibilities.

Incentives

States are utilizing various incentives for restructuring school improvement in the form of grants, differential pay, bonuses for individuals, salary increments, and regulatory relief itself. The benefits of incentives must be balanced with the unintended outcomes for students with special needs. For example, there may be pressures to exclude students with disabilities with group testing because of a concern about lower scores. In addition, differential pay for teachers of students performing at high achievement levels could serve as a disincentive to mainstream students with disabilities.

Report Cards

As another accountability variable, a number of states have begun to report the overall results and benefits of restructuring through the publication of state, district, or school report cards. For example, California is exploring the use of School Accountability Report Cards that include subjective and objective local data. Other states that are experimenting with a variety of school report cards include New Jersey and Maryland. The National Education Goals Panel has published the first Report Card of School Reform. Several states are producing or planning annual reports on the quality and effects of special education programs and services.

SUMMARY

The initial assumption of this chapter is that federal and state legislation passed since 1975 has resulted in quality programs and services for many students (infants, toddlers, children, and youth) with disabilities and their families. One unintended outcome, however, of the implementation of these laws is that special education has often been viewed as a separate system, not effectively coordinated and aligned with general education.

Special education has evolved from the 1960s with segregated programs or separate educational environments, curriculum, and instruction for students with disabilities. In the 1970s, access to common physical space was emphasized with resource programs and integration of students in regular buildings. The curricular and instructional agenda in special education, however, often continued to be separate.

The 1980s and early 1990s have focused on a more integrated, holistic approach. Adaptation of general education curricula is being explored for many students. For other students, intra- and interagency, coordinated programs are being implemented. The 1990s will continue to explore ways to better align the various educational support programs such as special education with each other and with general education, as well as to integrate educational, social service, and health services focusing on the "whole child." Special education will be viewed less as a "place" and more as a broad array of instructional and curricular supports to achieve better outcomes for children with disabilities and their families. Other evolutionary changes will include higher expectations and restructuring within the context of school reform.

Recognizing the importance for ongoing changes in special education to be made within the context of overall school restructuring, I have discussed four educational reform questions here. Based on twenty years of local and state-level experience in Idaho and Washington, as well as ongoing observations of school restructuring across the states, I wish to make sixteen final observations about the evolution of special education and its alignment with general education:

1. It is important not to be faddish but to focus on long-lasting change. Data collection is needed in order to allow for midcourse corrections depending on the positive or negative impact on various special and general education refinements on teachers, students, and families.
2. Outcome domains, indicators, and assessment systems developed and implemented within states should include, not exclude, students with disabilities.
3. Standardized testing and the focus on high achievement may not be appropriate for many special education students. Special education requires individualized instruction based on individual student learning needs.
4. Incentives provided for teachers for improved student outcomes such as differential pay, bonuses, and salary increments should be carefully analyzed for unintended negative outcomes for students with disabilities. Such incentives could encourage the exclusion of students with disabilities from participation in general education classrooms or from assessment and accountability systems because of concerns about lower test scores.
5. Sufficient staff development is needed before the implementation of change in school buildings.
6. Change should be encouraged but need not be mandated; rather, states, schools and communities should be empowered to initiate change.
7. Program refinements should be building based and led by school principals.
8. A single change model should not be imposed on educational systems; rather, tailor-made building and community-based change strategies should be encouraged and facilitated.
9. Program development and refinement involving collaboration across general education, special education, and other educational programs must be broad based and involve all stakeholders in the educational community.
10. Program collaboration models and program designs must involve interfaces with social and health services in order to foster a "whole child" approach.
11. Program change should not be done within the context of negative rhetoric about existing educational service delivery systems. It is important to build on the current or existing structures.
12. Clear communication is necessary prior to and during the early stages of change. It is important not to overestimate the merits of

change and minimize the demands and potential resistance of new collaborative practices.

13. The amount and quality of ongoing technical assistance support and networking is critical to the success of large-scale innovations.
14. The integrity of various educational programs (i.e., special education, Chapter I, bilingual instruction, and migrant education) must be preserved as the process of collaboration and change is explored in order to build on the successes of these programs achieved to date.
15. As we refine our programs to meet the complex educational needs of a changing student population, it is important to emphasize that parents are critical partners in the educational planning process.
16. The rights of students with disabilities and their families must be safeguarded during any process of change.

Many potential benefits are likely for students with disabilities as educational reform and restructuring occurs within each state. Special education, with its focus on programming for individual student needs and systematic involvement of parents in the educational process, has a rich contribution to provide school restructuring efforts. An important measure of the success of school reform will be the extent to which the educational system can align and coordinate its interlocking and interdependent educational, social service, and health components and the extent to which the educational system can improve outcomes for all students, including those with disabilities.

NOTES

1. U.S. Department of Education, *To Assure the Free Appropriate Public Education of All Children with Disabilities: Thirteenth Annual Report to Congress on the Implementation of the Individuals with Disabilities Education Act* (Washington, D.C.: U.S. Department of Education, 1991).
2. Regional Resource and Federal Centers Program, *Educational Reforms and Special Education: An Initial List of State Activities* (Lexington: Midsouth Regional Resource Center, University of Kentucky, 1991).
3. National Governors Association, *From Rhetoric to Action: State Progress in Restructuring the Education System* (Washington, D.C.: National Governors Association, 1991).
4. Council of Chief State School Officers, *Success for All in a New Century: A Report by the Council of Chief State School Officers on Restructuring Education* (Washington, D.C.: Council of Chief State School Officers, 1989).
5. Judith C. Bernison, *Testimony to the United States House of Representatives Select Committee on Narcotics Abuse and Control* (1991).
6. Linda B. Delapenha, *Testimony before the House Select Committee on Narcotics Abuse and Control on Drug Exposed Children Entering the School System* (1991).

7. Jeffrey Owings and Carol Stocking, *High Schools and Beyond: Characteristics of High School Students Who Identify Themselves as Handicapped* (Washington, D.C.: National Center for Education Statistics, U.S. Department of Education, 1985).

8. Mary Wagner, Lynn Newman, Ronald D'Amico, Deborah E. Jay, Robert Cox, Paul Butler-Nalin, and Camile Mander, *Youth with Disabilities: How Are They Doing?* (n.p.: SRI International, 1991).

9. James Wetzel, *American Youth: A Statistical Snapshot* (Washington, D.C.: William T. Grant Foundation Commission on Work, Family, and Citizenship, 1987).

10. Martin J. Kauffman, Edward J. Kameenui, Beatrice Birman, and Louis Danielson, "Special Education and the Process of Change: Victim or Master of Educational Reform?" *Exceptional Children* 57, no. 2 (Oct. 1990): 109–15.

11. Council of Chief State School Officers, *Success for All in a New Century*.

12. National Governors Association, *From Rhetoric to Action*.

13. National Education Goals Panel, *The National Education Goals Reports: Building a Nation of Learners. Executive Summary* (Washington, D.C.: National Education Goals Panel, 1991).

14. U.S. Department of Education, *America 2000: An Education Strategy* (Washington, D.C.: U.S. Department of Education, 1991).

15. Kathleen A. Fitzpatrick, "Restructuring to Achieve Outcomes of Significance for All Students," *Educational Leadership* 48, no. 8 (May 1991): 18–22.

16. National Center on Educational Outcomes, *Assessing Educational Outcomes: State Activity and Literature Integration* (Minneapolis: National Center on Educational Outcomes, University of Minnesota, 1991).

17. James Ysseldyke and Sandra Christenson, *The Instructional Environment Scale: A Comprehensive Methodology for Assessing an Individual Student's Instruction* (Austin: PRO-ED, 1987).

18. Barak Rosenshine and Robert Stevens, "Teaching Functions" in *Handbook of Research on Teaching*, ed. Merlin C. Wittrock, 3d ed. (New York: Macmillan, 1986), 376–91.

19. Jere Brophy, *Research Linking Teacher Behavior to Student Achievement: Potential Implications for Instruction of Chapter 1 Students* (unpublished manuscript; East Lansing: Michigan State University, 1987).

20. Nancy L. Karweit, *Time on Task: A Research Review (Report 332)* (Baltimore: Center for Social Organization of Schools, Johns Hopkins University, 1982); Walter Doyle, "Classroom Organization and Management" in *Handbook of Research on Teaching*, 382–431; Carol Sue Englert, "Measuring Student Effectiveness from the Teacher's Point of View," *Focus on Exceptional Children* 17, no. 2 (1984): 1–14.

21. See, for example, Catherine M. Voelker, Carol Chase Thomas, and Judy Smith-Davis, "Noncategorical Special Education Programs: Process and Outcomes" in *Handbook of Special Education: Research and Practice*, ed. Margaret C. Wang, Maynard C. Reynolds, and Herbert J. Walberg (New York: Pergamon, 1987), 287–311.

22. Jere Brophy and Thomas Good, "Teacher Behavior and Student Achievement" in *Handbook of Research on Teaching*, 328–75.

23. Claire E. Weinstein and Richard E. Mayer, "The Teaching of Learning Strategies" in *Handbook of Research on Teaching*, 315–27.

24. Jere Brophy, "Conceptualizing Student Motivation," *Educational Psychology* 18 (1983): 200–15.

25. Kathleen Cotton, *Instructional Reinforcement: School Reinforcement Series Close-up*, no. 3 (Portland, OR: Northwest Regional Education Laboratory, 1988).

26. Kathleen Cotton, *Monitoring Student Learning in the Classroom: School Improvement Research Series Close-up*, no. 4 (Portland, OR: Northwest Regional Educational Laboratory, 1988).
27. Richard Marliave and Nikola N. Filby, "Success Rate: A Measure of Task Appropriateness" in *Perspectives on Instructional Time*, ed. Charles W. Fisher and David C. Berlinger (New York: Longman, 1985), 217–35.
28. Walter R. Borg, "Time and School Learning" in *Time to Learn*, ed. C. Denhan and Anne Lieberman (Washington, D.C.: U.S. Department of Education, National Institute of Education, 1981), 33–72; see, for example, ERIC Clearinghouse on Handicapped and Gifted Children, *Academic Learning Time and Student Achievement* (Reston, VA: Council for Exceptional Children, 1985).
29. Nikola N. Filby and Leonard Cohen, "Teacher Acceptance and Student Attention" in *Perspectives on Instructional Time*, 203–14.
30. See for example, Wagner et al., *Youth with Disabilities*.
31. Cotton, *Monitoring Student Learning in the Classroom*.
32. Marliave et al., "Success Rate," 217–35.
33. Philip H. Winne and Ronald W. Marx, "Students' and Teachers' View of the Process for Classroom Learning," *Elementary School Journal* 82 (1982): 493–518.
34. Alan Hofmeister and Margaret Lubke, *Research into Practice: Implementing Effective Teaching Strategies* (Boston: Allyn & Bacon, 1990).
35. Northwest Regional Educational Laboratory, *The Effectiveness of Alternative Instructional Interventions for Washington's Low Performing and Mildly Handicapped Students*, prepared for the State of Washington, Office of Superintendent of Public Instruction (Portland, OR: Northwest Regional Educational Laboratory, 1989).
36. U.S. Department of Education, *What Works: Research about Teaching and Learning* (Washington, D.C.: U.S. Department of Education, 1986).
37. Robert Gaylord-Ross, ed., *Integration Strategizing for Students with Handicaps* (Baltimore: Paul H. Brooks, 1989).
38. American Association of School Administrators, *Learning Styles: Putting Research and Commonsense into Practice* (Washington D.C.: American Association of School Administrators, 1991).
39. Frederick J. West and Lorna Idol, "Collaborative Consultation in the Education of Mildly Handicapped and At-risk Students," *Remedial and Special Education* 11, no.1 (Jan.–Feb. 1990): 22–31.
40. National Association of State Directors of Special Education, *Role of the State Education Agencies in the 90s in Providing Leadership in Special Education* (Washington, D.C.: National Association of State Directors of Special Education, 1990).
41. Ron Brandt, "On Teacher Education: A Conversation with John Goodlad," *Educational Leadership* 49 (Nov. 1991): 11–13.

10

Teachers for Renewing Schools

John I. Goodlad and Sharon Field

The central thesis of this chapter is that teachers for our schools—all teachers—must be prepared to participate as colleagues in the four-part mission put forward in chapter 1. For schools to be healthy places, they must renew. For schools to renew, their teachers must not only understand this mission but be equipped with the knowledge and skills necessary to forward it. These include subject matter and pedagogy but go beyond to embrace what it means to be a schoolteacher in a social and political democracy and to be a moral steward in a compulsory system of schooling. It is reasonable to assume that teachers are more likely to possess these capabilities when they are the product of dynamic, renewing teacher education programs.

All of the preceding chapters have implications for how such teachers should be prepared. Several are quite explicit in their expectations. For example, chapter 1 calls for teachers who, once empowered by decentralization of authority and responsibility to the individual site, are aware of alternatives designed to encompass student variability and possess some common know-how with respect to effecting constructive changes. Chapter 3 suggests the broad role of schools in developing children and youths, the comprehensive curriculum, the instructional skills, and the range of evaluative techniques all teachers should understand and seek to implement. Chapter 4 goes so far as to recommend that the special education of special education teachers build on an initial preparation program designed for all future teachers. Chapters 6 and 7 add to the need for common preparation in the domains of curriculum, pedagogy, and evaluation introduced in chapter 3. And in chapter 8, there are significant implications regarding the moral sensitivity of teachers and, therefore, for the content and conduct of their preparation programs.

This chapter seeks to address all of these implications and more within the context of a comprehensive study that examined today's preservice preparation of both general and special education teachers in a representative sample of settings. It is organized into three major sections. The first describes the study, the second summarizes some of the findings that are particularly relevant to this volume, and the third addresses the renewal of teacher education.

A STUDY OF THE EDUCATION OF EDUCATORS

Description

In 1984 and 1985, hundreds of commission reports on the reform of schools surfaced, most stimulated by *A Nation at Risk*.[1] Many of these drew their conclusions regarding the poor conditions of schooling from three research-based books.[2] All three alluded to teacher education as a factor; Goodlad's *A Place Called School* singled out teacher education for special attention, noting the degree to which preparation programs perpetuate rather than challenge long-standing practices in schools. This and other conclusions motivated a follow-up study, this one directed to prevailing conditions and circumstances in programs preparing educators.

The study was named "A Study of the Education of Educators" because it went beyond general classroom teachers to include first-level special educators and administrators, specifically principals. The initial intent was to include findings regarding the last two groups along with those regarding the first in a single report. This plan was later abandoned for two reasons. First, this inclusion became perceived as upsetting the symmetry of a book that inevitably would have more to say about the character of teacher education generally than about the preparation of either special teachers or administrators. Second, the comprehensiveness of the whole inevitably would deny to these two important groups of programs the attention they deserve. Consequently, once the study had been completed and three, not one, general reports written, thought went to the missing pieces.

One of the major findings is the degree to which the teacher education enterprise is dispersed across the campuses of multipurpose universities. For example, a flagship public university we studied conducted teacher education in six separate schools or colleges, with little or no communication or coordination among them. Pugach and Warger point out in chapter 6 the degree to which general and special education exist in school districts as two largely separate systems. The separation begins in the colleges and universities where future teachers are educated.

A Study of the Education of Educators was conducted out of the Center for Educational Renewal of the University of Washington. We two authors participated. An initial inquiry into the history of reform in teacher education since the early 1890s revealed its disconnectedness with respect to school reform.[3] Even Conant, whose study of teacher education[4] followed on the heels of his study of high schools in the United States,[5] treated the two as separate entities. So adrift, teacher education has no clear mission.

Taking the minimalist position described in chapter 1, the research team conducting the entire study conceptualized the four-part mission for the education of educators described earlier: enculturation of the young into a social and political democracy, preparation to participate widely and deeply in the human conversation (a metaphor for the whole of living), comprehensive pedagogical competence, and the abilities essential to effective stewardship of schools. All four have moral dimensions; education is a normative, moral endeavor. Because schooling or the equivalent is compulsory in this nation, teaching in elementary and secondary schools becomes a very special case of teaching. No prospective teacher should be denied access to the education required to forward the mission described.

We then put our minds to determining the conditions necessary to the ebullient, robust conduct of teacher education programs geared to this mission. An institution of higher learning engaged in the preparation of teachers must do so seriously and proudly, providing the necessary resources and ensuring rewards for those who participate. Such runs quite contrary, however, to a century and a half of neglect and prestige deprivation. Teacher education must have clear and protected boundaries with respect to budget, students committed and enrolled, faculty members who accept responsibility and exercise authority, program identity and coherence, appropriate laboratory facilities, and the like. Currently, most of these are missing; the boundaries are ill defined at best. Some of the necessary ingredients are encompassed by no boundaries whatsoever. Finally, the quest for high quality becomes a sham when states set aside the very quality controls they prescribe in favor of ensuring no shortages in the supply of teachers. State policies must be such as to stimulate creativity and, indeed, competition in the quest for excellence among teacher preparing institutions. As Kauffman and Hallahan point out in chapter 4, these conditions are as necessary for programs preparing special education teachers as they are for those being more generally prepared.

We embedded these conditions in nineteen postulates and then used the postulates as part of the conceptual framework that guided our selection of questions for questionnaires and interviews.[6] The former were answered by students well along in their preparation programs and by faculty members, both groups identified with program units preparing the three types of educators referred to above in a representative sample of colleges and universities. Some 1,800 hours of interviews were conducted with presidents, provosts, faculty members in the arts and sciences and education, supervising and cooperating teachers, students, and administrators in nearby school districts. Additional data were derived from observations and hundreds of documents forwarded to us or picked up at the sites. Our files contain probably the largest body of field notes and other data regarding the education of educators ever assembled in a single study.

Publications reporting the whole include a dozen technical reports, one of which is devoted exclusively to the area of special education.[7] Findings, conclusions, and recommendations are presented in *Teachers for Our Nation's Schools*.[8] Moral aspects of teaching in schools are discussed in *The Moral Dimensions of Teaching*.[9] *Places Where Teachers Are Taught* provides a historical perspective regarding both teacher preparation institutions and the state context.[10]

Findings

Some general findings, reported next, describe the overall conduct of teacher education and note differences in degree, rather than kind, between programs preparing general classroom teachers and those focused on special education teachers. Most of these are rather subtle; some are quite distinctive. More specific data compare some perceptions of both students and faculty members connected with one or the other of the two programmatic divisions. The reader should keep before him or her the question of whether the mural that emerges conveys the impression of teacher education programs geared well or poorly to the expectations for teachers conveyed by the authors of preceding chapters. To the question, for example, as to whether future teachers in the programs we studied were being prepared to be moral stewards of our schools, the answer is a clear no. The answer to many other questions pertaining to adequacy of preparation likewise would be no.

Some Generalizations

Virtually all of the generalizations regarding the conduct of teacher education in the sample of settings studied apply to both general and special preparation. However, there were some differences in degree between the two. Although most of these were quite modest, they add up to some rather noteworthy differences.

Status and Prestige. On being asked to cite areas of strength, emphasis, and anticipated further development, presidents and provosts rarely mentioned teacher education or their schools of education. Those in the private liberal arts colleges perceived the preparation of elementary and secondary school teachers (special education teachers usually were being prepared elsewhere) as a service conducted in conjunction with the arts and sciences departments. On several of the multipurpose public university campuses, these administrators noted with some pride the research monies brought in by several professors in special education.

In these universities, public and private, education professors largely eschewed preservice teacher education, favoring advanced graduate teaching and research. Many students in teacher education programs complained about never seeing "star" faculty members; they were taught more frequently by adjunct, temporary, and part-time personnel. This was much less the case, however, in special education where professors tended to see some participation in preparing teachers, even at the undergraduate level, as a normal expectation. Indeed, tenure-track professors took major responsibility for planning the program. This same situation prevailed to a considerable degree, also, with respect to early childhood education and such subject specialties as music where rather extensive education in both the discipline and closely related pedagogy is required.

Our conclusion is that teacher education, regardless of the field of preparation, suffers considerably from the legacies of chronic prestige deprivation surrounding school teaching in our society and in higher education. This translates into low status for teacher education in the schools and colleges of education in our sample, but less so for special education, given the attention more frequently paid to it by tenure-line faculty members.

Ill-defined Boundaries. Strong programs of professional preparation have well-defined boundaries: an organized unit to which students are formally admitted and in which they are socialized into the profession, an intake of students tied to the availability of resources, a responsible faculty group representing the major program components, a reasonably coherent curriculum requiring a degree of sequential progression, and more. These boundaries were ill defined for teacher education to the point of near obscurity in most of the settings studied. They were somewhat clearer, however, in the small liberal arts colleges, where departments of education and teacher education are almost one, and in preparation programs in the larger institutions directed to such fields as early childhood education, special education, health and physical education, and the arts. It is interesting to note that both content and pedagogy in such fields tend to be in the hands of a single faculty much more frequently than is the case in the preparation of generalists.

It is important to note also that these somewhat clearer boundaries in regard to the preparation of special education teachers served both to narrow the scope of preparation and to separate these students from the mainstream of future teachers. The effects of separation showed up in interviews with mixed groups of students on the various campuses. Each group came as strangers to the others. It is only fair to add, however, that students in a given group were little more than casual acquaintances who showed up together in perhaps two or three courses. Even this much association was rare among future high school teachers majoring in academic subjects. This lack of a formal socialization process was paralleled by the near absence of deliberately planned informal social activities for all future teachers.

This absence leaves responsibility for the socialization process (regarded, e.g., as highly important in the preparation of doctors and lawyers) to the separate fields of preparation, should students and faculty members choose to assume it. This was more often the case in special education than in general elementary and secondary education in the institutions we studied. As an accompaniment of both a more coherent curriculum and a modest program of special lectures and events, students preparing to teach in this field appeared to be developing a relatively strong identification with it, according to data from our questionnaires and interviews.

Incoherent Curricula. Given the general absence of a comprehensive mission for teacher education tied to a mission of compulsory schooling in a democratic society, one would be surprised to find in place coherent teacher education curricula. We did not. We found in most programs a single "foundations" course, not always required, and much variation from institution to institution in what it sought to accomplish. Sometimes it addressed aspects of the history of education and schooling in the United States; sometimes it was more oriented to various philosophies of education; sometimes it dealt with both. More often, however, the introductory course was a potpourri designed as an orientation to the program and teaching, with class sessions devoted to everything from AIDS education to schools of thought such as realism and progressivism.[11]

All of the programs studied included a course in educational psychology that emphasized concepts drawn from the basic discipline rather than applications of psychology to teaching. Rarely in either of these first two courses were students exposed to ongoing practices in schools. Nor were these "introductory" courses always taken first by students.

Large numbers enrolled without any formal admission to a teacher education program; some had merely shopped for a convenient course as an elective or option in the social sciences. The goal of becoming a teacher appeared to be largely a matter of personal motivation not much augmented by a programmatic ethos.

Methods courses tended to bring with them some observations of classroom practices. Student teaching (often the point of formal entry into a program) brought students individually into increasing responsibility for classroom activities supervised occasionally by someone from the university but by the cooperating teacher on a daily basis. At this stage, students' interest in their preparation almost always peaked; both students and faculty members rated this field portion of preparation as more impactful than any other part. And, at this stage, students separated almost entirely from the professors who had taught the several on-campus courses—the so-called theory.

These rather depressing conditions were noticeably less present in special education. There usually was a sequence of courses to be taken in the order specified. There almost always was an apparent effort to adapt material from relevant disciplines to the specific problems of special education. More than in the professional courses for prospective elementary school teachers, for example, those in special education tended to address quite commonly from setting to setting the same content and readings. More than for other future teachers, those in special education dealt with the moral issue of equity, largely in the context of PL 94-142.

On the negative side, however, preparation in special education focused almost exclusively on the individual and especially on individual pathology. Unlike their counterparts in elementary education, for example, these courses dealt little with matters beyond, such as classroom management. Unlike their counterparts, they addressed the curriculum, beyond the teaching of reading and sometimes numerics, scarcely at all. But like the programs of other future teachers, special education students' preparation virtually ignored the stewardship of schools as a whole.

Program Autonomy. We found among professors of education considerable ennui regarding program renewal. Commonly, we found teacher education curricula to be little more than collections of courses tossed together to meet state certification requirements. It was less the specifics of these, we deduced, that worked against renewal than the fact of heavy state intervention. "Why spend two or three years revamping the curriculum," we were asked in various ways, "when the state will come in with a new set of regulations just as we complete our work?"

The field of special education appeared to be considerably less constrained, to be more autonomous in the domain of curriculum planning. And professors were found to be so engaged in many of the settings studied. They spoke much more to the expectations and requirements of PL 94-142 than to any straitjacket imposed by state regulators. The ethos surrounding the education of special education teachers appeared to be somewhat more professional than that surrounding the education of generalists for elementary and secondary schools.

Some Specific Comparisons

Before getting more deeply into a discussion of these findings and their possible implications for both better understanding some of the most unfortunate aspects of the separation of general and special education in schools and effecting constructive reform through redesigning teacher education, it is useful to examine some specific data. Of particular relevance to the concluding section of this chapter are comparisons of some student and faculty perceptions.

Some Perceptions Regarding the Preparation of General Educators. The data related to the confidence of students completing general teacher education programs to instruct students with disabilities in regular settings are striking. Students in our survey perceived themselves as ill equipped to deal with such students. They commonly viewed themselves as inadequately prepared in many of the specific skills that are generally considered to be important in providing instruction to students with special needs. It should be remembered that students responding to the questionnaires were either entering or in student teaching; a few had completed this requirement the previous quarter or semester.

These findings agree with those of our earlier study of schooling. Teachers in that study, especially at the secondary level, placed dealing with special needs and an array of behavioral problems at the top of their list in seriousness.[12] Few ranked high lack of subject-matter knowledge—an irony, given the degree to which policymakers almost invariably identify more general education and greater depth of subject matter as virtually panaceas for the reform of teacher education. In that earlier study, even teachers qualified for and teaching special education perceived themselves as needing more preparation in this area in order to deal with the problems confronted.[13]

In the study reported here, students being generally prepared to teach were asked to identify how well prepared they were in a variety of instructional skills. One of these was their ability to instruct students with disabilities in regular classrooms. They were asked to rate themselves on a scale of 1 to 7 (1 = very poorly prepared; 7 = very well prepared). Out of the twelve skills on which students were asked to rate their level of confidence, the item related to ability to instruct students with handicaps in regular classrooms was the lowest ranking of all, by far. The mean response for this item was 3.7. The next lowest ranking for general teacher education program students was 4.6 on the item that asked them to rate their ability "to communicate effectively with parents regarding their child's performance in school." It is interesting that this skill, which was ranked second to the bottom out of all twelve skills for students preparing to become general education teachers, is also a critical component in providing effective educational programs for students with disabilities.

A third skill on which students were asked to rate themselves, which is usually seen as a critical factor in successful instruction for students with disabilities, is individualization of instruction. When students in general preparation programs were asked to rate their confidence in their ability to individualize instruction, the results were somewhat more promising. On the seven-point scale, they ranked their confidence at 5.4. These students rated themselves at 5.0 or above on each of the nine remaining areas, which were focused primarily on skills used in traditional content-related classroom instruction (e.g., "explain material or lecture to a class," "engage in classroom discussions," "evaluate students").

When the responses of the special education students are contrasted with the responses of the general teacher education program students, it is not surprising to find that the former feel much more confident of their ability to instruct students with disabilities in general education settings and to individualize instruction than do the students who are preparing to be "regular" classroom teachers. The mean responses for students preparing to be special education teachers were 5.7 on ability to instruct students with disabilities in general education settings and 6.0 on ability to individualize instruction. It was surprising to find that special education students felt only slightly more confident of their ability to communicate effectively with parents than did students preparing to be general educators. Special education students rated their confidence on this skill at 4.9, lower than they did for any other. Given the importance of parental involvement in educational planning for students with disabilities, this is a discouraging finding, indeed.

It is interesting that students preparing to become general classroom teachers rated their competence in adapting instruction for students with disabilities lower than any other skill. Yet, one-fourth stated that they had not taken, and did not intend to take, any course work in special education. Of the eight types of courses or activities identified in the study (i.e., educational foundations, educational psychology, special education, general methods of curriculum and instruction, specific methods for specific subjects, field experiences, student teaching, and integrative seminars), special education was by far the area most often identified by students preparing to become general educators as the one in which they would not take more course work. In other words, they would carry their self-perceived inadequacies into employment as teachers.

The survey also indicated that students in our sample preparing to be general educators perceived that course work in special education would make a relatively weak contribution to their future success as a teacher. It was followed at the low end in perceived usefulness only by educational foundations.

When asked about the contribution of preparatory courses to their individual needs and how interesting each of the types of courses generally were, teacher education students in general programs rated special education course work at the same level that they ranked the contribution they perceived special education courses would make to their success as teachers. The mean response on these items by non–special education students placed special education course work seventh out of the eight course work areas. Once more, the only course work area receiving lower mean responses by these students was foundations.

An interesting contrast is evident in the student survey data. As noted already, most students preparing to be general educators stated that they had not taken and did not intend to take special education course work. Furthermore, they rated special education course work with respect to the contribution it would make to their success as a teacher and the attention given to their own individual learning needs consistently lower than most other course offerings in education. However, when they were asked about the attention that should be given to different course work areas in the teacher education program at their institution, 44 percent stated that special education should be given more emphasis. Of the eight instructional areas, only field experiences was rated higher as one deserving of more attention.

Sixty-two percent of the special education students stated that special education courses should be given more emphasis in a general teacher education program. The need for more emphasis in special education for all teachers was ranked higher by special education students than the need in any other program area, not surprisingly.

These findings raise many questions. Could it be that these students in "regular" preparation programs recognize the demands that will be placed on them to meet the needs of diverse learners in their classrooms but have found special education classes, as currently structured, inadequate to help them prepare to meet this challenge?

In most institutions, special education classes are still structured primarily to meet the needs of persons who will become special education teachers. In most cases, too, this practice is based on the largely unspoken assumption that special education is a separate educational system.[14] It is assumed that there will be some interaction between the two systems, but still they are largely separate and distinct. The very foundation on which these courses are based is in many cases diametrically opposed to the conditions that are necessary to help general education teachers develop the attitudes and skills necessary to adapt instruction to meet the needs of *all* learners enrolled in regular classrooms. Instead, through the way in which we structure our teacher preparation programs, we reinforce the notion that learners need to conform to the ways teachers now teach. Then, when students do not fit in, they are labeled handicapped and sent to the second educational system of special education. The very special nature of special education and its separation from the mainstream in teacher education reinforces the notion that students who deviate are largely the responsibility of special teachers in a separate system.

Responses of the general education faculty related to the importance of special education course work to their students' future success as teachers and the level of interest that they perceive their students have in special education courses mirror the students' responses. On a scale of 1 to 7 (1 = no contribution at all; 7 = a very great contribution), the mean rating by general education faculty for the contribution that special education course work would make to students as future teachers was 4.4. As for students, special education ranked seventh in perceived importance for teachers' future success, followed only by foundations. General education faculty also gave interest of their students in special education courses a relatively low rating. On the same scale of 1 to 7, the mean general faculty response to student interest in special education courses was 4.1. Again, of the eight areas, only educational foundations was rated lower.

In contrast to students' responses, however, general education faculty did not think special education course work should be given more emphasis. Of the general education faculty, only 14.8 percent stated that special education course work should be stressed more heavily, in contrast to 44 percent of the students. The majority of the general education faculty, 68.5 percent, felt that special education course work should be kept at its current level of emphasis—that is, very minimal.

Although there were some differences in the responses of general education students and faculty, there was an even sharper contrast between the responses of general education and special education faculty members. The latter were far more likely to state that special education courses should be given more emphasis in the preparation of "regular" teachers. Of the special education faculty, 53 percent responded that special education course work should be given more emphasis, as compared with the 14.8 percent of the general education faculty. Special education faculty members also rated student interest in special education courses and the contribution that course work would make to their success as teachers more highly than did the general education faculty. On a scale of 1 to 7 (1 = not at all interesting; 7 = extremely interesting), the special education faculty mean response to perceived student interest level in special education course work was 5.4. This rating is in marked contrast to general education faculty for whom the mean response was 4.1. The special education faculty also gave a much higher rating to the contribution special education courses would make to all future teachers. The average response for this group was 5.8, which resulted in a rank of fourth out of the eight course work areas. As stated earlier, general education faculty rated the contribution of special education course work to students' future success at 4.4, a rank of seventh out of the eight program areas. These data contribute significantly to the observation that there is a gulf between the programs preparing "regular" teachers on one hand and "special" teachers on the other.

Differences were also seen in the degree of emphasis that special education faculty and general education faculty members placed on different areas of content preparation. The former placed a stronger emphasis on theory as compared with practice than did other education faculty members. Fifty-nine percent of the special education faculty felt that a teacher education program should have more theory with some practice, while 60 percent of the general education faculty felt that the emphasis on theory and practice should be about half and half. Special education faculty members placed a stronger emphasis than did general education faculty on preparing teachers to teach career/vocational skills, developing students' skills in interagency collaboration, understanding legal issues and student rights, and adapting instruction for students with disabilities in general education settings. The most dramatic difference in these ratings was on the perceived importance of developing skill in adapting instruction for learners with disabilities. On the issue of adapting instruction for learners with handicaps as a component of a general teacher education program, special education faculty members strongly agreed (a mean of 6.2 on the seven-point scale). The mean rating of this item by general education faculty was 5.0.

The difference in perceptions of special education faculty and general education faculty is not surprising, but it is striking. It lends support to the notion that we have created a separate system for educating students with disabilities and for preparing the teachers who teach them. Even though changes are beginning to occur in the public schools to bring the two systems closer together, they are still in most cases markedly separated in universities, as evidenced by the variance in responses of general education and special education faculty members.

Assuming that there are, indeed, two separate systems of education, it is not surprising to find that students who are preparing to be general educators feel that their skills in adapting instruction for learners with disabilities are weaker than their skills in any other pedagogical competency. Clearly, more attention needs to be focused on helping them to build the capabilities they need to meet the diverse learning needs of the wide range of students who are, or should be, in their classes. This is critical if we are to provide services for students with disabilities in a manner that is consistent with the tenets of a least restrictive environment.

It is also necessary that teachers become more skilled at making adaptations for diverse learners if we are to meet the needs of the growing "at-risk" population.[15] Our schools are failing large numbers of students who are never given formal labels. These students usually either drop out or just barely squeak through the educational program with marginal success or accomplishment. Often students in this at-risk population are labeled "handicapped" and sent to the "second" educational system called special education. If our general education system fails to meet the needs of increasingly large numbers of its students, as evidenced by high dropout rates, low measures of achievement, and relegation to the second system of special education, where is the real disability? Does it reside in the students who are labeled, or is it a function of the inability of the system to acknowledge and respond to students' differences and needs?

Some Perceptions Regarding the Preparation of Special Educators. Special education faculty members perceived themselves as both more interested and more involved in the preservice preparation of special educators than did general education faculty. On a scale of 1 to 4 (1 = not at all involved; 4 = heavily involved), special education faculty members rated their level of involvement in the preparation of special educators at 3.4, while the mean self-rating of involvement for other education faculty in special education preparation was 1.6. Special education faculty also rated their level of interest in issues concerning the preparation of special education teachers much higher than did other faculty members. On a scale of 1 to 7 (1 = no priority; 7 = very high priority), the mean ratings for interest in special education teacher preparation issues were 6.3 for special education faculty and 3.9 for other education faculty. Such findings are to be expected, but they do emphasize the separation between these two groups.

Special education faculty members were also far more likely to state that special education course work should be given more emphasis, while other education faculty members were more likely to recommend that the emphasis on special education should remain as it currently is. Of the special education faculty, 52.8 percent responded that special education course work should be given more emphasis, 44.4 percent said that it should be kept as it currently is, and 2.8 percent stated that special education should be given less emphasis. This is in sharp contrast to the general education faculty responses. Of the general education faculty, only 14.8 percent stated that special education should be given more emphasis.

Although these differences between special education faculty and other faculty members in schools, departments, or colleges of education regarding the level of involvement and interest in special education preparation are not surprising, they further support the notion that there are separate systems for special education and general education in institutions of higher education. When we asked special education professors how it *should* be, we saw a very different picture. Generally, special education faculty members stated that there should be less separation between special and general education in teacher education programs. When asked to indicate their level of agreement with the statement that a special education program should be essentially separate from the general teacher education program and that it should focus solely on those competencies needed by special educators, 60 percent of the special education faculty indicated disagreement, 13 percent were neutral, and 26 percent expressed agreement.

Special education professors also stated strong preferences for program elements geared toward providing special educators with more integrated programs. These faculty members were asked to state their level of agreement with the statement that students in the special education program should be required to complete course work in the general teacher education program. On a seven-point scale (1 = strongly disagree; 7 = strongly agreed), 50 percent of the special education faculty responding chose 7. Thirty-three percent indicated lower levels of agreement, 10 percent were neutral, and only 7 percent expressed disagreement.

Special education faculty members told us also that, beyond formal course work, it is important for students who are preparing to be special educators to have the opportunity to interact informally with students in general education. Eighty-six percent indicated agreement with the statement that the opportunity to interact informally with students in the general teacher education program is an element of a successful special education program. Furthermore, 80 percent said that socializing special educators into the field of education as a whole is a characteristic of a successful special education program.

Finally, helping special educators develop skill in providing consultation to "regular" educators regarding strategies to assist learners with disabilities was rated by 89 percent of special education faculty members in our sample as an extremely important component of a successful special education program. The degree to which special education faculty members agreed that special education programs should be integrated with general teacher education programs seemed to be related to the severity of disabling conditions in question. Special education faculty members were asked to state their level of agreement with a "generalist" or a "categorical" view for teacher education programs preparing teachers to work with either mildly, moderately, or severely handicapped students. The following definitions were provided for the generalist and the categorical views:

> *The Generalist View*—Special educators should be trained primarily in issues affecting the education of *all* students with disabilities and in a variety of strategies that can be applied to the needs of individual learners. They should also be prepared to work cooperatively with general educators to meet the needs of the disabled.

> *The Categorical View*—Special educators should be prepared to deliver specially designed instruction for *specific* groups of handicapped students. They should have a comprehensive knowledge of the etiology, characteristics, and strategies appropriate for the specific disability area (hearing impaired, learning disabled, etc.) in which they are trained.

In our sample of special education faculty members, the generalist view was favored for teachers who are preparing to work with mildly disabled students, and the categorical view was favored for teachers preparing to work with students who are more severely disabled. The mean responses for rate of agreement with the generalist view were 5.8 for mildly handicapped, 4.6 for moderately handicapped, and 3.0 for severely handicapped.

These responses are to be expected, given that separate programming has been more accepted for students with severe disabilities than it has been for students who are more mildly handicapped. However, recent strides made in educational technology and in the development of program models that successfully integrate students with severe disabilities into general education classrooms may create changes in the way faculty members perceive the desired training of personnel preparing to work with students who are severely handicapped.

Comment. The picture we saw in this part of our study is one of some dramatic differences between what appears to be current practice and what special education faculty thinks is best practice. Some degree of coordination between general and special education certainly exists. For example, most special education students participate in general education course work; many programs for generalists require a course in special education. Furthermore, a small but growing number of universities have made a concerted effort to develop preparation programs that have placed an emphasis on developing skills in coordination with and collaboration between special and general education. Nonetheless, although some steps are being taken to close the gap between the two systems, it is fundamentally still there.

We learned that the general education faculty members in our sample generally perceived themselves to have little involvement in the preparation of special educators, yet we heard special education faculty placing a strong degree of emphasis on programming that would provide students preparing to be special education teachers a program coordinated with general education. We saw widely divergent views between special education professors and faculty members involved in other areas of education regarding the degree of emphasis that they feel should be placed on the preparation of teachers to meet the needs of students with disabilities.

All of this suggests a system that is failing to adequately prepare teachers to meet the educational needs of students with disabilities. It also suggests a sense of separateness between students, professors, and programs in institutions of higher education engaged simultaneously in preparing teachers for both general and special assignments in schools. Undoubtedly, this separation contributes to the separateness of general and special education in this nation's schools. Clearly, there is ample room for closer collaboration and a greater degree of integration.

TOWARD RENEWAL

Preceding chapters, together with the findings of the comprehensive study reported here—A Study of the Education of Educators—point the way toward necessary changes in preparation programs for all teachers, with special attention to effecting a closer relationship between those preparing generalists and those preparing specialists. Of particular relevance for reform are the breadth of mission, the demands of both sweeping changes in the total ecology of education and an increasingly diverse student body, an intensifying focus on the school as the center of change and teachers as its moral stewards, and heightened national and state attention to schooling and students' academic performance in the context of the nation's global competitiveness. Reasoning, fed by data, leads not to tinkering with present curricula but to sweeping changes in the teacher education enterprise.

No Quick, Easy Answers

First, it is necessary to consider the future locus of teacher education. That familiar bromide, mentoring future teachers with present ones, is before us one more time, backed by such high-level officials as President Bush and Secretary Alexander—this time under the rubric of alternative certification. Not surprisingly, given our findings regarding the low prestige given to school teaching and teacher education, some professors of education want to see teacher education out of the universities and in the schools.[16] The better answer is close collaboration between the two, not exclusivity on the part of one or the other.

Another highly touted panacea is to be a set of national examinations that when passed by an aspiring teacher assures both competence and, at long last, professional status. Ironically, its sponsors eschew for teachers, without explanation, the licensing, certifying, accrediting, and sustained socialization in a university-based program that they commend for the other professions.[17]

Teacher education today is near the crossroads confronted by medical education in the first decade of this century. Flexner, in his groundbreaking report, deplored the sorry state of the proprietary medical schools run by doctors as well as the conventional practice of mentoring an aspiring physician with a practitioner.[18] He came down firmly on the side of university-based schools of medicine linked with hospitals in such a way as to ensure these schools considerable control over the clinical side of medicine. Something quite comparable, with considerable attention to nurturing, is at the heart of our recommendations. But, with respect to most of the present conduct of teacher education, whether university-based or conducted alternatively largely in the schools, we say, "A plague on both these houses."

Chapter 1 argues strongly for a renewing stance on the part of schools—a continuing process of inquiry conducted with varying levels of participation on the part of parents, students, district and union representatives, teachers, and principals.[19] Recent rhetoric advancing site-based management, effective schools, and restructuring supports such a concept. But our data reveal glaringly that teachers are ill prepared for what is implied. And data not reported here reveal that the narrow management-oriented programs of most school principals prepared them poorly for the leadership role implied.[20] The data reveal also that both general and special education teacher candidates have misgivings about their readiness to deal with parents—an essential ingredient of a renewing school.

At best, it will be several years before even a small proportion of new teachers come into schools with an expectation for assuming this renewing role, let alone the necessary knowledge and skills. This is in large part because renewing schools conducted jointly by school districts and universities for purposes of both creating exemplary sites and preparing new teachers in them are in very short supply. And it is in part, too, because few teacher educators are driven by recognition of the need and especially the desire to get involved. The present reward structure stands against such, for one thing.[21]

School-University Partnerships and Partner Schools

The immediate necessity is to create school-university partnerships,[22] with the selection of the most promising sites as "partner" schools an immediate goal.[23] Into such must come professors in part-time residence who join with teachers there in receiving cohort groups of interns, now in their final year of preservice preparation.[24] Imagine, too, that these include intern principals, each engaged full-time in a completely redesigned preparation program such as that now to be found at Brigham Young University, the University of Washington, and the University of Wyoming, for example. Each group of aspiring principals in the one at the University of Washington, now several years old, has included several special education teachers.[25] It is reasonable to envision University X placing ten such teacher interns, with perhaps two of these planning careers in special education, and a principal intern in a partner elementary school staffed normally by thirty-five teachers—and, in a state providing truly enlightened policies, with three colleagues added to assist in the teacher education responsibility.[26] These interns not only participate in making schoolwide decisions but also include in their accompanying seminars discussion of how later, as an independent faculty group, they might handle comparable issues and problems, once in their own schools.

This is not a "dream" scenario. The articles comprising an entire 1991 issue of the journal *Metropolitan Universities* (vol. 2, no. 1) describe most of the pieces now developing or in place in a variety of settings. But these pieces have not yet come together anywhere in an integrated whole, although a number of settings across the country have committed themselves to their installation.[27]

Coherent Programs

Preceding paragraphs sketch the culminating portion of teacher education programs designed to prepare principals and teachers (including the various specialists) for the challenge of joining not only with one another but with others, especially parents and students, in renewing schools. We are talking about schools that provide comprehensively and individually for all children and youths except the few in homes, hospitals, and other institutions whose education must be brought to them. And even in these very special circumstances, neighborhood schools frequently play a part. The schools we need require teachers with preparation going well beyond what most are getting today.

There are at least two major directions for greater integration of general and special education in teacher preparation programs. First, regular classroom teachers clearly need a comprehensive introduction to the range of student individuality likely to be encountered in schools and more confidence than the student teachers in our sample expressed regarding their ability to provide satisfactorily for this variability. Their professional education should include an understanding of those areas of exceptionality likely to require the attention of special personnel.

Equally clearly, future special education teachers need a much broader grasp of their responsibilities to the whole of schools and classrooms—a

great deal more of what their professors believe is in the preparation programs of general education teachers. It would be interesting to know more
about what these professors have in mind. Our guess is that their expectations far exceed what this "mainstream" provides. As in schools, gaining
access to the mainstream often turns out to be insufficient.

In efforts to eliminate in-school segregation of minority children,
some critics have recognized the shortcomings of programs into which
they have been integrated but often have put aside this set of problems
for another day.[28] That day is here, whether we are talking about mainstreaming the economically disadvantaged or the disabled. The mainstream fails to provide for children and youths what it should, just as the
mainstream of educating teachers for our nation's schools fails to provide
what it should.

In order for us to have any hope that there will be in the near future
teacher education programs preparing all teachers for the four-part mission
previously outlined, the pieces now scattered about on university campuses
must be brought together. The first piece is a budget tied commensurately
to an institutional commitment to prepare a *fixed* number of teachers in a
finite number of areas. This would represent a radical departure from present sloppy practices of admitting virtually all those who meet certain academic standards and later seeking desperately for enough cooperating
teachers to supervise candidates now ready to begin the student teaching
portion of their programs.

This budget must embrace the time of a fully qualified faculty drawn
from the arts and sciences, education, and the partner schools. A beginning
inquiry into the budgets of schools of education suggests deprivation of the
teacher education component in regard to both faculty and dollar allocations.[29] The probability is that the common practice of relegating the
preparation of general elementary and secondary teachers to adjunct, temporary, and part-time faculty not only produces a disproportionately large
number of courses in relation to dollars spent but also deprives future
teachers of the attention they should receive from the most carefully recruit-
ed members of the faculty. In this regard, the programs in special education
appear to be in somewhat better shape.

Without there being a faculty of the kind suggested earlier representing the programmatic components now segmented, there can be little
expectation of a coherent, integrated curriculum. Segmentation, separation,
and incoherence are what we found, interprogram in virtually all fields and
intraprogram in the mainstream particularly.

What we envision, then, is a single faculty planning the common core
for all teachers—the core that addresses the common mission. Aware of this
core from participating in its planning and renewal, the specialists in each
area then arrange for the additional preparation required, much of it to
come after completion of the basic program and, indeed, teaching experience (see chap. 4). Similarly, faculty members drawn from the partner

schools provide input to the core and then seek later, with their professorial colleagues, to integrate theory and practice in campus courses, field experiences, and, finally, internships.

The current degree of casualness in placing and supervising student teachers is scandalous. University-based directors of student teaching invite, entice, and persuade teachers to take student teachers individually or, occasionally, in pairs. In large programs requiring many such cooperating teachers, there are few quality controls; it is virtually impossible to know the daily circumstances in the classrooms of teachers selected. Frequently, there is dissonance between school district policies and practices, on one hand, and campus-based values and teaching, on the other. If there is some coherence in the campus program, there is nothing to ensure its continuance once students go out into their classroom placements. Small, specialty preparation programs usually do better, building up over time collaborative relationships with the field. Nonetheless, this approach to what both faculty members and students consider to be the most formative part of teacher education must come to an end.

We already have pointed the direction: enough partner, renewing schools under the educational control of the joint faculty previously described to accommodate all students admitted who successfully complete the preparatory curriculum. A setting admitting 110 students annually and bringing 100 successfully to the intern stage might require ten partner schools—schools not yet adequately exemplary but, thanks to the combined efforts of university and school personnel, well on the way. These constitute the clinical settings, the "teaching" schools comparable to the teaching hospitals in medicine. They are not an option or a privilege granted but readily withdrawn at the whim of a school board or superintendent. Their role in the teacher education unit is part of a formal agreement under the umbrella of a school-university partnership.

Teachers for Our Nation's Schools proposes a center of pedagogy as the unit having a protected budget (in the same sense that medical school budgets are protected) tied to what it takes to operate in exemplary fashion a program that goes far beyond those of the arts and sciences in its need to supervise hands-on, teaching experiences. It would have the clearly defined boundaries with respect to student body, faculty, and teaching schools so lacking currently. It can be inside or outside schools and colleges of education, depending on individual institutional circumstances. Chapter 9 of *Teachers* describes the creation and early functioning of one such center in a fictitious, regional state university.[30]

A Five-Year Baccalaureate

What lies behind the assumption, explicitly revealed several times on preceding pages, of a five-year program? We studied in our sample a good many so-called four-year programs. Most advertised themselves falsely;

students complained about "lack of truth in advertising." They were not four-year programs in the sense that they could be completed in 120 semester or 180 quarter hours. Indeed, graduation with a B.A. or B.S. degree without any course work preparatory to teaching commonly required more. By meeting requirements for a teaching certificate as well, especially in elementary education, the course credits almost invariably exceeded 130 semester hours. The norm approached an additional semester, acquired by enrolling for up to twenty hours in several semesters and/or attendance at a summer session. And even under these circumstances, the feat required exceedingly careful planning and often squeezed regular graduation requirements to the minimum. Students entering teacher education programs late simply resigned themselves to as much as an additional year. The crowded, crammed, extended schedule represented the mode for most students in special education and for all seeking to combine such specialization with general preparation to teach in elementary schools.

Our conclusion is that there is just no way to prepare adequately for teaching by simply restricting electives and weaving teacher education courses in and out around other graduation requirements. Such a pattern assures teachers who are not liberally educated, who lack depth in subject specialties, and who are seriously wanting in the art and science of teaching (pedagogy). This is inexcusable for teacher education generally. It is outrageous in the preparation of those special educators who presumably are to take on some of the most daunting of all those daunting tasks teachers assume in seeking to educate this nation's young people.

We propose a three-year professional preparation program combining general education, specialized subject matter, pedagogy, field experiences accompanied by interpretive seminars, culminating in two markedly different internship placements, each of three or four months' duration accompanied by seminars conducted in the partner school settings, with an intervening university-based period of study and reflection between the two. These three years would be built on two years of carefully chosen general education studies, accompanied by various kinds of socialization pertaining to teaching and especially to the decision of selecting teaching as a career. In the last semester or quarter of these first two years, students would be required to declare their interest and engage in interviews and other activities relevant to a carefully conducted selection process.

There is no reason to believe that a decade or more from now, five years of preservice higher education will be considered sufficient but, at present, it appears to be appropriate in relation to the financial rewards of teaching and sensitive attention to supply and demand. This—not alternative certification and not a test after graduation from college and three years of teaching—we believe to be the route to the solid establishment of teaching as a profession and the preparation of first-rate teachers.

A Postgraduate Program

Although the route described probably would provide for about 75 to 80 percent of the future supply of teachers, there remains that other 20 to 25 percent who choose to prepare to teach after graduation from college, frequently after twenty or more years in military service, business, or some other occupation. They constitute an exceedingly important source of supply, but not if we continue to waive requirements deemed important for the larger five-year group. The experience one gains as an adult in work, play, and family life enriches a teaching career but does not substitute for competence in teaching a subject or in understanding and dealing with children and youths—prerequisites on everyone's laundry list of essentials. Yet, we appear willing in our policies and back-door routes to a teaching certificate to toss the list aside when dealing with the pleas of the many individuals who act as though teaching is a right rather than a privilege.

These individuals should be given every opportunity to display their qualifications through testing out of subject-matter prerequisites, joining teaching teams in partner schools as aides for periods of time, and enrolling in a program that does in two years, let us assume (less any time saved by demonstrating through examination high competence in general education), what we recommend be done for the younger group in three. Surely this should be sufficient provision for earnest, committed people who offer to the schools and the teaching profession important lessons from having lived longer, on the positive side, and a college transcript of studies completed two dozen years ago, on the negative.

Concluding Recommendations

At least two other important matters remain untouched. They interweave and carry us back to a recommendation put forward in chapter 4: namely, that special education teachers first be prepared as general classroom teachers and, indeed, that they gain some experience as such. We recognize that it is bound to be controversial in some quarters, but we view its implementation as an enormous step forward in seeking not only more comprehensive preparation for special education teachers but also schools that, more than today's, provide maximally productive learning environments for all children and youths. The present structure, curricula, testing practices, and narrowly restricted instructional repertoires of most teachers put many students at risk. Today's demands require teams of teachers who share some common background, who understand the mission and circumstances of schools sufficiently to apply widely and well an array of complementary specialties.

All future doctors share a common core of professionalizing content and experiences before embarking on one of a panoply of options. Similarly, future lawyers encounter case studies commonly, regardless of their later concentrations in criminal, constitutional, or international law. Future teachers share very little, not even being members of the class of '95, and come together in schools with little in common. Little wonder that crusades calling on teachers to join in restructuring and renewing schools leave so little change in their wake.

We recommend that special education teachers should be prepared as general education teachers first, as suggested by the authors of chapter 4. But it brings with it the problem of academic degrees. The practice of awarding a master's degree for one postbaccalaureate year of preparing to teach was established many years ago. James B. Conant and Francis Keppel significantly advanced the M.A.T. in the years following World War II by giving it the Harvard University imprimatur and attracting to it able students. But scrutiny of the one-year teacher education programs that subsequently sprung up all across the country gives one pause. What is there in such programs, providing more or less what undergraduate programs in teacher education provide, plus a few graduate courses in a subject field, that warrants the designation, "master"? Surely the graduates are not suddenly master teachers. Further, what degree does one get next in order to be designated a specialist or school principal, or perhaps a warranted master teacher? A doctorate? Thus is degree getting in the field of education inflated and ultimately denigrated by segments of society, including much of the academic world. Should practitioners' salaries be enhanced on criteria that can be only loosely connected, at best, with improved service to students and schools?

We believe that the interests of the public and the teaching profession could be better served by awarding candidates in the five-year program the B.A. or B.S. degree on completing the undergraduate requirements specified by the given college or university and a professional baccalaureate, such as a B.Paed. (bachelor's in pedagogy) or B.T. (bachelor's in teaching), on graduating successfully from the complete teacher education program, whether the five-year or the two-year variety as described. This would mean that unpromising candidates could be screened out before entering the internship year and still be awarded a degree for satisfactorily completing their academic studies. Similarly, it would mean that a promising candidate in an institution with restrictive requirements for entering graduate studies could continue to complete requirements for the fifth year and the professional degree in teaching, without entering or failing to enter graduate school.

Such a procedure ties nicely into the personnel preparation recommendations of chapter 4. The five-year program proposed in this chapter should provide much more preparation to deal with exceptionality than is now the case. Some of the students preparing for general teaching would carry from these educational experiences plans to pursue the field of special education. With the basic professional degree in hand and some teaching experience behind, they would then enter a truly specialized program leading to the master's degree in special education, "with all the rights, privileges, and responsibilities thereto appertaining."

We are well aware that these concluding two recommendations are controversial. We trust that they will stir lively dialogue among colleagues in both general and special education. We also believe that, implemented along with the rest of our recommendations, the resulting renewal of teacher education would go a long way toward providing the kinds of stewardship our schools so desperately need.

NOTES

1. National Commission on Excellence in Education, *A Nation at Risk* (Washington, D.C.: U.S. Government Printing Office, 1983).
2. Ernest L. Boyer, *High School* (New York: Harper & Row, 1983); John I. Goodlad, *A Place Called School* (New York: McGraw-Hill, 1984); and Theodore R. Sizer, *Horace's Compromise* (Boston: Houghton Mifflin, 1984).
3. Zhixin Su, *Teacher Education Reform in the United States (1890–1986)*, Occasional Paper 3 (Seattle: Center for Educational Renewal, College of Education, University of Washington, 1986).
4. James B. Conant, *The Education of American Teachers* (New York: McGraw-Hill, 1963).
5. James B. Conant, *The American High School Today* (New York: McGraw-Hill, 1959).
6. John I. Goodlad, *Teachers for Our Nation's Schools* (San Francisco: Jossey-Bass, 1990). See chaps. 1 and 8.
7. Sharon Field, *The Special Field of Special Education*, Technical Report 10 (Seattle: Center for Educational Renewal, College of Education, University of Washington, 1989).
8. Goodlad, *Teachers for Our Nation's Schools*.
9. John I. Goodlad, Roger Soder, and Kenneth A. Sirotnik, eds., *The Moral Dimensions of Teaching* (San Francisco: Jossey-Bass, 1990).
10. John I. Goodlad, Roger Soder, and Kenneth A. Sirotnik, eds., *Places Where Teachers Are Taught* (San Francisco: Jossey-Bass, 1990).
11. Kenneth A. Sirotnik, "The Eroding Foundations of Education," *Phi Delta Kappan* 71, no. 9 (May 1990), 710–16.
12. Goodlad, *A Place Called School*, 175.
13. Ibid., 184.
14. Margaret C. Wade, M. C. Reynolds, and H. J. Walberg, "Integrating Children of the Second System," *Phi Delta Kappan* 70 (Nov. 1988): 248–51.
15. Virginia Richardson and Patricia Colfer, "Being At-risk in School" in *Access to Knowledge: An Agenda for Our Nation's Schools*, ed. John I. Goodlad and Pamela Keating (New York: College Entrance Board, 1990), 107–24.
16. Chester E. Finn, Jr., "An Insider Grades Education Schools," *Christian Science Monitor*, 3 Dec. 1990, col. 1, p. 15.
17. National Board for Professional Teaching Standards, *Toward High and Rigorous Standards for the Teaching Profession* (Detroit: National Board for Professional Teaching Standards, 1989).

18. Abraham Flexner, *Medical Education in the United States and Canada* (New York: Carnegie Foundation for the Advancement of Teaching, 1910).

19. Bruce R. Joyce, Richard H. Hersh, and Michael McKiblin, *The Structure of School Improvement* (New York: Longman, 1983).

20. Karin Cathey, "Pre-service Programs for the Preparation of School Principals," source document (Seattle: Center for Educational Renewal, College of Education, University of Washington, 1990).

21. Roger Soder, *Faculty Work in the Institutional Context*, Technical Report 3 (Seattle: Center for Educational Renewal, College of Education, University of Washington, 1989).

22. Kenneth A. Sirotnik and John I. Goodlad, eds. *School-University Partnerships in Action* (New York: Teachers College, 1988); John I. Goodlad and Roger Soder, *School-University Partnerships: An Appraisal of an Idea*, Occasional Paper 15 (Seattle: Center for Educational Renewal, College of Education, University of Washington, 1992).

23. Holmes Group, *Tomorrow's Schools: Principles for the Design of Professional Development Schools* (East Lansing, MI: Holmes Group, 1990).

24. Carl Harris, "Educational Renewal: Not by Remote Control" in *Metropolitan Universities*, ed. John I. Goodlad, vol. 2, no. 1 (Summer 1991): 61–67.

25. Kenneth A. Sirotnik and Kathy Mueller, "Challenging the Wisdom of Conventional Principal Preparation Programs and Getting Away with It (So Far)," paper presented at the annual meeting of the University Council for Educational Administration, October 1991.

26. Neil D. Theobald, *The Financing and Governance of Professional Development or Partner Schools*, Occasional Paper 10 (Seattle: Center for Educational Renewal, College of Education, University of Washington, 1990).

27. John I. Goodlad, "Why We Need a Complete Redesign of Teacher Education," *Educational Leadership* 49 (Nov. 1991): 4–10.

28. Neil D. Theobald, *Allocating Resources to Renew Teacher Education*, Occasional Paper 14 (Seattle: Center for Educational Renewal, College of Education, University of Washington, 1991).

29. Goodlad, *Teachers for Our Nation's Schools*.

30. Ibid.

11

Retrospect and Prospect

Thomas C. Lovitt

In the foregoing chapters, we have attempted to identify and discuss issues that have to do with the integration of special and general education. We were interested in the impact of this involvement on all concerned, those in both general and special education. To deal with these issues we assembled authors from diverse backgrounds and perspectives. The authors of these chapters are associated with public schools, universities, private agencies, and the federal government. They have grappled with such issues as delivery systems, financing, teacher training and credentialing, curriculum, administration, and evaluation. Furthermore, they have addressed these issues and others from the perspectives of the past, the present, and the future.

Three parts comprise this chapter. In the first, I outline a few major points from each chapter and, when appropriate, relate them to educational programs recommended by agencies other than the public schools. This section of the chapter deals primarily with "outsiders," those not from the public schools. In the second part, an actual situation in a public school classroom is described, one in which the integration of disabled and nondisabled children is being played out. This section offers views from the "insiders." In the third part, I reflect on how we might merge the two sectors so that the energies of both are channeled for the common purpose of providing excellent educational experiences for our nation's children and youth.

THE BACKGROUND

In chapter 1, Goodlad sets the tone of the book by speaking of matters pertaining to equity, morality, ethics, and professionalism. With regard to those principles, he contends that schools of today are blemished, that many are in a state of disarray. Although Goodlad is heartened by the political energy devoted to education that keeps education and schools on center stage, he is not optimistic that the changes required to reshape society can take place within the context of America 2000 or other similar proposals for restructuring. Further, he is of the opinion that changes must take place within a context broader than only the schools if education is to change significantly.

Others are of a similar belief. Hodgkinson,[1] for example, uses a leaky roof metaphor to explain education's and society's plight. He maintains that attempts to rectify society's problems simply by altering a few instructional or administrative features of schools are like repairing the walls and floors of a house that were damaged by water but not taking the trouble to fix the leaky roof that caused the damage. To him, society's parallel of the leaky roof is the "one-third of preschool children who are destined for school failure because of poverty, neglect, sickness, handicapping conditions, and lack of adult protection and nurturance." Furthermore, Hodgkinson maintains that it will require the efforts of many individuals and organizations—health and social welfare agencies, parents, business and political leaders—to begin putting society back together again. Schools cannot do it alone.

In chapter 2, MacMillan and Hendrick trace the evolution of special education services for youngsters with disabilities, highlighting issues that have guided yet perplexed educators for over a century. Among them are the involvement of intelligence testing, the preoccupation with setting and corresponding treatments, the search for adequate definitions, and most recently, the impact of litigation. As astute historians, MacMillan and Hendrick note that the development of processes or themes—those relevant to special education in this case—are not always smoothly transitional or rationally stimulated. Likewise, as historians, they remind us that certain arguments that raged at the beginning of movements have often continued for quite some time. This is certainly true in special education. And as chroniclers of events, MacMillan and Hendrick remind us that certain notable figures have sometimes retarded progress of their respective movements as much as they have advanced it. In the case of special education, Terman and Goddard made about as many errors as they did hits.

In chapter 3, I identify seven recurring issues among special and regular educators, all of which are dealt with in considerable detail in other chapters. Following are the issues discussed in chapter 3 and an identification of the chapters in which they are primarily discussed. *Identification* is a major topic of chapter 2, whereas *evaluation* is the primary theme of chapter 7. As the major topic of chapter 5 is *funding*, the central theme of chapter 4 is *delivery systems*. The focus of chapter 6 is *curriculum*, and the *relationships* and *responsibilities* of teachers are emphasized in chapters 6, 8, 9, and 10. *Homogeneity* and *heterogeneity* and related notions of variability and tracking are given attention in chapters 6, 7, 8, and 10.

In chapter 4, Kauffman and Hallahan deliberate on the concept of "all" within the context of providing services to youngsters and youth with disabilities. They offer various meanings and interpretations of the term and bring the concept home dramatically by referring to rulings in the recent *Timothy W. v. Rochester School District* case. With reference to more general efforts toward school reform, the authors point out that special education has played a limited and insignificant role. Moreover, Kauffman and Hallahan believe that many of the arguments for restructuring are based on *misrepresentations, tortured ideologies,* and *conceptual confusions.* These authors are not as inclined to dismantle special education or merge it with general programs as are many others. They, in fact, see the movement toward integration as somewhat counterproductive in that service delivery and curricular options for children are being reduced at a time when alternatives for dealing with the increased variability and diversity of students are desperately needed.

In chapter 5, Bernstein offers a primer for financing education. His message is that if educators turn matters of finance over to mathematicians, they might as well give them license to make policy, for money goes with programs. Bernstein then goes on to explain matters of finance as they relate to special education in such a way that educators who intend to set policy can understand them. According to him, a special education program of finance should be equitable, comprehensive, flexible, compatible, and simple.

In chapter 6, Pugach and Warger remind us that any consideration of integrating special and general education must be well grounded in an analysis of curricular issues and that knowledge of curriculum is the basis on which instructional planning for students should take place. Relatedly, special education professionals, according to them, have shown little interest in either the form or content of the standard curriculum. For many special educators, the authors go on to argue, the individualized education program (IEP) is not only the means for acquiring the curriculum, it *is* the curriculum. Pugach and Warger then criticize special educators for confusing process with curriculum by claiming that they give inordinate emphasis to management techniques and strategy at the expense of providing instruction on meaningful content. The authors do, however, credit special educators with being more concerned about individual development and eventual outcomes of students than their regular education counterparts have been, intimating that those attributes should be shared by all teachers.

In chapter 7, Smith and Noble review a number of theories and approaches for evaluating educational programs: *positivism, interpretivism, multiplism,* and *critical theory.* They also comment on the role of four approaches for evaluating programs and reflect a bit on each: *value-neutral, value-relative, value-committed,* and *value-critical.* Smith and Noble then present a plan for evaluating the integration of regular and special education services that is characterized by panels and cycles. They describe the six stages of their model and outline examples of studies that could be set up within the model.

In chapter 8, Murray offers comments and suggestions on restructuring, particularly with respect to integrating youngsters of all types, from the perspective of an elementary school principal. When it comes to integrating special and regular education students, individuals with severe disorders significantly complicate the process, according to her. Murray gives emphasis to six pedagogical practices that may assist in the process of blending diverse types of students: *multiage grouping, authentic products and projects, integrated assessment, collaborative learning groups, peer and cross-age tutoring,* and *classroom management* and *disciplinary strategies.* Moreover, she expresses the belief that efforts to deal effectively with a variable lot of students will be accomplished best when teachers collaborate, either by forming teacher assistance teams, which enable specialists to offer direct intervention and increase the involvement of paraprofessionals, or by using other means. She, like other authors in our book, is of the belief that more flexibility, rather than less, is needed if educators are to accommodate effectively the diverse needs of today's children.

In chapter 9, Schrag offers suggestions for restructuring schools, more specifically on the alignment of general and special education, from the perspective of a federal official. She states that although there have been tremendous gains for individuals with disabilities since 1975 with respect to accessibility, it is now time to move forward and provide better services for them, services that are tied to outcomes that enhance individuals' lives. Schrag cites examples of states and school districts that have begun efforts of one type or another to revitalize their educational services and comments on a number of government-sponsored programs that reinforce those efforts. Furthermore, she advances several questions that, in her opinion, frame the challenges of continued refinement in special education. They deal with outcomes, learning experiences, service delivery approaches, and accountability.

The central theme of chapter 10, by Goodlad and Field, is that teachers for our schools must be prepared to take part in efforts to renew schools. As they see it, teachers are ill equipped to participate in dialogues on such matters as establishing school-based management, reallocating personnel or other resources, planning more relevant evaluations of pupils and teachers, or designing alternative curricula. Related to those concerns, Goodlad and Field present and discuss data gathered by the Center for Educational Renewal in its study of general and special teachers in training and of professors of the respective departments. A few paradoxical and disturbing views are brought out from these data. For example, although prospective teachers in general education believed that they were not adequately prepared to deal with exceptional children who might be enrolled in their classes, they were not convinced that it would help them to take additional special education classes. In general, the data show that the views of general and special education professors on what constitutes an acceptable program for teachers were quite different, which thus reminds us of the separation and lack of communication between the two camps.

Throughout these chapters most of the current educational movements, referenda, and initiatives that may influence the course of education
have been referred to. I will simply note those programs and a few others:

- America 2000
- The responses to it, *Voices from the Field*[2]
- The Oregon plan (based on "America's Choice") to revitalize education by expanding programs, lengthening the school year, allowing
youth to choose their curriculum at tenth grade, and other features
- The proposed New York plan that would give children in the state's
worst schools $2,500 that could be deposited at the school of their
choice
- The Texas plan to end the fiscal disparity between school districts
- The Kentucky plan that calls for school-based management, ungraded
classes, standards for teacher certification, emphasis on preschool, and
other features
- The proposed plan of Senator Gephardt that would pay states a boun-
ty for every child sent to first grade ready for school and for high
school seniors whose mathematics and science test scores matched the
highest standards
- The Regular Education Initiative (REI) that has to do with the integration of special and regular education

The origins of these plans, proposals, and recommendations have
come primarily from the "outsiders," not from the public schools where
they will ultimately be dealt with. They have been promoted by legislators
and other officials in the federal and state governments, professors in higher education, and executives in the corporate world. The major educational
stakeholders, the "insiders," have rarely been involved in prescribing their
destiny.

It is interesting to consider the forces that combine to form the "outsiders"; they indeed form an unholy alliance. It is difficult to come up with
a sociological, economic, or political parallel to it. Sociologically, that collection of agencies is not like the members of a team who strive for a common
goal, or even the members of a family who occasionally seek the same objective. Economically, they are like neither the confederation of nations that
form the European Common Market nor a conglomeration of stores that
make up a shopping center. Politically, the outside agencies that have profound impact on education are neither like the states of the United States,
nor do they resemble the republics that once constituted the Soviet Union.

Many teachers and not a few administrators in the public schools are
totally unaware of the plans and proposals from the "outsiders." They do
not know what others have in store for them. And just as teachers are generally unenlightened about what could be happening to them, the professors,
professional educators, politicians, and pundits of the corporate world—the
"outsiders"—are unaware of what is actually going on in schools. Although

they attended schools themselves and have sent their children to schools, not many of them have set foot in the schools of today, certainly not in the public schools. If they have, it would have been to visit a superintendent or high-level official at the administration building. Thus the information these individuals have about schools is probably secondhand, invariably biased, certainly unreliable, and possibly dated. In this next section we visit a public school classroom and witness a few of the events and circumstances that are happening.

THE SCHOOLS

While the articles are being written on renewal, the position papers on the REI are being circulated; as the pronouncements on dealing with diversity are being published and the other proposals are being argued, the reality of education is being played out daily in hundreds of thousands of classrooms throughout the country.

As I have indicated, teachers are unaware that others are out there trying to renew, revitalize, rejuvenate, and initiate them. If quizzed, they would be remarkable naive about all that is happening. In Seattle, for example, if teachers were asked if they knew of the REI, some of them might say that it was the outfit in town that sells camping gear, Recreational Equipment Inc. The same could be said of parents; they do not know about all the plans for rejuvenation. According to a survey carried out by the National Parent Teacher Association and the Chrysler Corporation, only 7 percent of the parents surveyed could correctly recall even one of the national goals set by President Bush and the governors.[3]

Certainly, schoolteachers have read in papers and magazines the reports about the plight of America's schools, and they have tuned in to television specials that lamented the sorry state of affairs. Teachers know, too, that although there are current rumblings about change, this is nothing new; there have been programs, referendum, and initiatives before, and for the most part they did not phase them. Add to this the fact that teachers do not have time to get involved with these plans for renewal, even if invited to participate. They have to get ready for Monday morning when their crowd of diverse youngsters shows up.

In order to help understand what is happening in schools today, I will describe a music class in an elementary school. Although this is not a typical classroom (I am not sure there is such a thing), it is a real one. There are two groups of students in this class: twenty-five general first-graders and eight youngsters who have developmental delays. They meet twice a week for thirty minutes each session.

The school, Mountain View, is in a suburban district. There are about 500 pupils in attendance, in grades kindergarten through sixth. The majority of families near the school would be characterized as middle class, but there is a fair number of families at the poverty level as well. There is quite an ethnic distribution of children in the school. In the past five or so years, great numbers of families from Southeast Asia, Europe, and Central and South America have settled nearby.

The music teacher of these combined groups has been in the business for over twenty years and has taught at all levels: primary, intermediate, middle school, and high school. Over the years, several youngsters with handicaps have been in her music classes. (It is important to point out that vocal music teachers have been the most dependable mainstreamers in schools. In 1964, when I was teaching a group of adolescents with mild handicaps in Kansas City, I could generally count on them to take in a few of my charges.) A few years ago, this music teacher worked with one class of mentally retarded children and a class of autistic children separately and with those children at another time when they were mainstreamed into second and third grade classes. She is willing to make what adaptations she can in order to accommodate children with special needs. This notwithstanding, the music teacher is sensitive to the needs of the other youngsters, those with no apparent or recognized disabilities, and desires that they, along with the special education children, have decent musical experiences.

The youngsters in the first grade class are a sample of the school's population in that there are children of several types in the group. Not only is there considerable ethnic and socioeconomic diversity in the class, there is a significant amount of motivational and ability variation as well. The first grade teacher has been teaching for about twenty years, having taught first grade for the past five years. She is acknowledged by the building principal and other teachers as one of the best in the school, and several parents request her class for their children every year. Although she has had a number of difficult children in her classes over the years, she has not dealt with any special youngsters who were mainstreamed into her classes.

The first grade teacher (referred to as "F" throughout this story) is sympathetic toward special children. She related an experience to the music teacher that may in part explain her willingness to work with those youngsters. She said that when her daughter was in elementary school, her teacher asked if she would help a special education boy with some of his schoolwork. The daughter refused, saying that she did not want to be near the special student, much less to work with him. Although F did not say that this experience had changed her daughter's life, making her more understanding or sympathetic toward individuals with disabilities, she still harbors a great deal of guilt over the incident. That episode apparently had a noticeable impact on F, however, for she is quite willing to work with these children.

Now a few words about the special education children who are mainstreamed with the first-graders. There are eight of them, four boys and four girls, most of them with Down syndrome. The youngsters are a year or two older than the first-graders but about the same size. Four of them have been together for about three years and have formed quite a clique. Nancy seems to be the ringleader. Since the children have been together for some time, so of course have their parents. They have their own advocacy group and often act as one. (This is not an unusual situation in special education. When I taught a class of children who were mentally retarded in Kansas City, there were two boys in my class whose parents had been in league for several years. They were quite aggressive and made it rather tough for an inexperienced teacher.)

Although the music teacher (hereafter referred to as "M") has seated the special education students amid the first-graders, they sometimes appear to act as one. This was particularly true in the first few weeks of school. One day, Nancy, their leader, flopped down on the floor and would not get up, and two or three of the others followed suit. On another day, she started singing at an inappropriate time, and a few others imitated her. The aide said that on another occasion, not in the music class, Nancy took off her shoes, and the others did likewise.

The teacher of the special group (hereafter referred to as "S") is a hard-core special educator; she appears to be a devoted advocate for her children. She wants them to have all the advantages and privileges that are available to children without handicaps and definitely wants them main-streamed into music, or "immersed," as she calls it. (S is a good reason for recommending that special education teachers be trained first in general education, for she has little understanding of what goes on in general class-rooms. She believes that whatever it is that other children do, her children should be given the opportunity to do it, whether they will gain from the experience or not.)

From the first day of school, S mainstreamed her charges into the music class. Although only two or three children came in the first few days, the whole gang joined in by the second week. She does not know a thing about the curriculum of the music class. She has not the faintest idea about what is expected of the children. (After the fourth week of school and after there had been some problems with the special children, M told S what the class rules were. M explained that she had a few basic rules: the children were to come in quietly and sit in their assigned seats, they were expected to participate in the activities, and they were expected to respect the rights of others.) As indicated, S's primary motivation is for her children to be main-streamed. (Unfortunately, this attitude of "let's all do the same thing" is held by many special education teachers. They simply want special educa-tion youngsters to be mainstreamed; they are not really certain why. Other special educators would argue that unless these special children are getting something out of a class into which they are mainstreamed, be it music or something else, they should be someplace else doing something else.)

One reason that S wants her children mainstreamed into the music class and into other situations is that she gets considerable pressure from some of her children's parents to do so. (It is doubtful that all eight sets of parents are asking for all-out mainstreaming, for most of the time there is not total agreement among parents of children with disabilities on what should be done with their children, any more than there is consensus among the parents of children without handicaps.)

When the eight children with handicaps come into the music class, they are accompanied by an aide. S does not set foot in the music room. Although the aide is a thoughtful person and generally effective with her charges, she has had little training to deal with youngsters of this type, or with any other type of youngster, for that matter. Whatever techniques she has picked up for working with these children have been learned from S in the classroom or picked up on her own. (Unfortunately, this is an all too familiar scene in special education, particularly with youngsters with the more severe types of disabilities. Aides do a lot of the real work. Too often they are not trained, and invariably, they are underpaid.) It appears then, that whereas S talks a good game about mainstreaming and gives others the idea that she really has children's best interests at heart, it is obvious that the music period is her time to relax.

One would think that S would come into the music class, determine what is going on, see what the music teacher is trying to teach, observe how she goes about it, learn about the classroom rules, and, certainly, become acquainted with the teacher. With this information, she could decide whether the setting was a proper one for her pupils. Following an observation or two, S could sit down with the music teacher and discuss the "immersion" of her students. Furthermore, S could give the music teacher thumbnail sketches about her pupils and tell the music teacher what she might expect from each of them and what she might do if they did something that was a bit out of the ordinary. Special education children should come with instructions. From this discussion, S would learn from the music teacher what her expectations were. With that information, S, or more likely her aide, could assist their children to develop behaviors that were requisite to participating in and gaining from the music class (e.g., taking their seats, staying seated when they are supposed to, participating in the activities, lining up when the period is over, walking quietly back to their classroom) in the special class so that when they arrived in the music class, things would go smoothly. It might also be that if S knew more about the music class and the activities they were working on, she would send in only those youngsters who would comply with the rules and could profit from the program. She might even consider the possibility that some of her youngsters would gain more from another program, at least for the time being, than they would from being integrated with first-graders in a music class.

After a few sessions the first grade teacher F expressed some concerns about the combined classes to the music teacher. She said that although she is sympathetic toward mainstreaming and her youngsters' being involved with those with developmental disabilities, she wants to be certain that the musical experience is a good one for her first-graders. The music teacher understood and said that she would keep her informed.

Although F does not come into the class either, she does ask the music teacher, from time to time, how things are going. That is more than can be said for S, the special education teacher, who had not asked about anything in the class until the music teacher reported to her, through her aide, that there were some problems with the children with disabilities. (Teachers do not have opportunities to talk to one another about the problems of children; times are rarely scheduled for that. The times they are not dealing with children—recess, lunch, music, physical education, library—are for their personal planning or for relaxation, not for talking with other teachers or visiting other classes.)

What are the possible gains for the first-graders of having an experience with a group of special children? A few come to mind. For one thing, they could be more understanding of people with handicaps. One day the school nurse came into the class and sat by one of the girls with Down syndrome. She took out some medicine, put it in a cup, and gave it to the girl, who swallowed it. The nurse then gave the little girl a wafer to eat. All the while the music class was going on. A first grade girl sitting by the girl with Down syndrome did not watch the process at all, whereas a girl seated behind the nurse and the girl with Down syndrome was fascinated by the episode. No one said a word, however, as all this took place. The music teacher had explained to the class before the event what would be happening.

The first-graders could also learn about differences and diversity. Glen, one of the special education children, has a hard time of it. Although he is generally under control, he does not appear to get much out of the sessions. When the other children are singing, using instruments, clapping, or moving about to music, he ordinarily sits and stares into space. One day the children were clapping to a song and having a great time. As usual, Glen simply sat, inactive and emotionless. Following the clapping activity, the children sang a patriotic song, one that did not involve clapping, but Glen decided to clap. Instead of being irritated with him, the music teacher, the aide, and the children were delighted. At last, he had done something that the others had done. Granted, he did it at a different time, but nonetheless he had in his way participated.

They could learn to help one another. One day the youngsters were taking turns with a few rhythm instruments, one of which was a guiro, a sort of gourd with striated edges. They were shown how to rub a stick across the edges in order to make a screeching sound. One of the girls with Down syndrome, when her turn came, had a hard time holding the guiro and rubbing the stick. A first grade girl sitting next to her watched for a while, saw that she was having problems, then reached over to help. It looked as though the first-grader had intended to hold the Down girl's hand as she held the stick and help her rub it across the rough edges of the instrument. The girl with Down syndrome would have none of this and quickly pulled the guiro away. She did not look at the first grade girl and said nothing to her, but it was obvious that she did not want to be helped. The first grade girl did not appear to be upset by the rejection. She seemed to be satisfied with her attempt to help and would probably give assistance of another kind on another day. (At least that is how I interpreted her expression.)

And what might be the down side for this, the first mainstreaming experience of these first-graders? They might not learn as many songs, dances, or rhythms as they would have had the group of special children not been around. Perhaps because of those missed opportunities one or two of them will not grow to love music the way they might have. Moreover, it is possible that a couple of them may learn to actually dislike special individuals, perhaps those with Down syndrome in particular, because of their sudden flare-ups and other interruptions. It could be that two or three of the first-graders will be like the first grade teacher's daughter; they will not be able to tolerate individuals with handicaps, but they will feel guilty about it later. And a few of them may become generally disgusted with school, believing that it is a place where one must adapt to unusual circumstances or wait for slower ones to catch up.

Not much thought and even less research has gone into the analysis of the positive and negative aspects of these mainstreaming experiences on so-called typical children. Personally, I think that society would be better off if we looked at the net effect of all these experiences.

While this scene is being played out in the music class, one might wonder what the building principal was doing about all this? What has she done to see that the mainstreaming process is a smooth one? Absolutely nothing. She has not come into any of the rooms: the first grade, the special class, the music class. There is no school policy on mainstreaming. She has not talked about it during faculty meetings and has not sent out memos on the topic to her staff. The principal could have encouraged the special education teacher to visit the music class so that she could see what was going on, and, likewise, she might have suggested to the music teacher that she visit the special education room. The principal could have taken over the classes of the teachers while they visited one another's situations. This building principal has elected to distance herself from a difficult situation, one that begs for leadership. In this case, she is acting as neither an outsider nor an insider. She has opted for benign neutrality.

It is mentioned in chapter 3 that, generally, schools do not have policies that deal with mainstreaming. Based on my experiences, and certainly the one just described, I share that view. Many teachers are simply expected to deal with mainstreaming as best they can, without guidance, support, or encouragement.

At the very least, the teachers and principal of Mountain View Elementary School should sit down and work out a plan. It should respond to the following questions, among others: What are the goals for the youngsters, those with and without disabilities? Who will be mainstreamed when and into what situations? What help is available for mainstreaming teachers? To what extent and about what should teachers collaborate? Will they be given time to do this? (In this school the teachers rarely communicate about the issues of mainstreaming, the principal is not involved at all, and no one else at Mountain View is working on a plan for mainstreaming. To complete this dismal picture, personnel from the central office have not offered to help the school work out matters of policy and procedure. Those who are involved are on their own.)

Although the class I have described may not be representative of many others with respect to curriculum and instruction, what is happening here is indeed similar to other situations in which mainstreaming is taking place: someone said that it was a good idea, someone got pressure from someone else to do it, and teachers are faced with doing it on their own.

Outsiders are unaware of the many complex incidents of classrooms such as those described here; they are generally unfamiliar with the real culture of schools. Outsiders talk about diversity, but they do not see it. They recommend individualized instruction, but they do not do it. They speak of the need to integrate youngsters with disabilities into the common track, but many of them do not mingle with individuals with disabilities in either their professional or personal lives. Outsiders address the need to collaborate and cooperate with others, yet most of them behave as soloists.

MAKING IT HAPPEN: A COLLABORATION BETWEEN THE OUTSIDERS AND THE INSIDERS

We are aware that there are two disparate forces that have something to do with education, the outsiders and the insiders. We recognize also that not only do the two groups differ from one another but also that there is a tremendous diversity *within* each group. But beyond simply recognizing this diversity, what could be done about it? What could we do to improve the educational experiences for all children, to arrange more equitable experiences for children, those in suburban, rural, and urban districts, those of all ethnic groups, from all economic levels, and those with handicaps? What could be done to provide those excellent and equitable services more efficiently? What could take place to guarantee better outcomes for all pupils: better quality of life, a citizenry that is more humane, productive, and cooperative, citizens who are in tune with the world and their planet?

Certainly, there is room for the improvement of education. In spite of the pushes for excellence of a few years ago and the many current programs referred to earlier and the fact that about half of many states' budgets go toward educational expenses, all is not well. According to a report on the progress of students in the United States summarized in the *New York Times*,[4] "American elementary and secondary school pupils have made some educational progress in recent years, but they are only now reaching the achievement levels of students in 1970. . . . Today's children seem to know about as much math and about as much science and read about as well as their parents did at that age about 20 years ago."

Relative to the attainment of the goals set by President Bush and the nation's governors in 1989, another report indicates that we are off the mark on all of them. About the only goal for which even modest progress has been made has to do with the rates at which students graduate; whereas numbers are up for white and black students, they are not for Hispanic students. With respect to the goal that schools would be free of drugs and safe environments for learning, the data are rather grim. According to a *New York Times* article, whereas marijuana use in schools by twelfth-graders dropped from 1980 to 1990, the use of alcohol increased in that period. With respect to violence, the article claims that this has remained a problem and that black students are more likely to be the victims of violent crime than Hispanic or white students.[5]

When it comes to renewing and rejuvenating the public schools, we need to expand our ideas about education. Our thinking now about education is guided too much by schools as we know them. Illich,[6] some time ago, lamented the fact that we often confuse and restrict our thinking about education when we equate it with schools, just as we limit our thinking about religion when we associate it entirely with churches. We need a much broader perspective on education.

As for today's educational goals, I am not convinced that we have identified those that are the most important. Of course, we need to learn to read, write, and cipher, but more importantly we must learn to live with one another and with our environment. We need to learn to respect one another and behave ethically. We are coming off a decade that will be noted for its greed and selfishness and remembered for its lack of moral principle and concern for community. And there is no indication that the nineties will be any better. Derek Bok, in his final presidential address at Harvard University, charged that an eerie indifference hangs over the land.[7] He lamented that instead of a popular outcry to end urban violence, poverty, homelessness, and the hunger of children, the loudest clamor we hear from the public is "no new taxes."

But for now, I will assume that we must work with the schools pretty much as they are and go on from there. It is at this point that I bring in a notion other authors in this book have referred to—that of collaboration—for that is our salvation, in my opinion. I am referring to collaboration in the broadest sense of the term: collaboration *within* the groups of outsiders and insiders and collaboration *across* the two groups.

Beginning with the schools, there is a great need for teachers to collaborate more with one another, special teachers with regular teachers, regular and special teachers among themselves, teachers with specialists, teachers and specialists with administrators. Not only do teachers, specialists, and administrators need to learn about collaborating within their own schools, they must learn ways to interact, share ideas, and cooperate with their peers at other schools in their districts, in other districts, and perhaps across the country. All this is possible today, with our advanced forms of telecommunicating and networking. There is no reason for any teacher to be enclosed in his or her room without keeping in touch with others. Taking advantage of today's methods of communication, the teacher could type in requests for techniques to enhance reading comprehension, better integrate reading and spelling, or establish cooperative learning situations. Others on the network could respond to those requests, and chances are that dozens of possible solutions would be sent.

There is also a need for teachers in public schools to collaborate and share information with teachers and consultants in private and parochial schools. Furthermore, teachers and administrators in public schools should collaborate and cooperate more with home teachers and private tutors. Many of those relationships are now adversarial.

Not only will public school people and other insiders need to collaborate if we are to pull this off, but college of education professors and other outsiders will have to do likewise. As we look around the country, there are too few examples of interagency coordination on behalf of education. To illustrate an example of what is unfortunately going on, I will note just a few practices in one of our states. At the state level, in this not-to-be-mentioned location, some staff members were drafting policy statements on assessment that would require districts to precisely identify youngsters who were learning disabled. Their idea was to locate only those students who were "truly" learning disabled. Meanwhile, down the hall from those staffers, other government workers were writing position papers that proclaimed the advantages of prereferral teams, one of which was to temper the need for precise diagnoses and, relatedly, simply recommend treatments and interventions for children who needed them, regardless of their label. While all that was happening at the capitol, there was a federally funded program at a nearby university to prepare consulting teachers. Not a bad idea, but none of the school districts in that state were operating programs of that type. There was more confusion. Certification personnel, back at the capitol, decided on their own to recertify regular teachers as special teachers if they took twenty-four credits in special education. Operationally, that meant that regular teachers could pick up a few credits at one place, two or three at another, and five or six at some place else. And lo and behold, they became special education teachers. Once they had their twenty-four credits, the state people swore them in, not the folks at the place or places where they obtained the credits. Sadly, I doubt that the experiences of that state, the total absence of an integrated effort to prepare teachers, are unique.[8]

In order to have effective collaboration, there are at least four factors that must be in evidence. First, each of the parties that intend to collaborate must have some body of knowledge or area of expertness. And relatedly, they must be willing to share it with others who recognize their knowledge or expertness as something worth knowing about. Obviously, if all parties knew the same things or were able to do the same things, there would be little reason to collaborate.

In schools, for example, within the context of prereferral teams, those organizations are successful to the extent that various members bring different expertness on different topics to the team. One member may know a great deal about reading techniques, another may be knowledgeable about disciplinary tactics, and a third could be expert in working with parents. With a group such as that, several important topics are covered. At the college of education level, collaborative teams could also be developed. One member may know a lot about language arts, another is an expert on evaluation, and a third is knowledgeable about administration. And perhaps the fourth member knows a great deal about exceptional children.

Second, all the parties involved in the collaborative arrangements must agree to share the "pain or gain" that could result from such relationships. If, for example, a team of college folks and a cadre of school people decided to revamp a school's or district's evaluation program—perhaps doing away with standardized tests and moving to forms of curriculum-based assessment—all parties must agree at the outset to do everything possible to make the project a success. They must all be committed to not only designing the approach but seeing to it that it is carried out reliably and efficiently, that data from the new program are analyzed, that decisions are made from the data, that changes are made if the data so indicate, and that implications and results from the research are communicated to parents and all others concerned. Along with those responsibilities, there could be mutual gain in the form of increased pupil performance; savings of time and money, satisfactions of parents, children, teachers, or administrators; recognition by other districts; and the publication of articles, chapters, and books. If, however, the approach is a failure, then all concerned must share in the pain and stay with one another to pick up the pieces. No one should walk away from the other.

Third, the efforts of the collaborative groups should be accompanied by data. Data must be available from which to make judgments and decisions. Too often, teachers or professors have changed a program or practice simply because they wanted to change it. They perhaps became bored with the current state, or their neighbor had tried something and they did not want to be left behind. Not a few school districts seem to be more interested in "staying ahead" or "keeping up" with other school districts, in that they start up new and different programs of all kinds, than they are in acquiring data to evaluate the effects of those programs. I happen to live in one like that.

School people and college folks must discuss all the projects in which they are collaborating and agree on ways in which to evaluate them. All concerned must know whether their efforts were totally, partially, or minimally successful or whether they were absolute failures. When it comes to evaluation, some university folks would have an opportunity to contribute their expertness in data gathering and analysis. They could propose a variety of ways in which to evaluate certain performances and programs and could give examples on how these various forms were used.

Fourth, all parties must be committed to studying those data relevant to their projects and willing, on the basis of that information, to make change. If one program at school is found to be more effective than another, teachers and administrators must be willing to adopt that method. If, through some collaborative effort, it is learned that it is more expedient and effective to train prospective teachers in one way than it is in another, university folks must change their practices. If school people knew that they had the muscle to change certain ideas, courses, or practices of folks in higher education, they would be greatly reinforced. With respect to one group influencing the other, a number of examples could be cited of schools changing their practices because of an arrangement with a university, but I am not as aware of examples of higher education people modifying their practices because of relationships with schools.

In collaborative relationships between schools and universities that I am familiar with, not all of these important and related elements are in place. This is particularly true of the last point, that all parties must be willing to change their practices based on acquired data.

To operationalize these school and university confederations, I would see a group of college professors, ones who had different abilities and areas of expertness, asking school people if they could come into schools to work with them. The university professors, after they had chatted a great deal with the school folks, listened to them, and informed them about their relevant abilities, would spend a fair amount of time in the schools. They would visit classes, talk with administrators, chat with specialists and visit their situations, and perhaps talk with parents (with the approval of the school people, of course). The professors should then relate their thoughts and observations to one another and, as a group, with the teachers and administrators. In the next phase of this process, school people and university folks would lay out a plan. In so doing, they would take into account the four points of collaboration that have been mentioned earlier.

Every important feature of education could be dealt with through these relationships. Aspects of education important to schools could be attacked collaboratively—those pertaining to curriculum, instruction, administration, finance, communication, public relations, and others. As for the professors, there would be enough work in teaching, service, and research for everyone. In the following sections, I will comment on and give examples of two major areas about which schools and universities could profitably collaborate, teacher training and research.

Teacher Training

With respect to teacher education, Goodlad and Field have strongly recommended that collaborative efforts be set up between public schools and universities. They are opposed to handing over the process of teacher education to the public schools, and they are critical of universities that take on the chore single-handedly. I agree, and furthermore I believe that the significant areas in which teachers need considerable experience before going into our nation's schools can be acquired within the framework of collaboration between public schools and universities. Following are four of those activities.

First, prospective teachers must have a number of field experiences closely tied to classes and seminars in a coherent, cohesive program. They should have these experiences throughout their programs, and they should be with excellent teachers. Moreover, they should have experiences in a variety of locations with various types of students. Every student should spend some time in preschools, elementary schools, middle schools, and high schools. Prospective teachers should have experiences in special education classes of all types, in urban, suburban, and rural locations, in lower and upper economic level schools, and perhaps in private and parochial schools. They should certainly work in schools in which there is a great deal of ethnic diversity. Students should observe and interact with teachers who work effectively with individual students, those who manage small and large groups effectively, and others who successfully incorporate microcomputers and other innovative aids into their instructional routines. Prospective teachers should interact with specialists: administrators, school psychologists, counselors, music teachers, special education teachers. (It might not be a bad idea if prospective teachers visited a few classrooms in which the teachers were not particularly good ones.)

Second, prospective teachers must be provided considerable training and be given a number of actual experiences with parents. Goodlad and Field report in chapter 10 that this is an area of weakness expressed by all prospective teachers in their research review. Teachers in training must learn to communicate and work with parents of all types: those who are affluent, highly educated, single, intimidated by schools, or who intimidate teachers and administrators. Prospective teachers must understand the power of parents and the important roles they can play in their children's education. As it is, most students in training programs do not take a single parent training course; they are rarely even assigned a book on the topic to read. Many prospective teachers are familiar with only the methods of interacting with parents that were the vogue in the 1950s: back-to-school night, school conferences, occasional notes home, and report cards. With today's children and their parents, those techniques alone are not at all sufficient.

Third, prospective teachers must be given a number of experiences in dealing with the extreme variability apparent in classrooms today. They must not only learn to *deal* with diversity, they must learn to *capitalize* on it, to use diversity in classes to the advantage of all their children. This is tough. Following is an example in a vocal music class of taking advantage of diversity.

One day a little boy from Peru came into the class. He had just moved to the country and knew only a few words of English. The music teacher, who can speak and understand a bit of Spanish and, more importantly, respects languages generally, happened to have a song in which the days of the week were in Spanish. She had the class sing it and told the youngsters what the words were in English. As they sang the song the little Peruvian boy's eyes lit up. Familiarity! They then sang the song with the days of the week in English. Following, the music teacher took the opportunity to talk about the Spanish language and inform the youngsters that there *are* languages other than English and that the new boy speaks one, Spanish. The music teacher then told the students a few Spanish words that sounded and meant about the same in English, words like *automóvil, rápido,* and *atención.* The children were excited that they were "learning" Spanish. For several weeks the music teacher and the Peruvian boy carried out a little conversation in Spanish, and then she translated what had been said, as best she could, for the other pupils. There came a time, however, when the boy signaled to the teacher that he did not want the special attention. He apparently wanted to be "immersed." Obviously, prospective teachers cannot learn every language spoken by the students who come into their classes and be highly knowledgeable about their cultures, for there will be dozens of them in some schools, but they can and must learn to respect other languages and cultures and convey that attitude to their youngsters. There are countless ways in which to capitalize on the diversity that comes about in all classes today, but it is shameful that teachers in preparation receive so little training on that score.

Fourth, teachers in training must have at their fingertips a great number of tactics for managing and controlling classes. They should have a large repertory of techniques for motivating youngsters. They should know a great number of procedures for teaching reading, mathematics, writing, and other subjects. Teachers in training must know dozens of ways to adapt materials from textbooks, tests, other media, and lectures, and know about modifying the ways in which students might respond to those materials. Furthermore, teachers in training must be familiar with a variety of approaches for evaluating student progress. Unfortunately, most teachers are woefully limited in their options for setting up and evaluating instructional environments.

Research

There are many examples of research that could be carried out collaboratively by public school people and university folks. Dozens of research studies could be set up that would pertain to important school matters and would satisfy the needs and ambitions of most professors and their doctoral students. I will comment on only four broad areas of research, ones that were mentioned in preceding chapters: arranging alternative delivery systems, developing alternative means of assessment, communicating with parents, and communicating and collaborating within and across staffs.

As for the first research topic, arranging alternate ways to deliver services, a school or district might be interested in setting up a prereferral system and perhaps comparing it with their current approach for providing services. When a prereferral plan is arranged, as explained in preceding chapters, a school organizes a team of individuals. The team could be made up of teachers, psychologists, or others; its composition would depend on the abilities and resources of the school. Once organized, teachers who have concerns about children in their classes go to that team. Following an appraisal of the situation, perhaps a visit or two to the classroom of the referred child, and an interview with the child's teacher, team members would suggest, in collaboration with the referring teacher, a few possible techniques that might be tried in an effort to solve the problem. This prereferral approach might be contrasted to a more traditional model in which teachers refer children directly to psychologists or others who test them, determine whether they are exceptional in one way or another, and, if they are, suggest that they be placed in settings that seem to be in line with the assessments. Data of several types could be gathered from such a comparative study: on the number or type of referrals; the number and type of treatments that are recommended; and of those, the ones that were attempted; and of those, the extent to which they were successful. Data could also be obtained on the money involved to carry out either process. Moreover, consumer satisfaction data could be acquired from participating teachers, administrators, youngsters who were a part of the process, and their parents.

For the second research topic, arranging alternative assessment approaches, a few teachers, several schools, or an entire district could collaborate with a group of university researchers. Research on this theme may have been stimulated by teachers and administrators who were dissatisfied with the data they were receiving from traditional, standardized measures. School people, particularly teachers, may have become disenchanted, frustrated, and even angry with the data they were being provided from the more usual measures. Although the teachers realize the importance of data and that data of different types have various meanings for individuals of different types, they are not at all pleased with the information they or others gather from these standardized measures, mainly because they are not of immediate (even long-range) use. They neither help them decide what to do with the tested youngsters, nor do they inform them as to the extent that youngsters have improved on the skills or behaviors that are being taught. Many teachers clamor for a more direct form of assessment.

Many parents are just as unhappy with the present forms of assessment as are the teachers, but for different reasons. Many of them believe that they are being bamboozled by the ways in which their son's or daughter's progress is measured and reported, particularly the latter. They are confused and frustrated by the *stanines, quartiles,* and *grade-level equivalents.*

Moreover, not a few administrators and school board members are displeased with the current evaluation system, the one that has been in place for several decades. To study this issue, school people, teachers, and administrators, along with parents, team up with a group from their local university to evaluate another approach, curriculum-based assessment, and compare it with the standard plan. Before deciding on the research design and discussing related methodological issues, the groups select measures that are important ones to obtain, some of which might have to do with pupil performance and the satisfactions of involved parties. Other measures could relate to time, money, and ease of communication.

The third research theme that could be carried out collaboratively by school people, parents, and folks from the university might have to do with communications between home and school. Although educators recognize the importance of these communications, both from the standpoint of assisting children and the more mundane motive of public relations, I am hard-pressed to come up with studies that have explored various means of communication and determined the relative effects of those styles. The reader will notice that I have included parents in with the school and university people to expand the collaborations in setting up the research. This is a must, for who could be more interested in the education of children than their parents? As with other investigations broadly outlined here, this research could be carried out with only a few teachers, with a number of schools, or with an entire district. Once the size of the project is determined, the collaborators could decide on the types of information that should be communicated, the frequency with which that information should be disseminated, the formats selected for the various types of communications, and other important variables. Relatedly, they could decide on how to determine the effects, comparative or otherwise, of the several options.

The fourth broad area of research on which individuals from schools and universities might get together has to do with collaboration itself. There is a growing realization that if we are to solve the problems of education, if we are to design effective programs for children (many of whom are difficult to deal with), we will have to draw on the collective wit and wisdom of many folks. Some of these collaborations could be among and between the school people—that is, the extent that teachers interact with one another about child-related matters and the extent that teachers interact with administrators or support personnel about children's concerns. Another level of collaboration in schools could pertain to the university people, those who are there to collaborate with teachers. It might be of interest to find out just how often the university people interact with one another about the common concern, helping children in schools. Another layer of collaboration, one on which additional data could be gathered, would pertain to the collaborations related to children that took place between university folks and school people.

University professors or other outsiders who collaborate with school folks about research will need to adapt. They will have to be satisfied with studies that are less elegant than the ones they have read or written about in their statistics and research design books. It is unlikely that the professors will be able to randomly assign students, subjects, teachers, schools, or anything else. They will probably have to deal with students, teachers, class schedules, assemblies, announcements, and other aspects of the school culture pretty much as they are or as they happen. Professors and other outsiders must keep in mind that teachers tend to be more spontaneous than professional researchers. This attribute has often frustrated many professors who go into schools intending to set up rigorous studies. But if it is any consolation, those professors can at any time, if their frustrations get the best of them, go back to school, get their teaching credential, find a job teaching school, and carry out the study of their dreams.

If education is to improve we must do it together. This is difficult, for all the various agencies, guilds, and associations that make up the insiders and outsiders have traditions and special interests. It could be, however, that in these times of recession, while we are all going broke (albeit slowly), we will be forced to work together for the commonweal whether we like it or not.

These changes for the betterment of education must come from the places in which education takes place. We cannot get by with the "theorizing at the kitchen table" schemes that we have promoted in the past. They will not work. Whether we like it or not, our sources of inspiration must be those locations where the action is: the schools, the homes, the other places where people are being taught. Many of the ideas and programs that have been cooked up for teachers and schools have been failures simply because they originated in boardrooms and other chambers that are far away from the action. Although it pains me to offer a military analogy, I am reminded of that long list of military exploits that were total disasters, largely because out-of-touch field commanders dreamed them up at places quite distant from the battlefields. We do not need any more educational "Pickett charges," "Charges of the Light Brigade," or "Gallipolies."

NOTES

1. Harold Hodgkinson, "Reform versus Reality," *Phi Delta Kappan* 73, no. 1 (Sept. 1991): 9–16.
2. *Voices from the Field: 30 Expert Opinions on America 2000, The Bush Administration Strategy to "Reinvent" America's Schools* (Washington, D.C.: William T. Grant Foundation Commission on Work, Family and Citizenship and the Institute for Educational Leadership, 1991).
3. Karen De Witt, "Most Parents in Survey Say Education Goals Can't Be Met," *New York Times*, 13 Nov. 1991, sec. B, p. 7. When interpreting these data on children's tests scores from one year to another, one must take into account the fact that the students in today's schools are more diverse, in many respects, than they were even five years ago. For an account of this phenomenon, see Gerald Bracey, "Why Can't They Be Like We Were?" *Phi Delta Kappan* 73, no. 2 (Oct. 1991): 104–17.
4. Karen De Witt, "U.S. Study Shows Pupil Achievement at Level of 1979," *New York Times*, 1 Oct. 1991, sec. A, p. 1.

5. Ibid., sec. A, p. 16.
6. Ivan Illich, *Deschooling Society* (New York: Harrow Books, 1970).
7. Fox Butterfield, "Harvard President Assails Urban Ills," *New York Times*, 7 June 1991, sec. A, p. 10.
8. Thomas C. Lovitt, "Reflections on Barsch's Perspectives, and a Few of My Own," *Journal of Learning Disabilities* 25, no. 1 (Jan. 1992): 23–28.

Index

ISBN 0-02-344771-0

90000>

9 780023 447716